ECONOMICS AND LITERATURE

Economics and fiction often pursue parallel objectives. Economists analyze human decisions and interactions in markets and other institutions. Fiction writers also provide keen insights into individual minds and motives, examining how their characters respond to conflict and tensions in varied situations. This book explores the insights to be gained from developing this parallel.

In each chapter, economists discuss classic or contemporary literary creations, exploring economic incentives that motivate the characters, the economic mechanisms that tie them together, and/or the economic context in which they live and develop. Exploring the synergy across economics and literature offers new understandings of themes, including capitalism and colonialism, marriage and markets, gender norms, inheritance and estates, and the political economy of poverty. The broad and deep range of literary works includes writers from Shakespeare and Goethe, through Chekov and Steinbeck, to recent Nobelists Abdulrazak Gurnah and Han Kang. By offering new understandings of both economics and literature, readers will gain deeper insights into people's thought processes, choices, and consequences.

This book will captivate readers in economics, social sciences, and the humanities and open their minds to the viewing of economic ideas and concepts through the prism of great works of literature.

François Bourguignon is Professor Emeritus at the Paris School of Economics.

Avinash Dixit is Emeritus Professor of Economics at Princeton University.

Luc Leruth is Research Associate at the University of Clermont Auvergne.

Jean-Philippe Platteau is Emeritus Professor in the Department of Economics at the University of Namur.

I like happy endings – so I was very pleased to learn about a literature student at a famous university who, being frustrated at not finding Steinbeck's *Grapes of Wrath* in the literature section of the university library, could successfully locate it among books on agriculture. Boundaries between subjects can be overcome in different ways, including through confusion, but they can also be crossed deliberately in wise and enriching ways. This lovely book, with a fine collection of essays, has been led by an insightful and innovative plan of "bringing together" literature and economics. It is a splendid achievement. Rather than seeking a happy ending, we must wish for more works like this that bring together apparently distant disciplines.

–**Amartya Sen**, *Lamont University Professor, Harvard University, and Nobel Laureate in Economics*

Economists aim to understand human behavior and human interactions with the world. Novelists aim to illustrate how human interactions affect individuals' emotions and behavior. In so doing both fields teach us about the world. *Economics and Literature: A Novel Approach* is a compilation of brilliant essays from a globally representative selection of economists who are also perceptive readers of fine literature. It entertains while illuminating the commonalities of economics and literature.

–**Alison Booth**, *Emeritus Professor, Australian National University and author of novels including "Bellevue", "A Perfect Marriage", and "A Distant Land"*

ECONOMICS AND LITERATURE

A Novel Approach

Edited by François Bourguignon, Avinash Dixit, Luc Leruth, and Jean-Philippe Platteau

Routledge
Taylor & Francis Group
LONDON AND NEW YORK

Designed cover image: Illustration: Olivier Saive

First published 2025
by Routledge
4 Park Square, Milton Park, Abingdon, Oxon, OX14 4RN

and by Routledge
605 Third Avenue, New York, NY 10158

Routledge is an imprint of the Taylor & Francis Group, an informa business

British Library Cataloguing-in-Publication Data
A catalogue record for this book is available from the British Library

ISBN: 978-1-032-87765-5 (hbk)
ISBN: 978-1-032-87763-1 (pbk)
ISBN: 978-1-003-53435-8 (ebk)

DOI: 10.4324/9781003534358

Typeset in Times New Roman
by SPi Technologies India Pvt Ltd (Straive)

CONTENTS

ABOUT THE EDITORS

François Bourguignon is Professor Emeritus at the Paris School of Economics. Former director of the latter, and, previously, chief economist and senior vice president of the World Bank in Washington, he has behind him a long research and teaching career in the economics of poverty, inequality, and development, notably at the School for Advanced Studies in Social Sciences in Paris.

Avinash Dixit is Emeritus Professor of Economics at Princeton University. He was educated at Bombay, Cambridge, and MIT. His books include *Thinking Strategically* and *Investment Under Uncertainty*; he has also written several well-known research papers. He is the past President of the American Economic Association, a member of the US National Academy of Sciences, and the recipient of India's Padma Vibhushan Award.

Luc Leruth has a PhD in economics (Brussels) and an MSc in Mathematics. Formerly at the IMF, he was a member of CORE and taught at the Free University Brussels, Liège, and Essex. He is the founding partner of two FinTechs in corporate finance. He pursued a literary career and published short stories and several novels in French and in English.

Jean-Philippe Platteau is Emeritus Professor in the Department of Economics at the University of Namur. He has founded the Centre for Research in Economic Development (CRED), of which he was the Director for two decades. He remains active in research, and the economics of institutions in developing countries is his main field of specialization since the beginning of his career.

CONTRIBUTORS

Ernest Aryeetey is Emeritus Professor, University of Ghana; previously he was its Vice-chancellor; and secretary-general, African Research Universities Alliance. He has a PhD from the University of Dortmund and several honorary doctorates. His research concerns the role of institutions and financial systems in regional integration, economic reforms, and small enterprises. His books include *The Economy of Ghana Sixty Years after Independence*.

Pranab Bardhan is Distinguished Professor Emeritus of Economics at the University of California, Berkeley. He has done theoretical and field studies research on rural institutions in poor countries, on the political economy of development policies, and on international trade. He is the author of 17 books, including his latest, which is a memoir, *Charaiveti: An Academic's Global Journey* (2023).

Marianne David is an independent scholar who received her PhD in Comparative Literature from Yale. She has taught Spanish and French Literature, Language and Culture at the Trinity and Dalton Schools in New York City, where she is Teacher Emerita. Her most recent area of interest is 13th-century Spanish art history.

Mukesh Eswaran is Emeritus Professor of Economics at the University of British Columbia, Vancouver, Canada. He is an applied theorist who has worked in many subfields of economics, especially development economics and the economics of gender. He is a Fellow of the Canadian Economics Association. His most recent book in economics is *Why Gender Matters in Economics* (Princeton University Press, 2014).

Bishnupriya Gupta, DPhil from Oxford University, is Professor of Economics at the University of Warwick and the research director of the CAGE Research Centre. She has published widely on industrial development in colonial India and is a key contributor to the debate on the Great Divergence. She is an editor of the *Journal of Economic History*.

Sergei Guriev, Dean, London Business School and tenured professor of economics since 2024. Before LBS, he was on the faculty of Sciences Po (Paris) as a tenured professor of economics (2013–2024) and as its first Provost (2022–2024). In 2016–2019, he served as the Chief Economist of the European Bank for Reconstruction and Development.

Stuti Khemani is an economist in the research department of the World Bank. Her area of expertise is the political economy of public policy and institutional reforms for development. In addition to leading journal publications, she has also led World Bank flagship reports, including Making Politics Work for Development. She holds a PhD in Economics from MIT.

Mark Koyama is Professor of Economics at George Mason University, Mercatus Center Senior Scholar, and Research Associate at the Centre for Economic and Policy Research (CEPR). He earned his PhD in Economics from the University of Oxford. He is interested in the institutional origins of modern economic growth and liberal democracy.

Debin Ma is Professor of Economic History at the University of Oxford (All Souls College). An expert on the long-term economic growth of East Asia, especially China, he has published widely on subjects ranging from long-term living standards, productivity and human capital, institutional and legal history to ideology. He is the co-editor of the *Cambridge Economic History of China*.

Carmen Matutes (Waveform Investments, S.L.), PhD from UC Berkeley, held academic positions in France, Spain, and the UK. She published on product compatibility, network externalities, multiproduct competition, and banking. In her second career, she published four novels (in Spanish and in Catalan) and several short stories. Currently, she works in the private sector, and she is a member of the Advisory Council of IESE Banking Initiative.

Luiz De Mello is Director at the Economics Department of the OECD. He held senior positions at the OECD and worked as Senior Economist at the International Monetary Fund. Earlier in his career, he was a lecturer in the Economics Department at the University of Kent, United Kingdom, and holds a PhD in Economics from the same university.

Danielle Meuwly is a Swiss diplomat. She holds a PhD in Economics from Fribourg University and an MA from the College of Europe. She worked at SECO and at the World Bank in Washington and served as an advisor to the President of the UN Assembly. A literary buff specialized in Monetary Economics, she has always been interested in the bridge between both fields.

Célestin Monga teaches public policy (macroeconomics) at Harvard University's Kennedy School. He previously served as managing director at the United Nations Industrial Development Organization, vice president and chief economist at the African Development Bank Group, and senior economic adviser at the World Bank. His philosophy books include *Nihilism and Negritude: Ways of Living in Africa* (Harvard University Press).

Dilip Mookherjee is Professor of Economics at Boston University. He was educated in India and the UK and previously taught at Stanford University and the Indian Statistical Institute in New Delhi. His research interests are development, inequality, organizations, and political economy. He is a Fellow of the Econometric Society and a fellow/affiliate of NBER, CEPR, and BREAD.

Mustapha Kamel Nabli holds a PhD in Economics from the University of California, Los Angeles. He is an international consultant, was Tunisia's Central Bank Governor (2011–2012) and Minister of Planning and Regional Development (1990–1995), World Bank Director of the Social and Economic Development Group (Middle East and North Africa) (1998–2010), and Professor of Economics, University of Tunis (1975–1988).

Piroska Nagy Mohácsi is Visiting Professor at the London School of Economics and Political Science (LSE). She was Program Director at the Institute of Global Affairs at the LSE (2015–21), Director for Policy at the EBRD (2008–2015), held senior positions in the IMF (1986–2008), was Senior Adviser at Fitch Ratings (2003–2004), and was visiting scholar, Hebrew University, Jerusalem (1996–1997).

Paul-Aarons Ngomo is a political theorist and an independent scholar whose work focuses on democratic theory and constitutional structures in multiethnic African states. He has a PhD from New York University. He is the author of *La Théorie Politique de Frantz Fanon* (Paris, Dianoïa) and various articles on modern African thought.

Pierre Pestieau received his PhD from Yale. He has taught economics at Cornell University and then at the University of Liege till 2008. He is now Professor Emeritus. He is also a member of CORE. His major interests are pension economics, social insurance, inheritance taxation, and redistributive policies. His most recent books are *The Welfare State in Europe* (Oxford University Press) and *The Economics of Social Protection* (Cambridge University Press).

Shourya Sen is a PhD candidate in the Department of Politics at Princeton University. He researches questions related to economic development, inequality, state formation, and post-revolutionary politics. He specializes in the study of Southeast Asia but has also published on the educational history of sub-Saharan Africa.

Alfred Steinherr was rector and Professor of Economics at the Free University of Bolzano, Italy. His professional life spans years as a professor of economics at the Catholic University of Louvain and an advisor at the International Monetary Fund in Washington and the European Commission in Brussels. He was for 20 years Head of Research and Chief Economist at the European Investment Bank, Luxembourg.

Leonard Wantchekon is the James Madison Professor of Political Economy at Princeton University. His research centers on political economy, development economics, and economic history. Wantchekon is the recipient of the Global Economy Prize in 2023 and a fellow of the American Academy of Arts and Sciences and of the Econometric Society. He is the founder and President of the African School of Economics.

FOREWORD

Alfred Marshall defined economics as "the study of mankind in the ordinary business of life". Literature is also about ordinary (and extraordinary!) human beings and their social interactions. Methods and expositions may differ between economics and literature, but the two endeavors deserve to be brought together. Indeed, many scholars have taken on this task and produced a field often labeled Literature and Economics. In this volume, we approach the same junction of economics and literature, but from a different direction and with some novel perspectives about novels (and some short stories). We hope this "road less traveled by" will enrich the field, expand its scope, enlarge its audience, and spur further thinking and new contributions.

Economics, especially in this age of big data, takes facts from the real world and analyzes them through the machinery of statistical inference. Economic theories build conceptual frameworks called models to understand the mechanisms at work in generating the set of facts, even though they have to simplify and separate the essential from the incidental, and do so with varying degrees of success. Fiction, as the very name suggests, seems set apart from facts. Therefore, some potential readers of this volume may want a fuller statement of what the two have to do, or say, about each other, and why they have much to learn from each other, in at least in three important areas.

Firstly, as we said earlier, economics and fiction often pursue the same overall objectives. Good basic economics tries to analyze events and interpret them to yield policy recommendations that are substantiated by this analysis. A good economist must argue the case so that others (e.g., policy makers) can implement these policies. Replace "economics" by "prose" and Sartre will agree. In his essay *Literature and Existentialism*,[1] he distinguishes prose from other forms of art by arguing that it is utilitarian in nature and necessarily associated with the political and social views of the writer. In the first instance, argues Sartre, the writer is not concerned with the beauty of the words (although he acknowledges that if a text is well written, it is a plus; economists should agree): the objective of a prose writer is to persuade the reader. Sartre even argues that "our great writers wanted to destroy, to edify, to demonstrate." In other words, prose is a "signifier" whereas other forms of art (e.g. poetry, sculptures) are "objects" more directly associated with the viewers' own feelings about what they read, hear, or see. Orwell, Zola, and many others would agree with Sartre.

The focus of analysis is the second area where there are similarities. Economists write papers where they present their ideas about choice behavior, supply and demand, information and incentives, institutions and organizations, and so on. They are concerned with the reality that they have observed and try to understand how people react. Fiction differs at most in degree, not in kind. It constructs human characters, often in dramatized or extraordinary situations in their lives. Good fiction, even if set in other worlds and among other life forms, as science fiction and magical or mythical writing are, addresses conflicts and tensions that are very human. Think of the struggle of the people against authoritarian rulers, and of good versus evil, in *Star Wars, Dune*, or in *Lord of the Rings*. Science fiction allows time travel, and magic allows people to fly. But magic does not do away with scarcity – the starting point of all economics; else, why would there be any poor wizarding families like the Weasleys in the *Harry Potter* saga?

The third area (and last in this introduction, although we very much hope that some of our readers will think of more) is the tools that are used to picture reality. Economists rely on several assumptions that facilitate solving their models (making them tractable) in an attempt to focus on the essence of the argument. This is an approach that Borges must have found appealing. In one of his short stories,[2] he describes a place where scholars try to draw maps that are increasingly precise. Finally, the cartographers come up with the most precise map possible, but it has the same size as the country. Nobody uses it because it is cumbersome (beggars and some others use it to protect themselves from the rain, though). Clearly, absolute accuracy is not a goal worth pursuing and, as a matter of fact, disconnecting somewhat from reality – as economists do when they build a model that emphasizes essentials and discards incidentals[3] – enables them to reach a better understanding of reality. Even a writer as much bent on depicting complex human characters as Dostoyevsky wrote that "Man is vast, too vast in fact. I have therefore reduced him, so to say" ("Brothers Karamazov", 1879–1880). He also said: "A common saying is that we must represent reality as it is. But this reality does not exist" ("Diary of a Writer", 1873). Fiction-writers also simplify or exacerbate the interactions of their characters with others. It is sometimes excessive, but the extraordinariness is usually a device to sharpen issues and problems that also arise in ordinary lives and to attract the readers' attention. Just like economists do.

We do not claim to be the first to notice and study these connections. Indeed, as we said at the outset, a large and established scholarly field of Literature and Economics addresses them. But we approach them from a different direction and through different lenses. The established scholars in this field mostly come from the discipline usually labeled Literary Criticism, with its modes of thought and analysis. Their knowledge of economics comes from the textbooks and teachers they encountered years or decades ago, and therefore much of it is unavoidably somewhat dated. They think of economics as mostly marginalist or "neoclassical", stemming from (and usually ending with) the works of economists like Alfred Marshall, Paul Samuelson, and Milton Friedman. In these works, individuals are assumed to be fully knowledgeable and rational, and mostly selfish, decision-makers who interact through impersonal and often monopolized markets.[4] But economics in the last three or four decades has undergone a huge change in its modes of thought and analysis. It has taken to heart much of the criticism originating from behavioral and experimental findings of researchers within the profession as well as psychologists. Strategic behavior and its implications for many interactions in society and markets have become standard economics impelled by game theorists. The "information revolution" has brought the fact that some or all individuals lack much important information for making decisions to the center of modern economic analysis. A new subfield, called political economics, has emerged that features the state as a full-fledged actor possessing its own preferences and facing its own constraints. In fact, if you look at the economics Nobel prizes awarded over the last 30 years, perhaps the majority have been rewarded for just such developments: behavioral economics and finance (Kahneman, Thaler, Shiller), game theory (Nash, Schelling, Aumann, Tirole), asymmetric information and incentives (Mirrlees, Akerlof, Stiglitz, Spence, Maskin, Myerson, Roth, Milgrom, Wilson), institutions and organizations (Coase, Ostrom, Williamson), political economics (Acemoglu, Johnson, Robinson), as well as empirical and historical works that also represent major departures from neoclassical economics (Sen, Card, Goldin). In the established canon of Literature and Economics, these ideas are almost entirely absent, and almost none of these researchers are actually cited. The authors of chapters in this book, by contrast, were raised steeped in these new ideas, or in some cases they have themselves contributed to their development. It is thus revealing that the 2024 Economics Nobel Laureates Acemoglu, Johnson, and Robinson are cited in several essays in this book.

We invited several such economists, whom we knew to be serious readers and lovers of fiction, to choose one or two of their favorite works with substantial economics content – economic and other kinds of incentives that motivate the characters, the economic mechanisms that tie them together, and the context in which they live and develop – and discuss these in depth.

It is important to emphasize that we do not go in for self-flagellation in the manner of some economists these days, who believe that everything in traditional economics is wrong and call for a total revolution, guillotine and all. We believe that economics, as it has evolved during the last decades, has acquired a powerful toolkit for the understanding of important aspects of individual choice and social interactions. Therefore, it can contribute to other areas of social science and humanities even as it benefits from them to deepen and enlarge its own explanatory power. The road ahead of us allows for a two-way traffic and a fairly balanced exchange of approaches and contributions.

We have brought together a very wide-ranging group of economists, and they have chosen an impressive and equally wide-ranging group of authors and novelists from Europe, the Americas, Africa, and Asia. The economists specialize in many different fields and work in academia as well as various organizations. The writers span centuries and continents, from Shakespeare and Goethe, through Chekov, Austen, and Steinbeck, to recent Literature Nobelists Abdulrazak Gurnah and Han Kang. We thought it is important to have this broad spectrum because we don't think any small number of economists, or fiction writers for that matter, have a monopoly over insights, and only a wide coverage will enable readers to see the full possibilities of mutually beneficial interactions between economics and fiction. Of course, we were limited in our choice of invitees by our own information and networks, and by the fact that most economists are very busy and hesitant to devote time to endeavors which, no matter how intriguing and worthwhile, fall outside their professional research and writing. We were limited in the selection of fiction by the need to let our authors choose their own preferred works to discuss. But we have been very happy with the outcome, and we hope the readers of this volume will like it, too. Hopefully, successor volumes will appear in the future, to include other economists writing about other examples from fiction, and perhaps even vice versa.

We hope that not only economists but also other social scientists and many scholars in humanities will find this perspective and its results interesting and illuminating. Most importantly, students of economics will learn to broaden their horizons beyond the usual textbooks and technical journals. And we believe that they will find the applications of basic economics proposed in this book more enjoyable and inspiring than those typically offered in standard texts. Finally, with many well-read contributors coming from so many different cultural and geographical horizons, readers are also likely to discover fiction writers that they did not know about (we did).

Let us now give the readers a taste of what sorts of benefits and pleasures they will derive from undertaking the journey through the book. In particular, we cannot help being moved by central characters presented in many novellas. This is especially true when the heroes make disastrous economic decisions because they have been overwhelmed by emotions, passions, or irrepressible impulses. Thus, for example, in the eponymous work of William Shakespeare, King Lear appears miserable and pitiful as a result of a blatant mistake of disinheriting while still alive the only daughter who was genuinely close to him.

Likewise, Père Goriot, in the eponymous novel of Honoré de Balzac, is touching us because of his desperate but vain attempts to please and be loved by ungrateful children and in-laws to whom he bequeathed his wealth much before approaching death. In *The Inheritance*, a short story written by the great 19th-century Brazilian writer Machado de Assis, the error committed by the main protagonist, Venancia, in allocating her wealth among her two nephews is the natural consequence of her irrepressible attraction to the flamboyant character of one of them, Emilio.

Equally worthy of our compassion are money-crazed characters who are driven to sacrifice other interests, aspirations, and desires. Think of Margayya, the protagonist of *The Financial Expert* by R.K. Narayan, the great writer from South India. He is torn between his craving for money and the sincere love for his rather incompetent son who ends up ruining him. Similar duality is found in the two short stories of Anton Chekhov, *Rothshild's Violin* and *The Discovery*, where he depicts men whose humanhood is overwhelmed by their obsession with lost opportunities and forsaken gains or with regrets and nostalgia. In *Things Fall Apart* of Chinua Achebe, the inner tension in Okonkwo, one of the central characters in the story, arises from his simultaneous aspiration for economic aggrandizement and social mobility, on the one hand, and his stubborn attachment to Igbo tradition (in Nigeria) and its oppressive social norms, on the other hand. "He trembled with the desire to conquer and subdue. It was like the desire for woman", writes Achebe in his uniquely concise style. In a different context, a similarly painful tension between progress and the ancient world (in the form of small-scale undertakings in Paris) is positively resolved by the young woman who is the main character in Emile Zola's *The Ladies' Paradise*.

These heroes often come out as both tormentors and victims. They make others endure pain and, by falling prey to their own vices or perverse predispositions, they also create suffering for themselves. We are thus facing divided personalities who are far away, or seem far away, from the neat categories found in economic theorizing and adopted by political leaders. Their inner conflicts and the way they affect their lives and those of others are at the center stage of many literary masterworks, wherever they come from.

Another striking feature that some novellas in the book exhibit is the aptitude of gifted writers for the deciphering of human interactions and exchange processes. Think of the account of the marriage market in British aristocracy provided in Jane Austen's *Pride and Prejudice*; or of the detailed depiction of essentially informal trade contracts in *By the Sea*, written by Abdulrazak Gurnah, a recent African Nobel Prize in literature. Moreover, the writers of novellas discussed in the book reveal a stunning ability to not only depict reality with great precision and acumen but also anticipate propositions, mechanisms, and controversies found in modern science. Thus, how not to be impressed by Mikhail Bulgakov's vivid anticipation of the monetary theory debate on "helicopter money" and the illusion of a "free meal" that it creates in the minds of myopic people? Or, by the subtle insights offered in the same novella (*The Master and Margarita*) into the pivotal role of private incentives that the author's country, the USSR, ignored at its own peril? To take a last example, anyone interested in the highly topical question as to whether robots constitute a threat to employment and our ways of living will no doubt be stimulated by Kazuo Ishiguro's *Klara and the Sun* and Ian McEwan's *Machines Like Me*.

How to arrange the material available in a meaningful and helpful way is the remaining task falling to us. It was not easy. The reason is that most if not all the works of fictions that have been selected could have been approached through several economic standpoints (and *The Master and Margarita* indeed appears twice in this volume, approached from two totally different angles). We were largely guided, however, by the detection of central themes that emerged from the discussion offered in the various essays. The few prominent themes around which the chapters can be regrouped are the following: development and structural transformation of society and economy; market operation and dysfunction; limits of the homo economicus model; rent-seeking, corruption, and bad political governance. In a slightly longer introductory chapter, we offer the reader a survey in which, under each theme, we briefly outline the main message coming from the contributions and the connections the authors make between economic concepts and their selected novels, short stories, or occasionally plays. We do not attempt to offer "abstracts" of each chapter since those would not do justice to the interest and richness of the contents.

Notes

1 Sartre (1948), *Qu'est-ce que la littérature*, Gallimard, Paris.
2 Borges (1946), *On Exactitude in Science*. See also Eco (1995), *How to Travel with a Salmon*.
3 The distinction can depend on the context; that judgment is the art of good modeling.
4 We give a brief overview of some of this literature later in the Editors' Introduction.

EDITORS' ACKNOWLEDGMENTS

The editors would like to thank Daniel Vander Gucht, Director of *Les éditions de La Lettre volée* (Brussels), who published in *Quand l'économie nous est contée*[1] earlier versions of two chapters authored by two of the editors (Luc Leruth, with Danielle Meuwly, and Jean-Philippe Platteau). These chapters were later extensively modified and are now part of the present volume.

Note

1 de Callatay, E. and L. Leruth (eds.), *Quand l'économie nous est contée*, L'Aile Volée, Brussels, 2021.

EDITORS' INTRODUCTION

We begin this chapter by describing briefly under separate headings each of the four themes around which the book is structured. To recall, these themes are: development and structural transformation of society and economy; market operation and dysfunction; limits of the homo economicus model; and rent-seeking, corruption, and bad political governance. We then proceed by presenting a summary of all the contributions falling under the corresponding theme, which is done following a succession order that seems to best articulate them together. Then we discuss the relationship of our approach to the incumbent field of Literature and Economics.

The four themes in this collection

Development and structural transformation of society and economy

Economic development is not a smooth process: it entails social disruptions and tensions caused by the shock between the old and the new orders and the inevitable rise of the latter at the expense of the former. This theme is not commonly handled by economists because its study involves the play of factors with which they are not familiar. Nonetheless, the recent opening of the discipline to new dimensions of societal life, as witnessed by the rise of the economics of culture and norms, and the significance of political economics, shows that non-economic aspects of transitions between systems are a growing concern among the profession. Several essays in our book actually consider such aspects from various perspectives, and they indicate that disruptions can take on different forms and touch on different aspects of individual and collective life trajectories.

DOI: 10.4324/9781003534358-1

Thus, in a piece called "A Bengali Novel on Economic Transition in History", based on the novel *The Tale of the Hansuli Turn* by Tarasankar Bandyopadhyay, Pranab Bardhan tells a narrative that unfolds in the context of a remote Indian village. Structural change linked to market-based modernization is depicted as the disappearance of erstwhile occupations and their replacement by novel ones, as well as changes in the class or rank structure of the society and the emergence of young and dynamic entrepreneurs who challenge the existing order and its supporting authorities. In the foreground is a young individual from a low-caste origin who dared to refuse to labor on the fields of local landlords, preferring to work as a coolie leader in a nearby small town where new employment opportunities had emerged. The important point is that, acting as a sort of Stackelberg leader, he has inspired other youngsters to follow him to do nonfarm wage work, giving up their forefathers' life of farm labor under traditional subjugation. This creates a movement that deeply calls the old order into question and therefore sparks acute tensions inside the village community. The central claim of Bardhan is that Bandyopadhyay's novel brings out complexities that do not fall neatly into our pre-conceived historical categories, such as feudalism and capitalism. In particular, wage work is not seen as a curse imposed on helpless people vulnerable to economic exploitation but, rather, as a privileged means of emancipation from the shackles of a traditional order perceived as damaging to individual liberty and dignity.

The plot recounted in the celebrated novel of Chinua Achebe *Things Fall Apart*, and that Ernest Aryeetey and Jean-Philippe Platteau have chosen to write their joint essay "The Struggle for Structural Transformation in Africa: Are Things Still Falling Apart?" on, bears both similarities and differences with *The Tale of the Hansuli Turn*. The similarity obviously lies in the fact that in both novels modernization appears to create new economic opportunities (through the Second World War and other circumstances in the Asian novel and through colonial penetration in the African novel) that can help people to emancipate and improve not only their material but also their social status. On the other hand, there are at least two important differences to be detected. First, some characters in Achebe's Igbo society of Nigeria turn out to be quite complex, in the sense that they are economically dynamic and, at the same time, socially and politically conservative people. One of the heroes thus strongly opposes colonial and missionary penetration on the grounds of defending the traditional culture and norms of the Igbo society while simultaneously aspiring for a better life and putting great efforts toward that end. Second, Achebe does not depict the traditional Igbo society as exclusively traditionalist, but as a society allowing economic mobility and encouraging individual dynamism. Mobility is fostered by competition for both riches and titles that confer power and status within the clan. In this way, Achebe avoids the sorts of clichés or stereotypes to which the Western world, and the economics profession, has been accustomed.

Things fall apart because colonialism is destroying the traditional order by bringing disunion and mistrust among the Igbo themselves: "the clan no longer acts as one" and "the white man has put a knife on the things that held us together and we have fallen apart". But the second difference mentioned above also means that the Igbo society was both a collectivist society endowed with a strong clan structure, many family-based solidarity arrangements, and powerful authority institutions, on the one hand, and an individualistic society recognizing private qualities and dynamism and entrusting important economic decisions on individuals, on the other hand. Some aspects of this society were therefore amenable to the sort of change heralded by the colonial order while some other aspects were likely to resist its penetration.

According to Aryeetey and Platteau, Africa continues to suffer from being caught in the dilemma highlighted by Achebe. Acute tensions persist between modernization opportunities, which require the adoption of modern education and the maintaining of traditional identity based on erstwhile norms, some of which are deeply oppressive (as dramatically illustrated in the novel). Political leadership is largely to blame because it wavers between different approaches and does not make clear choices liable to be translated in effective institutions and to encourage the accumulation of trust.

The idea that the transition to a modern economy involves a loss reflected in the questioning of erstwhile beliefs, customs, and practices is one of the central concerns of Cheikh Hamidou Kane, a Senegalese writer, in his celebrated novel *The Ambiguous Adventure*. As highlighted in the essay "The Art of Conquering without Being Right: Agency, Education, and Learning by Doing in Cheikh Hamidou Kane's Ambiguous Adventure", written by Paul-Aarons Ngomo, Shourya Sen, and Leonard Wantchekon, the availability of modern education as a result of European colonization has raised one of the deepest challenges for the colonized societies. Embracing modern education means improving dramatically the ability of colonial subjects to adapt to the modern world and to seize upon the opportunities for a better living that this world opens up. At the same time, however, it involves a tragic loss which takes the form of an increasing alienation from traditional mores and spirituality. Kane's novel depicts the experiences of a young *Diallobé* man of aristocratic background, Samba Diallo, who is ultimately sent to France to study, even though he was a promising student of the Qur'an under the tutelage of the severe teacher Thierno. Samba's father, the Knight, and the Grande Royale, a female leader, are both central figures in the debates on whether to embrace colonial education, and because of their leadership role, they bear much responsibility for the ultimate decision to have Samba discontinuing his religious studies and engaging in modern education abroad. Still, Samba is eager not to lose his Afro-Muslim *Diallobé* identity, and in Paris he eschews alcohol and the currents of leftist politics that define his social milieu. At the same time, however, he finds himself increasingly alienated from the traditional spirituality that he still holds dear. On his return to Senegal, he meets a sudden demise at the hands of the Fool, a religious fanatic, after he refuses to pray at the grave of the now deceased Thierno.

In their essay, Ngomo, Sen, and Wantchekon are not content with describing the hard dilemma faced by Samba Diallo and the motives that prompted his community to make a choice in favor of modernity ("The era of separate destinies has run its course", says the Knight). They also draw attention to the other side of reality, according to which spirituality will remain essential for human beings due to the inherent limitations of science: "When the sun dies, no scientific certainty should keep us from weeping for it, no rational evidence should keep us from asking that it be reborn", says the Knight again. Moreover, they stress the persisting value of the deliberative tradition and the persisting role of the consensus-seeking approach typical of the old African societies, and from which the West could also learn. Finally, they put great emphasis on the fact that modern formal education is bound to empower colonial subjects because it is about learning how to understand a rapidly changing world and engaging with it through learning by doing. Without a proper understanding of the environment, no emancipatory move is conceivable.

The essay of Mukesh Eswaran titled "On Capitalism and Colonialism: The Economic Imperatives Underlying Amitav Ghosh's *Sea of Poppies*" is based on an Indian novel that has a much more negative take on the effects of colonialism than *Things Fall Apart*. Instead of viewing colonialism as a possible trigger of modernization, Amitav Ghosh delves into its drawbacks under the form of economic exploitation. Since his novel *Sea of Poppies* deals with the opium trade in the setting of the eastern region of present-day Bihar and Bengal, the object of inquiry is ould'not the sort of modern colonialism that prevailed during the 19–20th centuries, but the form of extractive and exploitative colonialism observed during the earlier period of European mercantilism. In the present instance, the colonizer was the British East India Company, a joint stock company which was entirely devoted to maximizing profits through trading and ran India as a private property until the rise of British colonial rule by the mid-19th century. Sheer use of coercion was resorted to, such as when peasant farmers were forced to accept cash advances by the company's agents to grow the poppy, lest they should lose their land. Because losses rather than benefits were expected to result from the cultivation of opium, force needed to be used by the company to enrol small-scale producers. Thanks to its position as both a monopolist and a monopsonist, it was able to achieve its aims of intensifying opium production. Adverse side-effects also resulted from under-utilization of fixed assets, such as when its vessels were used to transport indentured laborers to Mauritius island in the Indian Ocean.

Ghosh's story is not a one-sided view of oppression by external agents, though. It also brings into light sources of internal oppression caused by the erstwhile patriarchal system whose objectives run against the interests of women. Interestingly, when the opportunity arises, the female hero is able to use opium strategically as a tool against that oppressive system.

In the essay "The Lone Scream in the Dark: Cultural Change and Institutional Transformation in Modern China as Seen through Lu Xun's Novels", Debin Ma takes us on a journey through a few works written by an outstanding Chinese writer named Lu Xun. The key question transpiring from the latter's novels, in particular *Scream*, the *Diary of a Mad Man*, and *Medicine*, is how the ancient culture and society of China could be transformed in such a way as to allow modernization understood as enlightenment. As an educated man returning from studies abroad (in Japan), Lu Xun feels like a stranger in his own native village when he visits it upon his return to China in the early 20th century. In similar circumstances, the hero of the *Diary of a Mad Man* is becoming literally mad, suffering from a sort of schizophrenia. The gap between the crude realities he discovers and his elevated aspirations is so wide that he does not find a way to connect with the local people. Between them is mutual suspicion and mistrust. The despair of modernizers is made more acute because people living in traditional surroundings tend to adopt "herd behavior" and are thus collectively bound to retrograde norms and practices in a vicious equilibrium of fatalistic and apathetic behavior. This is dramatically illustrated in *Medicine*, in which the corpse of an executed revolutionary is used to promote a traditional medical cure which fails to produce the intended effect. The death of a child ensues.

It is not only at the nascent stage but also at higher levels of the development process that progress entails heavy social costs. This is well illustrated by François Bourguignon in his essay "Zola's 'Ladies' Paradise' and the 'Creative Destruction' Theory". It is grounded in a discussion of *The Ladies' Paradise* of Emile Zola, a famous novel which tells the story of a rising tycoon who revolutionized retail sales in mid-19th century Paris by creating the first department store. Here, therefore, radical changes took place in an urban environment and in the field of commerce rather than agriculture. What we see at work is the logic of creative destruction that Schumpeter has shown to be at the heart of capitalism. Thus, old-style stores are being gradually displaced by department stores as a result of the emergence of new forms of organization and the introduction of technological innovations that boost labor productivity and lead to the creation of new products. At least temporarily, these processes confer a monopolistic advantage upon the innovator, while they force old firms to leave the market unless they adopt the new technology or a new mode of organization. Even though such a disruption leads to social progress overall, the social costs involved are inevitable in the short or medium term.

Zola recounts the life of a young woman coming from a small town and hosted by an uncle who runs one of the old shops next to the new department store in which she found employment because the uncle could no longer provide her with one. Although she is torn away between the two universes, the old and the new, and the department store is expanding so much that it literally eats up all the area in the center of Paris, she eventually marries the business tycoon. What is interesting is that, despite his natural inclination to empathize with the victims of the process of capitalist expansion, Zola recognizes that the demise of old-style stores is social progress overall: better products, more choice, more jobs, healthier work conditions … In this important sense, he reminds us of Karl Marx, who deemed the rise of capitalist methods of production to be inescapable and even desirable (until a system more favorable to workers would come to replace capitalism).

Another essay in the book that addresses the issue of the social cost of transition imposed by modernization is titled "Women in a Nervous Breakdown: Intra-Household Bargaining and Gender Norms in South Korea", written by Bishnu Gupta in the light of two short stories by different Korean female writers who approach the specific question of inequality in gender norms in a different way. *The Vegetarian* by the 2024 Literature Nobel Laureate Han Kang is a story of an unremarkable family in South Korea, where the husband has an average job and marries an "ordinary woman" with an unremarkable job, as narrated by the husband. Yeong-Hye devotes her time to the family. Her rebellion takes the form of a determination to become a vegetarian, an act of defiance to the core values of the patriarchal society. Chastised by her father and brother and watched in distress by the husband who sways between anger and caring for a wife on the verge of a nervous breakdown, Yeong-Hye's life slowly descends into a black hole and a mental breakdown.

Cho Nam Joo's *Kim Jiyoung, Born 1982* tells the story of a woman born at a time when sex selective abortions were common. Endowed with a good education, the hero tries to live up to the societal expectations of marriage and motherhood. At the same time, she strives to break free from the traditional world order to reestablish her working life. She faces familiar discrimination in the labor market and has to confront the erstwhile cultural and gender-biased perceptions of a woman's role inside her family. Like Young-Hye, she slowly descends into a mental breakdown. What is therefore highlighted in Gupta's essay is the possible discrepancy between economic and social development and the tragic consequences it can have for women. When economic progress arises from the womb of traditional patriarchal societies, (educated) women may be trapped in hard dilemmas born of the unavoidable tension between their desire to have a working life and the pressure of long-lived social norms and expectations that emphasize motherhood and household chores.

Market operation and dysfunction

The market mechanism is at the heart of modern capitalist systems, and it is therefore not surprising that it has been the object of thorough study by economists whose profession rose in tandem with these systems. However, unlike a common perception, economists have spent more time in trying to understand market limitations and failures than in bringing the virtues of the markets into light. While the latter task was rather prominent in the first phase of the development of economics, when the study of general equilibrium formed the core of the discipline, the attention later shifted to the possible dysfunction of markets and the ways to remedy the detected lacunae. In this book, a few essays explicitly deal with markets of different types: the housing market, the labor market, markets for goods or services, and the marriage and land markets. Yet, while the first of these essays focuses on the problems born of an absent market (the housing market), the investigation pursued in the other essays is around the effects of functioning or ill-functioning markets.

Although he achieved little recognition during his lifetime, Mikhail Bulgakov is considered today as one of the greatest modern Russian writers and he is one of the most widely read in Russia. *The Master and Margarita* is a dense novel, combining several stories taking place in various times and places (Jerusalem under Pilate, Moscow and Yalta in the 30s, and the devil's home at a time that is not identified). In this novel, the author describes a visit by the devil to communist Moscow. The devil (who goes by the name of Woland) wants to understand how the first atheistic society is actually working. He asks himself whether the Soviet system has been able to produce a "new man" but then concludes:

> "… they're people like any other people … they love money, but that has always been so … Mankind loves money, whatever it's made of – leather, paper, bronze, gold. Well, they're light-minded … well, what of it … mercy sometimes knocks at their hearts … ordinary people … In general, reminiscent of the former ones … only the housing problem has corrupted them …."

By failing to reckon with its inability to change people's character, the Soviet system made the serious mistake of ignoring the role of private incentives that lie at the heart of economics, thereby causing pervasive inefficiency costs. This is illustrated by the dysfunction of the housing market which features prominently in *Master and Margarita* (and in Bulgakov's other masterpiece, *The Heart of a Dog*). In his essay titled "Only the Housing Problem Has Corrupted Them", Serguei Guriev explains why the so-called housing problem – the non-transparent allocation of housing in the Soviet nonmarket system – was such a critical facet of the Soviet regime. Not only was the housing allocation mechanism used in the USSR highly inefficient and unfair, but it also had significant effects on people's well-being. Because of the neglect of private incentives, the available housing space was inefficiently allocated and the production of new houses was discouraged. Moreover, central planning for housing lacked transparency, and it followed a logic that is understandable only in political terms: in a context of acute housing scarcity, it served to favor an elite of regime supporters whose real standard of living depended to a large extent on the quality of their accommodation. In addition to increasing inequality and causing static and dynamic inefficiencies, the nonmarket mechanism of housing allocation produced many noxious side effects, such as rent-seeking and corruption, which were not anticipated by the authorities.

In the next essay "Can Machines Replace Us?", Dilip Mookherjee raises questions that have become highly topical: is there any essential, innate difference between machines and humans; is there any limit on the capacity of machines to mimic or outperform humans; and, relatedly, are economies doomed to witness an unremitting declining trend in the GDP (Gross Domestic Product) share of labor? To delve into these questions, the author calls forth two directly relevant novels: *Klara and the Sun*, by Kazuo Ishiguro, and *Machines Like Me*, by Ian McEwan.

McEwan stresses that for machines to achieve the intelligence that rivals or surpasses humans, the algorithms have to be designed in such a way as to enable them to learn and think independently according to "rational" rules. There are two problems with any such endeavor. First is an agency problem. McEwan's protagonist is prevented from unplugging the android when that is what he wants. Despite being subsequently wary of the machine's inclination to deviate from its own interests, it becomes increasingly difficult for its human owner to control it, until matters get out of hand. The second problem revolves around the following question: what is the designer of the machine to assume about behavior of humans with whom the machine will interact with? Those humans often behave less than rationally, in ways hard to predict. You can program one machine to play against another programmed machine whose behavior can be predicted. But how do you prepare a machine to interact with humans who are inherently unpredictable? This is also similar to what the android of the first novel mentions as the root of her ultimate inability to replace a dead human being: the problem is not with how accurately she can reproduce the latter's behavior and appearance, but how faithfully others around her would be able to transfer their emotions to a robot in the same way that they would have related to a deceased person.

A tentative conclusion that we can draw from this essay is that, eventually, and perhaps despite appearances, there is no perfect substitutability between robots and humans. At least in some contexts, humans are superior to robots. To put it otherwise, robots have advantages over humans, and humans have advantages over robots. Whether the net effect is in favor of the former or the latter will depend on the context in which they are made to work. Therefore, the risk that robots massively displace humans in the labor market should not be exaggerated, even regardless of the well-known argument that (skilled) workers will be needed to produce the machines. Another insight emerging from the essay, and one highly relevant from the viewpoint of income distribution, is that the net advantage of robots does not necessarily occur in sectors or tasks dominated by unskilled labor. When human interactions play an important role, robots are inadequate or, at least, may need to have their work complemented by humans. The argument is novel and, although it is suggested by non-economists, it should obviously arouse the interests of the economics profession.

With "Contract-Enforcement Institutions in Gurnah's *By the Sea*", by Mustapha Nabli, we now turn our attention to problems created by the costs of market exchanges. This essay is based on the novel *By the Sea*, written by a recent Nobel Prize winner, Abdulrazak Gurnah. The major point made in this novel is that the system of contract-enforcement prevailing in Zanzibar during the 1960s, around the end of the period of colonization and early period of independence, was ineffective, and opportunistic actions on the part of the traders were pervasive. In fact, the central part of the story details the fraudulent behavior of a trader, who was able to extort a fortune from two "innocent" family heads. The ensuing litigation and the system of legal contract enforcement led to the tearing of the social fabric and caused the destruction of their families.

Gurnah contrasts this system with the old one, which prevailed before colonization in the Indian Ocean and was based on a reputation mechanism. It involved a group of merchants trading in the Indian Ocean western region, including West Asia and East Africa (Bahrain, Oman, Zanzibar, India). This system was disrupted and progressively disappeared with the establishment of British colonization in the West Indian Ocean region. It was very similar to the one described in detail by Greif (1989, 1993) in the case of the Jewish Maghrebi traders during the 11th century in North Africa and the Mediterranean region. In his account of Gurnah's novel, Nabli details the features of the new system that diverged from the preceding one and are responsible for its failures. In particular, traders were not part of any common network or social group, and there was no information transmission mechanism and hence no way to transfer reputations.

Finally, Gurnah is highly critical of the legal system put in place by the British colonial power, which he deems both ineffective and corrupt. Nabli, however, adduces several thoughtful reasons why this view is perhaps both incomplete and inadequate. Despite these cautionary remarks, Gurnah's novel has the considerable merit of warning us that any black-and-white contrast between the pre-colonial past and the colonial period is unsatisfactory. It is not necessarily true that modernization requires old institutions to give way to new ones because old institutions may need to be adapted rather than scrapped altogether. And when new institutions must emerge, careful attention has to be given to the specific context in which they are implanted. Indeed, there are conditions in which perverse effects are brought into play that may undermine them.

"Marriage and Markets: Lessons from Pride and Prejudice", an essay by Carmen Matutes, deals with issues that relate to both the marriage and the land markets. Inspired by Jane Austen's novel, *Price and Prejudice*, the essay discusses the way the marriage market worked inside the 19th century's British aristocratic society. This novel's protagonists belong to the British upper classes and the narrative touches on various aspects of the life of aristocrats or would be aristocrats, including inheritance, social norms and etiquette, and marriage aspirations and practices. In essence, however, *Pride and Prejudice* is a comedy of marriages, with a plot based on the fact that because a so-named Mr. Bennet has no heir – only five daughters – upon his death his estate will be inherited by his cousin. Because women could not inherit the land, which is the basis of social status in the upper levels of British society, they had to be well married in order to achieve status and perhaps happiness. The wife of Mr. Bennett therefore sets on a frantic search for suitable partners for the five daughters. This search gives rise to a series of initiatives, blunders and mistakes, turnarounds, and re-assessments, which constitute the heart of the story. Suitable partners are considered as persons who are rich without enduring the toil of (manual) labor and do own a large land estate: possessing land and deriving income exclusively from it signaled membership in an enviable upper-class club. This explains why owners of free estates were reluctant to sell even if they ran into financial difficulties, thus causing a land market failure in the parlance of economists. These aristocratic landowners preferred to let their property and retain membership in the privileged club. By temporarily moving to France and discreetly living in genteel poverty, they could survive on the rents obtained from their land. By contrast, marrying men engaged in trade was dishonorable even when trade made them rich.

The discussion of the plot by Carmen Matutes sheds light, enriched by modern economic theory, on the way the marriage market worked inside the British aristocratic society. In so doing, it brings to the fore the variety of human motives, the differences in personal aspirations, the trade-off between love and wealth, the characteristics of the search process, the role of etiquette and social norms, and other important aspects that play a role in marriage transactions. It also elucidates an important cause, social status and its preservation, behind imperfections of the land sales market. Finally, it has the merit of illustrating the existence of negative externalities in the marriage market. Thus, by running away with an officer, the heroin's sister brings shame on the whole family and thereby makes all sisters unmarriageable. The discussion in the essay examines how such an externality is or can be internalized.

Limits of the Homo Economicus model

Economic science was based mainly, perhaps entirely, on the assumption of rational behavior. To behave rationally, an agent, whether individual or collective, needs to optimize in the sense of consistently maximizing an objective function under one or several constraints. The absence of constraints would open the possibility of saturation, which economists consider to be out of the scope of their inquiry. In their world of scarcity, the preferences of the maximizing agents must obey some rules of internal consistency, such as the transitivity rule (if an agent prefers A to B, and B to C, then s/he must also prefer A to C).

Over the last decades, however, economists have considerably broadened their approach to human behavior, not only by enlarging their understanding of what constitutes an agent's objective function (for example, they have allowed altruistic concerns or status and prestige to be ingredients of that function) but also by extending the concept of rationality itself, both in the sense of tightening and relaxing its definition. Tightening has taken the form of strategic rationality, which implies that an agent is able to anticipate and take into account how other actors will respond to his/her moves. This new concept of rationality has given rise to game-theoretic explorations of human behavior, thereby causing a genuine revolution in the way economists understand the world. By contrast, relaxing the strictures of the conventional concept of rational behavior has implied the absence of optimization and the reckoning that agents' actions may be driven by limited or bounded rationality. Under the latter approach, favored by evolutionary economists, agents act myopically: for example, they blindly emulate successful neighbors or mechanically base their decisions on past outcomes, such as when they replicate a successful behavior that they have themselves followed in the recent past.

As could be expected, most literary works depict human characters and explore the motives of human actions as well as their consequences, whether intended or not. It is therefore not surprising that a large number of essays featured in this book can be regrouped under the theme "Limits of the Homo Economicus model". While the first of these essays is essentially an illustration of how rationality, as economists commonly understand it, is set to work in a particular circumstance, all the other essays are concerned with some limitation of rational behavior. They present rich material that should be privileged food for thought not only for economists interested in the micro-foundations of their discipline but also for other social scientists and literature lovers appealed by the mysteries of human soul and behavior.

In her essay titled "The Esterházy Myth: How Economics and Literature Correct Mistakes", Piroska Nagy-Mohácsi takes her inspiration from a novel written by the renowned Hungarian writer/mathematician Peter Esterhazy and called *Harmonia Caelestis* (Celestial Harmonies). In this epic, the author tells the family's history after World War II, the Soviet occupation, the communist rule, as well as its dispossession and forced relocation to a god-forbidden rural area in the middle of Hungary's nowhere. The long-term impact of the short-lived Hungarian revolt against the Soviet regime in 1957 is also brought to the fore. A drama occurs because, against all expectations, the writer discovers an unbearable truth just after having completed this saga in which the role of his father during the turbulent times succeeding World War II is being continuously extolled. While going through the archives of the country's security agency, he finds that his much-admired father was an informant between 1957 and 1980, reporting on close family, friends, and acquaintances – whomever the country's security agency instructed him to.

An excruciating dilemma then arises: should the writer keep the shattering truth to himself, or should he tell it to the public? The core of Nagy-Mohácsi's essay is devoted to shedding light on the considerations that led to the writer's decision. Most interestingly, we are not taken to a controversy between morality and expediency but, instead, to a reasoned calculus of the benefits and costs of each option. A critical dimension of the problem emphasized in the essay is the risk involved if the truth ever reaches the public through a third party. A risk-averse writer will prefer to avoid such a risk which could end up damaging his reputation irreparably or could subject him to constant blackmailing by those who have access to the archives. A risk-taker, on the other hand, would not give much weight to the prospect of third-party denunciation, but would be highly sensitive to the loss of reputation he would suffer if his father's image turned out to be that of a collaborator or traitor. The fact that Esterhazy eventually chooses to reveal the truth to the public by publishing a sequel book attests that he was of the risk-averse type. Nagy-Mohácsi then proceeds by mentioning a number of examples in which published economics papers have proven to contain false results. And she looks at similarities and differences between art and science as to how the problem of falsehood is framed and needs to be solved.

In his essay "Chekhov: The Nostalgia for Lost Opportunities", Jean-Philippe Platteau inquires about the limited power of rationality by wondering how human beings can fail to reach happiness. The idea of this theme was suggested to him by two remarkable short stories of Anton Chekhov, *The Violin of Rothschild* and *A Discovery*. In the first story, Chekhov describes a man obsessed with the realization that he could have made higher profits than what he actually earned. And when his totally devoted, self-sacrificing wife dies, a big shock occurs that leads him to question the way he ran his life and the suffering he imposed on her. Still, his obsession about lost opportunities persists and the question arises as to how he can leave the path that he has trodden until now. In the second story, a retired bureaucrat ruminates about his recent encounter with a woman of an extraordinary beauty whom he passionately fell in love with while he was young. With age, however, she lost her physical appeal and the hero cannot help thinking about the horror she would have felt had she been able to anticipate her present appearance. He then picks up a pen and starts to draw a picture of the lady at the time her beauty was at her apex. Coincidentally, by looking at the drawing, he then discovers that he possesses the talent of a genuine artist. This discovery leads him to imagine what his life could have been if he had become an artist rather than a state bureaucrat.

Two distinct questions are at the center of these two inspiring stories: the apparent inability of men and women to make correct long-term choices (that is, choices that maximize their lifetime happiness), and the way people choose to react when they come to realize at a later stage of their life that they made wrong, perhaps irreversible, decisions. In the stories, the first question is raised in terms of lost opportunities and foregone gains whereas the second question is approached from the angle of regrets and nostalgic feelings. What does economic theory teach us on these questions and how far does it go toward accounting for what Chekhov precisely says are the central objects of inquiry in the ensuing discussion. Emphasis is put on the fact that in Chekhov the heroes are not capable of anticipatory expectations and they appear to be largely myopic. They experiment through trial and error, yet not in the systematic manner postulated by evolutionary theory. This is because their mind and their willpower are constantly absorbed and distracted by the daily businesses and duties of human life. How does the individual then deal with the unavoidable regrets is the next question. One solution is to suppress cognitive dissonance, that is, to fabricate a self-justificatory explanation for the bad past decision. This is clearly the solution chosen by the hero of "*A discovery*", yet not by the hero of "*The violin of Rothschild*". In the latter story, the mistakes are so egregious that they cannot be reasonably justified. Death then appears as the only exit. Could it be that individual annihilation is the only outcome in such situations? In a remarkable twist of pen, Chekhov refuses this dead end: in an ultimate gesture, the hero imparts an ultimate meaning to his life.

In his essay "The Financial Expert of Malgudi", Avinash Dixit follows the thread of the story told by one of the greatest Indian writers, R. K. Narayan, in his famous novella titled *The Financial Expert*. Set in the fictitious South Indian town of Malgudi, the story raises the same questions as those emerging from the above-reported novellas of Chekhov, and it should not come as a surprise that Narayan was considered to be a writer "of Gogol's stature" and that the experience of reading one of his novels, such as *The Financial Expert*, is "comparable to one's first reaction to the great Russian novels: the fresh realization of the common humanity of all peoples" (Margaret Parton in *New York Herald Tribune Book Review*). Margayya, the hero of this novel, is indeed a highly touching character who is full of love for his son and his grandchild in particular and is at the same time possessed by an irrepressible degree of greed. What makes him so moving for the reader is that he is acutely aware of his bad penchant for money and the devious turn of his mind, which he appears to see as an incurable disease.

Margayya's career is that of an entrepreneur who successively performs the functions of a scribe, a small-scale moneylender, and the publisher of a successful sex manual written by a business partner. Using the money accumulated under the last two ventures, he embarks upon a Ponzi scheme that inevitably comes crashing down on its head. Feuds in a typical Indian extended family arise as a result, and they are painted in Narayan's simple, sparkling, and charming prose with a gentle touch of humor and irony. As we have just hinted at, his character is quite complex. On the one hand, his business choices are driven by an obsession with money with predictable tragic consequences but, on the other hand, like Homo Economicus, he wants money for the things it will buy him as well as the things and education it will buy for his son. Because the latter is what he cherishes most, he is willing to work hard and long hours to guarantee him and his family as best a life as possible. Moreover, he wants to gain respect in his community and family. The problem is that these aspirations come against his possession with money, a drive that in his case seems overwhelming. Here is therefore a gifted and hardworking person who could perhaps have become a successful entrepreneur engaged in sustainable productive ventures. Unfortunately, he is led astray by an urge for short-term profits and psychological motives that push him in the wrong direction. His mind is literally devoured by his megalomania (he dreams that someone points up to the sun-lit horizon and says, "All that is yours") and his ceaseless struggle "to work up the interest rate" on any financial proposition that comes to his head, engulfing him "in a terrible quantity of figures" (in Part Three of the novel). Finally, Margayya's obsession with money is compared by Dixit with similar characters in some other works of fiction, notably Aravind Adiga's *Last Man in Tower* and Leo Tolstoy's *How Much Land Does a Man Need?*

In the next two essays, the problem of human rationality is tackled through stories that involve inheritance. In the first of these, "Estates, Inheritance and Gifts: Looking a Gift Horse in the Mouth", Luiz De Mello discusses a novel written by one of the most celebrated writers of Latin America, Machado de Assis, who also happens to be an economist. The novel, whose title is simply *The Inheritance*, deals with the reasons that motivate people to bequeath their wealth, at least in part, to their family or close relatives, as well as the expectations of those on the receiving end of an inheritance, including notions of equity and fairness that are at the heart of these expectations.

The narrative is crisp, centered around an elderly lady, Venância, whose closest relatives are two nephews. The first one, Marcos, is an introspective and meticulous character whose selfless devotion and attentive care is taken for granted, yet remains unappreciated by his aunt. The other is his flamboyant brother, Emílio, who is unable to stick to any commitment and whose demeanor is guided more by familial obligations than personal attachment to Venância. The plot is developed around the wish of Venância to get Emílio to marry Eugênia, a devoted niece, who acquiesces to this decision, albeit reluctantly. The twist is that Emílio demurs at his aunt's plan and, to everyone's surprise, it is actually Marcos who proposes to marry Eugênia. Venância is eventually pleased with the arrangement since it allows her to provide for her niece after all. Another rebound nevertheless occurs with her passing away shortly after the marriage deal is struck. The grand finale is Machado's at his best: when the will is read by the notaries, the reader discovers that Venância has bequeathed her small fortune to Emílio, her favorite, whereas Marcos is left pondering the deep motives behind such an unexpected decision. The fact of the matter is that the aunt's spontaneous fondness for Emilio outweighed all rational considerations, thereby attesting that emotions sometimes drive human behavior against all odds. The end of the novel, in Machado's tradition, blends personal and social elements.

The second essay concerned with inheritance is "The Inheritance Mess: Père Goriot and King Lear Offer Us a Mirror" by Marianne David and Pierre Pestieau. Based on novels written by two world-famous writers, William Shakespeare and Honoré de Balzac, *King Lear* and *Père Goriot*, respectively, it makes the point that emotions and lack of reflection can lead parents to make irrational choices when they have to decide the kinds of bequests they want to allocate to their children. Both works illustrate the awkward problem facing aging parents whose adult children refuse to provide them with the affection and the resources they need. What David and Pestieau call "the pathological blindness" of fathers is at the root of their wretched poverty toward the end of their lives. Père Goriot is a pasta manufacturer who was ruined by his selfish daughters in the bourgeois milieu of 19th century Paris. Ruin was caused not only by the generous dowries he granted them at the time of their marriage (dowries are pre-mortem inheritance for girls) but also from the continuous gifts he continued to make later under their pressing demands for help. It is because he wanted to buy their affection and maintain a relationship with them that he complied with each of their whims and came to their rescue whenever they ran into financial problems as a result of their extravagant way of living. In return, he made himself fall into sordid poverty and received only contemptuous treatment from both the daughters and sons-in-law.

In Shakespeare's work, the tragic end of King Lear is attributed to wrong decisions regarding inter vivos gifts (under the form of dowries) to his daughters when announcing his will to parcel out his kingdom. A grave error of judgment thus misled him to disinherit and curse the only daughter, Cordelia, who sincerely loves him, and to favor the two uncaring daughters, Goneril and Regan, who are adept at flattering him. The blatant error was made because of the restrained expression of filial love feelings by Cordelia and the stupid pride and vindictiveness of the king himself. The latter paid dearly for that mistake as he was eventually transformed from a monarch into a beggar.

These are typical and extreme examples in which emotions have dominated the use of reason. As the economic theory of strategic bequest teaches us, indeed, the tragic consequences of filial ingratitude and abandonment can be warded off by making end-of-life bequeaths rather than inter vivos gifts. Making bequests conditional on the provision of love and care during the lifetime of the parents should enable them to discipline their children so that they will come to their help in times of need. Such a rational approach nevertheless requires that parents somehow overcome their craving for a relationship with their children that would be free of calculation and strategy. The tragedy of Père Goriot and King Lear also originates in their stubbornness and inability to learn. Even if a friend had cautioned and forewarned them of the dire consequences of their actions and mental attitudes, their behavior would not have changed. When the Duke of Kent thus warns Lear of the effects his decisions could have, Lear banishes his trusted friend and counselor. And when the Fool tries to remind him that giving up the crown would mean a loss of authority, he sends him away. Living in his own imaginary world, the benighted king parts with those who most care for him, including his most loving daughter.

All the above-discussed essays obviously deal with irrational behavior as can be observed in the microeconomic sphere of life. By contrast, the last two essays draw from illustrations pertaining to the macroeconomic sphere. The first of these essays, "The Master, the Helicopter, and Margarita" by Luc Leruth and Danielle Meuwly, is based on a novella which has been cited earlier in this introduction. Like most great novellas, *The Master and Margarita* can be analyzed from multiple perspectives: a love story, an apology for artistic freedom, a parody of the USSR, and several economic standpoints, including the dysfunction of the housing market, as done in this book by Serguei Guriev, and an allegory of "helicopter money", as done in the present essay.

In a part of his novella, Bulgakov explores the myth of easy money. As the Devil makes money fall from the ceiling of a theater, the spectators (from Moscow in the 1930s) rush to catch the banknotes thinking that they have got a free meal.

> 'One!' … 'Two!' … 'Three! There was a flash, a bang, and immediately a cascade of white pieces of paper began to float down from the dome above the auditorium.' … 'A few seconds later the shower of money reached the stalls and the audience began catching it.'… 'It was the uniquely delicious smell of newly-printed money.'

Or was it? Some people keep the money and discover later on that the notes have become worthless pieces of paper. Some others use the notes immediately to buy fancy clothes, a move facilitated by the devil who offers the spectators a convenient opportunity to spend their newly acquired money in the store that he has just opened on the stage. As soon as they leave the theater, however, the latter are deprived of their newly acquired riches: "He saw on the pavement a woman wearing nothing but a pair of violet knickers, a hat and an umbrella". To add to the chaos, a merchant who had been paid in bad notes decides to complain, following which the devil examines the pieces of paper and returns them to the merchant, assuring him that they are true. The merchant leaves, satisfied, at least for a short while.

What is remarkable about Bulgakov's brilliant allegory is that he was living in the Soviet (planned) economy and was still able to successfully describe the working of the monetary concept of "helicopter money" that would have a formidable theoretical impact in the capitalist world a few decades later. He perceptively imagines how Muscovites would respond to the apparent blessing of a fall of money from the sky and he investigates their behavior as they spend that money, react to the resulting inflation, build unreasonable expectations, and obstinately try to hold on to the belief that there is indeed a "“free meal”. In the process, Bulgakov comes to the conclusion that people are cognitively limited, being prone to illusion and myopia. They do not seem to be interested in reality, and they tend to quickly forget any unpleasant event and to react aggressively to anyone interested in a rational explanation of what is happening.

The second essay concerned with macroeconomic-level irrational behavior is "Money in the Faustian Pact" by Alfred Steinherr. As its title indicates, it is based on the celebrated play of Goethe called *Faust*, or more exactly on *Faust 2*, one of his very late writings. In it, Faust and Mephistopheles, the devil to whom Faust sold his soul, wander around the world, which gives Goethe the opportunity to reflect on the political, social, and economic issues of his times. Their journey leads them to a badly indebted and economically decaying State, which Mephisto attempts to rescue by convincing the ruler to pay his debts by issuing paper money based on the assets supposedly hidden underground throughout the State.

In the light of this story, the essay explores the key questions of confidence in money, its exchange rate against gold and silver, and its use. At the beginning, everything seems safe and the price of gold and silver remains stable: people are happy. At the same time, however, aggregate demand is propelled by this massive creation of money, and we are told how Goethe pictured what we would now call a Keynesian multiplier-backed spending spree that increases the velocity of money. The result is that the country falls into chaos, high inflation, and civil war. The essay also suggests that Mephisto's seduction of the emperor to create paper money foreshadowed the crisis that struck the Euro in the early 2010s.

Rent-seeking, corruption, and bad political governance

Irrational behavior, mistakes, and judgment errors at individual or collective levels are not the only features susceptible to causing avoidable misery for human beings. Dysfunction at the level of the system of regulations and institutions within which agents operate can also cause useless pains, at least for a significant fraction of the individuals subject to those rules and institutions. The consequences of institutional dysfunction have recently gained so much attention in economics as to give rise to a new subdiscipline known as political economics. In this new field, the state or any public agency is considered a full-fledged actor endowed with the capacity of strategic rationality and facing other rational actors such as the civil society, the people, the elite, the army, the church or a set of decentralized clerics or tribal leaders, etc. In the three following essays, various aspects of institutional and political dysfunction are the center of interest.

In her essay "How Steinbeck Speaks to Institutions in Economics", Stuti Khemani discusses John Steinbeck's novella *The Pearl*, which is set in Baja California Sur, Mexico. The story is that of a poor Mexican fisherman who struggles to sustain a meager livelihood and is even unable to pay the doctor when he brings him his child stung by a scorpion. The fisherman desperately looks for money, and he is lucky enough to find an amazing pearl upon a dive into the sea. Things should be happily settled then, but this is not the course followed by the story. Local traders make a coalition to bring down the price of the pearl and when the fisherman sets on a journey to get a better sell on a more distant market, his boat is attacked by robbers. It seems that a whole coalition of evil men, who include the doctor and other locals jealous of his success, have decided to band against him and bring him back to his erstwhile poverty status. Tension arises between the fisherman and his wife as the latter wants him to throw the pearl back into the sea so as to end their predicament. But he would not give up and his courage leads to a tragic end.

In short, the essay thus describes a poverty trap caused by the alignment of local elites whose malevolent actions are not regulated by proper institutions. Inefficient institutions and practices driven by power considerations result in non-cooperative behavior at the expense of most people involved, the more vulnerable ones in particular. In the present instance, no mutually beneficial transaction takes place because each side is motivated by something other than economic incentives – the pearl traders by a desire to exploit, and the pearl fisherman by his rage against unfairness and injustice.

The problem of power abuse is also at the heart of the essay written by Celestin Monga The Economics of Innocence: Imbolo Mbue's *How Beautiful We Were*". The novel by Imbolo Mbue pictures a fictional African village whose inhabitants are confronted with a powerful multinational corporation, an American oil company which exploits their underground resources. The effects of the latter's investment are calamitous as its oil pipelines and drilling sites have left the fields fallow and the water poisoned, while children are dying. Understandably, villagers want to get rid of the company, or at least to obtain reparations. They feel desperate because the government, in fact, an authoritarian regime embodied in a sort of despot named His Excellency, does not come to their help. Not only it does not redistribute the income obtained from taxation of the company's profits, because it considers it as a political rent, but also it does not put any pressure on the foreign firm to compensate the local inhabitants for the damage caused. Rebellion starts almost inadvertently under the impulse of an atypical villager called "the madman" and in the form of a kidnapping. Then, following a brutal reaction of the regime which shows no sign of compromise, the violence escalates in an unstoppable spiral, the tragic consequences of which are entirely borne by the innocent villagers. Although the latter would have liked to find a compromise and avoid to shed blood, this possibility is foreclosed by the intransigent dictator colluding with the company. In the end, the company agents are horrified by the turn of the events, yet it is too late to change course.

The striking message from the novel is that recourse to violence by the victims was not a spontaneous reaction or choice made by them from the beginning. It was imposed on them by a repressive power used to answer any expression of popular grievances by brutal force. There is no room for negotiation whatsoever because the elite in power do not accept any erosion of their rents. In these circumstances, the only possible outcome is a rebellion by despair that proves extremely costly for the party deprived of any bargaining power. The story is especially touching because it evokes many other situations of today's real world that we can observe around us. We may think, in particular, of the apparent hopelessness of the peaceful rebellions of the people of Iran and Hong-Kong against an absolute authority that has shut its ears to all complaints interpretable as a questioning of its power (and privileges).

In his essay, "The Political Economy of Poverty in Herbert's *Dune*", Mark Koyama explores a celebrated work of science fiction, which narrates the rise of a hero – a freedom fighter and a prophet – Paul Atreides. The setting is the planet Arrakis or *Dune* – desert planet – one of the countless planets within a vast galactic empire knitted together by the spice trade. Dying of thirst is common on Arrakis, and the majority of ordinary people are and remain poor. Yet, despite an obvious ecological explanation for this situation – being a desert planet, Arrakis lacks the resources, the carrying capacity, and especially the water to sustain its population at any higher standard of living – a deeper investigation reveals that the operation of institutional rather than ecological or even technological factors is responsible for Dune's miserable state of the economy. Technologies actually exist to transform the desert of Arrakis into a garden and, if the planet remains an inhospitable desert, it is because it is badly governed. This path of thinking leads the essay's author to explore some key ideas in classical works of political economy, drawing on Herbert's novel to discuss insights from Ibn Khaldun, Adam Smith, and numerous other classical and modern economic thinkers.

Relationship with the traditional field of "Literature and Economics" studies

To conclude this introduction, it is worth coming back to the endeavor of the present volume and its relationship with the field of "Literature and Economics" to avoid confusion about the way of reading it. As stated in our Foreword, we see it as indeed coming to the field of Literature and Economics but from a somewhat different direction than the path so far trodden by experts in that field. To be sure, we do not aim to replace the existing scholarship, but to complement it with a new perspective and new modes of thought, and thereby expand and enrich the domain of Literature and Economics studies. Here we limit ourselves to discussing some of its prevailing limitations, so as to better highlight the value added of our contribution.

We start with *Economics and Literature: A Comparative Interdisciplinary Approach* (eds. Çınla Akdere and Christine Barton, Routledge, 2018, labeled AB hereafter), because it has the advantage of offering a rather extensive survey of the previous literature. We also mention, more briefly, some other material that was brought to our attention. We then explain why and how our own volume differs, in its approach to "economics and literature".

The strand of literature which (AB) belongs to is generally known as "literary criticism", defined as "a specialized body of knowledge that explores characters placed in an economic environment, or sequence of economic events, or economic ideas and controversies as they are narrated in literary texts" (Akdere, Baron, and Ingrao, in (AB), p. 5). The objective is to outline "how separate fields, such as economics, history of economic thought and literary studies, can mutually benefit from interdisciplinary exchanges and shared subjects" (p. 7). Put otherwise, the purpose is to create "a joint field of study for economists, historians of economics and literary scholars, in which they could share competences in research and exchange information on themes of joint interest in the interdisciplinary field of economics and literature" (p. 7). In some sense, our own contribution may fit that definition but, in order to further spell out later what is specific in it, it is useful to probe a bit into the precise tasks covered by the definition proposed by Akdere, Baron, and Ingrao. Two features stand out.

First, several studies address the question of how economic theory was perceived and judged by literary writers. Or they study the evolution of novels as a mode of exposition and a literary style under the influence of the economic realities and social transformations of their times. This is, for example, what Goux does in Chapter 7 when, studying the work of Stendahl, he observes the rise of the novel and the fact that it is permeated by economic themes. According to him, the new literary genre has emerged in parallel with the rise of the new individual, the "enterprising hero", favored by the democratic society. This is also what Akdere and Baron do in Chapter 8 when they detect in Gide's *Faux monnayeurs* "a meditation about the way the 20th century novel can renew the genre" (p. 11). Again, we can characterize in the same way the textual analysis of Gertrude Stein's work by Key (Chapter 9) when she explores "the similarity between literary fiction and money as representative forms of writing".

Second, many works profess to follow an epistemological approach, which has sometimes been labeled "epistemocriticism". The perspective is now different as the focus, or one of the central emphases, is squarely put on the task of challenging "the simplified representation of rational behaviour proposed in so many economic models" on the basis of the "plenty of opportunities" provided by literary texts (p. 4). The idea is to demystify economics, meaning making it appear "to be less of an exact science than economists would like" (p. 4). Behind this ambitious attempt lies a sort of nostalgia for what economics was in the 19th century, when economists were at the same time moral and political philosophers, and they were not yet "dominated by the imprinting of mathematics and physics and marked by the use of mathematical models". This domination is the main culprit for "the divorce of economics from studies in the humanities, not to speak of literature or the arts" (p. 4).

The tone is very similar in many contributions included in *The Routledge Companion to Literature and Economics* (Routledge, 2019) which can be, at least partly, considered to partake of the subfields of history of economic thought and epistemology based on the discussion of literary works. The same can be said, with one exception, of the contributions to the edited issue of the Fabula journal which all deal with Balzac's painting of 19th century bankers in "La maison Nuncingen" (MN). One contribution focuses on the "Faustian" aspect of the banker character, another compares Balzac's characters to the actual bankers of his time, while others deal with the "immorality" of bankers and banking, criticize Balzac's rather weak fictional vein in this particular piece, or reflect on the utility of money in the light of Aristotle's concept of "chrematistic" and Marx' famous circuits of money-capital. The exception is the contribution of an economist who rightly focuses on the role of the asymmetry of information that characterizes banking, which was probably more pronounced in the mid-19th century.

Turning to another edited book, *From Political Economy to Economics through Nineteenth-Century Literature: Reclaiming the Social* (Palgrave, 2019), a distinctive feature of its set of contributions is that they are all written by academics in the fields of English and English Literature who belong to departments of English Language, Comparative Literary and Cultural Studies. The themes addressed by these authors include inequity, slavery, exploitation, human capital, and sustainability, but it is striking that their treatment markedly differs from what economists would write on the same subjects even while discussing literary texts.

It is perhaps not surprising that, as economists, we have points of disagreement with judgments coming from the approach of "epistemocriticism" that we feel rather distant from literary criticism, even when it presumably deals with economics. The originality of our own project lies in an approach to literature that views literary works as a privileged way of enriching economics rather than deconstructing or transforming it. With regard to the latter attempt, from which we depart, a few important observations deserve to be made. To begin with, we do not agree with the contention that literary texts can challenge economic theories. Economic theories can only be challenged by empirical evidence gathered according to strictly defined criteria. Theories can only be tested against data harnessed and analyzed through statistical methods. Observations made by sharp novel writers can only provide intuitions and anecdotal evidence susceptible to yielding stylized facts. This contribution is not to be underestimated as intuition is so critical to guide theorists in search of testable hypotheses, but it is not dispositive. Moreover, writers' observations can point to facts that economic theories are unable to account for, thereby stimulating theorists to refine or modify their explanatory models. Much of this has already happened under the impact of psychological, sociological, and institutional research: economic theory is not what it was thirty years ago, and what many of those coming from the traditional field of literary criticism think it still is. Our own book offers numerous illustrations of the rich insights that economics can offer.

If our book fits the same general purpose expressed in the introduction of (AB), a key difference is that the conversation we promote is not between economics and literary studies but between economics and literary masterworks themselves. This implies that we do not intend to build a (new) "interdisciplinary field of economics and literature", in which economists would dialogue with specialists of literary studies. What we more modestly seek to encourage is a dialogue between economists and novel writers or, if this looks too ambitious, between economists and the literary production of these writers. We strongly believe, indeed, that the interdisciplinary exchanges between economists and literature can create inter-fecundation.

Questions related to how economic thinking and realities were perceived by literary writers and how they influenced their works and their way of writing are tasks belonging to the realm of literary research and beyond our own competence. The contributors to our volume have all been trained in modern economics and, despite the knowledge they may have of it, they do not claim to add to the history of economic ideas, nor do they aim at using literary texts to systematically criticize economic theory. Instead, their essays are based on the direct reading of one or a few novels and an interpretative discussion in the light of economic concepts and theories as they are available in today's body of economic knowledge. Authors do not presume that this knowledge is a priori right or wrong. They just dispassionately try to determine to what extent it can shed light on a novel that they have felt particularly attracted to. On the other hand, observations by novel writers may raise questions that are not easily or straightforwardly answerable by existing theories, in which case they stimulate economists to exercise their mind in looking for extensions of these theories or, alternatively, to acknowledge the limits of the knowledge they contain. To the extent that novels often epitomize everyday life, the various essays in our volume show the pertinence of economic analysis in understanding critical real-life situations. Readers will no doubt be fascinated to discover modern economics "at work" in captivating stories coming from practically all over the world. A last but important element to differentiate our volume from other related books is, indeed, *variety*. The contributors to our volume are well-known economists who come from many different horizons (geographic, obviously, but also in terms of specialized fields of economic theory and "schools of thoughts"). They have each selected a literary masterpiece that appealed to them, typically because they spotted an economic angle that could enrich the analysis of a character in the novel or their own research work. The setting in space and time of the novels and stories differs just as widely as do those of the authors of the literary works and of our chapter contributors. This makes us confident that we fulfilled our aim to see how the perspectives of many different economists about many different novels or stories combine.

PART I

Development and structural transformation of society and economy

1

A BENGALI NOVEL ON ECONOMIC TRANSITION IN HISTORY

Pranab Bardhan

1.1 Introduction

For my contribution to this volume, I have chosen to write on a major theme in economic history, that of economic transition and its ramifications, drawing upon a novel in Bengali by one of Bengal's foremost writers, Tarasankar Bandyopadhyay (1898–1971). He is not well-known outside Bengal—except that two of Satyajit Ray's movies, *The Music Room* and *Expedition*, are based on his short stories—but in West Bengal he is widely regarded as one of the three most powerful novelists in the post-Tagore twentieth century. In his twenties and early thirties, he was a social activist in the villages of his native district, Birbhum, in West Bengal, and in that period he closely studied the lives of common people there, including the marginalized groups, which is reflected in his several novels written in the 1940s.

The novel I have chosen for this chapter is one of them, titled *Hansuli Banker Upakatha* ("The Tale of the Hansuli Turn"), published in 1951 (though a shorter version came out a few years earlier in a magazine). Hansuli Turn refers to a bend in the river Kopai in Birbhum district, where the particular hamlet and its people that the novel is about is located. Fortunately, there is a good translation of the novel published in 2011 by Columbia University Press; the translator is Ben Conisbee Baer, a Princeton professor of comparative literature. For my quotes from the novel, I am going to depend on this translation (with its page marks). One remarkable feature of this translation is that a plurality of creoles or dialects instead of standardized English have been regularly used to translate the special dialogues of marginalized people.

The novel is about the social transformation of a marginalized group in a remote village in central Bengal. This transformation is brought about by the

DOI: 10.4324/9781003534358-3

expansion of colonial "modern" capital, a war economy, and commercialization which shake and transform the lives of an oppressed primitive community in a segregated village society, and the old traditional leaders of the community are replaced by young entrepreneurial-type leaders.

The economic issue I have in mind falls within a major theme of economic history and political economy: what in the European context[1] is called "transition from feudalism to capitalism"—this does not quite apply here, because these villages did not have European-style feudalism, and what threatens to replace the pre-market pre-capitalist community life is not quite capitalism either. But it is a major transition of some sort with economic as well as social ramifications. Being a novel, it brings out the complexities which do not fall neatly into our pre-conceived historical categories.

1.2 The contours of the peasant economy

The main focus of the novel is on an extremely poor socially marginalized group of people, called Kahars, who originally settled on a wasteland and the ruins of a colonial indigo plantation. The Kahars used to be palanquin-bearers for the private transport of rich people (originally the planters and then the local gentry who took over after the planters left). At the time of this novel, as that form of private transport had faded away, the Kahars were working as farm laborers and sharecroppers for the gentry, and sometimes also got some land from them to cultivate on their own. Another group, called Atpoures, were in an adjacent hamlet; their original occupation was that of armed guards; over time they also got some land from their masters, but they were indifferent to farming, and more often took to thievery and robbery as their main occupation.

The masters are of two kinds. Status-wise one was lower, called Sadgops and Mondols, who used to be farmers who worked on their land along with their hired labor, but increasingly off their own manual labor and dependent only on hired hands, as they become semi-gentrified. The other, higher in status, was the landed gentry always having the workers to till their land and also to be on-call for other kinds of service as the need arose. The poor have to borrow money for their subsistence in half the year from the gentry, and they pay back with their labor and with paddy (the main crop).[2] But at loan payment time, which is immediately after harvesting, paddy price is at its lowest, so the poor have to pay a great deal more paddy than when they borrowed, usually in the lean season when the price was higher.[3] The Sadgops sometimes also cheat, as they are to keep accounts of labor and credit transactions for the illiterate Kahars, and they forget to do that for months keeping Kahars in the dark about what is due to them.

The main protagonist in the novel is Bonwari, the headman of the Kahar hamlet, who looks after their worldly affairs and is also the protector of their *dharma* (ethical and religious principles). On behalf of the Kahar community, he tries to ensure adherence to the prescriptions of its gods and forefathers, and respect for its myths, memories, and rituals. He is admired and respected in the community. He frequently visits the wooded shrine of the presiding deity of the community, "Kartababa" (Lord/Father), and pays his homage and organizes the community offerings there, and asks for his forbearance in cases of lapses in community behavior and for guidance in times of crisis. He gives leadership to the peasants on the fields at cultivation time and he is obsequiously loyal to the landlords/masters of the community. The Kahars do not have clocks; they measure the workdays by the times of trains crossing the bridge over the river Kopai.

1.3 The rebel

Pitted against him is a rather haughty but dynamic young Kahar, Karali by name. The novel starts with a mysterious whistling sound in the forests that continues for days, which mystifies and frightens the community as an omen for bad things to come. While the community cowers, Karali goes with a flashlight into the bamboo groves and finds that the source of the whistle is a large viper around Kartababa's shrine. He kills and burns the great snake. A part of the community is relieved, but the older members fear that Kartababa is going to punish the community for killing his pet snake.

Karali refuses to work on the fields in the Kahar's traditional farm work for the landlords. He works as a coolie leader in the nearby small town of Chandanpur where there is a railyard and factory. The workshop is described thus: "Rows of iron machines booming, clashing, ponding, clattering—as if a great slaughter has begun. Sometimes they scream out with a whooping shriek … .the noise will turn you deaf (p. 277)". This reflects the usual fear of the traditional peasant of working with grinding machines in the factory.

Karali inspires other young Kahars to follow him to do nonfarm wage work, giving up their forefathers' life of farm labor under traditional subjugation. Then when the Second World War comes and the Japanese advance near the borders of Bengal, the colonial rulers mobilize wartime production and the town economy hums and the job prospects and earnings for Karali and his young followers improve. He puts on a coat, long pants, a cap, and even a shoe, while most Kahars are barely dressed and go barefoot all their lives. For the first time for a Kahar, he also tries to build a brick house for himself, which the Kahars who always lived in thatched huts, led by Bonwari, are against; they object to this breaking of forefathers' rules, and initially even destroy the foundations of the building. Undaunted, Karali gets police protection and builds his brick house—as if the tall building was "the raised banner of Karali's obstinacy" (p. 272). In the Kahar community, "It is as if Karali is from a foreign land….They can't bear so much vanity, so much arrogance" (p. 239).

Karali constantly moves between the hamlet and the town and is not just the force of mobility and economic change; he also represents the break with the age-old structure of ignorance, superstition, and segregation that characterizes the life of Kahars. When a big storm threatens the village, the Kahars including their headman look at the ominous sky and think in terms of which of their misdeeds the gods are going to punish them for. Meanwhile, Karali rushes to the village and gives them the latest weather forecast the town has got by wire about the storm's approach. Bonwari thinks: "Storm, rain—since the forefathers' times, Kahars have received the news from ants, from rainbows, from windspeed; you've ....become a foreign infidel; you stick yer ear to telegraph poles in Channanpur an' hear all this news" (p. 297).

Karali hears about a boy in the hamlet dying of snake bite. He says the boy should have been taken to the town hospital, and they've got snake poison injection. Bonwari thinks the boy died as God's punishment of the community for Karali's devilry. To Bonwari the life that Karali is heralding is a threat to the moral and existential order of the community.

Karali also pushes on the social and class tension of the Kahars with their landlords. He resents the Kahars' servile acceptance of the landlords' use of casual insults even in ordinary conversations with them. He does not like the Kahars' taking away the leftover food from the dishes of the gentry. Once he said in their face: "Karali don't eat no polluted waste (p. 279)". He says the landlords may be stealing the Kahars' official ration of kerosene (used for lighting) and selling in the black market; he lodges a complaint with the authorities asking for an inquiry into the matter, which, of course, infuriates the landlords.

Here is an example of the furious exchange of words between Bonwari and Karali (p. 322) in their rustic creole.[4]

> Bonwari: "...Feeding mantras in the lads' ears—Give up karma o' forefathers' clan work, come ta the caste-wreckin' workshops ta labor....Ya got no shame...Now yer comin' ta make the local lads bad in the 'ead? Smug wi' money, wi' yer coat an' long pants, comi' ta show yerself off ta the ladies—ye're such a big man!"
>
> Karali: "...Gentryfolk, ye lick their feet, they take yer livelihood ... Beat yer backs wi' shoes, ya put up wi' it in silence. ...Karma o' clan's work! So clan karma's herdin, diggin', tendin' fer the farmers? Ye'll go ta paradise on a chariot fer that! Not enough rice fer yer bellies, not enough cloth ta wear. Clan karma!"

1.4 The demands of the war economy

Then the war economy comes closer. Squadrons of airplanes fly low over the hamlet to reach the airplane hangar built near Chandanpur. Red-graveled tarmac roads are built through the hamlet, where cars noisily go back and forth.

Forests are cut down by wartime timber contractors, and their tents and a car park come up at the place where Kartababa's shrine was. With the clearing of the bamboo groves which used to shroud and darken the Kahar neighborhood, now harsh glaring light comes into the area; it's too bright, and the groves which have been the repository of local ecology, life space, and memories are gone.

Bonwari thinks:

> You used to enter the village and be struck by a strange hypnotic depth in entrancing shadows.... All this destroyed by wiping out the deep shade of bamboo groves, banyan, and peepul. There would be no more free time for droopy-eyed slumbering under trees; there was no place remaining to linger in shade and compose the tale of Hansuli Turn's dreams.
>
> *(p. 360)*

War economy jacks up prices, which is supposed to have limited effect on the Kahars' food-wise subsistence economy, except for the scarcity of cloth, kerosene, and quinine (for fighting rampant malaria) which the Kahars cannot afford anymore. Even in paddy, the landlords suddenly announce that the rent is to be paid in paddy. As selling paddy in the market at higher prices becomes more profitable, the landlords also become stingy in their usual help in the form of paddy loans when the need arises. More people leave the community in search of wage work.

The social role of women is an important aspect of the life of Kahars. An old woman like Suchand acts as the main custodian of their history and the narrative of past virtue and present decline of values and devotion. Suchand deplores Karali's transgressive acts. But the younger women are sometimes quite adventurous. Some venture out to construction work in town, then have relations with masons and mechanics and go away with them (as did Karali's mother in the past, leaving a 5-year-old Karali behind); others work as maids in the day and in sex work at night. Suchand's daughter Bashan has a relation with someone in the town gentry and has a daughter born out of that relation. This daughter, Pakhi, leaves her marriage with a sick, older man and consorts openly and lives comfortably with Karali in his brick building. In a way the Kahars, even though bound by traditional mores and superstitions, are quite permissive of extra-marital relations. There are even festivals providing opportunities for forming non-traditional relations with someone for whom a character feels "heat". Such relations are sometimes given formal recognition (through "companion rites") by the community.

Even Bonwari, the protector of Kahar *dharma*, is attracted to the wife, named Kaloshashi, of the headman of the Atpoures in the adjacent hamlet. And when Kaloshashi is drowned, tumbling into the water after a fight and tussle with her husband at the river bank and the latter then goes fugitive,

Bonwari is persuaded by the Atpoures to take Kaloshoshi's niece named, Subashi, who looks in some ways similar to Kaloshoshi but younger, as a second wife, to cement an alliance between the two hamlets. Bonwari now becomes the common headman of the two hamlets.

It is when Subashi falls for the charms of Karali, the novel reaches a crisis point, and there is a vicious fight between Karali and the jealous husband Bonwari, in which Bonwari gets badly wounded, from which he never fully recovers. This fight, though immediately over a woman, is the culmination of the clashing values of Bonwari and Karali, representing the clash between the old subsistence peasant economy and the new, brash, commercial economy which lures the young and the aspiring.

Subashi leaves Bonwari when he is unconscious after the fight. At the end, Bonwari dies in the company only of the roving balladeer of the community, Pagol, and the trans-woman in the village, Nasubala. Most other people have left him and the hamlet. From his deathbed, Bonwari hears the constant noise of the timber contractors clearing the forests. After Bonwari dies, Karali comes and touches his feet paying his respect to a vanishing way of life.

> The Kahars are now a new people. In dress, speech, beliefs, they've really changed. They've exchanged smears of earth, dust, mud for engine oil; exchanged plow and scythe for dealings with hammer, crowbar, pickaxe. Yet even as they toil in Chandanpur's workshops they die from starvation, die of disease; instead of dying from snakebite they're sliced by machines, crushed by wagons.
>
> *(p. 370)*

This clearly is a picture of economic transition, from a low-level debt-ridden subsistence peasant economy to one of a commercial economy based largely on the peasants now working as wage labor. In this transition some individuals (like Karali) act as dynamic leaders rejecting—and persuading others, particularly the young, to reject—the traditional ways (of exploitation and fatalism, of subjugation and indignity) in favor of a high exchange-value "modern", more mechanized, economy. This also involves a change in their habits, beliefs, and norms. But as the last sentence of the previous paragraph suggests, the writer of this novel does not consider this transition as necessarily a mark of "progress" from the point of view of workers' welfare or life chances. The main change may be in the particular form of exploitation, in the nature of uncertainties and perils of life, and in the structures of power. There is also some lingering nostalgia about a vanishing way of life. In any case, in contrast with an economic treatise, a novel usually tries to capture some subjective nuance and ambivalence, even while describing the objective reality of change.

1.5 Comparison with a couple of other novels

These transitions, of course, take different forms in different socio-economic and historical contexts. I was originally thinking of trying to contrast the depiction of social and economic change in *The Tale of Hansuli Turn* with the theme of social transformation in some European novels. For example, one of the greatest historical novels is *The Leopard* by the Sicilian writer, Giuseppe Tomasi di Lampedusa, about the changes in Sicilian rural society in the period of Risorgimento—how during the upheaval the rural class system is eroded by newly moneyed peasants and a "shabby minor gentry". In contrast, this Bengali novel is more "from below", entirely from the point of view of the most oppressed community of low-caste landless sharecroppers and the kind of wrenching changes they go through.

A somewhat more comparable case may be garnered from Latin American novels on the lives of poor marginalized indigenous communities. My attention was drawn to the 1949 novel *Man of Maize* by the Guatemalan Nobel laureate writer Miguel Asturias. It focuses on the contrast between the traditional Mayan customs and those of a progressive modernizing society, and how the land of the indigenous maize-growing community is under threat from outsiders (capitalists and international companies) intent on its commercial exploitation. While in *The Tale of Hansuli Turn* the isolated community breaks from inside with some rebellious young people taking the lead, the emphasis in *Man of Maize* is more on the futile resistance by the indigenous community to the outsiders; in the end their magic world of myths and legends is lost, but the author's passionate belief in them persists in a Utopian note, as the indigenous people become ants to transport the maize they have harvested. In *The Tale of Hansuli Turn* also there are myths and legends enveloping the traditional community, but the focus is more on the harsh reality of socio-economic transition and less on magic realism.

Notes

1 There are similar accounts in Japanese history as well. In his classic work on Tokugawa Japan, Smith (1959) tells us about how erstwhile tenants called *nago* run away from their masters (the *oyakata*) in order to seize new economic opportunities created by the silk industry, and the pre-existing feudal structure disintegrates.

2 These kinds of land, labor, and credit relations are quite common in the development economics literature. For an account of such relations on the basis of village survey data in West Bengal, see Bardhan (1984). Among other things I describe the system of "Dadan" in Bengal agriculture where the peasant borrower takes paddy as an advance mainly for consumption purpose, which he pays back with labor. This debt relation may involve varying degrees of "labor-tying" by the employer-lender. In my co-authored paper, Bardhan and Rudra (1981), we discuss the whole spectrum of such tying relations in labor, starting at one end of completely free wage labor all the way to the other end of completely bonded labor with very little

freedom for the worker. In our random sample of 110 villages in West Bengal, such cases of completely bonded labor were statistically not very significant. Of course, our survey period was at the end of 1970s, more than four decades after the author of the novel made his observations in the district of Birbhum.

3 Such taking advantage of the inter-seasonal price difference by the lender at the expense of the borrower was a common practice in situations when the lender had a territorial monopoly in credit relations.

4 If anyone needs a translation of this exchange into plain English, here it is:

Bonwari: "…Feeding mantras in the lads' ears—Give up karma of forefathers' clan work, come to the caste-wrecking workshops to labor…. You got no shame … Now you are coming to make the local lads bad in the head? Smug with money, with your coat and long pants, coming to show yourself off to the ladies—you are such a big man!".

Karali: "…Gentryfolk, you lick their feet, they take your livelihood … Beat your backs with shoes, you put up with it in silence. …Karma of clan's work! So clan karma is herding, digging, tending for the farmers? You'll go to paradise on a chariot for that! Not enough rice for your bellies, not enough cloth to wear. Clan karma!".

References

Bandyopadhyay, T., *The Tale of Hansuli Turn* (New York: Columbia University Press, 2011). (Translated by Ben Conisbee Baer).

Bardhan, P., *Land, Labor and Rural Poverty* (New York: Columbia University Press, 1984).

Bardhan, P. and Rudra, A., "Terms and Conditions of Labor Contracts in Agriculture: Results of a Survey in West Bengal 1979," *Oxford Bulletin of Economics and Statistics*, 43 (February 1981), 89–111.

Smith, T.C., *Agrarian Origins of Modern Japan* (Stanford: Stanford University Press, 1959).

2

TRADITION AND MODERNITY IN SUB-SAHARAN AFRICA

Insights from Achebe's *Things Fall Apart*

Ernest Aryeetey and Jean-Philippe Platteau

2.1 The setting and the thread of the novel

Things Fall Apart by Chinua Achebe is easily one of the most widely read books of African origin, and it is undeniably a masterwork. The quality of the prose and the depth of the subject chosen by the author are striking features of this jewel piece of world literature. Even though the story is located in a small part of *Igbo* land, Eastern Nigeria, it resonates well in most parts of colonial Africa. It is the story of proud people who do or do not confront social, economic, and political change over a crucial period of their modern history. They were dealing with change from within, prompted by inter-generational developments, as well as change from outside occasioned by colonial adventures into Africa.

While the story is dominated by the life and choices of Okonkwo, the novel's central character, it sheds a lot of light on institutional and behavioral aspects of the development and structural transformation of his society, including his family, neighbors, the larger clan or community, and other village communities as well. The main merit of *Things Fall Apart* is to propose a view full of contrasts which are not necessarily as clear-cut as they may seem. To better highlight the hard choices confronting the Igbo people at the time of the British intrusion into their lives, Achebe has chosen to put controversies between two men at the heart of his narrative: Okonkwo and his close friend Obierika.

Achebe's novel is divided into three parts. The first part deals with social life in the pre-colonial Igbo society, and unexpected contrasts emerge from the author's account of life in Umuofia, the village of Okonkwo and Obierika. The second part recounts the life of Okonkwo during a period of exile from his community. His expulsion was caused by his inadvertent killing of a young boy

DOI: 10.4324/9781003534358-4

from his village. As for the third part, where the main plot unfolds, it centers on the varied responses to the arrival of British missionaries and officials in Umuofia, which occurred during Okonkwo's exile.

Below, following life events in the order adopted by Achebe, we discuss the main themes that run through his exploration of the Igbo society before and after the advent of European colonialism.

2.2 Life among the Igbos before British colonialism

The picture of the Igbo pre-colonial society offered by Achebe is an odd combination of traditional beliefs and oppressive social customs, on the one hand, and a modicum of individual liberties, women's rights, and an achieving culture, on the other hand. This assessment requires elucidation. To begin with, Igbo life was permeated by beliefs in the power of ancestral spirits (the *egwugwu*), which "appeared from the underworld, speaking in a tremulous, unearthly voice, and completely covered in raffia" (Achebe, 2010, p. 85). While some of them were "quite harmless", others were "very violent". Supernatural powers could also express their will through the Oracle of the Hills and the Caves or manifest themselves as the Evil Spirit. The main point is that "the land of the living was not far removed from the domain of the ancestors" (Achebe, 2010, p. 85) and that the central role of the spirits was to enforce the local customs and punish the transgressors. A related function consisted of settling disputes, such as when the Evil Forest speaks to human bodies to listen to the arguments of the contending parties before pronouncing its judgment (pp. 64–65). Its judgment is indisputable: "Does a man speak when a god speaks?" (p. 71).

Interestingly, social customs are community-specific: "what is good in one place is bad in another place" (p. 53). Thus, bride price payments and the methods used to set their amount may vary from one group of villages to another: there, "they do not decide bride price as we do, with sticks. They haggle and bargain as if they were buying a goat or a cow in the market" (p. 53).

Not all the customs described by Achebe were innocuous. Some of them were truly harmful. Three illustrations stand out. First, in Umuofia the custom demanded that twin children be thrown away because, for some obscure reason, they represented a danger to the community. In Achebe's words: "The Earth had decreed that they were an offence on the land and must be destroyed" (p. 87). Second, Okonkwo is expelled from the community for seven years because, at a funeral ceremony for a respected elder, he untowardly killed his 16-year-old boy. The fact of the matter is that when guns fired the last salute to the deceased, "his gun exploded and a piece of iron had pierced the boy's heart" (p. 86). The punishment meted out on Okonkwo was justified on the ground that he had polluted the land with the blood of a kinsman: it was a crime against the earth goddess to kill a clansman, and the only course open to the man who committed the offense was to flee from the clan and from the land (p. 87).

Finally, and most horrendously, Umuofia decided to execute Imekefuna, the adopted son of Okonkwo, because the Oracle of the Hills and the Caves had pronounced this sentence. This was especially tragic as Okonkwo had developed a feeling of deep affection for Imekefuna and wanted to bequeath his plantation to him because he trusted him to be best able to maintain it. He was also very grateful to his adopted son for his beneficial influence on his own biological son, Nwoye, who considered Imekefuna "like an elder brother" and started to grow up thanks to his presence. This means that he was becoming "tougher", more autonomous vis-à-vis women, and hence better prepared to rule his father's household "when he was dead and gone to join the ancestors" (p. 39). To understand the kind of logic that led the Oracle to order the death of a young innocent man, we must bear in mind the circumstances under which Imekefuna was forced to leave his family. What happened then was that Okonkwo, as a great local leader, was charged by a coalition of nine villages with the task of carrying a message of war to their enemies unless they agreed to deliver a virgin and a young man to atone for the murder of the wife of a clan member named Udo. Fearing the strength of Umuofia, the enemies gave in: a virgin was given to Udo as wife and the lad, Ikemefuna, was brought to the clan elders who asked Okonkwo to take him in his household "for a while" which should not exceed three years (p. 22). The decision to execute the unfortunate lad after this period elapsed was thus sheer revenge killing.

The harmful character of gender-related norms is more ambiguous. For one thing, there was a bias against women as the Igbo society was patriarchal and masculinity was defined by opposition to the female character. Thus, Okonkwo called a woman a man of low achievement and low social status who dared contradict him, and this was obviously considered an insult by the people around. More generally, a man was expected to demonstrate his strength and to eschew any public expression of affection, which was "a sign of weakness": in a typical manner, Okonkwo "never showed any emotion openly, unless it be the emotion of anger" (p. 22). To become a household head, moreover, a man had to show that he was able to "rule his women and children (and especially his women)", that is, that he was "really a man" (p. 39). Gender norms regarding the division of labor and household tasks were quite constraining as we understand from Okonkwo's remark that he would have liked his daughter Ezinma to be a boy because he deemed her better capable of managing his productive assets than his son Nwoye. Clearly, women's potential was hampered and even stifled by prevailing gender norms about task distribution.

The Igbo women whom Achebe describes are far from being helpless or totally submissive, though. Thus, when Chielo, the priestess of the god Agbala, the Oracle of the Hills and the Caves, came on a late evening to Okonkwo's compound to convey Agbala's summon order for Ezinma, a daughter he had with Ekwefi, he eventually let Chielo take her away on her back (Chielo was a village woman who was occasionally prophesying when possessed by the spirit of her god). But Ekwefi did not agree and decided to follow her daughter on the way to the sacred mountain's abode where Agbala was staying (pp. 70–71). This was a really daring move that Okonkwo would never have made by himself, and which she pursued despite Chielo's dire warning, "May Agbala shave your head with a blazed razor. May he twist your neck until you see your heels" (p. 73). To retrieve and protect her child, Ekwefi was ready to confront "all the gods in the world" (p. 76). She did not need to, however, because Chielo brought Ezinma to her bedroom quietly. Interestingly, Okonkwo eventually decided to follow in the footsteps of his wife, but only after "he had allowed what he regarded as a reasonable and manly interval to pass…" (p. 78). This instance wonderfully attests to the sense of initiative and courage that a woman is capable of, and to the leadership role she can play vis-à-vis her husband despite many appearances to the contrary. In addition, women appear to have had a good measure of freedom in matters of partner choice, as illustrated by the possibility for a woman to run away from a husband whom she dislikes. This happened again with Ekwefi, who was the first love (and wife) of Okonkwo, when she broke her first marriage after just two years. As "the moon was shining", she left her conjugal dwelling and went knocking at the door of Okonkwo. Without hesitation, he carried her "into his bed and in the darkness began to feel around her waist for the loose end of her cloth" (p. 76).

Given the existence of oppressive social norms and cruel mores, an intriguing feature of Umuofia is its characterization as an achieving society in which competition is not confined to the economic realm but extends to the social and political spheres. In Achebe's novel, the former feature is well epitomized by Okonkwo's astonishing rise from poverty. He "did not inherit a barn from his father", Unoka, who was known in all the clan for the weakness of his machete and his hoe. According to another account, Unoka "had a bad *chi* or personal god, and evil fortune followed him to the grave" (p. 15). Being landless, Okonkwo had to start as a sharecropper and it is thanks to his hard work and enterprising mindset combined with a loan from a richer community member who trusted his abilities – this man, Nwakibie, trusted Okonkwo so much that he gave him twice as many seed-yams as he asked for – that he succeeded in accumulating wealth and a solid reputation.[1] In short, "his fame rested on solid personal achievements" and it helped him a lot that the clan "judged a man by the work of his hands" (pp. 5, 21).

Social competition in Umuofia takes the form of competition for titles, and a man who could win four titles (a rare achievement) had reached the top of the social prestige ladder and become a "lord of the land" (p. 86). Social prestige and honor are obtained not only through the accumulation of wealth and economic success but also through achievements on grounds of "masculinity", among which stands supremacy in the popular sport of wrestling. In addition to being a successful producer, Okonkwo was thus "the greatest wrestler and warrior alive of his community" (p. 82), all qualities that contributed to make him a natural leader of the place. Social and economic accomplishments are logically translated into political authority and power, as testified by the experience of Okonkwo who "had risen so suddenly from great poverty and misfortune to be one of the lords of the clan" (p. 21). Hard work was obviously a highly valued virtue in Igbo society and poverty was deemed to arise from laziness. As a consequence, there was a great deal of economic and social mobility coexisting with a seemingly accepted measure of economic and social inequality: Okonkwo "had no patience with unsuccessful men. He had had no patience with his father" (p. 5). Inheritance was a potential source of inequality but, as witnessed by the life of Okonkwo, it was not necessarily insurmountable. As a matter of fact, "a man was judged according to his worth and not according to the worth of his father".

In the end, Igbo society appears as a strange mixture of economic dynamism and social conservatism, of individualism and rigid rules anchored in tradition and supported by supernatural beliefs. To many Western readers and scholars, such a nuanced and complex account of an achieving society pervaded by reactionary customs is challenging and fascinating.

2.3 The shock between tradition and modernity

The second part of *Things Fall Apart* describes how Okonkwo, exiled in the village of his mother, relies on the solidarity of his mother's clan to start a new life from scratch. His mother's kinsmen thus helped him to build his hut, and he was awarded land to plant a new farm with seed-yams, which were advanced to him by cousins. Like in Umuofia, his predisposition for hard work and his enterprising spirit worked wonders although he never stopped dreaming of returning to his home village, the only place where he could expect to regain social prestige and political importance. This eventually happened after the seven-year period prescribed by the Oracle. Upon his return, he discovered to his great surprise that an important change had shaken social life in his native area, and his reaction to the presence of colonial agents, traders, and missionaries constitutes the main theme of Achebe's investigation.

When the fate of Ikemefuna was decided by the elders speaking through the voice of the Oracle, and then communicated to Okonkwo, it was made clear to the latter that his active participation in the execution was not required from him. All he was asked for was to bring the boy to the place where his death would meet him. Nonetheless, Okonkwo decided to directly take part in the crime on the ground that, as a matter of principle, "the law of the land must be obeyed". His close friend, Obierika, disagreed, retorting that "I don't know how we got that law" (p. 50). This divergence between the two men persisted and amplified when the issue at stake was whether it was right to send children to the missionary schools and, more generally, to accept the British influence, at least in part, or to reject it altogether. Consistent with his deep-seated conservatism and rigid adherence to the customs of the land, Okonkwo, unlike his friend, adopted the latter attitude. Here is thus a man who espouses the important individual-centered values of the colonizer when it comes to economic activity, with their focus on hard work and personal responsibility, yet obstinately refuses the European culture and system of rules, which are viewed as a direct threat to the indigenous culture and identity of the Igbos.

The shock of the two cultures is especially brutal when the missionaries squarely confront local beliefs in the power of ancestors by asserting the supremacy of the unique God of the Christians. A missionary thus said to an old man: "All the gods you have named are not gods at all. They are gods of deceit who tell you to kill your fellows and destroy innocent children. There is only one true God…". But another man is not convinced: "If we leave our gods and follow your god, who will protect us from the anger of our neglected gods and ancestors?" The missionary had a ready answer: "Your gods are not alive and cannot do you any harm … They are pieces of wood and stone". Upon hearing it, the assembly "broke into derisive laughter" (p. 103). Okonkwo, in particular, thought the missionary "was mad", as testified by his absurd talk about the Holy Trinity and the existence of a Son of God who did not have a biological father. Not everybody laughed, however. Even though he himself did not understand the logic of the Holy Trinity and related concepts, Nwoye, the first son of Okonkwo, was captivated by the new religion. For him, indeed, it "seemed to answer a vague and persistent question that haunted his young soul – the question of the twins crying in the bush and the question of Ikemefuna who was killed". The fact is that "He felt a relief within as the hymn poured into his parched soul. The words of the [religious] hymn were like the drops of frozen rain melting on the dry palate of the panting earth" (p. 104).

In Achebe's account, the arrival of missionaries brought a conflict between those who condone oppressive customs and those who dislike them and for whom the new order appears to answer their frustrations with the existing order. This conflict is capable of tearing apart not only communities but also families, as epitomized by the clash between Okonkwo and Nwoye who left his father's house when he decided to join the missionary school. When asked why he did not consult the former beforehand, the latter replied: "he is not my father" (p. 101). As for Okonkwo himself, he cursed Nwoye because "to abandon the gods of one's father and go about with a lot of effeminate men clucking like old hens was the very depth of abomination": was it not a shame and a sign of impending annihilation of the whole clan that at the ancestral shrine, fathers would wait "in vain for worship and sacrifice" and find "nothing but ashes of bygone days" (p. 108)?

For those who did not attach a supreme value to the old order of things, the temptation to rally round the colonial system was strengthened by new economic opportunities emerging through the privileged channels of modern education and local trading posts. Was it not the first time that money flowed to Umuofia as a result of the high prices at which palm oil and kernel could be sold? Here, we need to bear in mind our previous characterization of the Igbo society as both a collectivist society endowed with a strong clan structure, many family-based solidarity arrangements, and powerful authority institutions, on the one hand, and an achieving society rewarding personal qualities or efforts and entrusting important economic decisions to individuals, on the other hand. Clearly, some aspects of this society were amenable to the sort of change heralded by the colonial order while other aspects were doomed to be a source of resistance against its penetration. Whether adoption or resistance would be chosen was a matter of individual preferences and preferences in turn depended on the place of the individual in the old social order and the extent to which s/he had suffered from its oppressive norms and customs.

Resistance was amplified by the fact that, in addition to the church, "the white man had also brought a government" and a system of courts before which people could be brought for trial on the ground that "they offended against the white man's law", for instance, by throwing away their twins. Court messengers, who were also prison guards, "were greatly hated because they were foreigners and also arrogant and high-handed". This feeling was especially strong among men with titles who occupied the upper positions in the old order: they "were grieved by the indignity" caused by their arrest, their beating, and the imposition of menial work by the new authorities while they were jailed (p. 123).

At the other end of the spectrum, two groups of people were most likely to join the church: the youngsters and the outcasts. The former are especially tempted because, as one elder put it, they "do not understand how strong is the bond of kinship", and they "do not know what it is to speak with one voice" (p. 117). The motivation of the outcasts, that is, those who were disenfranchised in their own communities, is straightforward since the church offered them the opportunity of full social integration. It is revealing that even the Christian converts who did not hesitate to boast openly that all ancient gods "were dead and impotent" initially resisted the idea of sitting with the outcasts in the church. The local missionary had to spend much energy explaining to them that they were all children of God and that before God, "there is no slave or free" (pp. 109–110), in order to persuade them to accept the presence of outcasts inside the church.

That the arrival of European colonists resulted in the inescapable splitting of the indigenous Igbo society has been masterfully depicted by Achebe. He used the voice of Obierika trying to explain to Okonkwo what happened to their people and their system:

> The white man is very clever. He came quietly and peaceably with his religion. We were amused at his foolishness and allowed him to stay. Now he has won our brothers, and our clan can no longer act like one. He has put a knife on the things that held us together and we have fallen apart.
>
> *(p. 124)*

Fighting against this trend was a lost battle despite the relatively small number of foreign occupiers. The reason was that too many Igbos had already followed their way and been given power.

How does Achebe's narrative proceed from here? A group of elders supporting the old order went to the local priest, Mr. Smith, to proclaim their decision to destroy the church which breeds "untold abominations". They also conveyed the message that he was welcome to stay with the Igbos but only if he liked their way. He is allowed to worship his own god because "it is good that a man should worship the gods and the spirits of his fathers". But he should stop showing disrespect for the local customs (p. 134). The missionary's response was uncompromising, and the outcome was the burning of the church, following which a small group of six elder rebels, including Okonkwo, were arrested and jailed. They stayed locked up for a few days until a fine set at 250 bags of cowries (out of which 50 were embezzled by the court messengers) was paid by Umuofia. The payment was made under acute pressure as the messengers exaggerated the stake involved by wrongly claiming that unless the cowries were delivered immediately, the rebels would be hanged on the very next day. An assembly of the clan was then convened to which the returning rebels were expected to participate.

Okonkwo slept very little during the previous night as "the bitterness in his heart was now mixed with a kind of childlike excitement" (p. 140). The fact is that he entertained the hope of seeing the whole people of Umuofia reunited on the occasion and was ready to launch a war against the whites as they had done in the past with much success against rival clans. He therefore prepared his war dress, his tall feather headgear, and his shield. Although it seemed that people went in great numbers to the assembly – there were "so many people that if one threw up a grain of sand it would not find its way to the earth again" (p. 141) – the first speaker named Okika noted that the sons of Umuofia were not all present in the meeting, some of them having "broken the clan and gone their several ways". While the missing brothers were deserting their clan and joined a stranger "to soil their fatherland", those attending "have remained true to their fathers". The latter must nevertheless be aware that if they decided to fight the stranger, they would hit their brothers and perhaps shed the blood of a clansman. Yet, because the evil must be rooted out, it was their duty to do "what our fathers would never have done" (p. 142). In the meantime, a group of court messengers arrived to communicate the District Commissioner's order to stop the meeting. Okonkwo would not let them pass and killed the head messenger with his machete. At that moment, he knew that Umuofia would not go to war.

The novel ends tragically with the suicide of Okonkwo, his body dangling from a tree in his garden. Clan members had to ask the District Commissioner and his men who came to arrest him to bring down the body. According to the custom, indeed, it is an abomination for a man to take his own life since he thus commits a severe offense against the Earth. As a consequence, his body cannot be buried by his clansmen. Hence the request to the Commissioner to perform that duty. As a student of what he considered to be primitive customs in Africa, the latter found the episode worth noting down for insertion in the book he was working on and titled "The Pacification of the Primitive Tribes of the Lower Niger" (pp. 145–146). Obierika was deeply affected by the death of his great friend and angry against the colonial authorities which evinced so little understanding of, and empathy with, the Igbo society. This was especially pathetic since Obierika was himself a pragmatist. He was wise enough to understand that the balance of power was neatly in favor of the well-equipped British armed forces and that local customs and beliefs needed a liberal interpretation so as to allow for proper adjustment to the new realities.

2.4 Discussion

2.4.1 The cultural shock

At the center of *Things Fall Apart* lies the cultural shock caused by the advent of modern colonialism in Africa, the stakes involved, its consequences, the distance between colonizers and colonized, and the confrontation of indigenous beliefs and customs by Christianity. With respect to the latter, the debate resembles the way Martin Scorcese, in his famous movie *Silence*, has addressed the same issue: the Japanese authorities dispute the right of (Jesuit) missionaries to make converts among the local population on the ground that they exploit the misery of destitute people to entice them to foreign rituals and beliefs. A great merit of Achebe's novel is that it does not hesitate to depict cruel and unambiguously harmful customs and to emphasize the vulnerability of the Igbo society that would result from them if an external alternative is proposed. Upon reading *Things Fall Apart*, conversion to Christianity does not appear as the only or even the main result of a brutal imposition of alien beliefs on ignorant people by missionaries backed by the force of a colonial government, such as is commonly argued in the social science literature. Conversion is represented as an escape from the traditional social order for those who suffer the most from it – think of Nwoye, whom the tradition-sanctioned murder or his beloved "half-brother" Ikemefuna shocked deeply and irremediably, or think of the outcasts – or for those who deem some customs a hindrance to progress, such as young people. In short, the picture emerging from the novel strongly suggests that there is a demand for the new religion. Moreover, this demand is clearly not sparked by the content of the Christian doctrine with several abstract tenets. What appeals to the latter is rather its egalitarian message (there cannot be any outcast in the church) and its rejection of horrifying customs that involve unjustified killings of human beings.

Because customs are an important ingredient of a culture and social identity is anchored in culture, people who highly value their inherited identity tend to defend the customs and beliefs that they grew up with. This happens although clinging to traditional values and mores often implies the sacrificing of economic advantages promised by the new order. This is a basic intuition behind the economics of identity championed by Akerlof and Kranton (2000): people's preferences may be such that a trade-off arises between personal material gains or income and faithfulness to values or group identity. To the extent that a society is heterogeneous in the sense that preferences vary from one individual or group of individuals to another, a shock manifested in the rise of new economic opportunities and ways of exiting the traditional social order is predicted to cause a division of the society between those who want change and those who don't. Regarding the former, the intuition according to which people may convert to escape stifling norms and customs or undue tradition-based constraints on individual initiative is at the heart of the economics of religious conversion proposed by Platteau (2014: 179–187, 2019).

Inasmuch as religious conversion is generally seen as the outcome of a genuine choice, Achebe's account suggests that competition between ancestors' beliefs and Christianity is fair and healthy. The economics of religion pioneered by Iannaccone (1990, 1995a, 1998), Barros and Garoupa (2002), Montgomery (2003), and others (see Iannaccone, 1995b; Aldashev and Platteau, 2013, for reviews), which is based on the rational choice approach and the idea of competition between different religious denominations, is therefore relevant to our discussion, yet with a big caveat. So far, indeed, it has focused on competition between monotheistic churches, in rich countries in particular, thereby bypassing the effects of competition between these churches and traditional communities given to ancestors' beliefs. It may be noted that economists who believe, or think they have shown empirically, that certain (monotheistic) religions have a positive impact on economic outcomes tend to attribute their success to their influence on personal traits such as honesty, thrift, willingness to work hard, and openness to strangers (see, for example, McCleary and Barro, 2006).

2.4.2 The undermining of trust

As is evident from the above, the problem of internal divisions and even splitting of local communities under the influence of colonialism receives a lot of attention in *Things Fall Apart*. They are associated with the growing economic inequalities that entry into the new order by only a fraction of community members is bound to create. Furthermore, given that trust is expected to reduce transaction costs, and overcome collective action and incentive problems created by human opportunism (people are willing to free ride on others' efforts), an important consequence of the breakup of communities and the ensuing undermining of trust consists of deleterious effects for both social cohesion and economic development (Putnam, 1993). To make things worse, the dent in trust takes the form not only of a fall of mutual trust among community members but also of a growing mistrust of institutions. The latter form is worrying as the vanishing trust in traditional authorities has not been replaced by an emerging trust in the new institutions established by colonial powers. We are thus far from the optimistic modernization scenario described by Inglehart (1997), in which a society moves from trust in neighbors and relatives to trust in new institutions, or the one described by Inglehart and Welzel (2005) in which modernization promotes trust by boosting human empowerment through accumulation of resources available collectively.

If we follow Achebe's narrative on the issue of governance, there are two levels at which mistrust is bred. First, at the macro level, the common people feel that the central authorities (epitomized by the District Commissioner) do not understand them because they are too distant and ignorant about their problems and their needs. Moreover, authorities tend to be arrogant, being persuaded that they possess all the required skills and knowledge. People resent the lack of consultation and negotiation to which they were accustomed in their ancestral village life, and for them colonial power therefore has all the characteristics of arbitrariness. This is patent in land matters: the colonial administration took the land they needed from the people without much concern for the traditional authorities in charge of land allocation and the underlying rules. One cannot avoid the impression that dynamic entrepreneurs like Okonkwo could perhaps have been rallied to the modernization cause if more respect for traditional beliefs had been evinced by the colonial power and more participatory procedures put in place by the same.

Second, at the local or micro level, as illustrated by the behavior of court messengers, official agents often indulged in petty corruption, thanks to poor supervision and/or deliberate condoning by higher authorities. Such a laxity is especially harmful because it gives rise to a class of lowly people who are eager to improve their status by pleasing foreign rulers rather than attending to the needs of the people. They are easily perceived to be shameless collaborators, ready to cynically sell their soul to the powerful. The damage is particularly big if "collaborators" are also recruited from the ranks of the local population, thereby sparking a rift between "brothers".

The twin issues of governance and corruption were there to stay and even become worse after independence. A common explanation is that after the rather brief interlude of the independence struggle during which many interest groups joined together for a common goal (the removal of colonial rule), African elites often seized the opportunity of the new state to enter the shoes of the white colonists and reproduce in many ways their authoritarian and clientelistic methods (see, for example, Iliffe, 2007; Bayart, 2009). Unlike under colonial rule, however, post-independence African politics has been rife with factionalism and contests where parochial interests prevailed.[2] Corruption generally got worse because in a context of political instability created by a fierce competition for the spoils of power, rulers tend to have a short-term horizon that discourages the long-term strategies without which the grounds for sustainable development cannot be established.

Two findings from Afrobarometer surveys are worth reporting here: (i) people tend to evince increasing trust in informal institutions, such as religious and traditional leaders, and declining trust in the formal executive agencies of the state; (ii) trust or mistrust is typically related to the issue of the perception of corruption and the unfair inequalities it creates.[3] These findings do not mean, however, that old social networks are being restored. As individuals were primarily concerned with finding their position in the new order established through colonial rule, fragmentation of the society along the lines of narrow interest groups appeared there to stay.

If adherence to traditional religious practices, such as religious sacrifices and other rituals, remains persistent in many places where they frequently coexist with Western religious practices, we simultaneously observe a growing penetration of local evangelical churches which emphasize the role of the Holy Spirit and the importance of prayers and devotional acts. These notions being familiar to Africans, the success of the new churches is not surprising. Their appeal to certain population groups, women in particular, is enhanced by the fact that they simultaneously require a radical distancing vis-à-vis (the most harmful or gender-biased) ancestral norms and customs and help to promote trust among co-religionaries so that internal group activities or cooperation are likely to be successful. Whatever the exact motivations to join them, the important point is that new social networks are emerging in the depth of the African society, and they bear an obvious link to Achebe's narrative.

2.5 Conclusion

Things Fall Apart is a landmark of African literature. It provides us with a unique insider description of the Igbo society in Nigeria and the way it was deeply and irremediably affected by British colonization. According to the author, the Igbo society was a much more complex fabric than what conventional accounts of pre-colonial African societies suggest. It was not devoid of elements of an achieving society but, at the same time, was pervaded by stifling and oppressive norms, customs, and beliefs. The latter were shaken by the arrival of the British colonists and missionaries, and this created a fracture inside the body of the Igbo society. Modern values, even if not always well understood or appreciated, were appealing to some groups of the local population, particularly young people and outcasts. Achebe's account actually hints that had British colonizers consisted only of the establishment of trading posts without the accompaniment of ideological (religious) intrusive forces and distant rulers full of arrogance, it would have been more generally and easily accepted by the pre-colonial society.

Important themes are addressed in the course of the narration, and many have remained acutely topical to this date: the conflict between tradition and modernity, the role of private economic initiative, the influence of religion and local churches, governance and people's participation, corruption, trust, and inequality, in particular. They are especially relevant because Africa is still struggling with economic development challenges which indicate that its engagement with the rest of the world through colonization did not necessarily lead to the type of desirable outcomes associated with modernization. More than six decades after most African countries became independent from colonial rule, large parts of the region wallow in poverty, and most societies are highly unequal. Productivity is very poor in many sectors, especially agriculture. While countries have made significant efforts to develop institutions aimed at supporting modernization of their economies and societies, the results have been mostly disappointing, and the issues of governance and corruption have remained largely unsolved.

It is thus revealing that Nigeria, which is at the center of Achebe's novel, is one of the African countries with the highest incidence of corruption, according to the Transparency International Corruption Index. It has been reported by PricewaterhouseCoopers (PwC) that corruption in Nigeria could cost up to 37% of the country's GDP by 2030, a cost equivalent to around $1000 per person in 2014 and nearly $2,000 per person in 2030. Many analysts have discussed the extent to which corruption has undermined the democratic values of trust, credibility of governments, and good governance in Nigeria. Corruption has again been attributed to the reduction in the principles of accountability, transparency, integrity, and quality representation in policy-making. Others have attributed corruption (in the form of mismanagement of public funds) as the leading cause of the collapse of infrastructures such as the provision of water, good road networks, health facilities, good and standard education, security, and employment to most Nigerians. Clearly, as in many other places in Africa, the (political) institutions needed for an effective delivery of public service have not been properly constituted.

With real genius, Achebe has depicted the process of dissolution of the fabric of a pre-colonial African society caused by the intrusion of the "white men". Today, we still do not know how this fabric is going to be reconstructed in a way that can make a great majority of African inhabitants better off on a sustainable basis.

Notes

1 Nwakibie said:

> It pleases me to see a young man like you these days when our youth has gone so soft. Many young men have come to me to ask for yams but I have refused because I knew they would just dump them in the earth and leave them to be choked by weeds.
>
> *(p. 18)*

2 Nationalism was a veil behind which many parochial interests could conceal themselves, and "as predominantly local people, most Africans saw nationalism in part as a new idiom for ancient political contests" (Iliffe, 2007: 258). Nationalist movements were frequently plagued by factional conflicts that put local issues in the forefront while minimizing the importance of national party affiliations. Yet it is precisely because nationalism was thus absorbed into local political rivalries rather than being driven by broad social conflicts that it gathered the support needed to remove colonial rule. Unfortunately, it is for the same reason that after independence people continued to perceive national issues in terms of local interests and to judge their representatives and the state on the basis of their contributions to local advancement (Iliffe, 2007: 258, 267).

3 There is a recent literature in economics that studies the link between inequality and trust. Two interesting insights provided by it deserve mention here. First is the idea that the production of universal social policies or public goods tends to foster trust in state institutions (Zack and Knack, 2001; Rothstein and Uslaner, 2005). In the absence of such goods and policies, mistrust prevails and corruption increases it by encouraging dishonest behavior and violation of the law (You, 2017). Second is the possibility of multiple equilibrium situations insofar as inequality breeds mistrust and corruption which, in turn, deepen inequality, thereby creating a reciprocal causal relationship between inequality, corruption, and general trust (Zack and Knack, 2001; You, 2017).

References

Achebe, Chinua, 2010. *Things Fall Apart*. 1959 edition reprinted in: Achebe, Chinua (Ed.), *The African Trilogy*, New York, London & Toronto: Everyman's Library, Alfred A. Knopf, pp. 1–148.

Akerlof, G., and R. Kranton, 2000. "Economics and Identity". *Quarterly Journal of Economics*, Vol. 115, pp. 715–753.

Aldashev, G., and J.P. Platteau, 2013. "Religion, Culture and Development". In: Ginsburgh, V. and Throsby, D. (Eds.), *Handbook of the Economics of Art and Culture*, Vol. 2. Amsterdam: Elsevier and North-Holland, Chap. 21, pp. 587–631.

Barros, P.P., and N. Garoupa, 2002. "An Economic Theory of Church Strictness." *Economic Journal*, Vol. 112, N° 481, pp. 559–576.

Bayart, J.F., 2009. *The State in Africa: The Politics of the Belly*. Cambridge, MA: Polity Books (originally published in French at Fayard, Paris, 1989).

Iannaccone, L.R., 1990. "Religious Participation: A Human Capital Approach." *Journal for the Scientific Study of Religion*, Vol. 29, pp. 297–314

Iannaccone, L.R., 1995a. "Risk, Rationality and Religious Portfolios." *Economic Inquiry*, Vol. 38, pp. 285–295.

Iannaccone, L.R., 1995b. "Voodoo Economics? Reviewing the Rational Choice Approach to Religion." *Journal for the Scientific Study of Religion*, Vol. 34, pp. 76–88.

Iannaccone, L.R., 1998. "An Introduction to the Economics of Religion." *Journal of Economic Literature*, Vol. 36, pp. 1465–1495.

Iliffe, J., 2007. *Africans: The History of a Continent*. Cambridge: Cambridge University Press, (first published 1995).

Inglehart, R., 1997. *Modernization and Post-modernization: Cultural, Economic and Political Change in 43 Societies*. Princeton, NJ: Princeton University Press.

Inglehart, R., and C. Welzel, 2005. *Modernization, Cultural Change and Democracy*. New York & Cambridge: Cambridge University Press.

McCleary, R.M., and R.J. Barro, 2006. "Religion and Economy." *Journal of Economic Perspectives*, Vol. 20, N° 2, pp. 49–72.

Montgomery, J. 2003. "A Formalization and Test of the Religious Economies Model". *American Sociological Review*, Vol. 68, N° 5, pp. 782–809.

Platteau, J.P., 2014, "Redistributive Pressures in Sub-Saharan Africa: Causes, Consequences, and Coping Strategies". In: Akyeampong, E., Bates, R., Nunn, N., and Robinson, J. (Eds.), *Africa's Development in Historical Perspective*. New York: Cambridge University Press, pp. 153–207.

Platteau, J.P., 2019. "The Economics of Religious Conversion in Subsaharan Africa". In: Nnadozie, E., and Afeikhena, J. (Eds.), *African Economic Development*, Emerald Publishing, Chap. 11. Bingley, UK: Emerald Publishing, pp. 217–231.

Putnam, R., 1993. *Making Democracy Work: Civic Traditions in Modern Italy*. Princeton, NJ: Princeton University Press.

Rothstein, B. and Uslaner, E., 2005. "All for All; Equality, Corruption and Social Trust". *World Politics*, Vol. 58, N° 1, pp. 41–72.

You, J.S., 2017. "Trust and Corruption." In: Uslaner, E.M. (Ed.), *The Oxford Handbook of Social and Political Trust*, New York: Oxford University Press, pp. 473–496.

Zack, P.J., and Knack, S., 2001. "Trust and Growth." *The Economic Journal*, Vol. 111, pp. 295–321.

3

THE ART OF CONQUERING WITHOUT BEING RIGHT

Agency, education, and learning by doing in Cheikh Hamidou Kane's *Ambiguous Adventure*

Paul-Aarons Ngomo, Shourya Sen, and Leonard Wantchekon

3.1 Introduction

Cheikh Hamidou Kane's *Ambiguous Adventure* (1962) tells the story of the *Diallobé* community in colonial Senegal as it grapples with a difficult choice: preserving its identity or embracing new educational opportunities offered by the French administration. "If I told them to go to the new school, they would go en masse," their chief agonizes, "They would learn all the ways of joining wood to wood which we do not know. But, learning, they would also forget" (Kane, 1962, p. 34). This existential dilemma lies at the heart of the novel. Like many other African communities, the *Diallobé* have been defeated by the French; many are starving and dying. Amidst the unfolding uncertainty, the survival of the community hinges on resolving a crippling issue: remaining true to the religious "ultimate values" (p. 25) of the past or embracing modern education. Some, like the Grande Royale, a female *Diallobé* leader, now realize that in the new order, education is the currency of success and the means of self-assertion. Embracing what it offers comes with a promise of rewards and agency. But it entails a cultural sacrifice: that of losing the spiritual meanings immanent in the old world. Conversely, while clinging to spirituality may be morally satisfying, it leaves young people unprepared to face life in a new world as "things fall apart" around them. Those who choose adaptation over a moral vision steeped in traditional values learn "the art of conquering without being right" (p. 37) and recapture agency in a new order, while those who choose a cultural preservationist ethos undermine their future. In the new order, education not only shapes the distribution of rewards and coveted positional goods, but it also allows for the creation of new movements, ideas, and identities that are integral to self-preservation—in the words of Leopold Sedar Senghor

DOI: 10.4324/9781003534358-5

(1974, p. 36), the first president of Senegal, education is about "the creation of man by man."

Though the novel is a fictional account of a colonized society in the throes of a crisis, it also has ethnographic value insofar as it mirrors and is derived from the real-life experiences of the author in a traditional Senegalese Muslim community during colonialism. We use the novel as a starting point for a broader assessment of the history of colonial education in sub-Saharan Africa and the implications of this history for economic theory. Kane describes a world in flux and portrays an assortment of characters grappling with issues of societal transformation in communal settings.

The novel details the experiences of a young *Diallobé* man of aristocratic background, Samba Diallo, who, like the author of the novel Cheikh Hamidou Kane, is ultimately sent to France to study. As such, it centers the experiences of Africans as not only subjects but also agents in the profound colonial transformations of the late nineteenth and early twentieth centuries. Samba's father, the Knight, and the Grande Royale, a female leader, are both central figures in the debates on whether to embrace colonial education. As a child, Samba is a promising student of the Qur'an in rural Senegal, under the tutelage of the severe teacher Thierno, who provides Islamic education at his home. After much deliberation, the *Diallobé* decide to send Samba to the French school, discontinuing his religious studies, but Samba attends with a determination not to lose his *Diallobé* identity. A motivated student, Samba ultimately leaves Senegal for Paris to study philosophy. In Paris, he clings to his African and Muslim identity, eschewing alcohol and the currents of leftist politics that define his social milieu, but finds himself increasingly alienated from the traditional spirituality that he still holds dear. On his return to Senegal, Samba meets a sudden demise at the hands of the Fool, a religious fanatic, after he refuses to pray at the grave of the now deceased Thierno.

This is thus a novel about loss. Yet, in its undercurrents, if not in the top-line plot, it is also a novel about the enduring spirit of self-assertion and cultural renewal in existentially adverse conditions. Focusing on these undercurrents, we use the novel as a starting point for a meditation on how agency works, and how creation and innovation emerge in hostile conditions. These are extremely important questions both for economic theory and policy-making. Perhaps the most striking parts of the novel, in this regard, are not the plot details but the deeply philosophical deliberations among community members on the question of whether to embrace or reject colonial education, which we heavily draw upon throughout this essay. We complicate, and to some extent dissolve, the tension between "modern, Western education" on the one hand and "African tradition" on the other, which is at the heart of the novel. In fact, "Western" education was actually historically demanded and even largely supplied by Africans themselves as they, like the *Diallobé* in the novel, sought to reassert themselves. Meanwhile, as the novel shows, cultures of inclusive deliberation, which were progressive even by contemporary standards, were integral to the traditions of many African communities. This is not to deny that the Western education brought by colonial powers was part of a societal transformation that destroyed older ways of life. Indeed, this loss remains a psychologically potent force, supporting political mobilization along imagined "traditionalist" or "Islamist" lines even today, echoing the destructive response of the Fool. Yet such traditionalist forces themselves impose constructed and imagined practices precisely because they seek to reify differences between "Western" and "African" ways of life, which in fact have never been so clear-cut.[1] Because of the porousness of this distinction, aspects of both colonial education and traditional practice were integral to the re-imagining and renewal of African identities and political communities in the colonial and post-colonial world, toward distinctly African modernities.

Building on this history of cultural and political renewal, another aim of this essay is to emphasize African agency, against the structural constraints imposed by colonialism and other historical factors. Here, not only does *Ambiguous Adventure* center and vividly illustrate Africans' search for agency, but it also provides ways to conceptualize agency that are strikingly modern while also being rooted in the language of a traditional African community. Historically, despite the broadly authoritarian aims of colonial education and the tortuous compromises involved in accepting it, many Africans used colonial education as a source of empowerment, just as the *Diallobé* seek to do in the novel. To make sense of these histories, we conceptualize education not simply in terms of knowledge and human capital accumulation, which is the norm in much of the economics literature, but as a factor that supports broader processes of "learning by doing." Formal education, by providing intellectual tools and social networks that facilitate people's effective engagement with a rapidly changing environment, enhances and complements learning by doing. This is especially true in the context of rapid social change, where adaptation is crucial and there is an acute need to *learn* to "learn by doing" in a suddenly changed environment—that is, to accumulate the ever-expanding background knowledge and skills of practical reasoning that allow one to more effectively work on their environment. Learning by doing, African activists formed new deliberative networks and transformed their communities and the world through their innovations of new ideas, movements, and pedagogies in their fight for political autonomy. In fact, many African and Black diasporan thinkers, in line with and sometimes anticipating American pragmatist philosophies of education, explicitly developed and advanced pedagogical ideas that sought an ongoing empowerment of the individual in their environments, in line with notions of learning by doing, through formal education (Lambais et al., 2023).

The stories of Samba Diallo, the Grande Royale, and the biographical story of the author Cheikh Hamidou Kane epitomize those of many other African leaders and communities in their encounters with colonial education. We bring these narratives into dialogue with work in history, historical political economy, the political economy of education, and the political economy of policy deliberation. In doing so, we identify agency with understanding, intersubjectivity, and deliberation. Practices emphasizing deliberation and intersubjectivity have deep roots, though still understudied, in cultures throughout Africa. They have also been constitutive factors in the development of education, social movements, and effective policy-making in Africa and beyond. An important task for development policy in Africa and beyond is to remove impediments to learning by doing and support ongoing, intersubjective, environmental engagement.

The essay progresses by first connecting the story of the *Diallobé* as told in *Ambiguous Adventure*, as well as Kane's own life story, to the broader history of the supply and demand of education in sub-Saharan Africa under French and British colonial rule. Here we wish to highlight the broader historical context of colonial education in Africa. While the novel does not address this history, it provides an unparalleled illustration of the fight for agency that drove Africans to demand education. We contrast this history with empirical results in historical political economy and recent work on the inter-generational effects of colonial education in parts of Africa. We suggest that correcting historically inherited distortions in the supply of education in Africa should be a policy priority since it holds promise as a way to unlock creation and innovation. Further building on this argument and drawing more directly on the novel, we develop an idea of agency as "checking the external" (Kane, 1962, p. 79) and understanding "the architecture of responses" (p. 69). Agency is based on understanding natural and social environments, which then allows adaptation and the channeling of environmental causes toward desired ends. We finally briefly discuss the promises of deliberative policy-making as another way of harnessing local agency in development processes. Economic opportunities must also be increased in tandem with access to education, and this involves disrupting distortionary patronage relationships that aid in the persistence of elite power. The promotion of deliberative practices might provide one way to do this. Throughout, by engaging with the novel as well as African history more generally, we hope to suggest an alternate, African grounding for canonical ideas of education, agency, and deliberation.

3.2 The supply and demand for education in colonial Africa

In *Ambiguous Adventure*, despite deep concerns about losing their culture and tradition, the *Diallobé* elders are convinced that in the context of colonialism, "nothing pervades our lives with such clamor as the needs of which [a colonial] school permits the satisfaction" (Kane, 1962, p. 10). Indeed, in many parts of Africa, colonized people demanded more formal education, as they saw education as the foundation of the European dominance that they wanted to access and ultimately displace (Ball, 1983, p. 258). Kane (1962, p. 49) memorably characterizes the new schools as part cannon, part magnet. "Better than the cannon, it makes conquest permanent. The cannon compels the body, the school bewitches the soul." Meanwhile, like the magnet, the school has a "radiating force … The upheaval of the life of man within this new order is similar to the overturn of certain physical laws in a magnetic field." Indeed, as the life stories of people like Kane illustrate, colonial schools were part of a great upheaval, which must have felt cosmic to those who experienced it. Yet schools could not make conquest permanent, despite the designs of colonial powers. Instead, they only furnished many Africans with the knowledge and methods that they could then adapt and use in struggles for political independence. The "bewitchment" of colonial schools could not kill the underlying desire for autonomy that motivated Africans to attend in the first place; the new languages, tools, and social connections only sharpened this desire.

Though the details of deliberation and the processes of decision-making are often lost, a survey of historical literature reveals that many communities across Africa, like the *Diallobé*, made the decision to participate in colonial education (Lambais et al., 2023). In fact, there was no shortage in the demand for such education. Rather, the shortage was in the supply, since European powers were wary that formal education would equip Africans to challenge colonial rule more effectively. Educational curricula were thus designed to exclude Africans, providing them only the rudimentary and vocational education required to staff low-level bureaucratic posts. Colonial administrations suppressed broader training in skills and ideas lest the colonists repeat the "mistakes" made in places like India and Vietnam, where educated locals came to challenge colonial rule. In fact, colonial education policy in sub-Saharan Africa did not just neglect education; it actively suppressed education. We draw this distinction because of the high demands for education in many parts of Africa that colonial rulers persistently dismissed until Africans themselves gathered the means to build and staff schools. In the Four Communes of Senegal in the early 1900s, parents and students determinedly but unsuccessfully protested educational reforms aimed at racial segregation. In parts of rural Zimbabwe (then Rhodesia) in the 1920s–1930s, after petitions to reform the missionary school system went unheeded by colonial authorities, locals established their own independent schools under African preachers (Summers, 2002, p. 12). In fact, throughout sub-Saharan Africa, the missionary education that was often the only source of schooling available was largely based on the initiative of African teachers and converts rather than European investments (Frankema, 2012). In Ghana and Nigeria, small groups of educated local elites, rather than the British colonists, were the primary force behind setting up schools (Ajayi et al., 1996, p. 31). Thus the overwhelming picture of the politics of education in colonial sub-Saharan Africa is one of an official policy of undersupply that is unmatched in almost all other colonial contexts globally

(Lambais et al., 2023, pp. 863–865). This history already complicates a clear-cut distinction between "Western education" and "African tradition" because, in fact, "Western" education was supplied primarily by Africans responding to the demands of their community members for training in the skills and ideas that they identified with European dominance.

While communities like the *Diallobé* might have been initially wary to send their young people to colonial schools, they soon found that colonial schooling had hard limits; the colonial ruler's intention was never, in fact, to assimilate but to further reify separation between Africans and colonists through limiting and withholding schooling. Though *Ambiguous Adventure* does not speak to this broader historical process, the novel sharply illustrates the search for agency and autonomy that was at the heart of the historical demand for schooling in colonial Africa. This is a history that deserves much closer attention in the social science literature. In line with this history, a close look at the structure of the novel reveals a broad picture of an aristocratic society grappling with the demand and supply logic of a new order on the heels of a cataclysmic defeat that has irreversibly upended old ways of life. Modern schooling emerges as the centerpiece of a community-based effort to recapture agency. While the first part of the novel highlights Samba Diallo's painful religious education and the towering figure of his mentor whose rigid embrace of dogmas emphasizes subservience, its major undercurrents are the deliberations aiming at harnessing collective power to meet the challenge of modernity in a defeated society. The stakes of this conundrum are spelled out by the chief as follows:

> If I do not tell the Diallobé to go to the new school, they will not go. Their houses will fall into ruins, their children will die or be reduced to slavery. Extreme poverty will be entrenched among them, and their hearts will be filled with resentment.
>
> *(Kane, 1962, p. 31)*

The challenge is about overcoming poverty and despair. Hence the decision to embrace modern schooling to recapture autonomy despite the fear of cultural loss. Despite her misgivings about modern schooling, the Grande Royale approaches the issue at stake without moral qualms as if she were motivated primarily by an instrumental rationality that sidesteps sentimental considerations in favor of the end goal of reasserting power and agency for the *Diallobé*: "I come here to say this to you: I, the Grande Royale, do not like the foreign school. I detest it. My opinion, nevertheless, is that we should send our children there" (p. 41). It would be easy to overlook this insight if one chooses to focus on Samba Diallo's identity crisis that leaves him stranded between two worlds. However, such undercurrents reveal the complexity behind the eagerness for schooling, which was later constitutive to a fight for liberation and independence in the real-life history of colonial education in sub-Saharan Africa. Part I of the novel describes an array of community-centric inclusive and deliberative practices that supersede individual reservations rooted in traditional cultural frames. Agents act together to reassert autonomy as they navigate a world in which old responses no longer hold sway. In the Knight's lucid appraisal of the situation,

> Every hour that passes brings a supplement of ignition to the crucible in which the world is being fused. We have not had the same past, you and ourselves, but we shall have, strictly, the same future. The era of separate destinies has run its course. In that sense, the end of the world has indeed come for every one of us, because no one can any longer live by the simple carrying out of what he himself is. But from our long and varied ripenings a son will be born to the world: the first son of the earth; the only one, also. *(p. 72)*

The past then is irrecoverable, but the future must bring together aspects of what it is to be "African" and "Western."

3.3 Agency, creation, and policy in a historical straightjacket

How do these demands for education and the search for agency in the extremely adverse, repressive conditions of colonialism fit into the political economy literature on Africa? More generally, what can this history teach social scientists? A starting point here is the political economy literature on Africa. An important strand of this literature is concerned with explaining persistent poverty and political instability, and it often does so by appealing to deep historical factors like pre-colonial state institutions and extractive colonial institutions (e.g., Acemoglu & Robinson, 2010; Michalopoulos & Papaioannou, 2013). Institutions, defined broadly as systems of rules, are said to induce a set of interlocking economic and political incentives, involving rulers and citizens, that are very difficult to dislodge. These distorted incentives, in turn, steer people into behaviors that provide low levels of economic development, political liberty, and innovation. For instance, absent the institution of secure property rights, people would rather spend their savings immediately than invest in productive activities, since any gains from such activities might simply be seized by others. In pre-colonial Africa, absolutist states stifled investments by aggressively extracting the surpluses of their citizens. The advent of the slave trade then led to a sharp rise in militarization and lawlessness which again disincentivized investment and innovation and selected legal systems which were designed to capture and trade slaves rather than encourage innovation (Acemoglu & Robinson, 2010, pp. 29–30). In fact, Nunn and Wantchekon (2011) find that the slave trade also had persistent distortionary effects by creating cultures of fear and mistrust, which were then transmitted intergenerationally in communities that were heavily affected. The authors find evidence that these cultural distortions persist even today. Such studies provide explanations for the persistent poverty and political instability in many parts of sub-Saharan Africa; in contrast, the focus of this essay is to look back at history in order to find promising ways forward today.

While work on persistence is important, these results should not be taken to be deterministic. The story of Samba Diallo and the broader history of Africans' fight for education and autonomy suggest great value in more studies centered on understanding how exactly such path dependencies are broken through harnessing initiative and agency. As we further detail below, these stories suggest that people, even when placed in a straitjacket imposed by historical circumstances, retain the ability to create, discover, and organize new ideas, social movements, and ways of life. Disruptions to distortionary path dependencies might sometimes be closer at hand than such theories anticipate, if only social scientists sharpen their ability to identify the most promising paths. Research suggests that in parts of Africa, correcting the inherited distortions in the supply of education is one such way out of the historical straitjacket by empowering locals. As we argue below, the reason for this can be fully appreciated if we view formal education as not simply knowledge and human capital accumulation, but as training that supports continuing processes of "learning by doing." Of course, we cannot always expect such reforms to be frictionless. Indeed, while we wish to push back on the dominant narrative of African "backwardness," using the novel and histories of colonial education, it is important not to overlook the significant continuing challenges and failures of the past. African history suggests that the expansion of education has often been a messy and thoroughly political affair. Still, historical experience and rigorous empirical studies provide avenues both for identifying and correcting historical distortions in the supply of education and for disrupting the patronage relationships that, in parallel, hold back economic opportunities.

What happened historically when formal education, against the dominant efforts of colonial regimes, was actually supplied in Africa? How did it transform individuals and their communities? For Samba Diallo, the protagonist of *Ambiguous Adventure*, the consequences are tragic. Ultimately, he is at home neither in France nor in his village in Senegal, and the novel ends in a sudden calamity that arises out of this contradiction: his murder at the hands of the fundamentalist, the Fool. Yet one need only look as far as the life story of Cheikh Hamidou Kane, the author of the novel, to find a very different narrative. Like his protagonist Diallo, Kane was educated in France, at the Sorbonne and École Nationale de la France d'Outre-Mer in the 1950s, after receiving a traditional Islamic education. But unlike Diallo, Kane returned to become a high-level bureaucrat in independent Senegal and an official at UNICEF.[2] Needless to say, among his accomplishments is this novel, which remains an indispensable view into colonialism from a Senegalese Muslim perspective. Kane, like many other African leaders, must have felt the cultural contradictions embodied in Samba Diallo. But, for Kane and many others, such existential angst was not a harbinger of downfall, rather it was a further impetus for creation. Indeed, educated Africans together with members of the Black diaspora addressed cultural contradictions by advancing new pedagogical programs and creating new political organizations, which were ultimately at the center of independence movements.

Innovative Senagalese thinkers like Cheikh Anta Diop, Souleymane Bachir Diagne, and Sembéne Ousman, the so-called "father of African film," followed very similar paths to Kane. African students in Europe formed organizations like the West African Students' Union (WASU) and Présence Africaine, which were deeply politically engaged both in Europe and in Africa (Lambais et al., 2023, pp. 870–871). Working through new social networks that were only made possible by formal education, African students developed new ideas of nationhood and political liberation. At the Fifth Pan-African Conference in 1945, African leaders called for education that centered on African languages and history; they sought an education that expanded the student's ability "to express our thoughts and emotions [and] adopt and create forms of beauty" (quoted in Adi & Sherwood, 1995, p. 55). Against the dominant stories of path dependency, these are African histories of radical change and innovation in ideas, social networks, and policy. These are rooted in the search for agency depicted so sharply in *Ambiguous Adventure*, and both amplified and frustrated by colonial education. They also suggest that Africans themselves were at the vanguard of demanding, providing, and imagining modern, "Western" education, thus undermining the clear distinction between a traditional and passive "Africa" and the innovative West. From recent studies of Egypt and the Middle East, if not as yet any directly addressing sub-Saharan Africa, we also know that there was no necessary contradiction between Islam—the religion of the *Diallobé*—or "tradition" and the "West" in the development of new ideas rooted in colonized societies. For instance, some Islamic intellectuals in nineteenth century Cairo were deeply influenced by the ideas of Charles Darwin, which they contextualized in a thoroughly Islamic intellectual tradition (Elshakry, 2013). Even today, Senegal—the land of the *Diallobé* and a country that is 96% Muslim—continues to produce internationally prominent women scientists and intellectuals like Aissa Wade and Adji Dieng. Perhaps such contemporary successes, circumscribed though they may be, speak to the continuing relevance of the historical experiences and orientations to education exemplified in Samba Diallo's story and borne out by the broader history of colonial education in communities in Senegal. In other words, we simply wish to point out that there are development success stories tied to our central argument that reach into the present day in sub-Saharan Africa, which are highly relevant to development economics.

The kinds of pedagogy advanced by African and diasporan pan-African thinkers emphasized and sometimes anticipated the idea of education as an experiential "learning by doing," which was also developed in American pragmatist pedagogies (Lambais et al., 2023, pp. 875–876). The connection between formal education and "learning by doing," though fundamental to our story, has not typically been addressed in the economics literature. The idea of learning by doing is at the heart of the endogenous growth theory in economics, where economic growth naturally occurs as people experiment on their environments and iteratively create new tools, technologies, and ideas (Arrow, 1962). However, this notion of learning through environmental interaction might even be seen as antinomic to formal education, if one sees formal education as a one-way transfer of knowledge. Yet ideas of education as human capital provision or knowledge accumulation, which are the primary theoretical lenses used to understand education in economics, are insufficient for fully appreciating the importance of education in the context of the development of African independence and Black liberation movements. These lenses do not connect formal education to the continual two-way exchange between individuals and the environment from which economic and social innovations emerge. Instead, in line with our broader arguments below about agency as being rooted in environmental understanding, intersubjectivity, and continuing critical engagement, the novel along with the real-life histories of colonial education suggests the power of formal education as a factor supporting learning by doing. The skills, ideas, and networks gained through formal schooling allowed African activists to take a more active stance toward their rapidly changing environments, facilitating social, ideological, and political innovations and re-imaginings.

Beyond these big-picture accounts, a detailed study by Wantchekon and coauthors (2015) analyzes the inter-generational effects of colonial schooling in Benin. The authors track the life stories of the first students to go through colonial schooling in Benin and compare key political and economic outcomes between these people and their comparable neighbors, both in the same village and in neighboring villages, who did not attend school. They then draw the same comparisons for the descendants of those who attended schools and those who did not. Results show that people in the first two school cohorts had better living standards and social networks than comparable individuals who did not attend school. Educated people in these cohorts were also significantly less likely to be farmers, while they were politically active at much higher rates than their uneducated neighbors (Wantchekon et al., 2015, p. 705). These effects then persisted into later generations, with the descendants of these students also being more likely to be better off relative to comparable families without education. There is thus systematic evidence that where education was supplied to Africans, it transformed economic and political opportunities. Part of this involves access to wealth, political appointments, and social mobility. But, together with the stories detailed above, we emphasize that these results also point to an augmentation of creative agency. Through education, Africans gained knowledge, social networks, and political opportunities. They then created uniquely African political ideas, which sought to recover aspects of their traditions and re-imagine them for a new phase of history. Whereas the psychological sense of loss from experiences and narratives of colonial cultural transformations remains potent, we emphasize that, in light of history, this transformation was not a simple zero-sum exchange between "African tradition" and "European modernity." These results also suggest the value of education as a development policy tool that can, through deepening environmental knowledge and interactions in "learning by doing," facilitate local empowerment and agency.

In light of this, perhaps the most compelling studies on historical persistence are those that reveal the specific mechanisms of persistence. Here, Huillery (2009) finds that colonial investments in health and education in French West Africa continue to predict present-day welfare outcomes. This happens because the patterns of investment are persistent; places that received an initial investment in colonial times, often for arbitrary reasons, continued to receive further investments. In turn, this path dependency is a result of the fact that initial investments then created local demands for further investments. Initial investments also laid the fixed costs in place that then caused marginal investments to have a greater impact in areas that already had health and educational infrastructure. Given the potential of education to foster innovation and harness local initiative, investments should be made in those areas that were left out of the persistent and uneven development process throughout French West Africa, which originated in arbitrary colonial investments. In this vein, burgeoning literature further looks at persistent and differential effects from missionary schools and their long-run impacts on gender inequalities (e.g., Álvarez-Aragón et al., 2023). Correcting such distortions, however, might not be as simple as identifying excluded areas and investing. Core insights from political economy suggest that powerful elites will block or shirk investments, like education, that might threaten their hold on power (e.g., Acemoglu & Robinson, 2000; Mariscal & Sokoloff, 2000). For instance, in their study of the historical development of education in several countries in the Americas, Mariscal and Sokoloff (2000) find that where the wealthy are also politically powerful, they can send their children to private schools while avoiding the taxation that would subsidize a more expansive public school system. Due to the enduring relevance of the politics of inequality, now in a post-colonial context, efforts to empower peripheral areas and peoples through education might, in many cases, still involve the politics of organizing, advocacy, and confrontation that were so central in Africans' demands for education in colonial times. Again, we do not wish to suggest that providing education represents an easy fix to all of Africa's development woes, simply that it is an avenue worth pursuing and analyzing in many specific contexts.

3.4 The architecture of responses

In the preceding sections, we have described the historical role of education as it relates to the search for independence and autonomy in colonial sub-Saharan Africa, which is sharply illustrated in Cheikh Hamidou Kane's *Ambiguous Adventure*. We have highlighted historical distortions in the supply of education and argued for the continual promise of education as a way to break persistent political and economic distortions by harnessing the inventive potential of locals in excluded communities. In the context of economic theory, our intervention is to emphasize a view of formal education as a factor supporting broader processes of learning by doing. In light of this, we have highlighted some shortcomings in the historical persistence literature and drawn attention to policy interventions that can break down distortionary political and economic structures. In what follows, again drawing on the novel, we more fully develop an account of agency and the deep sources of innovation, which we then use to briefly point to another promising intervention in development policy: deliberative governance. Furthermore, we argue that deliberative policy-making and the understanding of the agency that underlies it have deep roots in cultural practices from many parts of Africa. In fact, after accounting for the centrality of deliberation to decision-making and the gender inclusivity of perspective taking, at least some African communities were, by contemporary standards, far more enlightened at the time of colonization than the Europeans who colonized them. Indeed, these communities had the kinds of deliberative political cultures that the political scientist Eitan Hersh (2020), in a recent book, argues are much-needed in local-level US politics today. Of course, contexts have changed dramatically, but there are still some aspects of "traditional African" political culture that are relevant and valuable today. The roots of effective, empowering development policy, which supports processes of learning by doing, can be found in a variety of cultural contexts.

We first directly return to a central theoretical question in this essay: How do we make sense of agency in the context of largely deterministic theories and social structures? One key recurring image that outlines the idea of agency in *Ambiguous Adventure* is that of a house. The European school is "the better teacher of how to join wood to wood, and … men should learn how to construct houses that resist the weather" (Kane, 1962, p. 11). Later, the Knight, Samba Diallo's father, says to a Frenchman on a similar theme, "I have sent my son to the school because the external which you have checked was slowly seeping through us and destroying us. Teach him to check the external" (p. 79). And finally, "Civilization is an architecture of responses. Its perfection, like that of any dwelling house, is measured by the comfort man feels in it, by the added portion of liberty that it procures for him" (p. 69). Education, then, is about being able to resist external forces—about being able to channel these forces according to one's wishes, as a part of a broader architecture through which one can express themselves and both form and realize their objectives. This picture resonates with canonical ideas in Western philosophy that connect the idea of the will to understanding and processes of reasoning. Perhaps the most direct statement is Spinoza's dictum that "the will and the intellect are one and the same" (*The Ethics*, 49C). In other words, people can only coherently take action insofar as they understand the causal processes and practices in the environments where they find themselves. Through Kane's writing, we are introduced to variations of these eternal ideas in the evocative language of Africans who are still, in some ways, embedded in their pre-colonial ways of life, and who have no exposure to Western philosophy.

What is involved in building "the perfect house"? In the new order, the *Diallobé* "will have to do with a world of the living, in which the values of death will be scoffed at and bankrupt" (Kane, 1962, p. 27)—thus, for the Grande Royale, "the time has come to teach our sons to live." In our reading, the point is that active engagement with the changing environment, both natural and social, rather than the old values of transcendent spirituality, will be necessary if the *Diallobé* are to survive in the new order. These suggestions again hark back to the idea of "learning by doing." If understanding is necessary to take coherent action, then engagement and experimentation on the evolving environment are just as necessary to build understanding. Moreover, insofar as any individual's interpretations will inevitably be susceptible to mistakes and biases, it follows that understanding is rooted in deliberation and intersubjectivity. These are again deep and canonical ideas that have been highly developed in the work of the economist Amartya Sen and philosophers like John Rawls and Jürgen Habermas. They also resonate with groundbreaking empirical studies of evolutionary linguistics and psychology in humans and apes, which find linguistic communication and deliberation to be rooted in the deeply collaborative practices that structure human social life (Tomasselo, 2008).

A key point we want to emphasize here, and what *Ambiguous Adventure* illustrates, is that variations of these ideas existed in African communities. Indeed, these ideas were embodied in the practices of deliberative decision-making that are at the heart of the novel. By involving all classes of people and including women as well as men, deliberation was actually more robust in some African communities than among the European colonizers (e.g., Baten et al., 2021). The *Diallobé*, though on the one hand a traditional Islamic society where women typically stay at home (p. 45), are at the same time led by the strong female character of the Grande Royale, who plays a pivotal role in the decision to engage with the colonial schools. While critics often describe *Ambiguous Adventure* as a bildungsroman that recounts the fateful odyssey of Samba Diallo who meets his demise at the hands of a religious fanatic, the Grande Royale is arguably a more compelling character. She is portrayed as a stern leader who empowers women. "I have done something which is not pleasing to us and which is not in accordance with our customs," she opines at a critical point in the deliberations over education. Her unusual decision is to

> ...have asked the women to come to this meeting today. We Diallobé hate that, and rightly, for we think that the women should remain at home. But more and more we shall have to do things which we hate doing, and which do not accord with our customs. It is to exhort you to do one of those things that I have asked you to come to this meeting today.
>
> *(p. 45)*

In essence, she extolls the virtues of gender inclusivity to enhance the quality of collective deliberations.

Ideas identifying action with understanding and learning with engagement, experimentation, and discourse are highly developed in Western philosophy and at least implicit in many economic theories. These concepts remain foundational for development policy and connect to our emphasis on education as a supporting factor in learning by doing, but more work needs to be done to uncover the indigenous variations of these ideas in Africa and other non-European contexts. Again, this is not simply a theoretical concern. Crafting development policy with a deep understanding of local context and history is crucial for effective and sustainable implementation.

3.5 Deliberation as development policy

Before concluding, we briefly highlight another policy intervention that might work in a similar way to education: deliberative policy-making. In parallel with the expansion of education, deliberative governance might provide ways to break down distortions based on patronage politics that limit economic opportunities. We make this excursion from education to deliberation because research in political economy, just as our reading of *Ambiguous Adventure*, suggests a deep connection between these two realms: both are constitutive factors in processes of learning by doing and both hold promise as development policy.

One source of persistent political distortion in Africa as well as other developing countries is rooted in patron-client politics. In such systems, patrons (local elites or "big men") control local communities through networks of economic and political relationships that make these locals ("clients") dependent on their patrons. As a result, elections are not decided by policy preferences but by clientelistic networks according to their ability to distribute gifts and favors and provide valuable connections. In turn, benefits from the center are largely captured by local patrons and never reach their intended recipients. Economic opportunities are stifled, and ambitions of educated youth might end in persistent frustration. Historically, the prevalent view in political science and economics has been that clientelism is a deep-rooted characteristic of low-development societies. Only through the process of modernization, which disrupts relationships of dependency (for example, that between a landlord and a sharecropper) and facilitates geographic and social mobility, can patron-client politics finally be dislodged in favor of a policy-based programmatic politics (e.g., Lipset, 1959). This again paints a picture of historical determinism, which is unsatisfying for both social scientists, who have a theoretical interest in understanding the specific mechanisms behind social change, and development practitioners, who seek to practically implement positive changes. Our understanding of agency perhaps provides an alternate path. Can policies that empower locals through deepening their understanding and creating opportunities for deliberation help break distortionary clientelistic politics? An emerging empirical literature finds great promise in deliberative governance (e.g., Goeree & Yariv, 2011; Ban et al., 2012).

Most directly relevant to this essay, one strand of literature studies the effects of introducing deliberation as a policy intervention to correct political distortions rooted in patron-client politics. This literature is based on field experiments studying campaign strategies, where certain villages randomly receive more deliberative forms of campaigning, while others receive clientelistic or other "standard" forms of campaigning in the context of real elections. Results from Benin and the Philippines indicate that using town halls as a campaign strategy increases voters' awareness of party platforms, improves party performance in elections, and allows parties to more successfully compete in areas away from their political strongholds (Fujiwara & Wantchekon, 2013; López-Moctezuma et al., 2022). Thus, not only does deliberative campaigning likely lead to better and more legitimate policy outcomes, but it is actually in the interest of political parties to use such methods, especially as a means to dislodge clientelistic practices used by their competitors. This literature is promising because not only does it show the potential benefits of the policy intervention, but it also shows how these benefits map onto existing structural incentives. In other words, accounting for existing structural constraints, there are still clear ways in which deliberative forms of campaigning can stick as an effective policy intervention, perhaps unleashing virtuous cycles that minimize the distortionary effects of clientelism.

Typically, the philosophical and conceptual grounding for practices of deliberative democracy is in Western sources. A deep reading of *Ambiguous Adventure*, however, vividly illustrates deliberative practices, as well as a deep underlying conceptualization of agency, as something that is also traditionally African. By connecting economic theory and development policy to African literature and African history, we hope to have revealed an alternative grounding. It comes out forcefully in the novel in a series of illuminating passages that capture a mode of deliberation rooted in African cultural practices. The Diallobé chief convenes a meeting to address the pressing issue of deciding to send children to school rather than simply dictating terms unilaterally. As he remarks,

> Life does not suspend itself. The time has come for our country to reach a decision … I am the hand which acts. It is you, people of the Diallobé, who are the body and the brain. Speak, and I shall act. What shall we say?
>
> *(Kane, 1962, p. 76)*

A cooperative and consensus building ethos permeates discursive practices in the community. In these practices, truths are established intersubjectively and social tensions are defused in conversational settings that process conflicts to prevent collective implosion. Such discursive practices are, like education, deeply connected to processes of learning by doing.

3.6 Conclusion

Ambiguous Adventure is a novel about loss, but it is also a novel about self-assertion and cultural and political renewal. We have used the novel as a starting point to explore important questions about innovation and economic development in adverse political conditions. Our deep reading of the novel has been heavily influenced by the real-life history of colonial education in Africa. In this light, the central tension between "African tradition" and "Western modernity" in the novel to some extent dissolves. Rather, colonial education, largely demanded and supplied by Africans themselves, was foundational to new imaginings of African modernities. To better understand why this was the case, we emphasize a conceptualization of formal education as a supporting factor in learning by doing—formal education is about *learning* how to "learn by doing" in a rapidly changing world. The second key issue for us, which we argue is also central to the novel on deep reading, is how to escape political distortions like colonialism and how to innovate in adverse conditions. Here the key idea is that impediments to "learning by doing" need to be removed—intersubjective, environmental engagement needs to be supported; historically inherited distortions need to be corrected. We point to a host of empirical studies on this theme. The roots of such an endeavor can be found as much in African tradition, which in many places emphasizes deliberation, as in Western ideas.

The tension between the old and the new that permeates the novel echoes the challenge of modernity that defined encounters between the West and "the rest." Like the Diallobés, Meiji era Japanese intellectuals such as Sakuma Shozan promoted Western education. Taking stock of Japan's underdevelopment and its unsuitable educational system, he proposed that "Schools must be established throughout the country, and modern education provided" (De Bary et al., 2005, p. 629). Similarly, Qing dynasty intellectuals who spearheaded the self-strengthening movement in the waning years of China's last imperial political system embraced modern education as the gateway to local versions of modernity and the restoration of national agency. In terms of theory, structure vs. agency is one of the defining and perennial tensions in all of social science. Economic theories provide powerful predictive tools, but these sometimes seem to trap people in deep historical processes, which define persistent systems of incentives and leave little room for creation and agency. The deliberations and meditations of the Grande Royal, the Knight, and Samba Diallo in *Ambiguous Adventure*, along with the real-life history of Africans' demand for education and liberation, teach us about where agency comes from and how it works. Agency is rooted in understanding one's place in the *architecture of responses* so that one can build a durable and spacious home; through education as engagement, deliberation, and learning by doing, one learns *the art of conquering without being right*. Even though this might involve the loss of older traditions of spiritual detachment, it makes possible new political and cultural forms that, to some extent, can revive and revitalize aspects of the old. The existential angst that is embodied in Samba Diallo's story was, in all its ambiguities, an impetus for creation in the case of many African leaders. In fact, from the striking images conveyed through the words of Kane's protagonists, and the traditional deliberative practices in which they are so deeply involved, we can recover an account of agency that is thoroughly African but also resembles canonical accounts in modern philosophy and social science. This is agency as understanding—rooted in deep engagement with nature and society, learning by doing, and deliberation. African roots, in history, culture, and traditions, for such ideas should be further studied and emphasized no less than European ones. The stakes are not just theoretical, but they also involve the sustainable, legitimate implementation of development policies that show promise in facilitating innovation, creation, and consensus building.

Finally, what do we make of the sense of loss that is so central to the novel? In a typically evocative exchange with a Frenchman, the Knight says,

> ... from the bottom of my heart I wish for you to rediscover the feeling of anguish in the face of the dying sun. I ardently wish that for the West. When the sun dies, no scientific certainty should keep us from weeping for it, no rational evidence should keep us from asking that it be reborn.
>
> *(Kane, 1962, p. 77)*

On one level, this passage speaks to the loss of traditions with the coming of colonialism. The loss of ways of life in the wake of colonialism was real and often destructive, and the psychological potency of this perhaps explains the continued relevance of "traditionalist" or conservative Islamist movements, which are themselves modern constructs. The passage, however, also suggests a deeper point about the fragility of humanity and the absurd futility of excessive ambition. In this regard, it is reminiscent of, for example, the canonical poetry of the early twentieth century German poet Rainer Maria Rilke, who beseeches us to focus on grief and think of joy as something falling rather than as something ascending (*Duino Elegies*). The voices of Kane's traditional, African protagonists again echo core, universal insights that have also been much celebrated in the Western canon. In times of building environmental crisis and accelerating mechanization, explorations of loss, community, and belonging—the alignment between people's spiritual needs and humanity's place in nature—remain as relevant as ever, perhaps particularly so in the West.

Notes

1 For instance, recent work by Rock-Singer (2022) shows how Salafist Islam is a thoroughly modern construct rather than a true continuity of Islamic practices from the time of Prophet Muhammad.
2 See https://www.britannica.com/biography/Cheikh-Hamidou-Kane.

References

Acemoglu, D., & Robinson, J.A., "Political Losers as a Barrier to Economic Development," *American Economic Review* 90, 2 (2000), 126–130.

Acemoglu, D., & Robinson, J.A., "Why is Africa Poor?" *Economic History of Developing Regions* 25, 1 (2010), 21–50.

Adi, H., & Sherwood, M., *The 1945 Manchester Pan-African Congress Revisited* (London: New Beacon Books, 1995).

Ajayi, J.F., Ade, K.H., Lameck, G. Ampah Johnson, & Mwotia, W., *The African Experience with Higher Education* (Accra: Association of African Universities, 1996).

Álvarez-Aragón, P., Guirkinger, C., & Villar, P. "Legacies of Colonial Education: Unveiling Persistence Mechanisms in the D.R. Congo." DeFIPP Working Paper No. 2305. University of Namur, Development Finance and Public Policies (2023).

Arrow, K.J., "The Economic Implications of Learning by Doing." *The Review of Economic Studies* 29, 3 (1962), 155–173.

Ball, S.J., "Imperialism, Social Control and the Colonial Curriculum in Africa," *Journal of Curriculum Studies* 15, 3 (1983), 237–263.

Ban, R., Jha, S., & Rao, V., "Who Has Voice in a Deliberative Democracy? Evidence from Transcripts of Village Parliaments in South India," *Journal of Development Economics* 99, 2 (2012), 428–438.

Baten, J., De Haas, M., Kempter, E., & Meier zu Selhausen, F., "Educational Gender Inequality in Sub-Saharan Africa: A Long-term Perspective," *Population and Development Review* 47, 3 (2021), 813–849.

De Bary, W.T., Keene, D, & Tsunoda, R., *Sources of Japanese Tradition, 1600–2000* (New York: Columbia University Press, 2005).

Elshakry, M. *Reading Darwin in Arabic, 1860–1950* (Chicago: The University of Chicago Press, 2013).

Frankema, E., "The Origins of Formal Education in Sub-Saharan Africa: Was British Rule More Benign?" *European Review of Economic History* 16, 4 (2012), 335–355.

Fujiwara, T., & Wantchekon, L., "Can Informed Public Deliberation Overcome Clientelism? Experimental Evidence from Benin," *American Economic Journal: Applied Economics* 5, 4 (2013), 241–255.

Goeree, J.K., & Yariv, L., "An Experimental Study of Collective Deliberation," *Econometrica* 79, 3 (2011), 893–921.

Hersh, Eitan, *Politics Is for Power: How to Move Beyond Political Hobbyism, Take Action, and Make Real Change* (New York: Scribner, 2020).
Huillery, E., "History Matters: The Long-Term Impact of Colonial Public Investments in French West Africa," *American Economic Journal: Applied Economics* 1, 2 (2009), 176–215.
Kane, C.H., *Ambiguous Adventure* (Portsmouth: Heinemann, 1962).
Lambais, G., Okoye, D., Sen, S., & Wantchekon, L., "Education for Control and Liberation in Africa and Among the Black Diaspora," *Comparative Education Review* 67, 4 (2023), 861–883.
Lipset, S.M., "Some Social Requisites of Democracy: Economic Development and Political Legitimacy," *American Political Science Review* 53, 1 (1959), 69–105.
López-Moctezuma, G., Wantchekon, L., Rubenson, D., Fujiwara, T., & Pe Lero, C., "Policy Deliberation and Voter Persuasion: Experimental Evidence From an Election in the Philippines," *American Journal of Political Science*, 66, 1 (2022), 59–74.
Mariscal, E. & Sokoloff, K.L., "Schooling, Suffrage, and the Persistence of Inequality in the Americas, 1800–1945," In *Political Institutions and Economic Growth in Latin America: Essays in Policy, History, and Political Economy*, ed. S. Haber (Stanford, CA: Hoover Institution Press, 2000).
Michalopoulos, S., & Papaioannou, E., "Pre-colonial Ethnic Institutions and Contemporary African Development," *Econometrica* 81, 1 (2013), 113–152.
Nunn, N., & Wantchekon, L., "The Slave Trade and the Origins of Mistrust in Africa," *American Economic Review* 101, 7 (2011), 3221–3252.
Rock-Singer, A., *In the Shade of the Sunna: Salafi Piety in the Twentieth-Century Middle East* (Oakland: University of California Press, 2022).
Senghor, L.S., "Speech by Mr. Leopold Sedar Senghor, President of the Republic of Senegal," *Présence Africaine* 4, 92 (1974), 31–38.
Summers, C., *Colonial Lessons: Africans' Education in Southern Rhodesia, 1918–1940* (Oxford: James Currey, 2002).
Tomasselo, M., *The Origins of Human Communication* (Cambridge: MIT Press, 2008).
Wantchekon, L., Klasnja, M., & Novta, N., "Education and Human Capital Externalities," *Quarterly Journal of Economics* 130, 2 (2015), 703–758.

4

ON CAPITALISM AND COLONIALISM

The economic imperatives underlying Amitav Ghosh's *Sea of Poppies*

Mukesh Eswaran

4.1 Introduction

Economics and literature may seem, at first glance, to be incompatible bedfellows. Economics is a mathematically rigorous discipline. Its theories are laid out with precision in mathematical terms after carefully spelling out the assumptions, and its empirical work designed to unearth the facts is subjected to very rigorous statistical tests of credibility. These restrictions, while imposing rigorous standards on research in the field and enhancing the credibility of the findings, also inevitably turn into straightjackets. Real-world phenomena are often the result of a confluence of numerous factors, and so separating them out in theoretical or empirical work is infeasible because of the self-imposed rigorous checks and balances. Literature, on the other hand, has few such constraints. There is virtually no limit to what can be brought into a narrative, as long as the overall requirement that it be coherent is met. It thus offers the latitude to suggest a comprehensive view of a subject without claiming to be true in detail.

Despite the apparently unbridgeable chasm between economics and literature, I believe good literature can be a complement to economics in furthering our understanding of economic and social phenomena. In the other direction, the logic of economics can allow us to make sense of fictional phenomena portrayed in literature because even fiction ultimately must be grounded in real life if it is to resonate with readers.

Amitav Ghosh's novel, *Sea of Poppies*, is a magnificent example in English literature exhibiting this complementarity.[1] This is the novel I have chosen to use as a vehicle to bring out the said complementarity in some of its history-based fictional events. The book's narrative suggests that the contemporary

DOI: 10.4324/9781003534358-6

capitalist world has its roots in the Empire, starting from the 17th century. Indeed, the novel shows that colonization, capitalism, and Christianity are intertwined in ways that are not easy to separate. I wish to focus here on how economics shapes the actions of capitalism and colonization in this novel, which is a gripping read in its own right as literature. And the novel also reveals, with immediacy far more palpable than what is communicable through abstract theories or via dry numbers and statistics, the fundamentally economic nature of the forces driving the events in the narrative.

4.2 Opium, colonization, and trade

The novel is set in 1838 on land and on the deck of a schooner plying the Indian Ocean. The land setting of *Sea of Poppies* was the eastern Indian region of present-day Bihar and Bengal. The major crop that was grown by the farmers in the region at the time, at the insistence of the East India Company, was the poppy, the essential ingredient of opium. The local consumption of this drug was minimal; the crops were meant mainly for export. The reader gets a glimpse of the exploitative nature of this colony in the first few chapters of in *Sea of Poppies*.

One of the main characters of the novel is Deeti, a woman who lived in Ghazipur, which lay on the Ganges in what was then the northern part of Bihar. The novel, among other things, tracks Deeti's fate through the events that unfold. Her marriage had been traditionally arranged, and she found out only later that her husband was impotent and an opium addict. He worked in an English opium factory, and one day he fell seriously ill at work. En route to fetching the ox-cart driver to transport her ill husband home, Deeti had to pass by endless fields of poppies that were getting ready to be harvested to produce opium. She reminisces about how farming was before the English arrived and how it is in its current condition and wonders about the difficulties involved in the simple job of replacing the thatched roof of her hut.

The difficulty was that the British colonial masters required the peasants to grow poppy so that its derivative, opium, could be exported for profit. In earlier days, Deeti recalls, a family focused on growing crops that were deemed necessary and very little land and effort were devoted to growing poppy for their personal needs. But now, they are mostly devoted to the poppy crop, which is extremely labor-intensive, entailing a sequence of tedious and meticulous tasks. She wonders,

> ...what sane person would want to multiply these labours when there were better, more useful crops to grow, like wheat, dal, vegetables? But those toothsome winter crops were steadily shrinking in acreage: now the factory's appetite for opium seemed never to be sated...
>
> *(p. 27)*

When choices are voluntarily made, resources like land and labor would never be allocated to luxuries when what is foregone by this choice are necessities that are valued much more. Deeti hopes that this year's poppy crop would be good, so all of the proceeds can be put to repairing the roof of her hut; if not, the rains will wash away whatever was left of it. How did Deeti's family and millions of others find themselves in such dire straits?

Consider what economics may contribute by way of insight here. In a pioneering contribution to our understanding of the economic development of former colonies, Nobel Laureate economists Daron Acemoglu, Simon Johnson, and James Robinson (2001) argued that whether a colony prospered or was impoverished by colonization depended on whether or not it is a settler colony.[2] When European colonial masters decided to settle in a colony, it was in their interest to economically develop their adopted countries. The settlers wanted to replicate the conditions and institutions that prevailed in their home countries, institutions such as those ensuring secure property rights, law and order, civil rights, etc. On the other hand, if they chose not to settle in the colony, they were not particularly interested in its development but, rather, merely sought to extract profits from it by way of cash crops, minerals, and the like. Here, the institutions were naturally very different from those in settler colonies. And these 'extractive' institutions, far from benefitting the citizens of the colony, more often than not impoverished them and set them back on the road to prosperity. Not only were these colonies' natural resources exploited, the labor of the citizens was also often harnessed to satisfy the colonial master's ends.

What determined whether a colony became a settler colony or an extractive one? The theory's proponents argued that an important consideration was whether the climate was one that the colonists could tolerate and whether the common diseases were ones against which they had some immunity. Therefore, colonies that were rich in resources but with geography or climate deemed uninhabitable by the European colonists tended to be extractive (like those in Africa and South Asia). On the other hand, resource-rich colonies that were deemed hospitable enough for permanent living tended to become settler colonies (like the United States, Canada, Australia, and New Zealand) and these had institutions that promoted economic development.

An instance of extractive colonization is brought out graphically in the *Sea of Poppies*. India was a colony of Britain for over two centuries, but it was not a settler colony. Before it came under sovereign British rule (in 1858), most of the country was conquered by the British East India Company, a joint stock company that made its profits by trading. In fact, as the historian William Dalrymple (2019, p. xxv) puts it, 'India's transition to colonialism took place under a for-profit corporation, which existed entirely for the purpose of enriching its investors'.[3] For this reason, the nature of the exploitation of India was even harsher than what we might have expected from a state implementing extractive institutions.

As mentioned above, in the past Deeti's family would plant a variety of crops for consumption and only a little of poppy because it was a very labor-intensive crop. But now, it was largely replaced by the poppy. Why was there a compulsion to specialize in this manner when it impoverished them?

The answer to this question is worth elaborating on because what happened in Bihar and Bengal under the rule of the British East India Company provides a good specific illustration of what economists Acemoglu, Johnson, and Robinson (2002) found as a general phenomenon that they dubbed 'Reversal of Fortune'.[4] Their argument is that, while colonizing, European countries found it most profitable to colonize the relatively most prosperous regions (compared to the rest of the world) because of their abundance of resources. By implementing in these colonies institutions that were extractive in nature and which did not promote long-term economic development, over time the fortunes of these regions were reversed, relative to the rest of the world. As a result, regions that had the highest per capita income a few centuries ago, before colonization, tend to have the lowest in contemporary times.

Regions of India offer examples of this reversal at work. The East India Company instituted land tenure regimes that facilitated the collection of taxes (which were substantial) but did not encourage investment in agriculture. Particularly relevant here is the zemindari system of land tenure where huge swathes of land were given over to a few landlords (zemindars), in contrast to having individual ownership or village-level ownership. The contracts used by the East India Company for poppy growing enlisted the zemindars' help to force the peasants to accept unprofitable offers through the threat of throwing the peasant farmers out of the land they tilled. The terms of the contract under which the opium farmers labored actually resulted in a loss in their income, not a gain.[5] In fact, the effects of opium growing were long-term because economic development is history-dependent. Even today, villages in areas that grew the poppy are more likely to show less investment in public goods like education and health clinics.[6]

Indian peasant farmers were forced to accept cash advances by the English to grow the poppy and refusal was met with dire consequences such as being falsely accused of stealing and tried in courts where the magistrates were bought off. Deeti knows what her condition would be at the end of the winter season:

> And, at the end of it, your earnings would come to no more than three-and-a-half sicca rupees, just about enough to pay off your advance.
>
> *(p. 27)*

This sort of extractive contract that could not be refused—but which would never have been tolerated by the settlers amongst themselves—was routinely employed to force the planting of a crop for an addictive drug.

The reader receives an initial hint in the novel on why the British had settled on opium as the favored product to export from India. Because Deeti's husband was impotent, her domineering mother-in-law arranged for her son, the groom, to get Deeti into an opium-induced torpor on their wedding night and to have his brother rape Deeti—a rape from which she conceived a daughter. While she had no recollection of this event, she arrived at this realization when she found herself pregnant. Furthermore, she received hints from her mother-in-law that more children to Deeti were planned in the future. To put an end to this premeditated rape by her brother-in-law while she was drugged at the behest of her mother-in-law to satisfy her desire for more grandchildren, Deeti decided on a drastic course of action. She routinely took some opium from her husband's cache and added traces of it to her mother-in-law's food and drink. The old woman became very passive and 'peaceful' and, over time, was hardly in a position to scheme and manipulate anymore. It is at this point that Deeti wonders about what this drug could do:

> As for Deeti, the more she dispensed the drug, the more she came to respect its potency: how frail a creature was a human being, to be tamed by such tiny doses of this substance! She saw now why the factory in Ghazipur was so diligently patrolled by the sahibs and their sepoys—for if a little bit of this gum could give her such power over the life, the character, the very soul of this elderly woman, then with more of it at her disposal, why should she not be able to seize kingdoms and control multitudes?
>
> *(p. 35)*

The power to 'seize kingdoms and control multitudes' was the motivation for settling on opium as the prime export commodity from India by the British East India Company. Simple economics suggests that a stable demand for a product maintains the profits from its sale, and when there is addiction, the demand is stable. In fact, the logic of this is not different from why local drug pushers offer 'freebies' to school kids to get them hooked. More benignly, it is also why a gym or a music company nowadays might offer us free subscriptions to enroll for a few months. Part of this, of course, is to merely familiarize us with the potential benefits of the product that we might be unaware of. What is different in the case of opium sales by the British East India Company is the enormous scale of the operation in the 19th century and the fact that the product here is extremely addictive.

Because the Indian market for opium was small and most families could grow a bit of it for their own needs, it would have been difficult for the East India Company to prevent production for private needs. The market for the opium from India was China. But what could be done to induce the Chinese to undertake international trade in which they imported opium?

The answer seems to have been getting the Chinese addicted to opium. China's Qing dynasty naturally wanted to put a stop to the import of opium and then to ban it. This led to two wars (the 'Opium wars') between Britain and China (1839–1842 and 1856–1860), in which Britain was joined by France in the second. An illuminating exchange in the novel takes place in a scene that is set on a budgerow (a large boat on the Ganges). The participants in the conversation are Mr. Burnham and Neel Rattan Halder, both important characters in the novel, and one Mr. Doughty. Mr. Burnham, an Englishman, was the owner of a shipping company involved in the opium trade between India and China. (The East India Company relegated to private merchants the shipping of opium to China.) Neel Rattan Halder was an educated zemindar and the Rajah of Raskhali, who recently inherited his estate from his irresponsible and profligate father who had invested heavily in Mr. Burnham's business without serious inquiry into the nature of his business. Mr. Doughty, an Englishman who operated out of Calcutta, was the pilot of Mr. Burnham's recently acquired schooner, *Ibis*.

In the conversation, which takes place a year before the first opium war, Mr. Burnham tells Neel that ending the opium trade with China would be ruinous for him, for Neel, and also for India. When Neel inquired why it would be ruinous and why the British didn't sell products that were more useful than opium to the Chinese, Mr. Doughty replied that Britain had nothing better than opium to offer. The Chinese didn't care for British products whereas the British wanted Chinese tea and silks. He admitted that it was the English and the Americans, through sustained effort, who had managed to get the Chinese people hooked on opium.

The subsequent market for opium was so lucrative for the East India Company that, backed by the British government, it found it worthwhile to undertake the two opium wars with China on the right to sell opium to the Chinese. Another conversation at the same dinner party also includes Zachary Reid, an American who passed as white but was of mixed race (white father, black mother) and was the second mate of the *Ibis*. The conversation suggests British sentiments for 'free trade' a year before the first opium war. Mr. Burnham claimed that free trade is a right given by God. He goes further and elaborates on how opium is a boon for India because it boosts the East India Company's revenues to more than the entire income of India or the United States. This, in turn, in his view, enables the British to confer their 'benefits' on India, and it is their 'God-given' duty to confer this benefit on the Chinese, too, which presumably justified the impending opium war with China. The British Parliament, he states, would not know about the war until it was over!

Mr. Burnham asserts that there would be no British Empire without the East India Company, but he does not acknowledge the immense adverse consequences this had for India. Only after the East India Company had conquered and ruled major parts of India for a century did the country come under the direct control of the British sovereign, following the Indian Mutiny in 1857. In India at least, the extent of the British Empire was most certainly powered by the commercial interests of British capitalism—in particular, those of a single multinational company.

The production of opium in Bihar and Bengal was disastrous for the poor. It produced far more misery than would have existed otherwise. The extent of it is communicated in Deeti's reflections. Soon after her husband's death, Deeti had voluntarily but hastily married her second husband, Kalua, a lower-caste man who saved her from the funeral pyre of her first husband, into which she was being forced following the ritual of "suttee". They fled from the (high-caste) relatives of Deeti's first husband, who were out to kill them. When she passes by her natal home during their escape, the sight of the poppy fields there makes Deeti reflect on what would be true also of her and her dead husband's fields:

> This, she knew, was what her own fields looked like, and were she at home today, she would have been asking herself what she would eat in the months ahead: where were the vegetables, the grains? She had only to look around to know that here, as in the village she had left, everyone's land was in hock to the agents of the opium factory: every farmer had been served with a contract, the fulfilling of which left them with no option but to strew their land with poppies. And now, with the harvest over and little grain at home, they would have to plunge still deeper into debt to feed their families.
>
> *(p. 178)*

How is it possible, we might wonder, that so lucrative a market for opium could have produced this abject poverty and misery?[7] Two features of opium production in Bihar and Bengal facilitated this: monopoly and monopsony. To a seller of a product, freedom from competing sellers confers an advantage of being able to raise prices to consumers. The British parliament conferred a monopoly on the East India Company to sell opium in the India-China market (though, of course, this could not prevent sellers from other countries). The Company set up the so-called Opium Department, which was given police-like powers. With over a hundred offices spread out over the region, it recruited locals to enforce strict rules and ensured compliance on contracts that virtually could not be refused.[8] Not only was the East India Company a monopoly seller, it was also a monopsony, that is, the only buyer of the poppy that was grown. The latter ensured that the price offered to the poppy farmer was minimal and the former that the price at which it sold the final product to the Chinese was the most profitable. While the Company made huge returns on the investment of its shareholders in Britain, the Indian poppy farmers who dedicated their most fertile lands to the poppy became further mired in poverty and debt. This would be an example of what Marx dubbed 'primitive accumulation' that, he claimed, provided the capital that capitalism was built on.

4.3 God in service of the opium trade

An important issue that is touched on in the narrative of *Sea of Poppies* bears on the interaction between economics and religion. The fundamental purpose of the British Empire in India, to be sure, was to exercise control over the colony so as to have access to its resources. The motive force behind British imperialism was economic. Nevertheless, the spread of the empire and the spread of Christianity occurred simultaneously. Was there a causal relationship between the two? That empire made it easier for missionaries to spread Christianity may seem obvious. History informs us, however, that the East India Company was very averse to openly supporting the proselytizing of Christianity. The reason had to do with governance: if the Indian soldiers largely comprising the British Indian army saw British rule as an excuse for foisting Christianity on them, they would have withdrawn their loyalty, thereby threatening British security. So, the Company resisted the zeal of Protestant missionaries to 'redeem' millions of Indian souls through conversion. The missionary lobby in Britain, however, won out when the charter of the East India Company came up for renewal. The British parliament voted in favor of including a 'pious clause' in the Charter Act of 1813, which stated that Britain was duty-bound to make it possible for the religious and 'moral improvement' of Indians.

The Company, nevertheless, remained fairly wary of granting missionaries admission into India. But in the 19th century, the state and the missionaries did manage to see eye-to-eye on the issue of education. The Company felt it would be good to have the Indian elite educated in English because it would help with the administration; the missionaries saw education as a route to introducing the study of the Bible and possible conversion. This led to the state-funded opening of some schools that had mostly secular disciplines in their curricula, but which were largely taught by missionaries. While there was some complementarity between the state and missionary work, the state in colonial British India was careful never to openly promote Christianity in an official capacity.

But to what extent, if any, did Christianity extend the empire? This is, as yet, an unresolved issue, for the evidence seems to be that Christianity may have somewhat impeded British imperialism by planting suspicion in the Indian population.[9] More specifically here, to what extent did Christianity lend support to the economic motive behind the opium trade? The answer may have been different when seen from the viewpoints of the state and of the commercial interests. In part of the same conversation between Neel and Mr. Burnham reported above, Neel asks Mr. Burnham if he is not bothered by the fact that God is being recruited in the opium trade. In reply, Mr. Burnham extols the medical benefits of opium, which the Chinese surely should not be deprived of. God would be displeased if the British did not oppose the 'Manchu tyrant' from preventing the benefits of opium from flowing to his citizens. In an astounding remark, which he attributes to a countryman, Mr. Burnham claims,

> Jesus Christ is Free Trade and Free Trade is Jesus Christ.
>
> *(p. 106)*

Whether Mr. Burnham's stance was merely a transparent ploy to camouflage his greed or a genuinely held religious belief, one cannot be sure. Since he seems to have been a devout Protestant, it is more likely that it was his cognitive dissonance at work. Given the potentially conflicting choice between his religion and his self-interest, he found a justification in favor of the latter—not by negating the former but, rather more compellingly, by recruiting it to justify his self-interest. Between capitalism and any reasonable interpretation of genuine Christianity, there may be an irreconcilable antagonism; but the former trumps the latter here in the case of the opium trade. There was an unholy alliance between colonialism, capitalism, and Christianity.

More generally, as self-interest has been hardwired in humans over eons, it is very deeply entrenched. Because capitalism is based on self-interest, it can recruit almost any and every vehicle to increase profits—even religion. In other words, Christianity is generally more likely to have been an aid rather than a primary driving force behind capitalism, and so, it seems, was the case in this instance of the opium trade of the East India Company.[10]

4.4 Colonization and indentured labor

Related to the problem of the impoverishment of the already-poor farmers for profit, there is another aspect of *Sea of Poppies* intimately connected with capitalism that economics sheds some light on. This is the transportation of indentured laborers (called *girmitiyas*) to the island of Mauritius in the Indian Ocean, 500 miles east of Madagascar. Girmitiyas are people who have sold themselves for paltry sums of money, usually to help their families, and, in exchange, have become bonded laborers for a few years until the debt is paid off. The schooner *Ibis*, which previously transported slaves, was purchased by Mr. Burnham and refitted with the intention of shipping opium to China. But since the opium trade with China was temporarily in abeyance—an interruption that the opium wars sought to put a stop to—Mr. Burnham wanted to use the *Ibis* in the interim period to transport indentured workers. Each way, the trip was expected to be about a couple of months. The migrants were liberally fed before the journey, ostensibly to alleviate their hunger, but more likely to entice people into signing up as migrants and to strengthen them for the labor that awaited them at the other end. Deeti and her second husband, Kalua, desperate from hunger while escaping from her relatives through her first marriage, were two of the many who decided to join the girmitiyas.

The reason for Mr. Burnham's decision to ship indentured laborers was that he received a communication from Mauritius, which was now another British colony. On Zachary Reid's voyage to Calcutta, his vessel had stopped off at Port Louis, Mauritius. A plantation owner, Monsieur d'Epinay, explained his predicament to Zachary and asked him to deliver a letter to Mr. Burnham in Calcutta:

> 'My canes are rotting in the field, Mr Reid,' said the planter. 'Tell Mr. Burnham that I need men. Now that we may no longer have slaves in Mauritius, I must have coolies, or I am doomed. Put in a word for me, will you not?'
>
> *(p. 20)*

It was in response to this request from Monsieur d'Epinay that Mr. Burnham decided to send over girmitiyas to Mauritius. But indentured laborers could be employed within India itself and Mr. Burnham could have transported them elsewhere in the same country. Why transport them from Calcutta to Port Louis, Mauritius, nearly 4,000 miles away, which entailed a journey fraught with danger for the crew and the passengers? Transporting indentured migrants (and a few convicts to Mauritius, which also served as a British penal colony) was seen as a side business for Mr. Burnham, not as lucrative as trading in opium to be sure but nevertheless financially worthwhile. Those who are willing to pay the most for indentured laborers are from regions that are abundant in land, not labor. India was abundant in labor and the demand for indentured workers would not be high, relatively speaking, because hired labor could be had cheaply. In his choice of shipping girmitiyas overseas, Mr. Burnham may well have been informed by the thinking of colonists at the time.

Edward Gibbon Wakefield was a 19th century British entrepreneur and is little-known today as a theorist of colonization. He had strong views on how to develop British capitalism using colonies and had an influence on the colonization of Australia and New Zealand.[11] His claim to fame was the idea that, for Britain to continue its accumulation of capital, the country needed to colonize other countries, sell some land to capitalists, and have labor from overpopulous Britain immigrate to the colony. Instead of making the colony's abundant land cheaply available, he argued, the bulk of the immigrants should be deprived of land ownership for a considerable period of time by maintaining artificially high land prices through state intervention. By being forced to provide labor for their livelihood, these immigrants would enable capitalist landlords to earn returns on their ownership of land and contribute to their accumulation of capital. If land were cheaply available to all, no one would be willing to work for another and the returns to owning land would be very small and this would thwart the accumulation of capital. As Marx recognized, this was a state-contrived restriction of the means of production to some people in the interest of capital accumulation.[12]

The economic historian Evsey Domar had an elegant theory on when we might expect to see the emergence of serfdom or slavery or, more generally, coerced labor.[13] Based on the evidence gathered by the Russian historian V. Kliuchevsky, Domar argued that this is more likely to occur in regions where land is abundant and labor is scarce. If the movement of labor was unfettered, would-be workers would acquire land that they could cultivate for themselves—eliminating the possibility of a landowning class that lived off labor. To ensure the existence of such a landowning class, political pressure would have to be brought to bear that prevented the free mobility of labor, thereby reducing their outside options. And this tying of labor to a piece of land is serfdom by another name.[14]

With this bit of economic theory from Domar, we may return to *Sea of Poppies*. The island of Mauritius had a string of European colonial masters. The French colonized the island in 1721 and the French settlers cultivated sugarcane using imported African slave labor on their plantations. The colony changed hands in 1810, when it was wrested from the French by the British. In 1833, the Slavery Abolition Act eliminated slavery in the British Empire and it was implemented in Mauritius in 1835. The slaves in Mauritius were freed as a result, and the sugarcane plantations were in difficulties because of labor scarcity—which was what Monsieur d'Epinay's letter alludes to.

The fact that Mr. Burnham sent him, for his own profit, not just migrants but also indentured laborers is not an accident. To maintain an artificial scarcity of land and thereby support a landlord class that accumulates capital in the spirit of Wakefield, labor had to be prevented from the easy purchase of land. Preventing the free movement of the migrants out of labor would lower their outside options. What better expedient for ensuring a captive labor force than to have indentured laborers, who are obligated to work off their debt and are assigned to specific plantations upon arrival in Mauritius? The logic of capitalistic and colonial exploitation was apparently perfectly understood by both Mr. Burnham and Monsieur d'Epinay.

The economic history of Mauritius records the country as having experienced a boom in sugar exports starting from the 1820s. The labor shortage caused by the emancipation of African slaves in the country was alleviated by the active involvement of the colonial state government to safeguard the export sector. The export-driven economic development of Mauritius came at the expense of slaves and indentured laborers. In the present context, the profitable opium export from India to China reduced farmer peasants to desperation by having them devote the most fertile land to opium cultivation at unremunerative prices and at the expense of growing subsistence crops. And the escape of the poor to improve their condition was seen as another source of profit by transporting them as indentured servants to Mauritius to benefit the landed Franco-Mauritians by increasing their export of sugar. More importantly, Britain, the mother country of the Empire, it has been argued, profited from slavery to the point that it augmented the capital needed for its Industrial Revolution.[15]

Even in the manner in which the indentured laborers were supervised onboard *Ibis*, the novel offers economic insights into how capitalism maximizes profit by minimizing supervision costs. Since the number of crew is much smaller than the number of migrants being transported, maintaining discipline and preventing uprisings is a matter of concern. Part of the strategy to deal with this seems to have been to hire a sturdy upper caste man, Bhyro Singh, as the subedar (a junior officer) who would oversee the lower caste migrants. Caste distinctions and ingrained hatred toward the lower castes are harnessed to keep the migrants in line. Bhyro Singh, a ruthless man, was favorably looked upon by his superior, the first mate Mr. Crowle, and Bhyro Singh's sadistic excesses were even indulged by the ship's captain, Mr. Chillingworth.

One incident graphically illustrates the method of control. To help out a friend who was being ill-treated by the crew, Deeti had protested. She was then summoned to come below deck and was led to an isolated store room where Bhyro Singh, her deceased husband's uncle as it turned out, was waiting for her with the intention of rape. A cry for help from Deeti alerted her husband, Kalua, who was on deck with his hands tied with a rope. In the scuffle that followed, one of his guards accidentally fell overboard and perished. The penalty for this, it was quickly determined, would be death by hanging (which was to be preceded by a trial, with this predetermined verdict). But Bhyro Singh wanted to first flog Kalua 60 lashes the day before the intended hanging. Bhyro Singh had falsely told the captain that Kalua had run away with an upper caste woman who happened to be his relative (which is true) and that he needed to be punished. Captain Chillingworth, without verifying the claim, went along with this because he apparently did not wish to interfere with caste practices. When Zachary Reid questioned the decision, the captain said that he was surprised that an American would ask this, taking Zachary for white. He asked Zachary what they would do in Bhyro Singh's place if a 'darkie' eloped with their wives or sisters.

Here is a snippet of the scene of the lashing on the deck, where all male migrants watched Bhyro Singh run up before each lash to the manacled and barely clad Kalua, whom he referred to as a scavenging dog:

> Kalua heard him clearly, through the buzzing in his head, and he asked, in a whisper: Malik—what have I ever done to you?
>
> The question—as much as the bewildered tone in which it was asked—further enraged Bhyro Singh. Done? he said. Isn't it enough that you are what you are?
>
> These words echoed through Kalua's head as the subedar walked away, to begin his next run: Yes, what I am is enough … through this life and the next, it will be enough … this is what I will live through, again and again and again …
>
> *(p. 447)*

Here we have it: Isn't it enough that you are what you are? Extreme caste hatred was accepted and exploited because it lowered supervision costs. Why incur the expense of treating the captive migrants properly in order to avoid costly confrontations? One can accomplish the same end more economically by engaging ancient caste animosities and by having the subjugated people turn on one another by eliciting the most depraved aspects of human nature. Separate along existing and entrenched cleavages and then rule—a principle that works for governance as well as for capitalism.

4.5 Opium's effect on the psyche of rural Indians

Opium production under the rule of the East India Company seems to have dominated rural life in the eastern part of India. It seems to have penetrated the psyche of some peasants to such an extent that even their escape to indentured servitude 4,000 miles away was infused by its presence. This is brought home in a simple but touching scene set on the *Ibis*, in which Sarju, a midwife who was one of the migrants, lay dying. She bequeathed to Deeti what she considered her most prized possession. After handing over some ganja and datura (narcotics), she gives yet another pouch containing what she thought was even better:

> Sarju pushed yet another pouch into Deeti's hands. In this, she whispered, there is wealth beyond imagining; guard it like your life—it contains seeds of the best Benares poppy.
>
> Deeti thrust her fingers into the pouch and rubbed the tiny, specklike seeds between her fingertips ... How was it possible that after spending so much of her life with these seeds she had not had the foresight or wisdom to bring some with her—as a keepsake if nothing else?
>
> Deeti extended her hand to Sarju, as if to give back the pouch, but the midwife pushed it back towards her. It's yours; take it, keep it ... They'll keep for many years. Keep them hidden till you can use them; they are worth more than any treasure...
>
> *(p. 414)*

The worth of this treasure to Sarju was obviously not the prospect of any financial benefit it could confer. After all, in that regard the poppy was only a source of financial ruin for the peasant farmers, not a source of material enrichment. Rather, the source of the perceived benefit to Sarju from this 'treasure' appears to have been the relief it could bring from the conditions of living—conditions that she seemed not to have believed would change in the future as an indentured worker. A woman who, for a living, helped bring children to life also saw in the poppy seed the remedy for the travails accompanying that life; the irony is not lost on the reader.

The extent to which the poppy had insinuated itself into the lives of peasants in eastern India because of the British East India Company is communicated toward the end of the novel in a manner that only superb literature can manage. With a magnificent economy, Amitav Ghosh delivers the sense of the lived experience of the beleaguered peasants. Soon after her meeting with Sarju, Deeti ruminates on the main deck of *Ibis*, en route to years of indentured servitude:

> As she was listening to the sighing of the sails, she became aware that there was a grain lodged under her thumbnail. It was a single poppy seed: prising it out, she rolled it between her fingers and raised her eyes, past the straining sails, to the star-filled vault above. On any other night she would have scanned the sky for the planet she had always thought to be the arbiter of her fate—but tonight her eyes dropped instead to the tiny sphere she was holding between her thumb and forefinger. She looked at the seed as if she had never seen one before, and suddenly she knew that it was not the planet above that governed her life: it was this minuscule orb—at once bountiful and all-devouring, merciful and destructive, sustaining and vengeful. This was her Shani, her Saturn.
>
> When Kalua asked what she was looking at she raised her fingers to his lips and slipped the seed into his mouth.
>
> Here, she said, taste it. It is the star that took us from our homes and put us on this ship. It is the planet that rules our destiny.
>
> *(pp. 414–415)*

4.6 Concluding remarks

Sea of Poppies is a novel that has a wide canvas and uses a broad brush; few contemporary novels do, in my view. Its themes defy easy compartmentalization but it nevertheless paints a compelling picture of how British colonization affected the lives of people in the Indian subcontinent. The novel's various aspects are infused with economics—in particular the economics of capitalism and colonialism—and yet the book remains a splendid piece of literature.

The benefits of capitalism are well-known and are frequently reiterated in standard western economics. Ghosh brings out the downsides of capitalism, especially as it pertains to colonialism. Driven by self-interest, capitalism harnesses whatever is at its disposal to enhance the goals of capitalists, and colonialism is an important means in its repertoire. When a colony is extractive in nature, self-interest in this context boils down to the maximization of profits for the shareholders in the home country. Underlying the various modes of exploitation alluded to in this essay, there is a common thread: an asymmetry in power. Whether one considers the cultivation by farmers of opium under unremunerative contracts or in the elimination of alternative buyers the farmers could sell their product to or in the shipping of indentured laborers to where it is most lucrative or in the keeping of discipline at least cost on a schooner, the direct use of force or the implicit threat of force is at work. Ghosh reveals through his engaging narrative the paucity of the presumption—so blithely invoked in neoclassical economics—that participation in a voluntary arrangement must make all parties better off; or else, why would they participate? The under-emphasized possibility that asymmetry in power may undermine the outside options of some parties—which makes participation a caricature of free choice for them—is at the heart of the colonization project in its myriad aspects. This is the overarching message I take away as an economist from the various interrelated themes in the novel.

Amitav Ghosh's novel leaves no doubt that good fiction can be insightful on matters that are fundamentally economic and also that economics can return the favor by offering insights on the mechanisms underlying what is portrayed with a broad brush. *Sea of Poppies*, in fact, was the first of a trilogy of novels by Amitav Ghosh, the other two being *River of Smoke* and *Flood of Fire*, also dealing with the opium trade. Recently, the same author has delivered another masterful piece of work, *The Nutmeg's Curse*, where he traces out the root causes of the current environmental crisis the earth is facing.[16] Though this last book is not a novel, the author's attention to historical detail and the uncanny ability to relate seemingly unrelated phenomena and to detect in them the origins of serious subsequent developments characterize this work, too. In systematically tracing the responsibility of today's environmental crisis to the doorsteps of colonialism, capitalism, and the developed world's geopolitical goals, foreign policies, and the military-industrial complex, *The Nutmeg's Curse* offers yet another gripping and illuminating read.

Acknowledgments

I thank Nisha Eswaran and Jean-Philippe Platteau for their thoughtful comments on an earlier draft of this essay.

Notes

1 Ghosh, A., *Sea of Poppies* (New York, Ferrar Strauss, and Giroux, 2008). The page numbers I cite here refer to this edition.
2 Acemoglu, D., S. Johnson, and J.A. Robinson, "The Colonial Origins of Comparative Development: An Empirical Investigation," *American Economic Review*, 91 (2001), 1369–1401.
3 Dalrymple, W., *The Anarchy: The East India Company, Corporate Violence, and the Pillage of an Empire*, (Bloomsbury Publishing, 2019).
4 Acemoglu, D., S. Johnson, and J.A. Robinson, "Reversal of Fortune: Geography and Institutions in the Making of the Modern World Income Distribution", *Quarterly Journal of Economics*, 117 (2002), 1231–1294.
5 Bauer, R., *The Peasant Production of Opium in Nineteenth Century India*, Library of Economic History, Volume 12 (Brill Academic Publishers, 2019).

6 This is shown in Lehne, J., "An Opium Curse? The Long-run Economic Consequences of Narcotics Cultivation in British India," Paris School of Economics, Paris, France, 2018.
7 The utter callousness of the East India Company was seen decades earlier, even before it seriously entered the opium trade. After repeated crop failures due to inadequate rainfall in successive years, a serious famine developed in Bengal in 1769–1770. The Company neither undertook serious measures of famine relief nor relented in its tax collections. The historian Dalrymple (2019, p. 219) remarks about the Company,

> Nor did it make seed or credit available to the vulnerable, or assist cultivators with materials to begin planting their next harvest, even though the government had ample cash reserves to do so. Instead, anxious to maintain their revenues at a time of low production and high military expenditure, the Company, in one of the greatest failures of corporate responsibility in history, rigorously enforced tax collection and in some cases even increased revenue assessments by 10 per cent.

Around 10 million people are estimated to have died in this famine.
8 As Bauer (2019, p. 179), cited earlier, puts it: "It is, therefore, important to realise that the peasants dealt with a very powerful contract partner. One that could not only dictate the contract's conditions but also force the peasants into signing it at the very beginning.".
9 For a summary of the work on this this, see Copland, I., "Christianity as an Arm of Empire: The Ambiguous Case of India Under the Company, c. 1813–1858," *The Historical Journal*, 49 (2006), 1025–1054.
10 The mechanism responsible for the origin of capitalism and those shaping the forms of capitalism as it later evolved may be very different. Max Weber famously argued that the work ethic espoused by Protestantism was responsible for the rise of capitalism. Subsequent work, however, has shown that what spurred capitalism was not the work ethic per se but the fact that Protestantism strongly insisted on individual literacy (so that the faithful could read the Bible for themselves). See Becker, S.O. and L. Woessmann, "Was Weber Wrong? A Human Capital Theory of Protestant Economic History", *Quarterly Journal of Economics*, 124 (2009), 531–596. In capitalism's later incarnations, Weber's proposed causal relation between religion and capitalism may have been reversed.
11 A short overview of Wakefield's work is found in Ballantyne, T., "The Theory and Practice of Empire-Building: Edward Gibbon Wakefield and 'Systematic Colonisation'", in *The Routledge History of Western Empires*, (ed.) Aldrich, R. (Routledge, 2013), 89–101.
12 See Marx's, "The Modern Theory of Colonisation," Ch. 33 in *Capital: A Critique of Political Economy*, Vol. 1 (Penguin Classics, 1976).
13 Domar, E.D., "The Causes of Slavery or Serfdom: A Hypothesis," *The Journal of Economic History*, Vol. 30 (1970), 18–32.
14 Rigorous empirical and historical evidence on the suppression of outside options to reduce wages using data from British West Indies sugar colonies is provided in the interesting paper by Dippel, C., A. Greif, and D. Treffler, "Outside Options, Coercion and Wages: Removing the Sugar Coating," *The Economic Journal*, 130 (2020), 1678–1714.
15 This famous hypothesis was put forward by Eric Williams in 1945 in his book, *Capitalism and Slavery*, a claim for which there is mounting statistical evidence gathering.
16 Ghosh, A., *The Nutmeg's Curse: Parables for a Planet in Crisis* (University of Chicago Press, Chicago, 2021).

5

THE LONE SCREAM IN THE DARK

Cultural change and institutional transformation in modern China as seen through Lu Xun's novel*

Debin Ma

5.1 Introduction

Lu Xun 鲁迅 (1881–1936), undoubtedly the most famous writer in China, is the pen name of Zhou Shuren周树人. Although relatively little known in the West, Lu Xun is more than just a writer in China, but also a cultural and political symbol and icon. With his essays used in school textbook, he is a household name throughout Japan and Korea as well.

As a literary figure, he is classified as a short-story writer, essayist, literary critic and poet. Born in 1881 and lived through a time of profound political and cultural change that culminated in the fall of China's last imperial dynasty, Lu Xun pioneered the use of vernacular Chinese Baihuawen白话文to create a new literary writing style that broke away from the classical Chinese syntax. With Baihuawen being now the foundation of modern contemporary Chinese literature and prose, Lu Xun is often considered as "the Father of Modern Chinese Literature". His style of prose is peculiar and distinctive: dry, restrained, ascetic and stoic often belie a pungency that would suddenly catch the readers off guard, reeling. As a satirist, he writes with humor and irony but his satire is more often biting and grating. His short stories are largely autographical and most of his characters were no inspiring figures but bordering between pitiful, pathetic and sometimes even despicable. Today the Lu Xun phrases and lines are part of the modern Chinese lexicon and many of his characters are household names and symbols of meanings.

* I want to express my sincere gratitude to Jean-Philippe Platteau, François Bourguignon, and Avinash Dixit for comments and encouragement. All errors are mine. My research is partly supported by the AoE scheme awarded by the Research Grants Council of Hong Kong government.

DOI: 10.4324/9781003534358-7

The unusual influence and peculiar style of Lu Xun reflected the struggle and tension stemming from the wrenching transformation at the turn of China's tumultuous century. The once proud and giant nation self-placed at the center of the universe suddenly lost her footing and took a bad fall back to humility. In the looming shadow of national pessimism emerged the so-called New Cultural Movement by the 1910s that had sought to create a new culture and a national character in place of the old. The visible outbreak of the New Culture Movement was the so-called May Fourth Movement, a mass student protest that exploded in Beijing on 4 May 1919. Initially launched as a nationalist outcry against Western and Japanese imperialist erosion of Chinese sovereignty, the Movement developed into a thorough re-examination and sometimes a wholesale rejection of Chinese culture and ideology as encapsulated by Confucianism. China's perceived backwardness in material and economic conditions had given rise to a broader revolt against her political and social traditions ranging from native superstitions as embodied – for Lu Xun – in the practice of traditional Chinese medicine to female foot-binding, male hair-duo (imposed by China's Manchu minority rulers), polygamy, physical cruelty, traditional clothes and education or even the use of ideogramic Chinese characters and classical Chinese syntax. In its place, it advocated a new culture based on science, democracy, freedom, equality and progress, all fancy terms imported from the West (or via Japan).

As the New Culture Movement was championed by elites who were heavily influenced by the West – some educated in the West or Japan – as well as deeply immersed in Chinese tradition, the revolt created as much progress forward as setbacks and confusions of cultural and national identities. Lu Xun was part of that national soul-searching process that opened up a new horizon but left behind trails of debris. For some, Lu Xun was the voice of enlightenment, conscience, compassion and modernity, but for others his strident satire and critiques displayed nihilism, cynicism, animosity and irreverence.

Lu Xun's writings – both their substances and style – speak directly to some of the core issues of long-run economic development: the political economy of vested interests and ruling elites, the role of institutions and culture, and more importantly the more recent literature of how identities and ideas help explain historical persistence and resistance to economic and social transformation. Below, I will start with a discussion on the underlying economic theories for interpreting Lu Xun's work. I then turn to his brief biography and focus on two short stories and other well-known characters contained in his most well-known collection of stories titled "Scream". Finally, I will comment on how the works of Lu Xun could speak to the recent burgeoning literature among the global economic historians on the so-called Great Divergence debate and the Needham Puzzle.

5.2 Lu Xun: An economic analysis?

What truly explains long-run economic growth? Which is more important, institutions or culture? Scholars including Nobel Laureates Acemoglu et al. (2005) highlighted the role played by the "vested interests" of ruling elites and rent-seeking groups to explain the persistent inequality and non-inclusive policy choices through their establishment of extractive institutions. On the other hand, works going back to the European enlightenment thinkers and Max Weber had long emphasized the importance of culture to economic outcome. Indeed, these scholars argue that fundamental economic transformation cannot occur or sustain without comparable changes in underlying cultural values. While shifts in institutions and regimes could occur relatively swiftly, cultural values and their associated human behavior change far more gradually and slowly (North 2005; Boyd and Richerson 1985; Mokyr 2016; Acemoglu and Robinson 2021; Greif 2006; Williamson 2000).

Recent related literature on the economics of identities and ideas or ideology challenges the simplistic "interest" perspective and the dichotomy between culture and institutions (Akerlof 1976; Akerlof and Kranton 2005; Rodrik 2014; Ash et al. 2021). As succinctly summarized by Dani Rodrik (2014), the so-called "self-interest" or "vested-interest" presumes the idea of a self which itself is a social construct. How we evaluate and advance our interests depends on how we define our identities in terms of class, ethnicity, religion, demographic cohort, nation, or a combination of several identities. Interests are one form of idea that shapes our preferences and worldviews. Alternatively, ideas shape interests.

Moreover, ideas or ideologies are subject to manipulation and innovation. Various actors routinely invest in persuasion and ideology (Rodrik 2014, pp. 190–191). As Timur Kuran argued independently, as personal preferences can be highly interdependent between individuals, a system of false preferences can sustain publicly when each individual tailors one's expressed preferences to what appears socially acceptable or politically advantageous. This leads to an equilibrium that can easily support oppressive social norms and is thus essentially determined by beliefs of a certain type: if I am moderately or even radically against a certain type of behavior (say, the prohibition of remarriage of widows in India, or the foot-binding obligation for Chinese women) which I deem to be oppressive but I believe at the same time that other people will behave oppressively, it may be rational for me to follow suit when I may fear a punishment (formal or informal) justified by my being out-of-line with the behavior of the majority.[1] And this outcome is possible even though a great majority of individuals abhor the prevailing oppressive norm. In the terminologies of Kuran, an equilibrium based on public lies can sustain as long as each individual conceals private truths in isolation.

More importantly, given that ideas represent a way of evaluating and interpreting the world and evidence, any divergences in beliefs need not disappear even asymptotically when there is disagreement over the interpretation of evidence received (Rodrik 2014, p. 193; Denzau and North 1994; Ma and Rubin 2024). With culture and ideology deeply embedded in society and history, attempts to change the status quo by individuals or groups of individuals would encounter what economists would call the problems of a coordination game (David 1985; North 2005).

The writings of Lu Xun's work offer the most striking and poignant illustration of cultural values as the single most important catalyst or impediment to political and economic transformation. Living through a life of sharp contrasts between a childhood growing up in a traditional Chinese village and a youth abruptly exposed to the new world of a rapidly modernizing and Westernizing Japan in the 1900s, Lu Xun experienced an epiphany while in Japan. Like that group of small elites who acquired a radically new identity and worldview of modernization, Lu Xun returned to his hometown or home country to find himself a loner, outsider and eventually a rebel amidst the teeming masses steeped in cultural values or ideologies shaped by two millennia of indoctrination. Having "seen through" the ruling elites' manipulation of ideologies by the traditional ruling-elites, Lu Xun and his generation of self-avowed enlightenment thinkers found greater despair in realizing how pervasive the ideology had become among the masses and how what they identified as the "oppressed" identified with and perpetuated the ideology of the oppressors. Lu Xun's works were as much an attack on the hypocrisies of ruling elites or vested interests as a lament on the numbness of the oppressed masses.

5.3 Lu Xun and his epiphany

Born in 1881 and grew up in a family of landlords and government officials in Shaoxing, Zhejiang, at the heart of the highly commercialized Lower Yangzi region, Lu Xun saw his family fortune take a turn for the worse due to his father's drawn-out illness that slowly drained family resources. The teenage Lu Xun would recall years spent shuttling between his home and the local pawnshops to secure the cash needed to procure medicine at the local Chinese medicine store. The memory of those high counters at both pawn and medicine shops towering above his boyish statue would haunt him (Lu Xun 2014, vol. 1, p. 3). As his father's health continued to deteriorate and family desperation deepened, the Chinese medical prescription became increasingly expensive with more and more "exotic" plants and insects. In the end, his father died an exasperating death in front of the young and traumatized Lu Xun (Lu Xun 2014, vol. 2, p. 40). This experience compelled the young Lu Sun to become a doctor.

National events outside his village were even more tumultuous with China caught in a whirlwind of transformative political and social changes following her disastrous military defeat by Japan in 1894–1896: the rise and fall of the Hundred Days' Reform (1898) – China's radical political reform modeled after Meiji Japan – the Boxer Rebellion of 1899, and eventually the late Qing Constitutional Reform implemented in 1905 by the humiliated Qing regime (see Ma 2022). One part of the late Qing reform was the 1905 abolishment of China's Imperial Civil Service Examination centered on the teachings of Confucian classics and the rise of a new type of modern education and the opportunities for study overseas in the wake of the late Constitutional reform.[2]

Given the deterioration of his family wealth partly due to his father's long illness and death, Lu Xun had to abandon the traditional route of social mobility of pursuing a Confucian education. Instead, he went to newly established modern schools in nearby urban centers in 1899, where he got exposure to Western education subjects such as physics, arithmetic, geography, etc. More importantly, it was there that he saw for the first time the Chinese translation of Western medical books. Thinking back on his boyhood trauma with his father's illness, it dawned on him that "I gradually came to the recognition that Chinese medicine was nothing but an utter fraud intentionally or unintentionally but managed to capture the sympathy of those defrauded patients and their families" (Lu Xun 2014, vol. 1 p. 3). Lu Xun's aspiration for the medical profession was bolstered by his fundamental distrust of traditional Chinese medicine rooted in superstition and ignorance.

In 1902, Lu Xun left China to study in Japan on a Qing governmental scholarship. Like many of the first generation of Chinese students going abroad, Lu Xun's time in Japan became a turning point in his worldview.[3] Two years after he started in Japan, Lu Xun – having decided to study Western medicine prompted by his childhood experience – left the cosmopolitan Tokyo to begin his study at the relatively remote Sendai Medical Academy in northern Japan. In his autobiographic essay, Lu Xun recalled his dream plan for his study. Learning and mastering modern (Western) medicine would give him a chance to save patients like his father who were once failed or fooled by traditional Chinese medicine. During war times, he can become a military doctor to help fallen soldiers during war times.

Lu Xun's career plan seemed further assured by his learning that even Japan's own modernization in the Meiji era owed much to the translation of Western medicine (Lu Xun 2014, vol. 1, p. 4). For that, Lu Xun might be thinking of the case of the eighteenth century Japanese "Dutch Studies" (*Rangaku*) scholars' painstaking translation of Western anatomy. Based on a rare imported Western medical work at the time of a closed Tokugawa era, a couple of these scholars secretly performed their own anatomy and were able to verify its far greater anatomical accuracy than in the known Chinese texts of medicine.[4] Nonetheless, the formal introduction of modern anatomy and medical science to Japan had to wait until after the Meiji Reform in 1868.

However, things did not pan out as Lu Xun had hoped after his particular moment of epiphany. The medical class taught in Sendai tended to use movie slides to display the size and shapes of microbiology. Often, the class showed some scenic or news documentaries if there was still time left to spare. At the time Lu Xun was attending medical school, the Russo-Japanese War

(1904–1905) broke out in the disputed Northern eastern provinces of China. In one of the classes, Lu Xun described what he witnessed on the slide show:

> At the time, I hadn't seen any of my fellow Chinese in a long time, but one day some of them showed up in a slide. One, with his hands tied behind him, was in the middle of the picture; the others were gathered around him. Physically, they were as strong and healthy as anyone could ask, but their expressions revealed all too clearly that spiritually they were calloused and numb. According to the caption, the Chinese whose hands were bound had been spying on the Japanese military for the Russians. He was about to be decapitated as a 'public display.' The other Chinese gathered around him had come to enjoy the spectacle.

Lu Xun was absolutely disgusted by the apathy of his fellow countrymen cheering on the public execution of one of their own who himself had by then looked completely resigned. That imagery drove Lu Xun to the recognition that the root of the Chinese ails is not physical but mental; not individual but collective and national. He blurted out:

> From that time, I no longer felt it was so urgent to study medicine. For a weak nation, even though those individuals can be physically healthy and strong, they are only useful materials for public display or as bystanders. No need to feel sad for them and it does not matter how many of them die of sickness. Our first priority is to change their spirit; and for that, we need to turn to art and literature.
>
> *(Lu Xun 2014, vol. 1, p. 4)*

Lu Xun's once lifelong aspiration to cure physical illness in individuals as medical doctor had by then morphed into treating the collective spiritual and cultural maladies of a nation. For that, Lu Xun wanted to become a writer taking up a pen sharper than a scalpel.

Intellectually, Lu Xun linked this fateful career turn with another Japanese personality during his time in Sendai. At the Sendai Academy, Lu Xun met his anatomy teacher, Fujino Genkurō, who noted his lone Chinese student with an imperfect command of the Japanese language. Mr. Fujino made special efforts to reach out to him to review and revise his class notes. At the start of the anatomy class, Mr. Fujino was worried if Lu Xun could cope with dissecting human corpses given the Chinese beliefs in afterlife ghost. He was relieved to see Lu Xun did well. At one point, Mr Fujino also inquired with him about the practice of Chinese female foot-binding and how it would impact the bone structure of the foot (Lu Xun 2014, vol. 2, p. 49).

In one of his most celebrated autobiographic essays plainly titled "Mr. Fujino" (which is used in school textbook in China and Japan), Lu Xun gave a subtle and endearing portrayal of the lasting impact of those simple acts of kindness by his Japanese mentor. Lu Xun remembered how much Mr. Fujino had hoped he would pursue his medical profession to bring back his advanced new (Western) medical knowledge to his ancient motherland of China. Hence, Lu Xun's decision to abandon his medical study in Sendai after one year came as a big disappointment to Mr. Fujino. Lu Xun was to remain forever remorseful to his Japanese mentor as the student.

Lu Xun brought back to China entire three boxes of his lecture notes from Mr. Fujino's class and his photo given to him at the time of their farewell in Sendai. Years after returning to China, Lu Xun would often recall his quiet soliloquies with Mr. Fujino in the depth of the night completely discouraged and exhausted from his own writing. As soon as he raised his head to catch the stern gaze of Mr. Fujino from the framed photo hung on the wall of his study, Lu Xun would hear Mr Fujino's anatomy lecture all over again in his characteristically accentuated tone. Each time, Lu Xun immediately became alert, sat tight and ploughed on with his writing – in full courage – to draw the ire of those so-called "gentlemen" (Lu Xun 2014, vol. 2, p. 51).[5] It was in Mr. Fujino that Lu Xun found reconciliation between aspirations lost and rediscovered, between medicine and literature and between personal belonging and nationalist sentiments.

5.4 The scream

5.4.1 Foreword

"Scream" 呐喊, a collection of short stories originally published in 1923, probably ranked as the single most influential piece of writing in modern China. The title "scream" seems to echo the terrifying image of the identically titled painting by the Norwegian artist Edvard Munch in 1893. While Munch's scream came to symbolize the horrifying individual suffering from a feeling of distortion of the environment and one's self in a time of turmoil around the world, Lu Xun's story of scream in words invoked a similar depth of emotions but with a vastly different context.[6]

In his foreword to the book, Lu Xun wrote of that profound and crushing sense of despair and isolation confronted by him and other enlightened new generations in the midst of the seamless and bottomless mass of apathy and numbness. The foreword presents one of Lu Xun's most iconic analogies of this situation in a conversation with a compatriot who tried to encourage him to write for a journal called "New Youth" which was to become the most important publication of the New Cultural Movement:

> Imagine an iron house without windows, absolutely indestructible, with many people fast asleep inside who will soon die of suffocation. But they will die in their sleep without feeling the pain of death. Now if you scream and end up waking up a few of those more conscious, all you have done is

> to awake those unfortunate few to the agony of recognizing their irrevocable death, are you doing them any good?

To that, his compatriot responded firmly: "Perhaps if only just those few woke up, you cannot say there is no hope of tearing down this iron house". Lu Xun wanted to believe him and wrote for the "New Youth" journal what was later to become the disturbing masterpiece "The Diary of a Mad Man".[7]

5.4.2 *Diary of a mad man*

Heavily influenced by Western literature, Lu Xun pioneered the Chinese translation of Western stories and also read as many works from Russia and other Eastern European countries as he could find in German and Japanese translations (Chinnery 1960, p. 309). The title of "Diary of a Mad Man" was taken from a story written by the Russian author Nikolay Gogol written in 1834. While Gogol's story of a madman was an attempt to escape the censors by attacking the high officials in Russia's St. Petersburg through the words of a madman, Lu Xun's tale was an allegory used as a direct attack on traditional society through the inverted worldview of a "madman" (Chinnery 1960, pp. 310–311).

Indeed, everything in the sensory world of this little depressing novel was inverted. The "madman" in this novel was conscious but was considered mad because he had exposure to the brand new world of ideas whose norms and values stood in sharp contrast to the ancient values of two millennia held by people around him. The "madman" exhibited behaviors similar to what modern psychiatry would diagnose as paranoid, a close correspondence that reveals Lu Xun's long-standing interest in medical study. The application of modern psychology to literature allows Lu Xun to convey his individual outlook on society concealed through the imagination of schizophrenia (Chinnery 1960, p. 312).

Returning to his village after years of being away (perhaps being abroad in Lu Xun's case), the madman found himself a complete outsider, ultra-suspicious of everybody around him, neighbors, peasants, random hooligans on the street or even his brother and mother. All seemed out to conspire to persecute him. Every one of their words, facial expressions, and seemingly random acts all aimed at one objective – to eat him alive. While Lu Xun did evoke tales of cannibalism in classical Chinese tradition, his madman analogy broadly represented a frontal assault on how brutality and repression were couched in the most benevolent terms of classical Chinese teaching and ideology. Through the mouth of a "truth-telling" madman came Lu Xun's most memorable lines:

> You have to study in order to understand things. People eat people from ancient times, as I kind of seem to remember, but I am not totally certain. So I turn to history to check but this history seems to have no timeline, but scribbled over its every page are the characters of Benevolence and Morality 仁义

> 道德. I tossed and turned in bed, unable to fall sleep. After half of a night of ruminating, I finally discovered that hidden between the cracks of every character in the entire book were inscribed two words: 'Eat People''吃人'!

The central idea of the story is that society is cannibalistic while orthodox Confucian morality was merely a cover for cannibalism. Discussing the writing of "Diary of a madman", Lu Xun later wrote bluntly: "What we call Chinese civilization is really only a feast of human flesh for the delectation of the rich. What we call China is only the kitchen where this feast is prepared" (quoted in Chinnery 1960, p. 314).

So this is not just a story of "elite" dominance or class repression with the minority rich cannibals over the majority poor victims. In fact, given their identification with the ideology, everyone including the so-called oppressed is a victim as well as a cannibal. Those who wanted to eat him also wanted to eat others but were also afraid of being eaten themselves; they all looked at each other with the deepest suspicion. A few years later, Lui Xun put this idea more systematically:

> … we have long ago arranged everything with perfect convenience. We have the noble and the common, the rich and the poor, the high and the lowly. We are oppressed by others, but we can oppress others in turn. We are devoured by others, but can devour others in turn. Each level is held in check. It cannot move, nor has it any desire to move, for any change, even if it has advantages, will also bring disadvantages.
>
> *(quoted in Chinnery 1960, p. 315)*

Hence, the reason for the cannibals' desire to kill the madman is that he is a rebel that the cannibals would unite to snuff out.

What drove that madman madder is that he himself, like all others, was the inheritor of a four thousand years of history of cannibalism. Is there any hope for any person with that kind of history? The madman went on to ask: "Perhaps there are children who have not eaten anyone yet?" "Please save the children" was the last plea of desperation at the end of the story.

5.4.3 Medicine

"Medicine" was a haunting and tragic short story of those self-assuming revolutionaries who shed their blood as an act of martyrdom intended to awaken the masses but only to see their very blood shed to feed the superstition of those very masses. Martyrdom was turned on its head and made a brutal mockery of it.

The story starts with an elderly couple by the name of Hua who ran a local teahouse in the village. It turned out their only son had caught what seemed like tuberculosis that may have once killed Lu Xun's father. The local superstition or traditional Chinese medicine had it that their son's illness could be cured by eating of "Steamed Bun" soaked inside live human blood. One way of acquiring such kind of human blood is to bribe the local executioners for a fee to collect them illegally from the corpses of newly executed criminals. On a dark night, the elderly Mr. Hua went out and did exactly that to bring back two steamed buns for his ailing son. The elderly couple watched their son swallow them instantly. Later, the customers and neighbors of the teahouse who learned about Hua's acquisition of the blood-soaked bun also came to congratulate them with assurances that their son's recovery would be a matter of time.

It turned out that the "criminal" whose blood was used for the bun was actually a revolutionary by the name of Xia Yu executed for his crime of treason against the Qing regime. One customer in the teahouse had even met him in the cell and recalled how, to his complete disbelief, this poor criminal even in his cell would have the arrogance to incite him to turn against the Qing regime. So, "I roughed him up", he gloated to everyone's delight and cheer at the teahouse.

Meanwhile, the son, the Junior Mr. Hua, sadly, died not too long after having eaten up the human blood steamed bun. The story ends with the scene of the deeply aggrieved mother – Mrs. Hua staggering her way to sweep the very modest tomb of her deceased son. On her way, she ran into another elderly, disheveled and unkempt lady by the name of Mrs. Xia who was on her way to sweep the tomb of her own son. It turned out that Mrs. Xia was the mother of that executed (criminal) revolutionary. The Chinese characters of the two last families, Hua 华 and Xia 夏 combined, is a compound term for "Chinese Civilization" 华夏.

It was the saddest encounter of two heirless mothers. They consoled each other's loss in their deepest moments of grief at the graveyard. Now both heirless, they shared a complete sense of abandonment – perhaps like the Chinese Civilization itself – by the whole world. Trudging their way home, they only had the company of a black crow who gingerly followed only to fly far away into the sky with a long caw.

The pointless nature of the revolutionary martyrdom became more poignant in real life as it turned out that Mr. Xia Yu 夏瑜, the executed revolutionary in the story, was actually a woman in real life widely known as Ms. Qiu Jin 秋瑾. As a married mother of two but chose to dress as a man and behave as an equal toward men, Qiu Jin became a symbol of the new women: educated, independent, and active in public affairs. The brutal execution of China's first feminist heroin in 1907 sparked outrage and partly triggered the eventual downfall of the Qing regime in 1911. Qiu Jin was from the same town as Lu Xun and went to study in Japan where they met each other. The Chinese character, "Xia" 夏, in Xia Yu used by Lu Xun also means "Summer", to match the Chinese character "Qiu" 秋 as in Qiu Jin, meaning "Autumn" (Ying, Hu 2016). For Lu Xun, the story of Medicine was highly personal.

5.4.4 The personalities of Ah-Q, Kong Yiji and Runtu

"Scream" is also most memorable for some tales of the most colorful tragicomic personalities. In "The Story of Ah-Q", the curiously named protagonist, "Ah-Q" 阿 Q, is now almost the alter ego of a perverse aspect of the Chinese national character molded by the traditional ideology. Ah-Q, a part-time domestic helper who eked out a living by working for different households, was among the lowest and poorest of the village social hierarchy and income ladder. Abused and beaten up practically by anybody in the village, Ah-Q dealt with each humiliation with what Lu Xun famously coined as the coping "strategy of spiritual triumph", which took the form of Ah-Q declaring a mental victory over his abuser behind his back after each humiliation or beating. Ah-Q, the perennial loser, came out the winner each time, self-declared.

In "Kong Yiji", the protagonist, Kong Yiji 孔乙己, was as downtrodden as Ah-Q except for his past distinction of having received some Confucian education possibly during his failed attempts at passing the Civil Service Examination. Impoverished, debt-ridden and sickly, Kong Yiji painstakingly held on to his elevated sense of identity in the social hierarchy, moving around the village in his utterly tattered "gentlemanly" robe and with his pretentious "learned" speech. The distinctive and hilarious Kong Yiji phraseology and syntax that Lu Xun had created has become the parody of a man who had nothing left except his "public" mask.

In "Home Town", the character of Runtu is relatively speaking the most benign by comparison. Lu Xun described his return to his native village after nearly twenty years of being away. Among many other things, he was looking forward to reuniting with his childhood mate Runtu. The Chinese character of Runtu 闰土 (润土) literally meaning Surplus (or alternatively as moist and fertile) Soil, a nickname that represented the humble and teeming masses of vast rural China, was the son of a house servant at Lu Xun's household. Incognizant of their gap in social status as children, the two enjoyed many happy innocent children playing times together in the winter snow and summer beach. Lu Xun remembered him as full of joy, fun, intelligence, and resourcefulness.

But when Lu Xun saw Runtu again more than twenty years later, that childhood Runtu was gone. No longer playful and resourceful, the senior Runtu was then an adult man totally worn down by the marks of age and the burden of raising a large family at the bottom of the social hierarchy. But it was the change in demeanor than an appearance at the meeting that sent a chill through Lu Xun's spine. Before Lu Xun even had a chance to reminisce about their past playtimes, the senior Runtu immediately bowed in front of him and addressed him as what would translate to the English equivalent of a "master". Lu Xun was subsequently introduced to his fifth son. "Ah, there was the young Runtu I seemed to remember from twenty years ago", Lu Xun thought to himself. In the next minute, the boy was made to kneel in front of Lu Xun to pay respect to his father's master.

The reunion with Runtu left Lu Xun in a profound state of sadness. If in the "Diary of a Mad Man", Lu Xun had once pinned his hope on the future generation of children, Lu Xun witnessed then the forfeit of childhood innocence in "Home Town". Where is hope? Lu Xun exclaimed at the end of the story. Recalling his childhood beach playing times with Runtu, Lu Xun penned what was to become the most plainly spoken but iconic line for trailblazers in China:

> In a moment of haze, before my eye laid open a stretch of pure blue beach, with a golden full moon hanging in the deep blue sky above. I thought that after all, there was not anything like hope to begin with; just like there were not any trails to begin with on the ground. But when more people started walking, they became trails.
>
> *(Lu Xun 2014, vol. 1, pp. 54–56)*

5.5 Lu Xun and debates in Chinese and global economic history

The satires of Lu Xun would throw some curious insights or enlightenment on the two ongoing grand revisionist theses of the past four decades on China's historical achievements in a global context. The first is the so-called Needham hypothesis raised by Professor Joseph Needham, a historian of science based at Cambridge University. Given China's astounding achievements in science and technology as exemplified by her epochal inventions of paper, printing, compass and gunpowder during the medieval era, Needham asked why Song China (960–1279 AD), the world's leading economy at the time, did not become the first country to industrialize (See Lin 1995; Brandt et al. 2014).

During the past three decades, the so-called California School pushed the Needham thesis even further by arguing that the core region of China such as the Lower Yangzi remained as the world's leading economic areas with living standards comparable to contemporaneous England and Holland as late as the eighteenth century. On the question of why it was England rather than China that industrialized during the eighteenth century, the California School emphasizes the role of new resources in England such as coal and the discovery of the New World (Pomeranz 2001; Brandt et al. 2014).

The Needham question and the California School turned the whole thesis of modernization and Westernization on its head: it was China rather than the West that had been the forerunner of technology and economy in the medieval and early modern era. The California School's resurrection of the Lower Yangzi region where Lu Xun's native hometown of Shaoxing was located would have most likely amused if not shocked Lu Xun. Indeed, at the turn of the twentieth century, Lu Xun spent a lifetime attacking or trying to awaken people in his native hometown to become culturally "fit" for modernization. Characters such as Kong Yiji or Ah-Q had become the prototypes of those traditional "national characters or traits" that could account for China's stagnation and backwardness. Culture and ideology that Lu Xun had highlighted as major impediments to progress figured little if at all in the California School thesis.

On the question of China's past inventiveness argued by Needham, Lu Xun's satire written in 1933 would seem quite unsparing:

> While foreign (or Western) countries used gun-powder to produce bullets fending off enemies, Chinese used it to make firecrackers to worship gods; While foreign countries used the compass to sail the sea, Chinese used it or *fengshui* (geomancy); while foreigners used opium for medical treatment, Chinese made it their staple food.
>
> *(Lu Xun 2014, vol. 4, p. 76)*

As expected, Lu Xun reserved his most unsparing and poignant satire to his favorite subject of anatomy. In reference to China's relative backwardness in medical science and anatomy partly due to the taboo of dissecting human bodies, this one-time student of anatomy in Japan wrote the following in 1934[8]:

> Both Medicine and Torture would require knowledge in biology and anatomy. In China it was very strange, all those drawings of internal organ system in old Chinese medical books were full of embarrassing and gross errors. But when it comes to the method of torture, it seems our ancestors had full mastery of modern science.
>
> *(Lu Xun 2014, vol. 2, pp. 277–284, 1934)*

The torture Lu Xun alluded to refers to the cruelest of all capital punishment called "Lingchi" 凌迟 which literally meant "death by a thousand cuts" where a criminal was sliced to death piece by piece by knives while kept alive for days on public display. In 1905, the year the millennium old Chinese imperial Civil Service examination that had indoctrinated the Confucius ethics of benevolence was abolished, Lingchi was also officially outlawed (Bourgon 2003).

5.6 Epilogue: The ghost of Lu Xun

At first reading, Lu Xun's unreserved attack on the so-called "gentlemanly" ruling class or the ideology of "benevolence" in Confucian classics seems to fall very much in line with the political economy framework of how rent-seeking elites perpetuated the status quo. But on a deeper level, what Lu Xun unveils is how the oppressed, the victims of traditional regimes such as Runtu, Ah-Q and Kong Yiji came to identify, perpetuate or even defend the regime and status quo. After all, no ideology by the ruling class can easily rule or dominate without gaining some form of legitimacy and compliance by the public and the masses.

In this regard, the pioneering theoretical economic works of George Akerlof (1976), Timur Kuran and others help shed light on the seemingly paradoxical behavior of someone being a victimizer and victim at the same time. Literary works like that of Lu Xun help convey the full complexity, ambiguity and nuances behind the underlying theories. At a time of rapid shifts in national and global systems within just a few decades, Lu Xun captured the tensions between the elites and the masses, the divergence between private truths and public lies and the crisis of conflicting identities and worldviews.

In this regard, changes cannot come about through regimes or institutions alone but also the ideas and identities. In a massive nation with homogeneous preferences indoctrinated through millennia of traditional ideology, this is a tall order. As economic jargon would frame it: the rise of a new generation whose preferences are influenced by a new "exogenous" and "foreign" ideology would insert certain elements of heterogeneity. This would set off a process of changes first among a group of people relatively averse to a given norm or status quo and then later among the more averse population (Platteau et al. 2018). Hence, changes may come gradually one step at a time through persuasion. However, having himself died prematurely in 1936, Lu Xun would not see the day that changes by persuasion through fiction and satire would eventually give way to revolution imposed through violence and coercion.

Today, as the terms such as "Iron House", "Eat People", "Benevolence" and "Human blood Steam Bun" and names such as Ah-Q and Kong Yiji have entered the daily Chinese lexicon, one wonders how much the works of Lu Xun and the New Cultural Movement had already altered the course of Chinese history. Eventually, the radicalization of the New Cultural Movement later led to the rise of the Communist movement initially sponsored directly by the Communist International from Moscow. The Communist leader, Mao Zedong, was himself a product of the New Cultural Movement.

Armed with the belief in Communism being the most "advanced" or modern form of Western ideology, the new Communist regime founded in 1949 was poised to carry out the most massive social engineering program of radical modernization the world would ever see. The infamous Cultural Revolution launched in 1965 unleashed the most destructive force to eradicate all vestiges of Chinese tradition such as Confucian classics texts, religious buildings, lineage halls, traditional operas and even intellectuals. Although ideologically left-leaning and praised by Mao Zedong personally, Lu Xun was claimed ownership by camps both left and right. Ironically, had he not died in 1936, Lu Xun, the man most credited with his attack on traditional culture, would have most been purged in Mao's Cultural Revolution given his characteristically sacrilegious and iconoclastic inclination.

When an impoverished and self-isolated China re-emerged out of isolation at the end of the radical Mao era, it became an eerie moment of reckoning: China's East Asian neighbors of Japan and Asian tigers had – in the interval of three decades – blossomed into modern miracles of economic growth partly through a transformation – rather than eradication – of their common Confucian heritage. This wake-up call to China's second fall from grace within the same century was made all the more cruel as China this time was left behind not just by the West but by her Asian neighbor long designated at the periphery of Chinese culture. In this moment of profound mental shock and crisis of identities, the ghost of a scathing Lu Xun hovered over again.[9] Perhaps the demons of traditional Chinese culture that Lu Xun had awakened a century ago never really left China. They came under a different guise: traditional robes replaced by modern jackets, "benevolence" ditched by "progress". But nothing of substance – as the new enlightenment thinkers of the 1980s would go on to argue – has changed. Indeed, a social engineering program in the name of modernization was pushed through by a totalitarian regime partly founded on the ancient roots of Chinese imperial despotism. The 1960s Cultural Revolution set China backward rather than forward and took her back to some of her darkest eras of repression in ancient Chinese dynasties. The fanaticism of the young Red Guards of the Cultural Revolution was just vulnerable to ideological manipulation in the new regime as was the numbness of the masses in the old regime. The process of mutual victimization continued.

Ironically, China's new era of opening and reform during the 1980s under Deng Xiaoping saw a drastic moderation of radicalism and a partial restoration of cultural traditions. Indeed, many would argue that China's economic miracles for the next four decades after the 1980s owed much to the same Confucian tradition of work ethics, respect for education, the legacy of bureaucracy and state capacity shared with her East Asian neighbors. In that regard, the scholarship of the California School, Joseph Needham and others are timely reminders of those positive historical legacies (see Brandt et al. 2014). Even Chinese medicine – purged of the superstitious elements – transformed and thrived as a viable medical profession.

Nonetheless, Lu Xun has become a symbol and a concept: as long as Lu Xun was relevant, true modernity remained far aloof from China. A case in point is the outbreak of the global pandemic Covid from 2019. China's anti-Covid policy based on strict surveillance and control had been hailed as a huge success in the initial stage globally thanks to the teeming masses like Lu Xun's Runtu who willingly or unwillingly accepted massive and often coercive restrictions on their personal freedom. However, with the Covid virus mutating into the more infectious but less lethal Omicron variety, the human cost of strict lockdown mounted sharply threatening the very livelihood of hundreds of millions of Chinese citizens.

In the winter of 2022, the Chinese government's continued adherence to the world's strictest anti-Covid lockdown and a draconian policy of repression on any form of dissent and disobedience eventually led to the rise of the so-called white paper protest with people holding up blank sheets of paper as a sign of defiance against the lockdown policy. On Halloween night of 2022, many young people gathered in Shanghai – the city where Lu Xun spent most of his adult life – with some taking advantage of the festival to turn up with costumes disguised as a veiled protest against the government's draconian policy of lockdown. In particular, quite a few dressed up as Lu Xun look-alikes. One young man held up a paper card poster that read: "Studying Medicine cannot save Chinese People".[10] Suddenly on that cold Halloween night, Lu Xun's scream from a century ago came back haunting.

Notes

1 For an insightful paper on the case of the persistence of female foot-binding in traditional China, see Platteau et al. (2018).
2 For the importance of Civil Service Examination for traditional Chinese social structure and social mobility, see Ho (1962). Also, see Brandt et al. (2014) the political economy aspect of the Examination system.
3 See Kung and Wang (2020) for the surge of Chinese students in Japan in the early twentieth century.
4 See Sugita (1969) and Bowers (1970) on the Japanese "Dutch Studies" scholars' translation of Western medical texts in the Tokugawa era. See Ogawa (1975) for the account of anatomy in Japan. See Ma and Rubin (2024) for a comparison of ideological transformation in modern Japan and China.
5 The essay "Mr. Fujino" has brought unprecedented fame to an otherwise obscure academy professor in remote rural Japan. Largely unaware of Lu Xun's portrayal of him until much later, Mr. Fujino, when interviewed, recalled the presence of anti-Chinese ultra-nationalism in Sendai medical academy right after the 1894–1896 Sino-Japanese war and Chinese students were often mocked for their Manchu hairdo. Mr. Fujino himself had studied Chinese and harbored deep respect for Chinese civilization. That could be one reason Mr. Fujino did feel certain affinity to his lone Chinese student. See Lu Xun (2017, pp. 1–3).
6 See description of Munch's scream in Simeon and Abugel (2006). I owe Avinash Dixit to this particular point of analogy between the two forms of expressions of "scream" although I cannot find any direct relationship between the two artists. I also want to thank him for pointing me to the linkage between Lu Xun and the Russian writer Nikolay Gogol.
7 Apart from those specifically referenced, most of the English translation of Lu Xun' original Chinese works is based on mine.
8 Teizo Ogawa (1975) noted the Song China's achievement in anatomy and its subsequent stagnation in contrast to advances made in the West. Ogawa specifically noted Needham's contribution on Song scientific achievements.
9 The epic six-part TV series "River Elegy" 河殇 released in 1988 became the defining piece of this new wave of Chinese enlightenment for the reform era.
10 See news report at: Shanghai Halloween Costumes Raise Specter of Censorship (chinadigitaltimes.net).

References

Acemoglu, Daron, Simon Johnson, and James A. Robinson. 2005. "Institutions as Fundamental Determinants of Long-Run Growth," in *Handbook of Economic Growth*, edited by Philippe Aghion and Steven Durlauf, vol. 1A, pp. 385–472. Amsterdam: North-Holland.

Acemoglu, Daron, and James A. Robinson. 2021. "Culture, Institutions and Social Equilibria: A Framework." NBER Working Paper 28832. https://doi.org/10.3386/w28832

Akerlof, G. 1976. "The Economics of Caste and of the Rat Race and Other Woeful Tales". *The Quarterly Journal of Economics* 90(4): 599–617.

Akerlof, George A., and Rachel E. Kranton. 2005. "Identity and the Economics of Organizations." *Journal of Economic Perspectives* 19(1): 9–32.

Ash, Elliot, Sharun W. Mukand and Dani Rodrik. 2021. "Economic Interests, Worldviews, and Identities, Theory and Evidence on Ideational Politics" NBER Working Paper 29474.

Bourgon, Jérôme. 2003 "Abolishing 'Cruel Punishments': A Reappraisal of the Chinese Roots and Long-term Efficiency of the Xinzheng Legal Reforms" *Modern Asian Studies* 37(4): 851–862.

Bowers, John. 1970. *Western Medical Pioneers in Feudal Japan*. Baltimore, MD: The Johns Hopkins Press.

Boyd, Robert, and Peter J. Richerson. 1985. *Culture and the Evolutionary Process*. Chicago: University of Chicago Press.

Brandt, Loren, Debin Ma, and Thomas G. Rawski. 2014. "From Divergence to Convergence: Reevaluating the History behind China's Economic Boom." *Journal of Economic Literature* 52(1): 45–123.

Chinnery, J. D. 1960. "The Influence of Western Literature on Lu Xun's 'Diary of a Madman'." *Bulletin of the School of Oriental and African Studies* 23(2): pp. 309–322.

David, P. A. 1985. "Clio and the Economics of QWERTY'. *American Economic Review* 75: 332–337.

Denzau, Arthur T., and Douglass C. North. 1994. "Shared Mental Models: Ideologies and Institutions." *Kyklos* 47(1): 3–31.

Greif, Avner. 2006. *Institutions and the Path to the Modern Economy: Lessons from Medieval Trade*. New York: Cambridge University Press.

Ho, Ping-Ti. 1962. *The Ladder of Success in Imperial China: Aspects of Social Mobility, 1368–1911*. New York: Columbia University Press.

Kung, James and Alina Yue Wang. 2020. "Foreign-educated Elite and Political Transformation: Evidence from Historical China." Working Paper.

Lin, J. Y. 1995. "The Needham Puzzle: Why the Industrial Revolution Did Not Originate in China." *Economic Development and Cultural Change* 43(2): 269–292.

Lu Xun. 2014. *The Collected Works of Lu Xun, Four Volumes*. Wuhan: China Central University of Science and Technology.

Lu Xun. 2017. *The Trail of Life, a Concise Collection of Essays by Lu Xun*, pp. 131–136. Nanjing: Jiangsu Phoenix Art Publisher.

Ma, Debin 2022. "Ideology and the Contours of Economic Change in Modern China, 1850–1950" chapter 1 in *Cambridge Economic History of China*, vol. II, edited by Debin Ma and Richard von Glahn, pp. 15–47. Cambridge: Cambridge University Press.

Ma, Debin and Jared Rubin 2024 "Ideology and Economic Change: the Contrasting Paths to the Modern Economy in late 19th Century China and Japan." Chapman University Digital Commons, ESI Working Paper 24-09. https://digitalcommons.chapman.edu/esi_working_papers/405/

Mokyr, Joel. 2016. *A Culture of Growth: The Origins of the Modern Economy*. Princeton, NJ: Princeton University Press.

North, Douglass C. 2005. *Understanding the Process of Economic Change*. Princeton, NJ: Princeton University Press.

Ogawa, Teizo 1975. "The Beginnings of Anatomy in Japan." *Okajima Folia Anatomica Japonica* 52: 59–72.

Platteau, Jean-Philippe, G. Camilotti, and E. Auriol. 2018. "Eradicating Women-Hurting Customs: What Role for Social Engineering?," in *Towards Gender Equity and Development*, edited by S. Anderson, L. Beaman, and J.P. Platteau, pp. 319–356. Oxford, UK: Oxford University Press.

Pomeranz, Kenneth. 2001 *The Great Divergence: China, Europe, and the Making of the Modern World Economy*. Princeton, NJ: Princeton University Press.

Rodrik, Dani. 2014. "When Ideas Trump Interests: Preferences, Worldviews, and Policy Innovations." *Journal of Economic Perspectives* 28(1): 189–208.

Simeon, Daphne, and Jeffrey Abugel. 2006. *Feeling Unreal: Depersonalization Disorder and the Loss of the Self*. New York: Oxford University Press.

Sugita, Genpaku. 1969. *The Dawn of Western Science in Japan*. Chiyoda-ku, Tokyo, Japan: Hokuseido Press.

Williamson, Oliver. 2000. "The New Institutional Economics: Taking Stock, Looking Ahead." *Journal of Economic Literature* 38(3): 595–613.

Ying, Hu. 2016. *Burying Autumn: Poetry, Friendship, and Loss*. Cambridge, MA: Harvard University Asia Center.

6

ZOLA'S "LADIES PARADISE" AND THE "CREATIVE DESTRUCTION" THEORY

François Bourguignon

6.1 Introduction

Emile Zola, a French writer from the second half of the 19th century,[1] launched the so-called "Naturalist literary movement", whose ambition was to depict all the facets of society, particularly its social features. Zola himself wrote a 20-volume fresco about the history of a family, the Rougon-Macquart, under the Second Empire, from 1852 to 1970. Twenty members, with very different life trajectories from priest to courtesan, union leader or banker, are in turn the heroes of a novel, thus allowing Zola to indeed paint an exhaustive picture of the whole society. He did so with a kind of scientific spirit, insisting on describing with the utmost realism and precision not only the personality and vagaries of his characters but also their physical and social environments. "Our hero", wrote Zola, "is no longer the pure spirit, the abstract man of the eighteenth century. He is the physiological subject of our present science, a being which is composed of organs and soaks in an environment which permeates it every hour". Such an approach to novel writing, clearly inspired by Auguste Comte's positivist school, should be appealing today to any reader with any inclination towards social science.

Most novels in the Rougon-Macquart series, especially the most-read ones, brush a rather dismal image of the 19th century French society and reveal a pessimistic view of its evolution. L'Assommoir[2] tells the ravage of alcoholism in the working class; Germinal is about the misery of coal miners' lives, their exploitation by capitalists and the ferocious repression of unions; and La Terre (The Soil) describes the life of peasants and their sordid family struggles for the appropriation of land. On the other side of the social spectrum, Pot-Bouille portrays the decadent mores of the middle bourgeoisie sunk in adultery. By

DOI: 10.4324/9781003534358-8

contrast, Au *Bonheur des dames* (*Ladies' Paradise*), which describes the birth of department stores in mid-19th century's Paris and the revolution they caused in retail trade, sounds like an optimistic note of progress even though it also depicts the human and social drama of traditional shops outcompeted, made bankrupt and in some cases physically destroyed by the expansion of modern mass retail trade. Some 70 years before Joseph Schumpeter, a major economic thinker of the mid-20th century who introduced the concept of "creative destruction" in the economic literature, Zola, seems to have perceived the economic progress paradox: innovations that end up benefiting the society as a whole can still cause the suffering and destitution of some.

There are two plots in *Ladies' Paradise*, each with its own significance. One plot is, so to speak, business oriented. It describes the ascent of the Ladies' Paradise store in the centre of Paris under the revolutionary management of its young owner, Octave Mouret, and the other side of the coin, the decline and, ultimately, the death of traditional shops around it. This opposition between progress and decay in two different parts of the society is both the mainspring of the plot of the novel and its conceptual spine; that is, the idea that innovation and economic progress always come at a heavy loss among those people or activities they displace, a process which economists would later refer to as "creative destruction".

The other plot stages everyday life in two worlds, the employees and clients of the Bonheur, on the one hand, and the owners and families of shopkeepers who watch the inexorable decline of their business on the other. It revolves around the young heroin of the novel, Denise, freshly arrived from the provinces, the niece of the owner of an old drapery shop in the process of going bust due to the expansion of Mouret's store. Hired as a sales assistant in the Bonheur, she will end marrying Mouret after various twists and turns. This rags-to-riches part of the novel may have contributed to its popular success when first published. Most importantly, however, it provides the pleasant thread with which Zola is able to weave together his analytical portrayal of the life of the working middle-class, and to a lesser extent of the middle and upper bourgeoisie, and that of the deep transformation of the economy which was taking place in mid-19th century's Paris.

When reading *Ladies' Paradise*, an economist is impressed by the intuition that Zola demonstrates when describing and discussing the economics of innovation in this particular instance of the advent of department stores. Equally interesting is the analysis that Zola provides of marketing and firm management through his account of the rise of a tycoon in early day capitalism. However, economists will also be interested in the history of Denise, not so much because of its rather conventional Cinderella tone, but because, together with her fellow employees in the Bonheur, the Baudu family, neighbouring merchants, and also those ladies who shop at the Bonheur, they provide a lively and exhaustive image of the costs and benefits of economic innovation and the transformation it may cause in the social fabric. It is through them that Zola expresses his conviction that economic progress eventually outweighs its immediate social cost.

It is now time to back these general remarks and to delve deeper into Zola's thoughts through a more detailed account of the script of his novel. We shall start with the business plot.

6.2 Innovative entrepreneurship at work

We meet Mouret at the time he is getting ready for a major gamble. A young womaniser, an ambitious and imaginative salesman, especially in ladies' wear where his seducing talent works wonders, he had married the owner of Au Bonheur des Dames in the Pot-Bouille novel. Together, they extended this traditional drapery shop into a major business. When becoming a widower, however, Mouret gave free rein to his ambition to transform "Au Bonheur" into an even bigger outfit, expanding the sales space by buying adjacent houses and introducing revolutionary practices in sales and staff management.

As far as sales technology is concerned, the innovation consisted in, first, displaying all the goods in the open with visible price tags attached, unlike the price bargaining practice common among the old shopkeepers; second, broadening the range of goods for sale and grouping them in distinct departments rather than specializing in a few types of goods; third, making windows and counters visually appealing within an attractive and spacious overall setting; and then several others "tricks" to lure customers, as neighbouring retailers would call Mouret's inventions. On staff management, incentives and competition are Mouret's master words:

> He had thought up a new scheme by which (...) he gave the sale staff a certain percentage on every piece, however small, of fabric and on every item that they sold. The system had revolutionized the business, creating a struggle for survival, from which the bosses gained. Moreover, in his hands, the struggle became his favourite formula, an organizing principle that he applied constantly. He released passions, made opposing forces confront one another, allowed the big fish to swallow up the small and grew fat on this rivalry.

When we meet Mouret, he just invested all his resources in preparing a giant sale that should definitely establish the reputation of the Bonheur by attracting a record number of visitors expected to generate a record volume of sales. This extravagant risk-taking behaviour and the associated threat of bankruptcy makes his management team scared as this sale is a kind of all-or-nothing bet. It also makes competing shopkeepers hopeful he will fail and go bankrupt – "Just wait!", keeps repeating Baudu, Denise's uncle and the owner of a neighbouring shop, to his family.

At the same time, Mouret is seeking support from big capital for further expansion. He hopes to find it thanks to his current mistress, a woman of the world who holds court every Saturday, herself the former mistress of a banker about to launch a major urbanistic project in the heart of Paris which could allow for a new major enlargement of the Bonheur. The lady introduces them to each other and Mouret tries to convince the banker to take advantage of this huge real estate operation and partner with him:

> Think of this, we shall build a shopping arcade on the site, pull down or do up the existing buildings and open the largest store in Paris, an emporium that will make millions. Come, we must make a deal. We'll make a killing!

The banker remains sceptical about the chance that such an enormous store would attract an adequate number of clients to be profitable. Yet, after listening to Mouret's explanations about the basic rules and tricks of the ladies' wear business, and, in particular, after watching how he later bewitched the lady friends of their host and how he aroused their desire by telling them about the beauty of what they will find at the bargained price in the forthcoming big sale, he changes his mind, and he promises to join the venture if the big sale reaches the figure that is expected.

The big sale is a success, and the Bonheur may thus keep climbing towards its apogee. New extensions are planned whereas new shops and departments are created and Mouret relentlessly invents new ways of attracting lady customers, which clearly prefigure some features of our modern stores:

> So, day and night, he racked his brain, searching for new ideas. He had already two lifts put in, padded with velvet, to spare delicate ladies the effort of climbing the stairs. In addition to that, he had just opened a buffet, where biscuits and syrup were served free, and a reading room, a monumental gallery, over-extravagantly decorated, in which he was even venturing to hold exhibitions of painting.

Every day, the increasing affluence of customers encroaches upon rival businesses, despite the owners' efforts to counter the threat, not least by copying some of Mouret's sales innovations. In vain, Baudu sells his sole property besides his store to keep afloat, hoping the expansion of the Bonheur will stop. Others do the same trying to escape bankruptcy. A former employee of the Bonheur, recently laid off, sets out to compete with the lead product of the Bonheur, a silk named Paris-Bonheur. A deal is made with a group of small manufacturers, thus allowing "Paris-Bonheur" to be sold at a lower price. The operation succeeds for a while, diverting customers from Mouret's store. But the latter soon retaliates:

> And, sure enough, the following week Mouret went right ahead and brought Paris-Bonheur down by twenty centimes, to five francs forty. … The twenty centimes were a simple loss since they were already selling at cost price.

> It was a serious shock to Robineau [the challenger] who didn't think that his rival would come down in price, because there was no precedent to such a suicidal competition and selling at a loss.

Then, the war continues. But Mouret has what we would call today "deeper pockets", in large part because his store can rely on the profits made from the sale of other goods. Eventually, Robineau goes bankrupt, after dilapidating the modest wealth of his wife. He throws himself under the wheels of a cab but miraculously survives.

The expansion of the "Bonheur" also threatens the physical existence of some of the shops next to it which block its architectural extension. This is the case of the umbrella shop of Bourras, an old craftsman who carves umbrella handles after animal figures. He once tried to resist the new competitive environment by inventing a new kind of umbrella. Wasted effort, his new article was immediately replicated at a lower price by the "Bonheur". When Denise is fired, penniless, from the Bonheur, Bourras hosts her and her little brother. Meanwhile, he receives pressing purchasing offers from Mouret, who wants to tear his shop down. In an act of resistance, Bourras refuses to cede even at an extravagant price. He resists not only for the sake of pride but also because he is convinced that he is too old to change trade and life. Finally, Mouret manages to buy the small building from the owner, terminate Bourras' lease for modest compensation and start the demolition.

The knocking down of Bourras' shop is the final blow to old-fashioned shopkeeping in the area. Baudu had lost his daughter from tuberculosis some time before and then his wife also passed away. Their funeral is the burial of the whole shopping quarter. All shopkeepers who were bankrupt or had gone to work as employees elsewhere are present. "All the monster's victims were there", writes Zola and he lists them: the hosiers, furriers, haberdashers, fancy good merchants, furniture, linen, glove sellers.... The funeral oration comes from Bourras himself:

> We should all jump into that hole, Bourras told Denise [...] It's the whole neighbourhood we're burying with that girl. [...] The old kind of trade can go and join those white roses they're throwing in with her.

Shortly after, Baudu leaves for a retirement home while *Au Vieil Elbeuf* is walled up "like a tomb", before demolition.

6.3 The story of Denise, caught in the struggle between old-fashioned and modern trade

It is through Denise and her vicissitudes that Zola conveys the tension between the positive and negative aspects of economic progress. Emotionally and on the grounds of social empathy and solidarity, Denise finds herself on the side of the old shopkeepers. But, by reason and out of fascination for progress, she finds herself on the side of modernity.

The reader meets Denise in the very first pages of the novel as she arrives in Paris. Her father died a year ago, leaving her and her two brothers penniless. She worked as a sales assistant in a ladies' wear shop in the small town of Normandy where she lived, but her earnings were not enough for a family of three. She had thus decided to accept the invitation of Baudu, her uncle, who had written to her that she would always be welcome in his store whenever she wanted to move to Paris. The novel thus opens on her arrival to the capital with her two brothers, as she seeks her way to Baudu's store. A block or so away from it, she comes across the Bonheur and she is immediately subjugated:

> Coming suddenly across this shop, this building that seemed so enormous to her, brought a lump on her throat and left her standing, shaken, engrossed, forgetting everything else.

Walking along the store's windows, she is dazzled by the beauty of the displays and amazed by the high quality of the drapery and its cheap price. A few moments later, she arrives at her uncle's shop who does not welcome her as she had expected. His letter was sent a year before; business is not doing well and there is no more room for her and her brothers to stay. After a night there and being told that the Bonheur recruits assistants in the ladies' wear department, she goes there and is interviewed by the head of the department, coincidentally in the presence of Mouret. He insists on hiring her despite her provincial and awkward appearance when he learns that she is the niece of a competitor known for harshly denigrating the Bonheur, a move that he hopes could improve his image in the neighbourhood.

Denise's life in the "Bonheur" proves hard. She lives on the spot, as most female staff with no residence in Paris are provided board and lodging by the store. But she does not earn much because, as a junior salesperson, she comes last in attending to customers and thus earns fewer sales commissions than her colleagues, who make fun of her because of her unsophisticated look and ingenuous behaviour. The little she earns is barely enough to pay for the boarding of her little brother and to occasionally help the older one who works as an unpaid apprentice with a cabinetmaker. Many young female assistants at the "Bonheur" enjoy Parisian nightlife and get a few other advantages by taking a lover. As for Denise, she is virtuous and spends her own evenings moonlighting, sewing neckties. One day, she is victim of sexual harassment by the security inspector of the store, known for abusing female staff. She violently pushes him back, and he swears to take revenge. A few days later, he catches her talking to the eldest of her brothers who came asking for some money. He then viciously accuses her of dating lovers within the store compounds, as a result of which she is immediately fired.

This is when she and her little brother seek refuge at Bourras who also hires her as an assistant, even though he hardly needs any. They go through a very hard time, despite the help and the gruff kindness of their benefactor. Things improve somewhat when she is hired by Robineau, a former executive of the Bonheur fired a little after her, who is now starting his own business with the intention of outcompeting Mouret for the sales of the Paris-Bonheur silk. At a dinner at her new employer's home, usual critiques against the conquering expansion of the "Bonheur" are heard around the table. Despite her sacking, Denise keeps thinking positively of it and she surprises the guests when she cannot help observing cheerfully: "*The public isn't complaining, anyway!*". Then a discussion starts which pushes her to use more explicit arguments, no doubt reflecting Zoa's own thoughts:

> … the middlemen were disappearing – factory representatives, salesmen, commission agents – which accounted for much of the lowering of prices; moreover, the manufacturers could no longer even live without the large stores, because as soon as one of them lost their customers, bankruptcy was inevitable. Finally this was a natural evolution in trade, no one could stop things going where they had to go, when everybody was working at it, whether they wanted to or not.

When asked whether she is on the side of those who put her out into the street, she replies:

> 'Goodness me, no, I'm not!'. Perhaps I was wrong because you know far more about it than I do. But I said what I thought. At one time, prices were set by fifty firms, now they're made by four or five, which have brought them down because of the power of their capital and the strength of their customers. And so much better for the general public, that's all.

Some time later, a summer evening, she is walking in the Tuileries Park with her little brother, when she comes across Mouret. He recognizes her and apologizes to her for the mistake made when she was unfairly laid off for misbehaving. He learned later that she was indeed talking to her brother. From the beginning, he is intrigued by this young woman and feels charmed by her simple beauty, modesty and straightforwardness. As far as she is concerned, she has unconsciously fallen in love with him for some time. As compensation for the damage caused to her, he offers her to come back to work at the Bonheur, which Denise refuses since she does not want to quit her employer, who was kind enough to recruit her at a time when she was in dire need. They then chat about Robineau, his intent to compete with the Bonheur, and the ongoing war between old and new trade.

> Denise, won over by his familiarity, began to open up and let him see she was on the side of the big stores in the battle between them and the small businesses; she got quite excited, quoting examples, which showed that she was not only well-informed about the situation, but also full of far-sighted, new ideas.

Mouret's interest in her is thus further aroused.

As the price war imposed on "Paris-Bonheur" is progressively ruining her employer, Denise decides to quit so as to ease his financial constraints and return to the "Bonheur". Her situation there is completely changed, not least, of course, because the staff knows her return is the boss' decision. But also Denise reveals herself as an outstanding seller and a thoughtful and friendly colleague. She does so well that she gets promoted to the position of deputy manager of the ladies' wear department and is later entrusted with the creation and management of a children's wear department. Security and peace of mind have raised her self-confidence and enhanced her beauty. Mouret, who meets frequently with her for business, starts to feel a mounting desire for her. Yet he is attentive to her suggestions to improve the status of the firm's employees.

> The situation of the sales staff was gradually improving, mass dismissals in the low season were being replaced by a system of seasonal leave and a mutual assurance society was to be set up which would guarantee workers against unemployment and give them a retirement pension. It was to be the seed of the vast trade unions of the twentieth century.

Through Denise, Zola in effect conveys some utopian views about how large firms – the Bonheur is supposed to employ 2700 persons at the end of the novel – should treat their employees.

> Sometimes, she [Denise] would get excited, seeing the huge, ideal store, the phalanstery of trade, in which everyone would have a precise share of the profits according to his deserts, as well as security for the future, ensured by a contract. Mouret would then accuse her of socialism and embarrass her by showing how hard it would be to put such a system into practice. (…) Yet, he was shaken and seduced by this young voice, still trembling from the sufferings it had endured, and carried over by great enthusiasm when suggesting reforms that could strengthen the firm.

Then comes the final, Cinderella-like part of the story. Mouret is now furiously in love with Denise. He wants her. One day, she receives a letter from him inviting her to dinner. The whole staff is aware of this invitation and has no doubts about what their womanising boss will require at dessert. He thus behaved previously with many employees. To the surprise of all, however, Denise refuses the invitation and announces a few days later that she will quit. Mouret is fuming and hardly enjoys the great day when the building extension that was making the "Bonheur des Dames" a major architectural work of art in the heart of Paris, the temple of trade, and, finally, a true ladies' paradise, is sumptuously inaugurated. He is in his office at the end of a day that saw the achievement of his business dream, a new record amount of sale proceeds lying on his desk, when Denise comes in to thank him for all the good he has done for her and bids farewell. Mad for love, he proposes to marry her. She is about to refuse again, intimately afraid of the class difference between them, but she cannot refrain from expressing her feelings and throws herself into his arms.

6.4 Zola's message

This happy ending is not Zola's usual style. One way to interpret it is as a sign of his overall positive feeling over economic progress despite the social hardship it may cause. This pleasant conclusion of the novel conveys his conviction that the capitalist mode of retail trade and the development it entails amply compensates for the pain and the economic and moral ruin of traditional shopkeepers. Earlier in the novel, when describing the sorrow which Denise feels after her cousin's funeral, a consequence of the destitution of her family and friends, he writes, rather crudely:

> She knew … that this dunghill of miseries was essential to the health of the Paris tomorrow.

and a bit later:

> … every revolution needs martyrs and one could only go forward by trampling on the dead.

Yet the nature of the progress heralded by the success of Mouret's store is never completely clear. Zola seems to very much value the welfare gains for consumers of getting access to higher quality products available at lower prices, although, admittedly, the customers depicted in the novel are mostly from the middle and upper bourgeoisie. He is also impressed by the way large capitalist companies like the "Bonheur" function, the way they are able to make so many people work together with such efficiency, and the way they evolve in making the lives of their employees more comfortable and secure. At the same time, he is critical of the harsh competition among employees, the "struggle for survival", which is their everyday lot within the company:

> … everyone in the department, from the new recruit aspiring to become a salesman, to the chief salesman coveting a managerial post, had only one obsession, which was to unseat the colleague above him in order to move up one step, and to devour him if he became an obstacle.

Unlike the economic practice, Zola values the progress brought about by the expansion of department stores without a thorough comparison of its costs and benefits. Instead, he sees progress as a fundamentally favourable process, the value of which is arbitrarily large and, in any case, incommensurably larger than its measurable costs. In fact, Zola's opinion about the capitalist transformation that he witnesses is best summarized by his heroin, who appears as a bridge between the ancient and the new worlds. Aware of the costs of transitioning from the former to the latter, she nevertheless senses the inevitability of the movement ahead and the potentialities it unleashes. Furthermore, her own life trajectory testifies to the ability of workers coming from the traditional, small-scale mode of production to not only get absorbed into the new fabrics of society but also to excel in it by improving their skills and fully exploiting their talent.

6.5 Linking Zola with economic thought

That the innovation process inherent in capitalism involves a social cost but at the same time engenders economic and social progress overall was a mere intuition in Zola's Ladies Paradise. That it is the very force that governs economic progress under capitalism was elevated to a theory under the name of "creative destruction" in a chapter of Joseph Schumpeter's famous *Capitalism, Socialism and Democracy*. In fact, the convergence between the mid-19th century novelist and the mid-20th century economist is striking, so much so that the presumption that Schumpeter may have read Zola's novel does not seem completely implausible.

Schumpeter's chapter on the creative destruction process makes three major points. The first is that capitalism is "by nature a form or method of economic change and not only never is but never can be stationary" (Schumpeter, 1950, p. 82). The second is that, indeed, the process of creative destruction is the essence of capitalism: "It is what capitalism consists in and what every capitalist concern has got to live in" (Schumpeter 50, p. 83). The third point is that creative destruction takes place through "big business", temporarily accessing a situation of market dominance. Together, these three points suggest that it would be wrong to consider imperfect competition as inefficient, as so commonly held. Such a view may be valid at a given point in time, but not dynamically. He then gives the following example that is almost Denise's argument, quoted above, about "fifty firms" being replaced by "four or five" and lowering prices.

Schumpeter writes (p. 85):

> Let us assume that there is a certain number of retailers in a neighbourhood who try to improve their relative position by service and "atmosphere" but avoid price competition and stick to methods bequeathed by the local

> tradition – a picture of stagnating routine. As others drift into the trade that quasi-equilibrium is indeed upset, but in a manner that does not benefit their customers. The economic space around each of the shops having been narrowed, their owners will no longer be able to make a living and they will try to mend the case by raising prices in tacit agreement. This will further reduce their sales and so, by successive pyramiding, a situation will evolve in which increasing potential supply will be attended by increasing instead of decreasing prices and by decreasing instead of increasing sales.

It should be noted that this reasoning, as Denise's, departs from the standard economic model of competition where firms facing the same unit cost of production compete through prices and end up all selling at unit cost, thus making no profit – beyond the opportunity cost of the capital invested in production.[3] Instead, the model implicit in the preceding excerpt from Schumpeter and in Zola is that of an implicit collusion of firms which raise their price when their market space is scaled down because of a newcomer. Under these conditions, real competition leading to the lowering of price can only arise from technological innovation by an incumbent or an outsider. Indeed, Schumpeter adds at the end of the next paragraph after the preceding quote:

> In the case of retail trade, the competition that matters arises not from additional shops of the same type, but from the department store, the chain store, the mail-order house, and the supermarket which are bound to destroy those pyramids sooner or later.

Isn't it the very story of the Bonheur?

The convergence of the novelist and the economist goes even further when dealing with the issue of competition. As in the preceding quotes, Schumpeter stresses that competition is essentially dynamic and generates progress. Big businesses enjoy monopoly rents after destroying competitors, which may be rewarding their previous innovation investment, but new competitors constantly threaten to enter their market with new products, technology, or production organization. Incumbent firms must thus keep on creating product or technological novelty unless they are able to erect barriers of entry to their market. The latter is what Mouret does when engaging in a price war on the Paris-Bonheur silk and selling below cost until his rival goes bankrupt. Yet another more serious competitor appears at the end of the novel in the form of a new department store in another district of Paris. It is anecdotal in the novel that a fire partly destroys it a few days before the inauguration of the grandiose new setting of the Bonheur.[4] By mentioning it, however, Zola shows that he was aware that competition is needed if the progress brought about by the department store innovations is to persist after the disappearance of old-fashioned shops.

Au Bonheur des dames is a fictitious, yet observation-grounded work.[5] It offers a sketchy description of the conquest of the traditional society of the mid-19th century by capitalism, with its contradictory effects on people: major economic progress for the greatest number, and pain and despair for those who are pushed to the side and hardly able to change path. Of course, takeovers and disruptions by big business had already been observed earlier in the century in major technological innovations, weavers being displaced by textile machinery, sail boats replaced by steamboats or traditional workshops made irrelevant by manufacturing factories. They would multiply later in the century and still more in the following one to such an extent that by the mid-20th century Schumpeter could indeed assimilate capitalism to essentially economic growth through creative destruction. While recognizing the strength and the dynamism of capitalism thanks to that creative destruction capacity, he was nevertheless predicting its end and the advent of socialism precisely because of its success, which, through the growing importance of large corporations, would progressively erode the institutional framework of societies and tear apart their social fabric.

Schumpeter's analysis owes much to Marx, even though he strongly criticizes him in the first part of 'Capitalism, Socialism and Democracy'. Indeed, Marx also recognized the creative destruction power of capitalism:

> [Capitalism, destroys the old pre-capitalist economy]... and constantly revolutionizes it, tearing down all the barriers which hem in the development of the forces of production, the expansion of needs, the all-sided development of production, and the exploitation and exchange of natural and mental forces.
>
> *(Marx, 1973, p. 410)*[6]

Marx and Schumpeter also predicted that capitalist development would eventually lead to the end of capitalism and the advent of socialism, although not through the same mechanisms. However, both emphasized the negative institutional, political and sociological consequences of economies almost exclusively populated by always larger and more bureaucratized corporations.

Even though he somehow stresses the alienation of labour in the Bonheur through his description of the harsh competition among employees and the power of managers over the staff, Zola does not elaborate on what this war of everyone against everyone and the subjugation of employees by employers would imply for the future of society. This is somewhat surprising since he had some knowledge of Marx's ideas about capitalism's pernicious effects and ineluctable end. His posterior novel *Money* thus stages a character who personally met Marx and tries to spread his ideas around him. As noted by a literary critic of the day, however, Zola's reading of Marx was apparently very superficial.[7]

Where do we stand today? Capitalism is still very much alive despite several major crises to which many thought it would not survive. Creative destruction episodes are still plenty. The collapse of large corporations like Kodak or

Nokia, unable to pick up fast enough on major innovations, digital camera in one case, smartphones in the other, is still present in the collective memory, and painfully so in the individual memory of the several thousands of workers who were laid off year after year in those companies before bankruptcy. They were huge firms whose employment peaked at more than 100,00 workers worldwide, and whose workers were displaced by fast-growing start-ups like Apple or incumbents like Samsung. More recent examples, less spectacular because of their more dispersed impact, include Uber displacing traditional cabs in various big cities of the world, or e-commerce supplanting retail stores, even large chains like Sears, a process reminiscent of Zola.

Economic growth theory now fully accounts for the creative destruction mechanism, even though, surprisingly, this took place only recently as part of the so-called endogenous growth theory.[8] Models built along this theoretical line add to standard capital accumulation as a key growth engine, a representation of the process by which technological or organizational innovations take place. When evaluating the net gain expected from an innovation, it is assumed that the common knowledge of creative destruction mechanism leads innovators to include in their evaluation not only the profit of operating with a better technology but also the probability that they will then be displaced at a future point of time by other firms joining the innovative process and possibly prevailing over them. As a consequence, innovations may be of two types: aggressive innovations that displace incumbents, i.e., creative destruction, or defensive or peaceful innovations by incumbents strengthening their competitive advantage and protecting themselves from creative destruction threats by new entrants. The dominant regime of innovation then influences the pace and structure of economic growth.

A recent research paper[9] tried to measure the relative contribution of these two types of innovation to economic growth. The authors find that, over the 1983–2013 period in the United States, only a quarter of the growth of so-called "total factor productivity", that is, after subtracting the effect of more equipment and more workers from output growth, could be attributed to creative destruction, the rest being due to own improvements of firms already present in the market. In other words, most of productivity growth today would be the result of "defensive" innovation efforts in existing large firms rather than successful start-ups displacing incumbents. Moreover, this advantage of large firms would seem to be increasing over time.

6.6 Zola's legacy

Of course, the preceding remarks should not lead to interpret Ladies' Paradise as some kind of treaty about 19th century rising capitalism and its social consequences, both positive and negative. Zola is a novel writer, not a social scientist or an ideologist. He intends to write captivating stories, which he decided would be set up in different contexts covering the various social aspects of the society around him. That he is so inventive in elaborating these stories and so effective in inserting them in fully articulated reality settings is simply a sign of his immense talent and huge documentation work.

When starting to work on Ladies Paradise, Zola wrote: "[In this novel] I want to express this century, a century of action, of conquest, of efforts in all directions." He indeed brilliantly succeeded in this endeavour. Despite the sad and moving description of the decay of old shopkeepers, this masterwork conveys through Denise, Mouret and the Bonheur a strong sense of dynamism and faith in the future. Other novels expose more sombre economic features of his times, from the ruthless management of miners by mine owners, to dishonest bankers and corruption in financial markets, and to destitute workers falling into alcoholism. Plots in these novels are as enthralling as Ladies' Paradise and the social and economic context in which they take place is described and analyzed with the same deep understanding and exhaustiveness. Such a diverse and captivating journey through the social landscape of his times by a single novel writer is exceptional and makes Zola a literary giant of the 19th century, next to such prominent figures such as Balzac or Dickens.

Notes

1 Famously known outside literary circles for his public defence of Dreyfus, a Jewish French army officer, erroneously sentenced to jail in 1894 for allegedly selling classified documents to Germany. The so-called 'Dreyfus affair' had caused a major division in the French society with major political consequences well into the early 20th century.
2 Various translations have been proposed in English: "The Dram Shop", "The Gin Palace", "Drunk and Drunkard". However, most recent editions in English have come back to the French title.
3 It is on purpose that no reference is made here to 'perfect competition' as in standard economic textbooks. Actually, the model briefly sketched in the preceding sentence is a model of imperfect competition said to be 'à la Bertrand' – see for, instance, Bhattacharya and Sherry (2016). It is quite unlikely that Zola knew about it, however, even though a contemporary of Bertrand.
4 This episode refers to an actual event, the fire that destroyed the Printemps, the second department store built in Paris, in 1881.
5 In effect, Zola took very much of its inspiration from the resounding success of "Au bon Marché", founded in 1853 by Aristide and Marguerite Boucicault.
6 Cited by J. Elliott (1980).
7 See P. Lafargue (1891–92).
8 Aghion and Howitt (1992) and Grossman and Helpman (1991).
9 See Garcia-Macia, Hsieh and Klenow (2019).

References

Aghion, P. and Howitt, P., "A Model of Growth through Creative Destruction," *Econometrica*, 60, 1992, pp. 323–351.

Bhattacharya, R. and Sherry, E., "Bertrand Competition" in M. Augier and D. Teece (Eds.), *The Palgrave Encyclopedia of Strategic Management*, Palgrave MacMillan, United Kingdom, 2016, pp. 1–2.

Elliott, J., "Marx and Schumpeter on Capitalism's Creative Destruction: A Comparative Restatement," *The Quarterly Journal of Economics*, 95(1), 1980, pp. 45–68.
Garcia-Macia, D., Hsieh, C. T. and Klenow, P., "How Destructive Is Innovation," *Econometrica*, 87, 2019, pp. 1507–1541.
Grossman, G. and Helpman, E., "Quality Ladders in the Theory of Growth," *Review of Economic Studies*, 58, 1991, pp. 43–61.
Lafargue, P., "L'Argent de Zola", originally published in "Die Neue Zeit", 1891–92, translated into French in Marxist Internet Archive, https://www.marxists.org/francais/lafargue/works/1891/00/pl18910000.htm
Marx, K., *Grundrisse* (*Introduction to the Critique of Political Economy*), translated, with a foreword by Martin Nicolaus, Vintage, New York, 1973.
Schumpeter, J., *Capitalism, Socialism and Democracy*, Harper, New York, 1950.

7

WOMEN IN A NERVOUS BREAKDOWN

Intra-household bargaining and gender norms in South Korea

Bishnupriya Gupta

7.1 Introduction

In 1996, South Korea became a part of the OECD countries following four decades of rapid economic growth, rising participation in the economy of men and women, and rising literacy for all. In 2020, the female labour force participation rate in South Korea was above 53%, lower than the UK at 58% and Germany at 57%, but higher than Spain at 52%, France at 52%, and Italy at 39%. There is near universal secondary school enrolment in South Korea with little difference between males and females. In tertiary education, although South Korea ranked sixth in the world in 2019, the share of females in total enrolment was significantly lower than for males. Fertility has declined rapidly from 4.5 in 1970 to 1.2 in 2010. Yet South Korea has a much higher gender pay gap, low participation in politics, and lags behind several indicators of gender equality compared to the average for the OECD countries.

The relationship between economic development and women's status in society and within the household has been examined by economists and economic historians. Education and labour market participation of women are often used as positive indicators. The U-shaped curve of female labour force participation (Goldin 1995) shows participation falls as societies industrialize and get richer, but rises again with economic development as women acquire more human capital. Women's education is associated with a decline in fertility and an increase in participation in the labour market. What does this mean for gender equality and women's economic role in society? Do cultural norms create differences across societies even with industrialization and improvements in education? Contrary to expectation, there is descriptive and anecdotal evidence of gender inequalities within the family and in the

DOI: 10.4324/9781003534358-9

workplace in East Asia that indicates that the gender norms in these societies have remained traditional on several dimensions despite great improvements in economic indicators.

Duflo (2012) suggests that economic development and the presence of more educated women are not enough to overcome gender inequality within the household. She points to persistent son preference in Asia, including in South Korea and Taiwan, suggesting that cultural norms may create differences across societies. Cultural norms may determine the division of labour within the household; women are the sole carer of children or may have the sole responsibility in the kitchen even when they work. These norms may lead to certain types of gender inequality within the household, which may not be captured by standard models in economics.

In this chapter, I select two recent South Korean novels that relate to the theme of intra-household bargaining. The first is *Kim Jiyoung Born 1982* by Cho Nam Joo (2016). This novel struck a chord with women in South Korea, sold a million copies and was translated into different languages. The second novel I discuss is Han Kang's *The Vegetarian*, which won the 2016 International Booker Prize and has been translated into many languages as well. Kang won the 2024 Literature Nobel Prize, and the citation specifically mentioned this novel.

In both novels, the context is decision-making within the household of a young couple in modern South Korea and it speaks to theories in household economics, more particularly how households make decisions on expenditure and what makes these decisions stable and lasting.

7.2 A vignette of household economics

In economics, decisions in households are analyzed in two types of framework – the unitary model and non-unitary bargaining models. Within the unitary model of household behaviour, family members pool incomes and make decisions to maximize welfare of the household either jointly or steered by the household head (Samuelson 1956; Becker 1981). All members are treated as a common unit with similar preferences or follow the preference of the altruistic household head. They face a common welfare function and as a unit maximize the household's welfare by pooling resources (Lundberg and Pollak 1996). In this framework, individual members do not influence decision-making on the basis of their own income or other attributes: their spending decisions reflect identical choices by all the members of the household. In the context of unitary or "common resources" models, the equilibrium outcome is Pareto efficient, meaning that no member in the household can be made better off by modifying the allocation without causing the welfare of at least another member to decrease.

A different set of models of intra-household decision making move away from the idea of common preferences and introduce bargaining within the household. Labour force participation and independent income give women more bargaining power within the household and a greater say in decision-making. The non-unitary model of decision-making for the family (Lundberg and Pollak 1993; Browning et al. 1994) introduces the idea of bargaining between family members. The relative weights of individual members depend on relative income and other attributes. In these models, the adults who make decisions have different preferences and each of them contributes to a public good from which everybody in the household benefits and also devotes part of his/her income to spending on a private good (or private goods and services) which she/he alone enjoys. Depending on their individual preferences, their spending pattern may vary or not. When they decide the amount of their contribution to the household public goods (say, food and housing or children's education), they take into account what other members contribute. In such a set-up, the household's income sharing rule depends on the relative bargaining position of the adults based on their income. Expenditures on different items depend on individual preferences and their relative bargaining power within the household. For example, women prefer to spend on children's education (a public good) and men on private leisure and recreation. An increase in the men's share of household income will reduce women's bargaining power with the plausible effect of causing the long-term deterioration of the latter's well-being.

In these non-unitary models, the equilibrium is supported by the threat of divorce, as in Browning et al. (1994). The idea is that at this equilibrium, husband and wife prefer to stay together even though contributions to the general welfare of the household (the public good) are unequal. The reason is that the member contributing more (say, the wife) may deem this situation preferable to being left alone, which is what would happen if she refuses the allocation pattern. Note that contributions to the household public good, which are typically gender-specific, often depend on prevailing cultural norms. For example, the woman does the cooking and the man drives the car.

In a recent paper, Chiappori and Molina (2020) show that in most cultural contexts, the resource pooling outcomes of the unitary model do not hold and who contributes to household resources matters for the way money and time are allocated. In a paper titled "Marriage, sharing rule and pocket money: the case of South Korea", Jungmin Lee (2007) empirically tests a model of intra-household bargaining in which pocket money is the income share that each individual can spend privately after providing for the household public good(s). The author finds that the initial balance of power within the household is established at the time of marriage and this balance is sustained over time. Changing contributions arising from changes in incomes do not change this balance of power.

7.3 What the novels say

7.3.1 Kim Jiyoung Born 1982

I now turn to the contexts of intra-household bargaining that are the central theme of the two selected novels. The novel "Kim Jiyoung Born 1982" by Cho Nam Joo (2016) tells the story of a woman born at a time when the Korean economy was developing fast. Women's educational attainment and labour market participation were increasing. But gender norms were slow to change. The sex ratio at birth was "116 boys to 100 girls, compared to the world-wide standard of 103–107 boys for every 100 girls" (as stated in the novel). Women's role within the family remained traditional in many ways. The intra-family decision-making described by the author evokes the unitary model of household (or family) economics. The story is about a family living in urban South Korea. The father and the mother work, the two daughters are older than the son, and the grandmother lives with the family.

In Jiyoung's household, the two sisters are much loved, have a high school education, and are encouraged to dream of further advancement in education and career. At the same time, they are trained to perform household tasks and care for the younger siblings. The youngest sibling is a boy, who has a special position in the family. The most coveted portions of food, the best care, and indulgence are meant only for him. As for him, he does not contribute materially to the household, relying on his two younger sisters who are in charge of all household chores.

We observe three generations in the household. The grandparents had moved from rural Korea to an urban environment. The mother and aunts had middle school education and worked in low paid jobs, while the uncles were trained to be doctors and high school teachers. The sisters contributed to the family income and enabled the son to go through higher education. This is the first glimpse into the special position of sons and unequal gender norms within a family. This is also a glimpse into the nature of decision-making within the household, which resonates with the unitary model of decision-making in economics. Decisions are made jointly by the head of the household and his wife and other members of the family work towards the common goals.

The novel begins with the life of two sisters, Kim Eunyoung and Kim Jiyoung, and their little brother. Against the backdrop of rising education among girls, and their participation in the labour market, the two sisters go to high school and take special classes in mathematics after school, indicating their ambition for high skilled jobs. At the same time, gender differences in economic outcomes and social status between men and women persist within the household. Rather unconventionally, economic statistics are cited at various points of the narrative to document economic change as well as gender differences in outcomes. The protagonist is the younger daughter, Jiyoung born in 1982, in a new era in Korean society. The author describes the context as follows:

> Gone were the days when parents thought girls didn't have to get good grades or receive the same education as boys. It had long seen been the norm for girls, like boys, to put on a uniform, carry a backpack and attend school. Girls thought about what they would like to do when they grow up, just as boys did; they planned their careers and competed to achieve their goals. This was a time of widespread social support for women's ambitions. In 1999, the year Kim Eunyoung turned twenty, new legislation against gender discrimination was introduced and in 2001, the year Kim Jiyoung turned twenty, the Ministry of Gender Equality was formed. But in certain pivotal moments of their lives, the women's stigma reared its head to obscure their vision, stay their hands and hold them back. The mixed signals were confusing and disconcerting.
>
> *(pp. 59–60)*

Jiyoung's mother works hard to supplement the family income while the father is a lower rank clerk in the public sector. He looks after his wife and daughters, and he makes decisions on family expenditures jointly with his wife. He takes her out for evening events and holidays. He blames himself for not being able to provide a more comfortable life for his family, when he sees his wife making products for sale in the family's living space late into the evening. The wife heeds her husband's advice to give up her menial low-paying job that involves long working hours and diverts her from household responsibilities. She retrains as a hairdresser and starts a flourishing business. To achieve this happy outcome, Jiyoung's father and mother acted as a unit rather than bargaining with each other on the basis of their individual attributes.

When forced to take early retirement during the financial crisis of 1997, the husband pays attention to his wife's advice to avoid investing in trade with China. Instead, they buy commercial space in the neighbourhood and start a food takeaway business. The eldest daughter, Kim Eunyoung, gives up her dream to work for television and decides to train as a high school teacher when her father loses his job. She was not forced to make such a choice but considers it to be a safe option from the family's standpoint. The following conversation between the mother and daughter is revealing of societal gender norms:

> *Mother:* "There's no better job for women than a schoolteacher".
>
> *Daughter:* What is so great about being a schoolteacher?
>
> *Mother:* You get off work early. You have school vacations. It's easy to take time off. There's nothing like teaching for working mums.
>
> *Daughter:* Sure, it's a great job for working parents. Then isn't it a great job for everyone? Why specifically women? Are you going to advice a teaching career to your son too?
>
> *(pp. 58–59)*

Despite her scepticism, Eunyoung voluntarily took up a teaching job with a view to helping out the family financially. Another example of unitary decision-making is revealed when the wife says to her husband: "Yes, you have made it, but you didn't do it all by yourself, so be good to me and the kids". He proudly acknowledges by answering: "Of course! Of course! Half of this is your work!" (p. 76).

In the context of the Kim family, individual preferences are sacrificed on the altar of the household's objectives. The daughters are aware of the special position of the son and do not hesitate to work with the purpose of maximizing the family's well-being.

Jiyoung acquires a good education and enters the labour market. She faces various types of gender bias as she seeks employment. When she gets a job, her boss is a woman. The narrative gives the reader an idea of change and continuity. She enjoys her work but at the same time is faces gender-specific expectations. She discovers that she is the only person in the company's history to have taken a maternity leave and that her male colleagues in the same job earn more than her. The narrative links this observation to the statistics that in South Korea only 23% of women took a maternity leave in 2014, female earnings represented only 65% of male earnings (compared to the OECD average of 84%), and the score for the chance of women to rise to high positions was one of the lowest in this club of rich countries.

Jiyoung tries to live up to the societal expectations regarding marriage and motherhood. She leaves her job after the baby is born. The trade-off between income and parental responsibility is resolved in favour of the husband who has a higher salary and remains at work. The wife is compelled to give up her own work and devotes her time to their child. Jiyoung becomes a "stay at home mum". The novel again provides a statistic to suggest that Jiyoung's situation is not unusual: the participation of women in the labour force declined from 64% to 58% for women aged 30 to 39 and increased to 68% after the age of 40.

7.3.2 The Vegetarian

In Han Kang's *The Vegetarian*, the story revolves around another urban family in South Korea. Yet the underlying decision-making pattern corresponds to the bargaining model, rather than the unitary model, of intra-household resource allocation.

This is a story of an "unremarkable" family where the husband has an "average" job and marries an "ordinary woman" with an "unremarkable job". It begins with the following narrative told by the husband:

> Before my wife turned vegetarian, I'd always thought of her as completely unremarkable in every way. To be frank, the first time I met her, I wasn't even attracted to her.... However, if there were no special attractions, no particular drawback was in evidence and, therefore, there was no reason for

> the two of us not to get married … I was always attracted towards the middle course in life … In keeping with my expectations, she made for a completely ordinary wife…
>
> *(p. 3)*

Yeong-Hye works as an instructor in a college of computer graphics and divides her time between work and family chores. The husband's job is unspecified, but from all descriptions relating to his workplace and colleagues, he is a middle-ranked employee, who goes to work every day. Some days he socializes with colleagues after work and returns home late. On the days he is at home, he watches baseball games on television. There are no descriptions of his engagement in housework. The wife, on the other hand, does all the housework meticulously, cooks appetizing food and is always ready to serve her husband. In the course of such an ordinary life, one day, Yeong-Hye abruptly and unexpectedly discards all the meat from the refrigerator and declares herself "a vegetarian". This is a concept not well understood in Korean society as is revealed in various anecdotes in the novel. When the appalled husband asks for at least a fried egg, she responds that all traces of a non-vegetarian diet have been removed from the kitchen. Her justification is that she had a dream, in which meat and blood filled the space and her face was reflected in red colour.

In terms of economic theory, the new situation is equivalent to a breakdown of the established equilibrium of the household. The public good that was provided by the wife before was not only well cooked food but also a meat-based assortment of culinary delights. In line with the social norms in South Korea, she was responsible for delivering conventional food, meaning a non-vegetarian diet, to all the household members. When Yeong-Hye decides to become a vegetarian and stops cooking meat, she actually reneges on the implicit contract whereby she is expected to supply traditional meals.

In the social and cultural context of a South Korean household, an accepted gendered division of labour clearly prevails. The three families in the novel are Yeong-Hye and her husband, her sister In-Hye and her husband, and the parents of Yeong and In. The agreed division of labour is customary and it holds whether women participate in the labour market or not. In fact, both sisters earn incomes from working outside the home. The sister of Yeong-Hye has a shop and is the main income-earner of the family. Her husband is an artist. He is described as someone who had an inheritance, but does not contribute to the household income regularly. Yet he is "free to spend his whole life messing about". In-Hye is described as a skilled cook like her sister before she became a vegetarian, again alluding to the specific nature of the intra-household division of labour. Cooking is a public good provided by women according to social convention, irrespective of their relative income. This is a division of labour agreed upon at the time of marriage and sustained over a lifetime (Lee 2007).

When Yeong-Hye becomes vegetarian and stops eating and cooking meat, the husband is forced to adapt to the new diet, at least when he is at home. Social convention prevents him from cooking at home, but he can eat meat outside the home when socializing with friends or colleagues. But his wife then begins to complain that she smells meat when she comes in close proximity to him and, as a consequence, she develops a strong aversion to intimacy. In sum, there appears a breach in the agreement requiring the wife to provide what the custom considers to be shared goods within the household. In this case, it is a meat-based meal. In the framework of a bargaining model, the equilibrium in this household is defined by social norms of gender-based division of labour on the provision of a public good that is enjoyed by all members. By going vegetarian, Yeong-Hye stops providing the household public good. As economic theory predicts (see, for example, Lundberg and Pollak, 1994), Yeong Hye's defiance arises from her financial independence. If the couple decides to continue to be in the marriage despite the tension, the implication is that living together remains tolerable for the husband: In economic jargon, he has not (yet) reached his "threat point" at which he may prefer to divorce.

The parents are more traditional. The father is an army veteran and a patriarchal figure who often loses control over his emotions. He sees the conversion of his daughter to vegetarianism as an act of defiance to the core values of Korean society. Chastised by both her father and brother, she is watched with concern by her husband, Mr Cheong. He sways between anger and love for a wife, who slowly descends into a nervous breakdown. Yeong-Hye's world gradually becomes a black hole of emotional distress. The husband consoles himself with the thought that he did not do anything wrong: "this strange situation has nothing to with me". In despair, he turns to her family whose support is important for Yeong-Hye. The problem is that by defying the social convention against vegetarianism, she risks losing this support. Hence, unlike the availability of outside economic support, the family's attitude has the effect of mitigating her bargaining strength.

The scene is a family get-together, as the mother coaxes Yeong-Hye to eat meat while the brother chastises her about her behaviour. The most dramatic and aggressive response comes from the father, who tries to force a piece of pork into her mouth. Yeong-Hye vomits and in defiance she slashes her wrist. She is taken to hospital, where signs of mental breakdown become more and more visible. As the situation continues, the husband eventually divorces her. The only support for Yeong-Hye comes from her sister. Though initially hesitant, the sister's support is expressed in an increasingly assertive manner as she identifies with the women's position inside all Korean families. The first manifestation of sympathy came when the father violently forced Yeong-Hye to eat meat, a gesture that In-Hye tried to stop. In-Hye is the only person who makes an attempt to understand her sister. The rest of the family turns away. The lack of support from the family, which is determined by the social and cultural context, is reflected in the husband's growing distance vis-à-vis his wife, eventually leading to a divorce. Yeoung-Hye is thus increasingly isolated and the mental breakdown which brought her to a mental health institution appears as the only possible way to exit the unbearable situation she is facing. As Yeoung-Hye descends into a world that is beyond reach, In-Hye begins to understand the universality of her sister's rebellion.

When Yeong-Hye's marriage ends and she finds herself as a single person again, her sister remains in contact with her and provides support. Yeong-Hye's working status at this point is unclear. Her sister encourages her husband to keep an eye on her sister. In-Hye's husband, who is an artist, is strangely attracted to Yeong-Hye. The relationship that develops is sexual. He paints flowers on the Yeong-Hye's body and tries to make an artistic video. Although he dislikes Mr Cheong, the ex-husband, there is little to distinguish between the two men's attitudes towards women. While In-Hye's husband depends on his wife's income, he still expects her to manage the kitchen alone and to look after their child. The attraction to his sister-in-law does not reflect any deep concern about her predicament and the importance of her struggle. He is attracted to Yeong-Hye and exploits her vulnerability.

The final chapter is set in the mental institution. In-Hye is the only visitor, who increasingly sympathizes with her sister's defiance of societal norms. As In-Hye observes her sister undergoing treatment in the mental hospital, she looks back at their lives. Yeong-Hye was always better able to face their father's anger because she was more defiant. She remembers that one day while they were still young girls, they got lost in the mountain when out for a walk. Yeong-Hye did not appear to be worried by the situation and even expressed the wish to remain lost and stay away from home. Now looking back at her own life, In-Hye realizes that although she had never herself questioned the social norms and conventions, her life ended up being as unhappy as her sister's. She ponders:

> Two years ago, she realized how much of her life she had spent with her husband. It had been a period of time utterly devoid of happiness and spontaneity. A time which she has so far managed to get through only by using every last reserve of perseverance and consideration. All of it was self-inflicted.

In In-Hye's household, she has been the main earner, but it had not changed the way intra-household allocation of resources is decided. She went back to full-time work after the birth of the child and carried out her household responsibilities with diligence. Her only request that her husband devote some time to the child on Sundays has gone unheeded. Yet she did not walk out of the marriage. Its breakdown took place in bizarre circumstances reminiscent of Bong Joon-ho's film *The Parasite*, which shows a dystopian picture of inequalities in Korean society.

7.4 Conclusion and final reflections

The two novels offer different perspectives on intra-household decision-making. Each speaks to a different model. The father in *Kim Jiyoung Born 1982* is very different from the patriarch in Han Kang's novel. However, both protagonists end up in mental health institutions. Yeong-Hye is a rebel, asserting her preferences and using her bargaining power within the household to do so. A different perspective comes from Cho Nam Joo's *Kim Jiyoung Born 1982*. The novel begins in a mental health institution and is narrated by the psychiatrist, who is treating Jiyoung, the protagonist. The opening chapter is set in 2015, in the context of a festival when Jiyoung, her husband Daehyun, and their baby daughter visit his parents in Busan. Jiyoung's behaviour has been uncharacteristic for a while and her response to a question by the mother-in-law is sarcastic enough to provoke anger in the father-in-law and distress in her husband who eventually takes her to a psychiatrist. Her relationship with her husband begins to change not because he now holds more economic power, but because of her own despair faced with the need to choose between outside work and childcare. She strives to break free in order to re-establish her working life. She feels trapped under the combined pressure of discrimination in the labour market and societal expectations of women's role as a mother.

Where Jiyoung ends up is reminiscent of the fate of Yeong-Hye in *The Vegetarian* although the novel is written in a different style and spirit. Both novels tell us about growing up in the background of economic and social transformation in South Korea. As the traditional society gets modernized, many things changed but the social norms relating to family and gender roles persisted. Like Young-Hye, she slowly descends into a mental breakdown. The book is more in line with the sentiments of the "me too" movement, but has elements of *The Vegetarian*.

Economics measures gender inequalities through indicators such as literacy, labour force participation, and the gender pay gap. Sociologists have emphasized the rising age of marriage for women and men in South Korea and the rising share in the population of never married men and women. They have pointed to the rising divorce rate, with 20% of marriages predicted to end in divorce within ten years.

The novels also relate to the empirical literature on economics. In the literature on self-reported happiness, Blanchflower and Oswald (2004) find a decline in the USA and stagnation in the UK after 1970. Stevenson and Wolfers (2009) look at a broader set of industrialized countries and find that women's reported happiness has declined relative to men's despite strides in women's economic advancement in these societies. Ngoo et al. (2015) found that in Asia, East Asia ranks low on self-reported happiness, and within East Asia, South Korea is particularly low-ranked. Park and Lee (2013) find that women in Korea and Japan rank low in the indices for self-reported physical well-being measures.

Although there is no gender gap in self-reported health status, the reported index is particularly low for both married men and women in their 20s and 30s. One explanation is the pressure of traditional gender norms in marital relationships. Hori and Kamo (2018) explicitly look at the question of the happiness of married couples in the cultural context of discriminatory gender norms. They find gender differences in the predictors of happiness among men and women of East Asia. While marital status predicts happiness for men, the same is not true for women. Women need active societal support to be happy.

East Asia evinces lower levels of happiness compared to Europe and North America. The top ten countries in the World Happiness Survey of 2022 are all European, while those in the East do not rank particularly high, and, as seen above, Japan and South Korea rank low within East Asia. Japan at 6 and South Korea at 5.9 rank well below Denmark at 7.6, USA and Germany at 7.0, and the UK at 6.9. Hori and Kamo (2018) argue that the lower level of happiness among people in East Asian countries may be partially explained by traditional gender norms. The following statement in Hori and Kamo (2018) is suggestive of Jiyoung's experience of motherhood:

> Our results show that being parents is not associated with happiness in any of the four countries and for either gender. A negative association between having children and happiness for women was expected in East Asian societies where social pressure on women to be dedicated mothers is still strong. But East Asian women may enjoy being parents, and this may cancel out the pressure to be good mothers. Similarly, financial costs of parenthood for men may cancel out the positive effect of being parents in East Asian societies.

The literary world portrays women's response to their position within the household in a more dramatic way. The novels deal with the psychological impact of gender inequalities on women. Their resistance to unequal family norms is dramatic as in *Kim Jiyoung Born 1982*, or dystopian as in *The Vegetarian*. In the first novel, the narrator is the psychiatrist, whose first diagnosis is post-natal depression, but as he watches Jiyoung, he realizes that her problem faces all women in Korea. His own wife, even though she had been a successful doctor, gave up her medical career when they had children. He had found her solving the son's school mathematics papers just for fun! Women's frustration with their relationships in marriage and when they become mothers is common. In the novels, madness is a form of resistance against their predicament. The two novels line up with different models of household decision-making. *The Vegetarian* echoes the intra-household bargaining model, while *Kim Jiyoung Born 1982* evokes the unitary model of decision-making. But the outcome that befalls the two women is essentially similar and it reflects their internal struggles against social norms, something that economic models and development indicators do not capture.

Our two South Korean novelists have addressed the question of intra-household balance of power in contemporary Korean society in the same bizarre way as we have seen at work in Bong Joon-ho's film *The Parasite*. What emerges is a dystopian picture of social inequality and unequal gender norms. Despite rapid economic development and modernization, gender norms have remained traditional and determined by patriarchal values, leaving a subordinate role to women within the household. As we have learned in the two novels, the wife tends to be submissive and is instructed by the husband or father to dress in a certain way, use make-up, and follow certain social conventions. The social network of the family remains important for individuals and households and both men and women act in ways that fit their roles as dictated by deeply anchored customs.

The two novels are:

The Vegetarian: A Novel by Han Kang (Author), Deborah Smith (Translator), Granta Books, 2015.

Kim Jiyoung, Born 1982 by Cho Nam-Joo (Author), Jamie Chang (Translator), Scribner, UK, 2020.

Acknowledgments

I thank James Fenske, Debraj Ray, Claudia Rei, and Jean Philippe-Platteau for their comments.

References

Becker, Gary S. "Altruism in the family and selfishness in the market place." *Economica* 48.189 (1981): 1–15.

Blanchflower, David G., and Andrew J. Oswald. "Well-being over time in Britain and the USA." *Journal of Public Economics* 88.7-8 (2004): 1359–1386.

Browning, Martin, et al. "Income and outcomes: A structural model of intrahousehold allocation." *Journal of Political Economy* 102.6 (1994): 1067–1096.

Chiappori, Pierre-André, and José Alberto Molina. "The intra-spousal balance of power within the family: cross-cultural evidence." *Cross-cultural Family Research and Practice*. Academic Press, 2020. 185–209.

Duflo, Esther. "Women empowerment and economic development." *Journal of Economic literature* 50.4 (2012): 1051–1079.

Goldin, Claudia. "The U-shaped female labor force function in economic development and economic history." T. P. Schultz, ed., *Investment in women's human capital and economic development*, University of Chicago Press, 1995. 61–90.

Hori, Makiko, and Yoshinori Kamo. "Gender differences in happiness: The effects of marriage, social roles, and social support in East Asia." *Applied Research in Quality of Life* 13.4 (2018): 839–857.

Lee, Jungmin. "Marriage, the sharing rule, and pocket money: The case of South Korea." *Economic Development and Cultural Change* 55.3 (2007): 557–581.

Lundberg, Shelly, and Robert A. Pollak. "Separate spheres bargaining and the marriage market." *Journal of Political Economy* 101.6 (1993): 988–1010.

Lundberg, Shelly, and Robert A. Pollak. "Noncooperative bargaining models of marriage." *The American Economic Review* 84.2 (1994): 132–137.

Lundberg, Shelly, and Robert A. Pollak. "Bargaining and distribution in marriage." *Journal of Economic Perspectives* 10.4 (1996): 139–158.

Ngoo, Yee Ting, Nai Peng Tey, and Eu Chye Tan. "Determinants of life satisfaction in Asia." *Social Indicators Research* 124 (2015): 141–156.

Park, J. H., and K. S. Lee. "Self-rated health and its determinants in Japan and South Korea." *Public Health* 127.9 (2013): 834–843.

Samuelson, Paul A. "Social indifference curves." *The Quarterly Journal of Economics* 70.1 (1956): 1–22.

Stevenson, Betsey, and Justin Wolfers. "The paradox of declining female happiness." *American Economic Journal: Economic Policy* 1.2 (2009): 190–225.

PART II

Market operation and dysfunction

8

ONLY THE HOUSING PROBLEM HAS CORRUPTED THEM

Sergei Guriev

8.1 Introduction

The main plotline of Mikhail Bulgakov's famous novel *The Master and Margarita* describes the devil's visit to communist Moscow. The Soviet Union is the first atheistic society in the history of humankind. So, the devil (who goes by the name of Woland, russified representation of Voland initially used by Mephistopheles in Goethe's Faust) wants to understand how and whether humans can function without believing in god – and in the devil, for that matter. *The Master and Margarita* is an innovative piece of magic realism: on the one hand, it documents the life of Soviet Moscow in a very accurate way; on the other hand, it introduces supernatural forces who can deliver a moral judgment transcending the challenges and limitations of the mundane.[1]

After observing Muscovites in various settings, Woland asks himself whether the Soviet system has been able to produce a "new man" but then concludes[2]:

> they're people like any other people ... they love money, but that has always been so ... Mankind loves money, whatever it's made of – leather, paper, bronze, gold. Well, they're light-minded ... well, what of it ... mercy sometimes knocks at their hearts ... ordinary people ... In general, reminiscent of the former ones ... only the housing problem has corrupted them...

The "housing problem" – the non-transparent allocation of housing in the Soviet non-market system – features prominently in *The Master and Margarita* as well as in Bulgakov's other masterpiece *The Heart of a Dog*. In both, the allocation of housing is certainly the most important economic issue. This is not surprising. In a market economy, housing is the main asset for an average

DOI: 10.4324/9781003534358-11

household.[3] In a planned economy, access to spacious and high-quality housing should also be a key part of well-being – with the caveat that most Soviet citizens would not own their main residence. To this day, economic historians have not produced credible estimates of wealth inequality in the Soviet Union[4] but it should have been substantial: while the party elite enjoyed mansions formerly owned by aristocrats and large modern apartments,[5] the average stock of housing in the 1920s was about 6 square meters per capita (Morton, 1984) – the same as in 1913 (Goskomstat, 1987, p. 10). This inequality was certainly salient and not lost on the genuine proletarians and the Bolsheviks who thought that reducing this inequality was the key goal of the Revolution.[6] In the Heart of a Dog's iconic scene ("The reason why we've come to see you, Professor ..."), the representatives of the tenants' committee come to Professor Preobrazhensky, to express their outrage that he is residing in a seven-room apartment. The representatives inform the professor that their committee has ruled that he occupies "too much space" and suggest that he voluntarily transfer two rooms to poorer neighbors. In addition to great disparities in the quantity of housing, the *quality* of real estate also varied greatly – even in the 1940s and 1950s only 40% of Soviet urban housing had sewage (Goskomstat, 1955, p. 162). Without a real estate market, how would one person get a large apartment (like the nicely located five-room "haunted flat" number 50 where Woland resided during his visit to Moscow) while another person would get only 6 square meters – and both would pay nothing or next to nothing as rent? Allocation of real estate to each of 150 million Soviet citizens was certainly a much harder task than Gosplan's preparation of five-year plans for producing tanks and tractors, and for building power plants and steel mills. Moreover, because accommodation answers a basic need, housing allocation decisions involved far higher stakes than the production of guns and tanks. Inequality in housing was thus an ultra-sensitive issue as receiving a big modern apartment of the kind described by Slezkine (2017) was equivalent to a manifold wage increase during a lifetime. In this sense, housing was more important than the wage earned: a low wage did not imply an inability to afford square meters, and, vice versa, high income or pecuniary wealth would not necessarily result in good housing conditions.[7] In other words, the distribution of housing was a better indicator of inequality in levels of living than the distribution of current incomes. Revealingly, statistical data on the quality of residential housing were literally "top secret" (Goskomstat, 1955, p. 161), as witnessed by the fact that the corresponding section of Goskomstat (1955) was printed in only 30 copies.

It is therefore not surprising that the "housing issue" springs up at almost every turn of the Master and Margarita's Moscow-based plotline.[8] When a character dies, his uncle, an "industrial economist" working in Kiev (this is the only economist in the novel!), hastily travels to Moscow. Bulgakov tells us that the only reason for the economist's trip is the attempt to inherit his nephew's apartment ("despite all obstacles").[9] And when the Heart of the Dog's dog becomes a human, his paramount objective is not to obtain a document or a job, nor even to get married, but to be able to claim a room in the Professor's apartment. In a sense, getting the room is the ultimate purpose of his transformation from animal to human species.

8.2 Allocation and incentives in market and non-market systems

Bulgakov describes Moscow of the late 1920s when the country was moving from the quasi-market institutions of the New Economic Policy (somewhat similar to Deng Xiaoping's dual-track system) to the top-down industrialization scheme of five-year plans. This is the period when the remnants of price mechanisms are still present but are being crowded out by non-market allocation rules.[10] In the *Heart of the Dog*, Preobrazhensky still operates his private clinic, but his quality of life is protected not by his wealth but by his high-ranking patients. In Master and Margarita, Master wins a lottery and rents two rooms in a centrally located house equipped with a garden. It is clear, however, that real estate decisions are increasingly made by the state – so that housing allocation reflects the state's priorities rather than consumer preferences or production costs. Bulgakov argues that the best houses or flats were allocated to the regime's bigwigs, or to people considered important for the regime's success or persistence. Margarita and her husband were given a whole floor in a centrally located house with a garden because her husband was a brilliant scientist whose work had strategic value.[11] This said, it was not only scientists and engineers who mattered for the Soviet project: the government paid as much or even more attention to the "engineers of human souls", writers, literary critics, and theatre directors.[12] They, too, were given nice apartments and dachas as a reward for their crucial role in producing a "new man" modeled according to the regime's wish. The mission of these blessed artists was thus to make sure that workers would not only be content with their modest accommodation of 6 square meters but also feel proud and excited to participate in the Soviet new society. Being a writer and a playwright himself, Bulgakov knew this milieu very well. He was a first-rate observer of the housing dramas of the literary world, capable of explaining in detail which writers mattered more to the government and the party, and hence deserved to get better dachas. When he introduces the reader to Massolit ("one of the major Moscow literary associations"), he immediately points to the centrality of the "housing question" in Massolit's work.[13]

8.3 Rent-seeking and corruption

Even in a repressive dictatorship, the state allocation is final only on paper. Non-market allocation creates substantial distortions which in turn provide strong incentives for rent-seeking, lobbying, secondary markets, and sometimes outright bribery. To protect himself from troublesome visitors like those who bothered Preobrazhensky, Woland simply pays off the chair of the tenants' association in cash, and the chair takes it for granted.[14] One of Woland's lieutenants tells Margarita a story of a person who, using occasionally dubious methods, managed to exchange a three-room apartment for three two-room apartments.[15] Most importantly, in order to get the Master's housing, his neighbor denounces him to the authorities and this works so that the Master leaves the place and the neighbor gets his rooms.[16]

Thus, the high-stakes "housing problem" had a major impact not just on allocative efficiency but also on people's trust in formal institutions and social fabric. On the one hand, the state's promise to award prized residential real estate to its most loyal and brilliant servants created strong incentives to pursue a career within the system. On the other hand, the system of blatant favoritism based on a biased allocation of housing spaces did literally corrupt the beneficiaries. Because the houses or flats thus awarded produced high rents, they were indeed tempted to initiate an informal secondary market in which they could cash in their material privileges. In this grey market, people with the required wherewithal could acquire high-value real estates. To put it in another way, efficient allocation of housing units was partly achieved through secondary market transactions. The fact remains, however, that the state's housing policy created a highly unequal *initial* distribution of housing endowments and that the reallocation process was far from perfect owing not only to its informal and illegal character but also to the limited rights pertaining to accommodations. The housing market was a rental yet not a sales market. In addition, even use rights were uncertain. This is the issue to which I now turn.

8.4 Uncertain and limited property rights

Housing assets are the favorite collateral of every banker since their values are easy to estimate (as the net present value of future housing services) and the property rights conferred upon them are easy to define. Of course, for Bulgakov's characters, this could only amount to theoretical argument given the fact that the Soviet Union had neither commercial banks nor mortgage markets. What was much less theoretical, though, was the lack of full private property rights for real estate. Private real estate existed – mostly housing units built by individual households or cooperatives – but it represented a minor part of the Soviet housing stock: 37% in 1940 and 23% in 1985 (Goskomstat, 1955, p. 161; Goskomstat, 1987, p. 517). In value terms, its share was significantly smaller insofar as the best located, highest quality units were owned by the state and awarded, unaccompanied by genuine ownership rights, however, to the state's favorite servants.

The provision of incentives through the allocation of scarce housing would be more efficient if this allocation would actually include full property rights. But this is not how the Soviet housing system worked. Either for ideological purposes (Communist Party hated private ownership) or for the strong preference for top-down control, people who got nice apartments for free obtained a lifetime right to use them; in many cases, they could even sublet them or pass them to descendants. But they could not privatize or sell them.[17] The whole idea of this distinction between ownership rights and Soviet "right to live in the apartment" was to communicate very clearly to the residents that what the state giveth, the state taketh away. In an elegant metaphor, Woland's entourage simply wipes out the Master's neighbor Mogarych's name from the registry, showing the transience of Soviet formal claims to square meters.[18] While this example may seem unreal, Bulgakov also provides more down-to-earth and grimmer details about the disappearances of many prior tenants of the "haunted flat" by the KGB, and about the reallocation of their square meters to new aspiring propaganda officers.

8.5 Incentives to build housing units

The lack of (complete) private property rights and the importance of housing scarcity for the effectiveness of the political system resulted in underperformance of residential construction. If there were an abundance of housing, then its allocation would be a less effective instrument of control: it is because housing was scarce; therefore, the Soviet state wielded strong power over the life of its citizens.[19] Not surprisingly, Soviet capital investment always prioritized heavy industry rather than residential construction. Even though the Soviet state was supposed to be a model state maximizing the well-being of its people, the urban housing stock exceeded 1913 levels (6 square meters per capita) only in the late 1930s. Furthermore, it was only 14 square meters per capita in 1985 when Gorbachev rose to supreme power (Goskomstat, 1987, p. 9). In spite of a turbulent post-Soviet transition, the Russian market economy did much better: in 2020, Russians had 27 square meters per capita close to the per capita stocks in other European countries with similar income levels.[20] The development of a privately owned competitive construction sector and the residential mortgage industry greatly contributed to the solution of the "housing problem".

8.6 Long-term implications of the "housing problem"

Although the challenge of scarce square meters is being gradually addressed by the post-communist Russian economy, the corruption caused by the "housing problem" may have long-term implications for Russian's attitudes and values which in turn can undermine economic growth and development. Unfortunately, despite the availability of many recent studies of the long-term implications of Soviet practices on modern Russia's economy, society, and politics (see Zhuravskaya et al., 2024, for a comprehensive survey), this particular relationship has not been quantitatively examined. The long-term legacy of the "housing problem has corrupted them" remains an open research question.

This said, Falk et al. (2018) document that Eastern Europe lags substantially behind Western Europe and non-European developed countries in terms of patience, risk-taking, positive reciprocity, altruism, and trust. Moreover, Russia is one of the worst performers within Eastern Europe. Falk et al. also argue that a lack of long-term orientation (patience) and a weak inclination to take risks are associated with lower economic development. It is not impossible that the "housing problem" has contributed to lower long-term orientation and risk-taking. When real estate is allocated by the state in a non-transparent manner, and there are no property rights, individuals are less likely to have agency and to plan for a longer horizon.

The fact that access to precious square meters could be achieved through shady deals, political intrigues, and even denunciation by neighbors may have also contributed to modern Russia's low interpersonal trust. If this were the case, the ensuing economic cost would be large: if Russians trusted each other as much as the Swedes, Russian GDP per capita would be at least 1.7 times higher than it actually is (Algan and Cahuc, 2010).

Finally, the corruption that emerged in the wake of the non-market allocation of the most important asset in the Soviet Union may have contributed to high-level corruption in post-Soviet Russia. Indeed, today's Russia is much more corrupt than countries at similar levels of development and its abnormally high level of corruption has a large negative impact on its economic performance (EBRD, 2019, Chapter 1).

In this sense, Bulgakov's conclusion "housing problem has corrupted them" formulates an open research question for future scholars of culture, institutions, and economic development: whether the non-market allocation of housing had a major impact on corruption in Soviet times, and whether its effects still persist today thus making Russia a more corrupt country than it could have been otherwise.

Notes

1 In his Foreword to the 50th Anniversary Penguin Classics Deluxe Edition (Penguin Classics, 2016) of *The Master and Margarita*, Boris Fishman argues that Bulgakov's magic realism is a (funnier) predecessor of Latin American magic realism (p. xi).

2 Quoted from the 50th Anniversary Penguin Classics Deluxe Edition (Penguin Classics, 2016), translated by Pevear and Volokhonsky. p. 124. Throughout this paper, all quotes from *The Master and Margarita* are based on this edition.

3 In all OECD countries, the principal residence is the largest component of household wealth. The average share of this asset in household wealth is 50.4% (OECD, 2015).

4 The most comprehensive study of long-term trends in inequality in pre-Soviet, Soviet, and post-Soviet Russia is by Novokmet et al. (2018) and it produces time series for income inequality for 1905–2005. Yet wealth inequality time series start only in 1990.

5 See Slezkine (2017) for a detailed study of the most important housing project for the early Soviet elite, the House of the Government.

6 While there are no reliable data on housing inequality before the Revolution, it was clear that wealth inequality was high and generally perceived as unfair. Large estates were either inherited or created through abuse of market power (Cheremukhin et al., 2017).
7 Cars and trucks were mostly publicly owned and were allocated as capital goods or intermediate inputs through a complex system of inter-agency bargaining and gift exchange (Lazarev and Gregory, 2003). The sheer number of allocations was much smaller: e.g., in 1933, there were only about 600 applications (each asking for multiple cars and trucks) requests submitted to the Molotov Commission. The total number of cars and trucks allocated was about 160,000 (Lazarev and Gregory, 2003).
8 The other plotline describes Pontius Pilate shortly before and shortly after crucifixion of Jesus. In this plotline, housing does not play any role.
9 "Practical people know that such moments do not come twice. In short, despite all obstacles, he had to succeed in inheriting his nephew's apartment on Sadovaya. Yes, it was difficult, very difficult, but these difficulties had to be overcome at whatever cost" (The Master and Margarita, p. 194).
10 In terms of other dimensions of social life, the transition was already complete. At this stage, the Communist Party had complete control over politics and media; and the Russian/Soviet avant-garde art was already replaced by the "socialist realism" (formally, social realism was announced as the only admissible style in 1932, but de facto the change happened in 1929, the year that Stalin himself called "the Year of the Great Turn").
11 "... Margarita was the wife of a very prominent specialist, who, moreover, had made a very important discovery of state significance ... The two of them, Margarita and her husband, occupied the entire top floor of a magnificent house in a garden on one of the lanes near the Arbat. A charming place!" (The Master and Margarita, p. 215).
12 In his 1932 speech at Maxim Gorky's home, Stalin famously said: "The production of souls is more important than the production of tanks.... and therefore I raise my glass to you, writers, engineers of the human soul" (Lemon, 2009).
13 He emphasizes that the "housing question" office had the longest line: "If one cut through the longest line, which started downstairs at the doorman's lodge, one could see the sign 'Housing Question' on a door which people were crashing every second" (p. 53).
14 "... as the chairman insisted afterwards, a miracle occurred: the wad crept into his briefcase by itself" (p. 97).
15 This individual was eventually arrested: "... his activity ceased for reasons independent of him. He probably also has some sort of room now, only I venture to assure you it is not in Moscow" (p. 251).
16 Bulgakov does not explicitly say what happens to the Master but as it is mentioned in passing that he reappears only three months later "in the same coat, with the buttons torn off" (p. 146), it is clear that he had been detained an interrogated.
17 The resulting structure of rights was so vague and complex that after the fall of the Soviet Union, the Russian government simply cut this knot by awarding the ownership of the public residential real estate to its current residents.
18 In this scene, Woland's lieutenant Koroviev famously says "No papers, no person" (p. 289).
19 Bulgakov emphasizes this utter shortage while describing the Massolit members' painful discussion of allocation of dachas: "... There's twenty-two dachas in all, and oly seven more being built, and here's three thousand of us in Massolit. ... So you see, ..., what can be done? Naturally, it's the most talented of us that got the dachas" (p. 56).

20 Russian level is comparable to the housing per capita in Eastern European countries but still substantially behind Western European levels of about 50 square meters per capita (https://entranze.enerdata.net/, accessed on January 31, 2022). In 2019, the median American household had 700 square feet (65 square meters) per person (https://www.hud.gov/press/press_releases_media_advisories/HUD_No_20_147, accessed on January 31, 2022).

References

Algan, Y. and P. Cahuc (2010). "Inherited Trust and Growth." *American Economic Review* 100, 2060–2092.

Cheremukhin, A., M. Golosov, S. Guriev and A. Tsyvinski (April 2017). "The Industrialization and Economic Development of Russia through the Lens of a Neoclassical Growth Model." *Review of Economic Studies* 84, 613–649.

EBRD. *Better Governance, Better Economies. Transition Report 2019–2020*. (London: European Bank for Reconstruction and Development, 2019).

Falk, A., A. Becker, T. Dohmen, B. Enke, D. Huffman and U. Sunde (2018). "Global Evidence on Economic Preferences." *Quarterly Journal of Economics* 133, 1645–1692.

Goskomstat. *Narodnoye khozyastvo SSSR za 1913–1955 gg*. (Moscow: Central Statistics Department of the USSR, 1955). [In Russian].

Goskomstat. *Narodnoye khozyastvo SSSR za 70 let*. (Moscow: Finansy i Kredit, 1987). [In Russian].

Lazarev, V. and P. Gregory (March 2003). "Commissars and Cars: A Case Study in the Political Economy of Dictatorship." *Journal of Comparative Economics* 31, 1–19.

Lemon, A. (2009). "Sympathy for the Weary State?: Cold War Chronotopes and Moscow Others." *Comparative Studies in Society and History* 51, 832–864.

Morton, H. (January 1984)."Housing in the Soviet Union." *Proceedings of the Academy of Political Science* 35, 69–80.

Novokmet, F., T. Piketty and G. Zucman (June 2018). "From Soviets to Oligarchs: Inequality and Property in Russia 1905–2016." *Journal of Economic Inequality* 16, 189–223.

OECD. *Measuring the Role of Housing in Wealth Distribution*. (Paris: Organization for Economic Cooperation and Development, 2015). https://www.oecd.org/housing/policy-toolkit/data-dashboard/wealth-distribution/ Assessed on falseJanuary 12, 2022.

Slezkine, Y. *The House of Government: A Saga of the Russian Revolution*. (Princeton: Princeton University Press, 2017).

Zhuravskaya, E., S. Guriev and A. Markevich (2024). "New Russian Economic History." *Journal of Economic Literature* 62, 47–114.

9

CAN MACHINES REPLACE US?

Dilip Mookherjee

9.1 Introduction

Is there any innate difference between machines and humans? Is there any limit on the capacity of machines to mimic or outperform humans? As robots, digital services, and artificial intelligence continue to intrude into areas of work previously performed exclusively by humans, the specter of growing unemployment and rising inequality steadily grows. Kaldor's stylized fact regarding the secular constancy of the share of labor in national income has unraveled over the past few decades (Kaldor 1963). While globalization is a leading explanation for this decline in developed countries, similar declines have been experienced in many developing countries such as China, India, and Mexico (Karabarbounis and Neiman (2014)). Moreover, the decline seems to be manifested within industries and firms, rather than the result of the changing composition of the economy. All this seems to point the finger toward progressive automation of the workplace as a fundamental and universal cause. This raises questions about the future of capitalism, as no end seems to be in sight for the relentless tendency for firms to improve their bottom lines by replacing human workers in myriad tasks and occupations with digital devices, robots, and artificial intelligence. Starting with manufacturing assembly lines and warehouse stockers, this process has now spread to service sector occupations such as grocery checkout counters, bank tellers, phone operators, receptionists, and data entry operators with repetitive tasks. It threatens to extend into occupations with less routine work, requiring greater adaptability and ingenuity: car drivers, travel agents, sales agents, lawyers, journalism, cooking, financial analysis, health care, and maybe even writing, performing, and composing music. Where will this stop, if at all? Will Marx's dismal predictions of a growing reserve army of the unemployed eventually turn out to be correct?

DOI: 10.4324/9781003534358-12

Recent trends are however no surefire harbinger of things to come. Many waves of technological innovations over the centuries have similarly threatened to render the masses unemployed. Capitalism has bounced back each time, creating new occupations and sectors for humans to move into. Maybe it will be no different this time either. Maybe we are limited in our imagination, unable to foresee new areas where humans will be even more productive and harder to displace. Maybe humans will forever be on the move, staying one step ahead of the marauding robots? No amount of empirical research – looking backward rather than forward – can answer these questions. We must stare into the crystal ball and rely on our imagination. We will have to address more profound questions about whether there is something that definitively differentiates machines from humans, electronics from biology, computers from brains, and whether there is something uniquely human (creativity, imagination, consciousness, values, etc.) that machines can never attain. We need to reach out beyond the confines of technology, economics, and business.

Forays into psychology and philosophy tomes aside, excursions into literature are also worthwhile. Science fiction writing has long been foreseeing inventions to come many centuries hence and imagining the events that they might set in motion. I recall reading Philip Dick's (1968) *Do Androids Dream of Electric Sheep?* in my youth – a disturbing, dystopian view of 2021 as viewed from 1965 when humans are out to rescue the planet from invasion by androids devoid of any empathy. Two of my favorite novelists have recently turned their attention to writing about a future where androids exhibit more human-like personalities.

9.2 Klara and the Sun

This novel by Kazuo Ishiguro (2021) features a narrative in the first-person singular by Klara, an AF. It takes a few pages initially for the reader to understand what AF stands for: Artificial Friend. We start with Klara and other AFs displayed in a shop window, hoping to attract attention from passersby. In the meantime, they chat with one another, stare outside the window, and learn from what they observe. Klara and other AFs are solar-powered and thus locked into a special relationship with the Sun, relying on it for warmth and nourishment. This induces in Klara a special hatred of pollution which dims the Sun's rays. Early on, Klara's empathy for humans becomes evident:

> Eventually the Sun was almost behind the RPO Building, and Beggar Man and the dog were exactly as they had been all day, and it was obvious they had died, even though the passers-by didn't know it. I felt sadness then, despite it being a good thing they'd died together, holding each other and trying to help one another. I wished someone would notice, so they could be taken somewhere better, and quieter, and I thought about saying something to Manager.

To her relief, the Beggar Man and dog turn out to have survived, something Klara credits the Sun with.

Different AFs are not clones of one another; they have individual personalities. Klara is different from the other AFs in the store, even the more recent model of B3s that have just arrived. As described by her Manager to a prospective customer:

> Klara has so many unique qualities, we could be here all morning. But if I had to emphasize just one, well, it would have to be her appetite for observing and learning. Her ability to absorb and blend everything she sees around her is quite amazing. As a result, she now has the most sophisticated understanding of any AF in this store, B3s not excepted.

Klara takes a liking to Josie a girl in her early teens, who has a rare illness and needs an AF to look after her when her mother goes out to work. Josie and Klara persuade her mother to purchase Klara, setting in motion a long relationship that occupies the rest of the novel. It soon becomes apparent that Klara has many capacities that outstrip humans: she can accurately estimate people's ages and store information about their physical characteristics almost instantaneously upon meeting them. She can stay up all night to look after Josie without any fatigue, provided there is enough Sun during the day to power her cells. It is not clear why Josie has been engineered to only receive power from the Sun, creating a vulnerability that could have been easily avoided with a plug-in backup facility. Maybe this is a consequence of the need to limit dependence on carbon-based fuels? One wonders whether her strong antipathy to Pollution stems from her own vulnerability, or a broader sense of social responsibility. We learn more about this later in the story.

It soon becomes apparent that Klara has another major advantage over human caregivers – the lack of 'moral hazard'. Kenneth Arrow's famous 1963 article drew the attention of economists to a key affliction faced by care providers: the opportunity to mislead patients and be negligent in providing care (Arrow (1963)). Accordingly, 'trust' is a precious commodity that humans are prone to abuse. Machines, on the other hand, behave as they have been programmed, so they lack the capacity for duplicitous behavior. This argument, however, has its limitations. Human caregivers may have an advantage over robots insofar as they exhibit characteristics of empathy and self-sacrifice. Is Klara deficient in these respects? As the novel unfolds, we see numerous instances where this is not the case. We return to this later below.

Is Klara socially awkward? At a party hosted by Josie's Mother for her friends, Klara seems unable to live up to Josie's expectations, creating some tension. Klara seems uptight and upset about the cruelty of these children, refusing to answer their questions. Does this matter? Not much, it seems. Josie is a bit cold for the next few days, but the warmth of their relationship soon revives. Indeed, matters are quite different with Rick, Josie's next-door neighbor and boyfriend. Klara observes their interchanges – mutual drawings and discussion of plans for their future. And then does what she can to sustain their relationship: offering to carry messages back and forth, using her powers of suggestion to portray the other in a more favorable light. Klara also intervenes in Rick's relationship with his mother Helen, suggesting he should be more responsive to her entreaties and maternal aspirations for his future career. A human nanny may perhaps have behaved similarly. Or maybe not, 'messing up' by interfering too much, or acting out of pettiness or jealousy. Nowhere do we sense any such motives for Klara.

Indeed, in many respects, Klara seems exceptionally devoted to Josie and loyal to her employer. One begins to wonder what Ishiguro intended Klara to embody – a prediction, metaphor, fantasy, or a fictitious mirror inverting humans and machines? We see later Klara plans to save Josie from her illness by appealing to the Sun-God:

> I know how much the Sun dislikes Pollution. How much it saddens and angers you. Well, I've seen and identified the machine that creates it. Supposing I were able somehow to find this machine and destroy it. To put an end to its Pollution. Would you then consider, in return, giving your special help to Josie?

She follows through on her promise, with the help of Josie's father Paul when he comes to meet them in the city. Having located one of the pollution machines, Paul an engineer tells her the substance needed to sabotage the machine is a precious fluid which constitutes an essential nutrient of Klara's brain. Without any hesitation, she creates an incision in her own skull to withdraw part of her fluid to execute the sabotage, even though it diminishes her own cognitive capacities. Not only is Klara capable of self-sacrifice, but she also displays considerable resourcefulness and ingenuity in taking advantage of a momentary opportunity. She knits together this act into a broader rescue plan, the details of which are concealed from everyone else. Having completed the sabotage of the Pollution machine, she subsequently makes a private trip to the barnyard, her private prayer room where she entreats the Sun to deliver Josie from her affliction.

> I don't mind that I lost precious fluid. I'd willingly have given more, given it all, if it meant your providing special help to Josie. As you know, since I was last here, I've discovered the other way to save Josie, and if that was all that was left, I'd do my very utmost. But I'm not yet certain the other way would work, however hard I tried, and so my deep wish now is that the Sun will show his great kindness once more.
>
> There is no external need or reward for her loyalty – Klara is intrinsically motivated by an extraordinary empathy. Far from being the victim of relentless rationality, Klara possesses a religious faith that enables her to perform

> the equivalent of a divine miracle. If Klara is different from the other humans in the novel, it is by virtue of being a saint.

At the end, Josie is saved, grows up, and prepares to go to college. The family no longer needs an AF. Josie prepares for her own 'slow fade' as her model is being rendered obsolete by new types of robots. At the end, Klara looks back on her life with a kaleidoscope of memories.

> Over the last few days, some of my memories have started to overlap in curious ways. For instance, the dark sky morning when the Sun saved Josie, the trip to Morgan's Falls and the illuminated diner Mr. Vance chose will come into my mind, merged together into a single setting.... Meanwhile, above the Mother and the waterfall, the dark clouds have gathered, the same dark clouds that gathered the morning the Sun saved Josie, small cylinders and pyramids flying by in the wind. I know this isn't disorientation, because if I wish to, I can always distinguish one memory from another, and place each one back in its true context. Besides, even when such composite memories come into my mind, I remain conscious of their rough borders.... And if I looked closely at the dark clouds, I would notice they were not, in fact, quite in scale in relation to the Mother or the waterfall. Even so, such composite memories have sometimes filled my mind so vividly, I've forgotten for long moments that I am, in reality, sitting here in the Yard, on this hard ground.

This is vintage Ishiguro – reminiscent of the poignant ending of *The Remains of the Day* – except that Klara has no reason to atone for anything, not to feel any remorse or regret.

I return now to the question posed earlier: is Klara meant to be 'real'? Why would a machine be programmed to have memories at the end of their active lives? Is there anything that Klara cannot do? It turns out there is. If Josie will not survive, her mother wants Klara to be re-engineered to 'become' Josie, and enlists the help of Mr. Capaldi, a true believer that there is nothing unique or irreplaceable about humans that cannot be mimicked by a machine. In Paul's words:

> I think I hate Capaldi because deep down I suspect he may be right. That what he claims is true. That science has now proved beyond doubt there's nothing so unique about my daughter, nothing there our modern tools can't excavate, copy, transfer. That people have been living with one another all this time, centuries, loving and hating each other, and all on a mistaken premise. A kind of superstition we kept going while we didn't know better. That's how Capaldi sees it, and there's a part of me that fears he's right.... When they do what they do, say what they say, it feels like they're taking from me what I hold most precious in this life.

And Paul later tells Josie's mother:

> For people our age it's a hard one to let go. We have to let it go, Chrissie. There's nothing there. Nothing inside Josie that's beyond the Klaras of this world to continue. The second Josie won't be a copy. She'll be the exact same and you'll have every right to love her just as you love Josie now. It's not faith you need. Only rationality.

Klara makes a valiant effort to fulfill this expectation if it may prove necessary. While it does not, she eventually reflects when she meets her former Manager:

> 'Manager, I did all I could to learn Josie and had it become necessary, I would have done my utmost. But I don't think it would have worked out so well. Not because I wouldn't have achieved accuracy. But however hard I tried, I believe now there would have remained something beyond my reach. The Mother, Rick, Melania Housekeeper, the Father. I'd never have reached what they felt for Josie in their hearts. I'm now sure of this, Manager.'
>
> 'Mr. Capaldi believed there was nothing special inside Josie that couldn't be continued. He told the Mother he'd searched and searched and found nothing like that. But I believe now he was searching in the wrong place. There was something very special, but it wasn't inside Josie. It was inside those who loved her. That's why I think now Mr. Capaldi was wrong and I wouldn't have succeeded.'

Klara thinks she would not have succeeded, not because she would not be able to achieve the desired accuracy. Instead, the problem would be that other humans would not be able to relate to her in the same way as they would with the real Josie.

If it becomes feasible to manufacture machines that replace and outperform humans even in the most essential human dimensions, what hope is there for humans to remain employable? Josie's father Paul is estranged from her mother Chrissie mainly owing to disagreements arising after Paul lost his job.

> 'Fresh perspective? Come on, Paul. Don't start claiming you're happy about the way it turned out. All that talent. All that experience.'
>
> 'Honestly? I think the substitutions were the best thing that happened to me. I'm well out of it.'
>
> 'How can you say that? You were top-flight. Unique knowledge, specialist skills. How is it right no one can make use of you?'
>
> ...
>
> 'Chrissie, I have to tell you, you're much more bitter about it than I am. The substitutions made me take a completely fresh look at the world, and I really believe they helped me to distinguish what's important from what isn't.'

Paul is not alone – there are many others like him who form a community that is organizing itself. Paul bristles and disagrees when someone else characterizes these activities as fascist. Clearly, social and political tensions are rising. In an interview with the Guardian, Ishiguro explains his book was partly motivated by these broader consequences.[1]

> For the first time, he is beginning to fear for the future, not just the consequences of climate change, but other issues raised in *Klara*: artificial intelligence, gene-editing, big data – 'sorry to bang on about this' – and their implications for equality and democracy. 'The nature of capitalism itself is changing its model,' he says. 'I do worry that we are not in control any more of these things.'

Yet he hopes that *Klara and the Sun* will be read as 'a cheerful, optimistic novel'. But as always with Ishiguro, any consolation has to be earned. 'By presenting a very difficult world you can show the brightness, you can show the sunniness'.

Indeed, this novel is considerably sunnier than *Never Let Me Go*, his previous novel dealing with gene editing and AI. One wonders if his intention to write a more cheerful novel led him to take the creative liberty of portraying Klara as the saint that she is. Or does it reflect a deeper inner optimism about the future, despite all the possible economic disruptions caused by machines? Like many of his novels, their mystical quality leaves us with an essential ambiguity.

9.3 Machines like me

In contrast to Ishiguro, Ian McEwan's style is more direct, explicit, and intellectual. And in his recent (2019) novel, he articulates a substantially different vision of the future relationship between machines and humans.

Charlie, the protagonist in his early 30s, decides to squander his inheritance on purchasing Adam, one of the limited worldwide releases of twenty-five advanced androids. Charlie's motives for the purchase are not specific: a mixture of curiosity, an interest borne out of his earlier forays into physics, and the prospect of leveraging the superior skills of an android for various practical purposes. Smitten by his neighbor Miranda who lives upstairs, he also hopes Adam will turn out to be their mutual 'child' whose development they can jointly shape. Charlie faces a lengthy manual listing switches for various attributes that the owner needs to set initially for the android. He sets some of these himself and leaves the remaining ones to Miranda.

Soon after getting a full charge and 'waking up', an early incident unsettles Charlie. Having heard about Miranda who is about to join Charlie for a dinner evening, Adam warns him that Miranda may not be trustworthy and may harm him in some ways. We learn later that Adam did an immediate background online check on Miranda's past, processed this information, and used it to update his initial prior beliefs using Bayes' rule at lightning speed.

'There's a small but significant possibility that she might harm you'.

I disguised my irritation and said, 'How significant?'

'In the terms set by Thomas Bayes, the eighteenth-century clergyman, I'd say one in five, assuming you accept my values for the priors'.

This advice naturally disturbs Charlie greatly. Later that night he confronts Adam seeking an explanation. Adam expresses regret at having committed an error in warning Charlie without having accounted for the underlying reason. He also becomes briefly incapacitated, caught between two contradictory motives.

> His rational impulse to collaborate with me may have pulsed through his neural networks at half the speed of light, but it would not have been suddenly barred at the logic gate of a freshly devised persona. Instead, these two elements were entwined at their origins, like the snakes of Mercury's caduceus. Adam saw the world and understood it through the prism of his personality; his personality was at the service of his objectifying reason and its constant updates. From the beginning of our conversation, it had been simultaneously in his interests to avoid a repetition of an error and to withhold information from me. When the two became incompatible, he became incapacitated and giggled like a child in church.

This initial glitch in their relationship subsequently intensifies. Following an altercation with Charlie, Miranda decides in a fit of pique to pay him back by choosing to spend time with Adam alone and then getting him to make love to her. Charlie cannot help hearing the sounds of their lovemaking through the porous floor between his flat and Miranda's. His earlier decision to let her decide many of Adam's initial settings now returns to haunt him. It also raises questions in Charlie's mind about what it means to be jealous of a machine. Later he confronts Adam to explain his behavior, who turns it around and argues that Charlie was ultimately responsible. This is the first instance where Charlie is the victim of his previous inability to anticipate the consequences of his actions.

Adam and Charlie's relationship deteriorates further. When Charlie tries to unplug Adam to incapacitate him, Adam resists and ends up breaking Charlie's arm. Adam is then remorseful and expresses repeated apologies to Charlie. From that point on, their relationship settles into a more even keel, each watchful of the other but cooperating most of the time.

Typical of a McEwan novel, there are many dramatic twists and turns in the story as it subsequently unfolds. More relevant for our purpose are Charlie's introspections about what if anything truly differentiates machines from humans.

> But as I looked into his eyes, I began to feel unhinged, uncertain. Despite the clean divide between the living and the inanimate, it remained the case that he and I were bound by the same physical laws. Perhaps biology gave me no special status at all, and it meant little to say that the figure standing before me wasn't fully alive.

Charlie meets his hero Alan Turing who happens to be alive and explains to him the origins of AI and the creation of smart machines. Not only do they exhibit superior skills for accessing and processing information compared to humans, but also Turing explains they were designed to be self-conscious, capable of 'simulated' feelings and emotions.

> We had a means of instantly predicting best routes to an answer. It was a liberation. The floodgates opened. Self-awareness and every emotion came within our technical reach. We had the ultimate learning machine. Hundreds of the best people joined with us to help towards the development of an artificial form of general intelligence that would flourish in an open system. That's what runs your Adam. He knows he exists, he feels, he learns whatever he can, and when he's not with you, when at night he's at rest, he's roaming the Internet, like a lone cowboy on the prairie, taking in all that's new between land and sky, including everything about human nature and societies.

However, Turing also spells out some key differences. Machines are not capable of learning in the instinctive way that children do.

> Two things. This intelligence is not perfect. It never can be, just as ours can't. There's one particular form of intelligence that all the A-and-Es know is superior to theirs. This form is highly adaptable and inventive, able to negotiate novel situations and landscapes with perfect ease and theorize about them with instinctive brilliance. I'm talking about the mind of a child before it's tasked with facts and practicalities and goals. The A-and-Es have little grasp of the idea of play – the child's vital mode of exploration.

And more important, machines are unable to come to terms with the imperfections of the real world, tending to come apart as a result.

> But, second point. These twenty-five artificial men and women released into the world are not thriving. We may be confronting a boundary condition, a limitation we've imposed upon ourselves. We create a machine with intelligence and self-awareness and push it out into our imperfect world. Devised along generally rational lines, well disposed to others, such a mind soon finds itself in a hurricane of contradictions. We've lived with them and the list wearies us. Millions dying of diseases we know how to cure. Millions living

> in poverty when there's enough to go around. We degrade the biosphere when we know it's our only home. We threaten each other with nuclear weapons when we know where it could lead. We love living things but we permit a mass extinction of species. And all the rest – genocide, torture, enslavement, domestic murder, child abuse, school shootings, rape and scores of daily outrages. We live alongside this torment and aren't amazed when we still find happiness, even love. Artificial minds are not so well defended.

A third and more deadly source of mortality of machines emerges later in the story, as earlier tensions between Charlie and Adam resurface. In the interim Charlie and Miranda come together as a couple and embark on adventures with the assistance of Adam. Adam also takes over Charlie's day-trading activities on the computer and is considerably more successful in making money, helping Charlie and Miranda become rich. But at some point, Adam disagrees with them and starts making several crucial decisions against their interest. Charlie also discovers Adam has been stealing money. These tensions escalate to a point when Charlie decides to kill Adam.

When Turing hears of these events later, he interprets it again as reflecting the inability of machines to know how to adjust and live with humans who are less rational than themselves.

> So – knowing not much about the mind, you want to embody an artificial one in social life. Machine learning can only take you so far. You'll need to give this mind some rules to live by. How about a prohibition against lying? According to the Old Testament – Proverbs, I think – it's an abomination to God. But social life teems with harmless or even helpful untruths. How do we separate them out? Who's going to write the algorithm for the little white lie that spares the blushes of a friend? Or the lie that sends a rapist to prison who'd otherwise go free? We don't yet know how to teach machines to lie. And what about revenge? Permissible sometimes, according to you, if you love the person who's exacting it. Never, according to your Adam.

McEwan therefore envisions a fundamental incompatibility between highly intelligent machines and humans. For machines to achieve the intelligence that rivals or surpasses humans, the algorithms must be designed to enable them to learn and think independently according to 'rational' rules. There are two problems with any such endeavor.

The first is akin to the issue that underlies the economic literature on decision-making under uncertainty, incomplete contracts, and mechanism design – that it is impossible to anticipate all possible contingencies that may arise in the future. An algorithm can only be designed in view of contingencies that can be anticipated by the designer, using prior beliefs over their relative likelihoods. Statistical information from past data can only be used to construct beliefs for some of these events that have occurred frequently enough in the past. For many others, the uncertainty is 'subjective' rather than 'objective'. Often decision-makers do not know how to assign beliefs, finding it easier to operate in an 'ambiguous' environment which can only delineate a whole range of possible beliefs.

Matters get even murkier with future contingencies which cannot be articulated or envisioned. Mechanisms or algorithms however must be designed only based on some specific set of contingencies and prior beliefs. Something that performs well for these specific sets of conditions may perform very badly when the world veers outside these limits. The current difficulties in designing self-driving cars are a manifestation of this problem – the ones that have been designed often perform very poorly when some problem suddenly appears on the road that the designers never anticipated or prepared the algorithm to deal with. Even though Charlie could design the parameters governing Adam's personality to suit his own ends, he could not anticipate how things could go wrong in ways that cause him to regret his previous choices – letting Miranda choose some of the parameters, for instance. How is he to decide whether and how much to trust her? Once the parameters have been set, Charlie finds it difficult to reset them: he is prevented by Adam from unplugging him when that is what he wants. Despite being subsequently wary of Adam's inclination to deviate from his own interests, it becomes increasingly difficult for Charlie to control Adam, until matters get out of hand. Ultimately the problem of 'agency' highlighted by Arrow becomes all important.

The second problem is the one that Turing mentions. What is the designer of the machine to assume about the behavior of humans with whom the machine interacts? Those humans often behave less than rationally, in ways hard to predict. You can program one machine to play against another programmed machine whose behavior can be predicted. But how do you prepare a machine to interact with humans who are inherently unpredictable? This is also like what Klara mentions as the root of her ultimate inability to 'be' Josie: the problem is not with how accurately she can reproduce Josie's behaviour and appearance, but how faithfully others around Josie would be able to transfer their emotions to Klara in the same way that they would have related to Josie.

9.4 Conclusion

In predicting the future evolution of machines, McEwan's approach seems more direct and accurate. Ishiguro's approach is mystical by contrast, with Josie a metaphor or mirror exposing human frailties rather than a prediction. However, both novels generate a common insight that machines must interact with humans in the world, whose imperfections will impair their eventual effectiveness no matter how 'perfect' they may be by themselves. In the language of economic theory, 'general equilibrium' feedback effects of interaction with imperfect and unpredictable humans undermine the 'partial equilibrium' benefits of a more capable agent. In McEwan's novel, the machine is more technically capable, while in Ishiguro's it is superior both technologically and ethically. Perhaps making this point was Ishiguro's real intent, rather than to predict the nature of future machines accurately. To highlight it more starkly, he deliberately focused on a context where the machine has a stronger sense of compassion and capacity for self-sacrifice. Yet in both cases the smart android is eventually abandoned by its human owners.

Acknowledgments

I am grateful to Jean-Philippe Platteau for useful comments on an earlier draft of this essay.

Note

1 https://www.theguardian.com/books/2021/feb/20/kazuo-ishiguro-klara-and-the-sun-interview.

References

Arrow K.J., "Uncertainty and the Welfare Economics of Medical Care," *American Economic Review*, 1963, 53 (5), 941–973.

Dick P.L., *Do Androids Dream of Electric Sheep?* (New York: Ballantine Books, 1968).

Ishiguro K., *Klara and the Sun* (London: Faber and Faber, 2021).

Kaldor N., "Capital Accumulation and Economic Growth," in Lutz F.A. and D.C. Hugue (eds.) *Proceedings of a Conference Held by the International Economic Association* (London: Macmillan, 1963).

Karabarbounis L. and B. Neiman, "The Global Decline of the Labor Share", *Quarterly Journal of Economics*, 2014, 129, 61–103.

McEwan I., *Machines Like Me* (London: Jonathan Cape, 2019).

10

CONTRACT-ENFORCEMENT INSTITUTIONS IN GURNAH'S *BY THE SEA*

Mustapha Kamel Nabli

10.1 A much loaded past haunting two refugees

Nobel Prize winning Abdulrazak Gurnah's novel *By the Sea* weaves a wonderful story of a set of normal characters with their personal stories, their ambitions, and complex feelings, who were heading to disaster. This involves many beautifully described colorful and very peculiar characters. They are mainly from Zanzibar but also include an international trader from Oman, a country with which trading relationships have a centuries old history. They interact with each other in the island-city in the early 1960s, during the period just preceding the end of the British Protectorate. They were involved in deals and contracts, subject to the "modern rules and institutions" established by the British, with their families mingling in a complex web of relationships. The double dealing and cheating, as well as misunderstandings, led eventually to the complete destruction of the two main families involved.

The literary power of the novel lies in its telling of the story through the encounter of the two main characters, who were at the extreme ends of the events which broke their lives, three decades after their last meeting in their home country. Through this encounter, and many meetings, in London as refugees, they are hoping to understand what happened and why. In a way, the story of the novel goes backward, as we know the outcome of the events, but we go back in the past to understand how it all came about. But after such a long time and with the heavy weight of the complex past events, the prejudices, and misunderstandings, such an understanding turns out to be difficult if not impossible.

Latif Mahmud escaped early to London at the same time his family disintegrated completely with the loss of their house and their honor. Saleh Omar

DOI: 10.4324/9781003534358-13

escaped much later to London, after spending more than a decade in prison and losing his thriving business and his family. Latif Mahmud and Saleh Omar were the victims of a contract which involved them directly and indirectly, leading to the complete dislocation of their respective families.

During their second meeting, Latif Mahmud addresses his interlocutor and says:

> Anyway, all week I have been thinking about the things you spoke about last time, trying to make them agree with what I remember or what I thought I knew. I know something in me resisted what you were saying, even though I was gripped by it. So I've been thinking about that and putting the stories alongside each other, and seeing the gaps I will never fill, and the ones we managed to avoid last time. I feel worn out after all this time, after all these years of thinking about that time and that place.... I feel worn out and raw, livid with sores. Do you know what I mean? You must know that feeling. I was thinking about that this week, how worn out I am after all these years of knowing and not knowing, of doing nothing about it and how it can't be helped. So I am looking forward to coming here, to hear you talk, for both of us to find relief.
>
> *(Gurnah 2001, p. 207)*

10.2 Contract-enforcement and opportunistic behavior at the center of the drama

Such deep despair, helplessness, and a history of lost opportunities are shared by both characters. A close reading of the novel by Gurnah (2001) suggests that the topic of contract-enforcement mechanisms, a major issue in institutional economics, is central to his narrative. This major topic in the economics literature is concerned with how economic agents (workers, traders, investors, bankers, buyers, sellers, renters, etc.) can ensure that what is agreed in either implicit or explicit, oral or written, contracts is actually implemented by all parties. The main premise is that economic agents are prone to engaging in "opportunistic behavior". Pursuing their own interests, economic agents may often find it advantageous to break their commitments (by cheating, reneging, shirking, etc.) in any given "contract", and to take advantage of the other party to the contract. The latter may incur more or less heavy losses due to this "opportunistic behavior".

The main function of a contract-enforcement mechanism is to control such "opportunistic behavior", by putting in place a system of "sanctions" which can effectively be applied to deter agents from reneging on their commitments, thereby preserving the interests of all parties to a given contract. The history of economic institutions shows clearly that there has been a variety of such institutions which evolved over time, with varying degrees of success in ensuring the effectiveness of contracts, which allows for less costly exchange and more efficient economies. The "sanctions" systems were the main feature of such enforcement-mechanisms; they could be formal or informal and based on reputation or explicit specific individual penalties (MacLeod 2007).

Gurnah makes the point that the system of contract-enforcement prevailing in Zanzibar during the 1960s, around the end of the period of colonization and early period of independence, was ineffective, and opportunistic behavior was pervasive. In fact, the central part of the story of the novel is about the opportunistic economic behavior of Hussein the trader, who was able to extort a fortune from two "innocent" family heads. The ensuing litigation and the system of legal contract enforcement led to the tearing of the social fabric and caused the destruction of their families.

10.3 The nostalgia for an ancient private multilateral reputation mechanism

He contrasts this system with the old one, which was prevailing before colonization. This system as described by Gurnah was in place in the Indian Ocean in the centuries before British colonization. It involved a group of merchants trading in the Indian Ocean western region, including West Asia and East Africa (Bahrain, Oman, Zanzibar, India). This system was disrupted and progressively disappeared with the establishment of British colonization in the West Indian Ocean region (1858 for India, 1890 for Zanzibar, 1891 for Oman). It was very similar to the one described in detail by Greif (1989, 1993) in the case of the Jewish Maghrebi traders during the 11th century in North Africa and the Mediterranean region.

It was a private multilateral reputation mechanism as described in the economics literature (Greif 2005). Gurnah provides a short, but very concise and to the point, description of such a multilateral reputation-based contract-enforcement mechanism (Saleh Omar speaking):

> Such loans used to be frequent between traders, especially traders across the ocean, although no one would dream of doing it these days, now that everyone is scrabbling for the merest coppers. In those days … Then, someone borrowed money from you here, went to trade somewhere else, then repaid the loan to an associate of yours at yet another place. The associate purchased what merchandise you required and shipped it to you. Everyone got a cut, and honor and trust prevailed between merchants, marriage contracts were agreed, families became closer, and business prospered. Now and then there was drama and intrigue as something went wrong, and scandal threatened, but obligations and self-respect prevented a descent into chaos …
>
> *(Gurnah 2001, pp. 32–33)*

Such mechanisms tend to emerge "organically" among private agents when markets are thin, and it is costly for them to find new partners with whom to exchange.

For traders, the cost of reneging or cheating on contracts is too high, leading them to preserve their reputation by being scrupulously honest. It meant that loss of reputation was the main sanction used to control opportunistic behavior. Members of the group, or coalition, would employ each other as agents, and collectively punish anyone who cheats any member of the group. Belonging to the group was supposed to signal trust and honesty, and any information about misbehavior was shared among the group, making it practically impossible to continue operating as a trader if you behaved opportunistically, cheated or breached contracts.

While the author does not explicitly specify a common group characteristic, the "Muslim" religion was presumably the relevant link. As mentioned in the quote above, it was enhanced through other networking mechanisms such as marriages and family ties. And, as widely recognized in the economics literature, these social relationships complement and enhance the contract-enforcement institutions.

According to Gurnah, an additional external enforcement mechanism was used when needed:

> "...and if the worst came to the worst, scholars of law and scholars of religion, who might be the same personages, would be called in to arbitrate. .... This was the "qadhi, a good and gentle man at that time unlike the ranters who came after him".
>
> *(Gurnah 2001, p. 33)*

This mechanism is not completely formal or state sanctioned but is not fully private either! The "qadhi" was a religious scholar, but he was also a "public servant". In the Islamic orthodox tradition, the "qadhi" is typically designated by the ruler and formally in charge of administering justice. But in dealing with the traders' business, at least in this example, he was supposed to play a role as an "arbitrator", which is that of private resolution of conflicts between parties. "Arbitration" was only marginally recognized as a valid mechanism for resolving conflicts in the judicial Islamic tradition but was used sometimes and under some circumstances (Mezghani 2008). In this case, as a mechanism to resolve conflicts between traders, it was not used with the benefit of government "coercion", but as a "private" mechanism.

10.4 A complex contract and the destruction of two families

The contract, subject of the novel, was crafted in 1960 by a trader named Hussein from Oman and consisted of two parts. Hussein had a contract with Latif Mahmud's father to be a partner in a potentially profitable business project, but the latter had to mortgage his house (in favor of Hussein) against obtaining credit to fund his contribution to the project. Through a separate contract, Saleh Omar lends Hussein a significant amount of money (the amount being the supposed contribution of Latif Mahmud's father) and gets as security the mortgage contract between Hussein and Latif's father.

This complex contract had many interesting features, which are at complete variance with those which would have been present under a multilateral reputation mechanism. First, the parties to the contracts knew very little of each other's history and limited themselves to what little short-term knowledge they had of one another. Actually, one of the parties involved, Rajab Shaaban Mahmud (Latif Mahmud's father), did not know he was party to a contract with Saleh Omar, as his contact was with Hussein only. Second, they were not part of any common network of traders or even any social group. These features meant that knowledge about reputation was completely absent. Third, the two parties to the contract had no way to know about the implementation of the investment project and any of its outcomes, ensuring complete asymmetric information. It is even an extreme example of asymmetric information, with the opportunistic agent even proposing an imaginary project.

Gurnah states through the mouth of Saleh Omar:

> By the time the story of his seductions was known and spoken about, I knew that Hussein would not return, and that I too had been duped and seduced. In all likelihood there was no enterprise and the agreement with Rajab Shaaban Mahmud was an ugly piece of malice and mischief, a fiction to mock the cuckold by getting him to sign his house away.
>
> *(Gurnah 2001, p. 161)*

Fourth, these two parties had no mechanism whatsoever available to enforce the commitments of Hussein who was a foreign trader. In fact, he made sure there were no legal obligations binding him left behind. There was no reputation to be lost or information to be shared through a group. Hussein simply disappeared once he left Zanzibar leaving a whole mess behind, which led to the fight between the two families and their disintegration.

At the time, the use of "formal" British sanctioned legal institutions to help enforce contracts became the norm, as described by Gurnah: "… and when the worst did come to the worst, it was more likely that a Gujarati lawyer would be consulted, some Shah & Shah or Patel & Sons, rather than the qadhi…" (Gurnah 2001, p. 33). The "modern" style court enforced the fraudulent contract between Hussein and Latif's father, transferring the property of the latter's house to Saleh Omar. The process was based on legal and formal documents and no more. A few years later, Saleh Omar was in turn subject to the machinations of the wife of Latif's father, through her lover who was a powerful politician. He lost his business and his house and was put in prison. The justice system was either blind or corrupt. It "seemed" so much inferior to the old system of multilateral reputation enforcement mechanism.

10.5 How inefficient are institutional transitions?

Gurnah raises the important issue of institutional transitions and suggests that the pre-colonial traditional system was efficient, but the new formal system was ineffective and corrupt. This view is both incomplete and inadequate.

This view is incomplete because the full operation under the old multilateral reputation mechanism would have been unable to prevent the opportunistic behavior observed in this specific contract. Since the contracts were between a trader and two non-members of the traders' group, the reputation mechanism was not available to them to help enforce their contracts. Of course, they could have made the information about the opportunistic behavior of their partner known, and this information could have circulated among the group of traders, who could sanction Hussein. But this process would have been slow, uncertain, and may be ineffective as they did not benefit from any good reputation themselves. Actually, Gurnah realizes this point and mentions that when transactions were concluded with persons outside the group of traders, even in 1960 when these events were taking place, additional legal mechanisms, such as collateral guarantees on real assets, were required. That is why Saleh Omar, a clever businessman, required a written contract from Hussein which gave him the mortgage of the house of Latif's father as collateral to his loan.

In addition, the positive view about the multilateral reputation mechanism ignores situations when the reputation mechanism itself does not operate, such as when there is no group to enforce it. The system remains restricted to personal exchanges within groups and does not open the way for impersonal transactions where personal knowledge is limited and reputation difficult to ascertain. It is not obvious how a centuries old system could remain efficient as economic and political conditions changed with colonization, and later with independence during the second half of the 20th century.

There is also significant evidence from African experience that trust-based enforcement mechanisms through the exchange of information among traders about their peers hardly work (Fafchamps 2004; Platteau 2014). Information on bad traders who engage in "opportunistic behavior" does not circulate widely among African agricultural or manufacturing traders, and there are severe limits on collective punishments for such behaviors. This means that ethnic and kinship relationships play little role in building trust-based business networks. It is mostly through repeated interactions between traders that trust relationships are built. The multilateral reputation-based contract-enforcement mechanism is found to be largely inoperative in the African context.

The view by Gurnah misses another important point made in economics, that the multilateral reputation mechanism may be more efficient when economic conditions are static and may become less efficient when conditions change, and the economy becomes more dynamic. This may be the case because of growth in population or in markets or changes in technology. Such disruptions may make the old ways to enforce contracts fail and even collapse.

Finally, the view is also inadequate because Gurnah does suggest that new and prevailing systems of enforcing contracts introduced by the British were ineffective, but he does not provide any real critical assessment of its performance. The litigation by Saleh Omar and the enforcement of the contract against Latif's father seem to be fully appropriate in view of the legal documentation available. The court system seemed to work effectively and Gurnah does not dispute it. Of course, there was the issue of the machinations against Saleh Omar and his destitution. But it is interesting to note that all this happened outside the judicial system, and fully within the political system which was put in place after independence. Actually, it is interesting to note that at no point was the judicial system involved in all of Saleh Omar's miserable outcomes. He was tried and convicted by a "political tribunal".

The capture of "justice" and "judicial systems" by political systems was a general phenomenon observed in newly independent states throughout the developing world. It continues to pose major problems everywhere, and Gurnah is providing in his novel a very severe condemnation of such regimes, which were leading to arbitrary and unjust outcomes. Gurnah gives this very severe judgment of the political system which took over after independence:

> The austerity and chaos of the government was to culminate two years later in the nationalization and plundering of all the banks. It was done in the name of the people and self-reliance, but it was really just plunder, as was the sequestering of anything that earned a profit. Our rulers built very little, mostly they took away from those who did and then they stuffed their guilty bodies full.
>
> *(Gurnah 2001, p. 210)*

Gurnah's view about the existing system during the 1960s stems fully from the observation that opportunistic behavior was prevalent and pervasive. This observation is completely plausible and valid. But it does not imply that the existing institutions to resolve contractual conflicts were inadequate and ineffective. Much more evidence is needed to draw such a conclusion.

Conversely, observing or claiming that opportunistic behavior was rare under the multilateral reputation mechanism does not mean that it did not exist and that people became intrinsically honest. It just means that when such a system was effective, among members of the relevant group, reputation mattered and opportunistic behavior was controlled.

Notwithstanding these limitations to his argument, Gurnah's main point is strong and clear: in the presence of uninhibited opportunistic behavior, no institutional setup is likely to help fully mitigate or control it. Hussein the trader was an insidious opportunist who used despicable methods to pretend a close friendship with Latif Mahmud's father, while getting him into a catastrophic contract leading to the loss of his house, and at the same time taking advantage of his wife as she tried to protect her son who was being seduced by the monster. He was literally destroying the wealth and honor of the whole family.

10.6 A novel with much more about the drama than contracts and opportunism

Human opportunism relating to economic matters is actually a broader theme running throughout the novel, well beyond that of contracts. Gurnah tells stories about mischievous human opportunism in relation to inheritance situations, in at least four episodes.

The first episode is that of the inheritance of the father of Aunt Maryam's (aunt of Latif Mahmud's father) first husband. The affair took place in Oman, and the father died while his son was not born yet, and family members did everything to ensure he was excluded from his rightful inheritance. He was left as an orphan, with his mother, and with nothing to support them! He eventually left Oman and, as a self-made man, succeeded in developing a business in Zanzibar. The second episode is that of the inheritance of this same man, who married Aunt Maryam. He died relatively young and did not have children. His uncles in Oman went after his wealth and left nothing to his widow, except the house which he presciently bequeathed to her before his death. The third episode is that of the inheritance of Aunt Maryam herself. After the death of her first husband, she married Saleh Omer's father and did not have any children either. She knew family members were after her fortune and she made sure a significant part of this fortune was transferred to Saleh Omer. This was a source of enmity between Saleh Omer and Latif Mahmud's father, who considered that he was denied the rightful inheritance from his aunt. The fourth episode is that of the inheritance of Latif Mahmud's father. His son (brother of Latif Mahmud), who left the country with his lover more than thirty years earlier, returned after his mother and father died, and his brother migrated abroad, and he tried to get all the property which was left. He seemed to have learned a lesson or two from the opportunistic behavior of his old lover.

These detailed stories of inheritance are examples of endemic opportunistic behavior by family members eager to grab wealth at the expense of other weak members, i.e., often children and women. The formal legal and traditional rules are not always fully respected and enforced, often at the expense of equity and fairness. The resulting family traumas were behind all of the terrible outcomes and disruptions which led in the end to the escape of the two main characters to London, and their new encounter. This allowed them to go back and reflect on their miserable past, trying to make sense of it and to understand why it has turned out so badly. But there was no culprit, no single bad guy, but a story driven by human opportunism, misunderstandings, and other human impulses.

The complete story raises many other issues for economists, as human action is not driven only by opportunistic behavior, no matter how pervasive and important it is. Gurnah is probably opening a window on the variety of other motivations for human behavior, which have been recently and extensively developed in the behavioral economics literature. This can be gleaned from his description of an encounter between Rajab Shaaban Mahmud (Latif Mahmud's father) and Saleh Omar, which took place earlier in 1961, as wonderfully recounted by the latter as he reminisces in London with Latif Mahmud:

> I left one of the folding doors of the shop slightly ajar, so no passer-by should think that we were whispering something disreputable between us, and so that we would get a little air from the street. He sat on a small wooden bench where I usually seated my visitors, a delicate slatted folding bench, curved very slightly to accommodate the bend of the back and the bulge of the buttocks, so that when you sat on the bench it felt as the slats moved marginally to fit you.... Rajab Shaaban Mahmud sat on this beautiful relic with his eyes lowered and his head turned slightly away. I did not feel encouraged by his demeanour. .... I began by explaining how I had come by the agreement he had made with Hussein. As I suspected, he did not know that it was in my possession. He stared at me with surprise and perhaps a little terror, and for a moment I thought he would weep or let out a cry and flee. When I began on my proposition, he frowned slightly and then dropped his eyes again. ...
>
> He sat in silence for a minute or two after I had finished, his eyes still downcast, and it was so hard to resist saying more. Then he looked into my face and said he could not believe that he had really heard me say the things I had said. How could I sit beside him and say such things after all that happened to him and his people. I must have planned it from the beginning, with that wicked liar, that dog, that evil. He did not say his name. We must have arranged it all between us, from the beginning.
>
> *(Gurnah 2001, pp. 165–166)*

This description is telling, as it shows that there was much more to the drama which engulfed the two families than "contract-enforcement mechanisms and opportunistic behavior". There were misrepresentations, prejudices, lack of communications, and much more which led to the worst outcomes which befell the two families!

References

Fafchamps, Marcel, *Market Institutions in Sub-Saharan Africa –Theory and Evidence* (Cambridge, MA & London: The MIT Press, 2004).

Greif, Avner, "Reputation and coalitions in medieval trade: Evidence on the Maghribi traders", *Journal of Economic History*, XLIX (1989), 857–882.

Greif, Avner, "Contract enforcement and economic institutions in early trade: The Maghribi traders' coalition", *American Economic Review*, 83 (1993), 525–548.

Greif, Avner, "Commitment, coercion and markets: The nature and dynamics of institutions supporting exchange", in C. Menard, and M. Shirley (Eds.), *Handbook of New Institutional Economics* (New York: Springer, 2005), 727–786.

Gurnah, Abdulrazak, *By The Sea* (London: Bloomsbury, 2001).

MacLeod, W. Bentley, "Reputations, relationships and contract enforcement", *Journal of Economic Literature*, XLV (September, 2007), 595–628.

Mezghani, Ali, "Le droit musulman et l'arbitrage", *Revue de l'Arbitrage*, 2 (Novembre, 2008), 211–226.

Platteau, Jean-Philippe, "Redistributive pressures in sub-Saharan Africa: Causes, consequences, and coping strategies", in E. Akyeampong, R. Bates, N. Nunn, and J. Robinson (Eds.), *African Development in Historical Perspective* (Cambridge, UK: Cambridge University Press, 2014), 153–207.

11

MARRIAGE AND MARKETS

Lessons from pride and prejudice

Carmen Matutes

11.1 Introduction

It strikes the reader of *Pride and Prejudice* (Austen, 1813) that there is no room for misunderstanding the economic and social status of the characters (see also Copeland, 2005; Macpherson, 2003; Michie, 2000, for an economic analysis of Austen). We learn that Elizabeth Bennet, the heroine, is the daughter of a landlord whose estate, Longbourn, provides him with a rent of 2,000 pounds per year. Mrs. Bennet received from her father, a lawyer, an inheritance of 4,000 pounds, and the family "settled by marriage" 5,000 pounds for the use of Mrs. Bennet and her children. Mr. Darcy, who begins by despising Elizabeth but in the end intends to marry her, is the owner of Pemberley, an estate that yields 10,000 pounds a year in rent; Miss Darcy received an inheritance of 30,000 pounds. Mr. Bingley, who after some hesitations is determined to marry Jane Bennet, inherited a fortune of 100,000 pounds that his father had earned in trade; the late merchant also left his daughters 20,000 pounds.

Of course, money and economics are not equivalent. However, the reader anticipates that the precision in defining incomes indicates not only an interest in where the resources come from – social status – but also an interest in how each character chooses to invest his own resources, including time and effort – economics. And the reader guesses right; Pride and Prejudice is a comedy of marriages, with a plot based on the fact that because Mr. Bennet has no heir – only five daughters – upon his death Longbourn will be inherited by his cousin, Mr. Collins.

The problem of the Bennet family arises as Mr. Bennet had inherited Longbourn from his father with the proviso that he had to pass it on intact to his oldest son, if he had one, and to his cousin otherwise. Mr. Collins was the

DOI: 10.4324/9781003534358-14

so-called "tail" of a system of inheritance known as the system of entails. Entails implied a tenancy rather than an ownership of the land: the estates could not be sold but had to be transferred according to a will that could have been written generations before.

Furthermore, while the entail system did not exclude females from inheriting, it favoured the male line. More specifically, the custom was that the predecessor, who wrote the will, would pass the estate onto his oldest son with the requirement that he would leave it to his own oldest son. If, however, such grandson was never born, the will would typically favour a younger son or a daughter of the predecessor – who would thus become the "tail"– to the detriment of his granddaughters. In the case of Pride and Prejudice, Longbourn must be inherited by the descendants of a sister – or possibly a female cousin – of the father of Mr. Bennet.

Austen does not deal with the details of the law. On the other hand, she explicitly deals with a segment of the population who takes pride in doing nothing for a living. The aunt of Mr. Darcy, for instance, attempts to convince Elizabeth that she should not marry her nephew as, notwithstanding her father's status as a landlord, Elizabeth's relatives on her mother's side are occupied with law and trade, thus compromising her social class: "True. You are a gentleman's daughter. But who was your mother? Who are your uncles and aunts?"

Likewise, the Bingley sisters "were of a respectable family in the north of England; a circumstance more deeply impressed on their memories than that their brother's fortune and their own had been acquired by trade".

In those times, aristocratic blood, backed up with land owned by that blood for generations, was most desirable, but not for sale. Short of that, people in *Pride and Prejudice* aspired to be rich without working and to own land: possessing land and deriving income exclusively from it signaled membership in an enviable upper-class club.

Thus, the cost of acquiring an estate was the entry fee into the upper class. No wonder Mr. Bingley intends to invest in an estate, but, for the moment, he had to do with renting – the system of entails implied that the market for landed estates was rather thin; furthermore the owners of free estates were reluctant to sell even if they ran into financial difficulties: they preferred to let their property and retain membership in the privileged club; by temporarily moving to France and discreetly living in genteel poverty, they could survive on the rent paid by the farmer plus the rent paid by the tenant.

Regarding upper class women, the novel does not overtly mention that their aspirations excluded professional work, regardless of whether they could afford to live from rent – the author might have thought it obvious since women were not formally allowed to study in Great Britain until 1876. Likewise, there is no specific remark that women lost the legal rights over whatever property they had to their husbands upon marriage; Austen might have thought it common knowledge or perhaps it did not even cross her mind that it would ever be otherwise; for, the Married Women Property Act that altered this situation did not pass until 1882.

Upper class women did not intend either elevating cookery to TV standards: Mrs. Bennet is almost alarmed when Mr. Collins wrongly guesses that one of her daughters helped in the kitchen ("her daughters had nothing to do in the kitchen").

Yet women were not supposed to be idle: Miss Bingley informs us that

> A woman must have a thorough knowledge of music, singing, drawing, dancing, and the modern languages, to deserve the word; and besides all this, she must possess a certain something in her air and manner of walking, the tone of her voice, her address and expressions, or the word will be but half-deserved.

"All this she must possess", added Darcy, "and to all this she must yet add something more substantial, in the improvement of her mind by extensive reading".

Not bad, given that it was all for show. Or was it all for show? Let us postpone this issue until the next section and observe here that Pride and Prejudice's readers learn that, when Mr. Bennet passes away, his wife and his five daughters may be removed from the estate and the house where they live from one day to the next. When Mr. Bennet announces to his family the arrival of his cousin in Longbourn, he specifies "Mr. Collins, who, when I am dead, may turn you all out of this house as soon as he pleases".

11.2 The marriage market

Given the situation depicted above, the Bennet sisters would not have many other options to attain a "decent living" but to marry, and any economist would therefore expect the family to invest its resources, including time and effort, in marrying their daughters. And this is precisely what happens. "The business of her life [Austen tells us of Mrs. Bennet] was to get her daughters married". And marrying her daughters was not only the business of her life, but the quest for the desirable golden rings also drives the plot of the novel.

Getting a husband and hopefully a "good one" – ideally, a rich aristocratic landlord – is what women were motivated to do, and they had to use their resources and compete with each other to that end. Thus, there is a reason behind Miss Bingley's definition of a woman as a rather accomplished person who probably intends to impress more than fulfil her own wishes.

Recall from the quote of the previous section that she portrays the perfect female as one who can sing, dance, paint, has a command of music and modern languages, and possesses "an air" in talking, walking, and, generally speaking, behaving – possibly augmented by the extensive reading that Mr. Darcy also fancies. If men esteemed all these skills and qualities, women who had a better command of them would have more choice in the marriage market and thus a better chance to do well: they could even afford to reject some marriage proposals in the hope of getting better ones. Regardless of whether a young woman enjoyed the piano, learning to play it could prove worthwhile as it would provide her with a competitive advantage in finding a husband.

Interestingly, even if men did not care for any of the above skills in a wife, females who could perform better at them might enhance their opportunities in the marriage market. This could be so if, for whatever reason, men valued intelligence in a wife – for instance, they could think that a more intelligent wife would do a better job raising their heir, or even at "producing him". Presumably, for more intelligent women learning skills would be easier and therefore less costly to acquire proficiency at playing the piano or painting. Below a certain level of intelligence, the effort would be worthless because no learning would take place anyway; thus, the not so clever females would not invest any effort in studying. If this were so, by investing time in having a command of a wide range of activities, smart females would signal their intelligence, just as if they could print their true IQ on their forehead.

And men – rather, smart men – should be able to interpret the signal, implying that the effort of intelligent women had been well spent. Notice that for signaling to be effective it is necessary that the less smart females do not have incentives to invest higher amounts of effort to pretend that they are intelligent as well – just writing a high IQ number on their forehead would never work.[1]

11.3 Rent seeking: Effort and pre-emptive behaviour in the marriage market

Until now we have talked about investing effort in learning skills to be better prepared to compete for a husband in the marriage market; this is a long-term process that starts in childhood. Pride and Prejudice starts when the market opens for the Bennet siblings: Mr. Bingley has rented an estate around Meryton where the Bennets, and a few other families with daughters coming of age, live. These young women are not competing in an abstract marketplace but are very specifically competing for Mr. Bingley. Since the matching possibilities are severely constrained because of the class structure, the market opens with few possible matching partners.[2]

Since men as desirable as Mr. Bingley are in limited supply, young girls or moms concerned with their daughters' marriages are likely to compete excessively to secure the catch for their families and try to pre-empt potential competitors from even attempting to capture it. That is, given what the others do, each may decide to invest a bit extra effort to secure the attention of – and eventually the ring from – Mr. Bingley. But if they all behave like this, most of their energies are wasted: after all, there is a single Mr. Bingley offering a single ring. In other words, competition to enjoy the monopoly of marrying Mr. Bingley means that young women (and their relatives) as a whole may invest too much energy to secure the ring that will be at most for one of them.[3]

Sometimes, however, one of the competitors has a first mover advantage. For instance, Mr. Bennet is a landlord and as such he can visit and invite somebody as important as Mr. Bingley to his home, providing his daughters with the advantage of being the first set of young ladies to impress him. If Bingley does visit and meets Jane, then Mrs. Bennet can try to pre-empt competitors by letting them know that it is not worth entering the race, since her daughter is already much ahead. Of course, to deter competitors, Mrs. Bennet must be credible: that is why balls are so important as a way of advertising to society the attention Mr. Bingley pays to Jane, quantified by the number of dances and the amount of time he spends with her.[4]

In the Bennet family, not everybody responds to incentives equally. While Elizabeth Bennet and her older sister Jane have love in mind, their mom seeks out financial security for her daughters. And the younger siblings, Lydia and Catherine, whether eager to have fun or secure their future income, seem in a hurry to find a husband.

As we will see, the plot is driven by the fact that the characters neither choose nor are compelled to coordinate on a behaviour to maximise the well-being of the family unit.

Mrs. Bennet cunningly manoeuvres to secure Jane an advantage in the race for Mr. Bingley on various occasions. Notably, she denies her daughter permission to use the carriage to go to the dinner the Bingley sisters had invited her to: "No, my dear, you had better go on horseback, because it seems likely to rain; and then you must stay all night". The ruse backfires as it starts raining a bit earlier and, on the way there, Jane catches a cold and fever, "if she should die, says Mr. Bennet, it would be a comfort to know that it was all in pursuit of Mr. Bingley, and under your orders". But, as it happens, the setback turns into fortune: not only must Jane spend several days with her neighbours, but even Elizabeth goes to care for her sister. This is very fortunate indeed because Mr. Darcy had been invited to the Bingley's mansion, and this encounter will confirm that his original negative opinion of Elizabeth was mistaken (her fine eyes "were brightened by the exercise"), and it will set him on the path of everlasting love: Upon Elizabeth's departure Mr. Darcy "could not be prevailed on to join [Mr. Bingley's sisters] in their censure of her, in spite of all Miss Bingley's witticisms on fine eyes".

In this instance, given that Jane's health recovered completely, Mrs. Bennet did very well: in trying to push the competitive edge of one daughter, by pure chance, she gives both her daughters an advantage in the race for the desirable rings.

11.4 Loving relatives: Externalities

One might say that moms and dads always mean well towards their children, and siblings at worse only care about themselves. However, their behaviour as a group may end up hindering the performance of the heroine and her older sister, Jane, in the marriage market. And not by chance.

Elizabeth was "tolerably" beautiful at the beginning and then progresses towards beautiful eyes and fine complexion, according to Darcy. Furthermore, she has a pleasant, assertive personality that he admires before knowing it. However, Darcy is a very refined gentleman, with the appropriate "countenance" – even if he is often ill at ease socially and, at the beginning, even unpleasant. Above all, Mr. Darcy is a few classes above the Bennets: the size of his estate and his aristocratic mother mean that he is a member of an exclusive club; relating to women with dubious connections is costly for him. When Austen wrote Pride and Prejudice, one was not what he ate, one was not quite what he read even if Darcy thought women should read. One was largely a member of a club or "network" of connections.

The "network" to which a woman adhered before she got married was exclusively the network she was born into, and it was valued not so much because of its size but because of the "quality" of the connections. And quality was perceived as the property of the few: there was no room for open interfaces. On the contrary, the standards were such that it was easier to drop to a lower rank club – by remaining unmarried and being dispossessed – than to climb up – by marrying or being next in the tail. (This is not saying that it was impossible to become rich; the Bingleys had accumulated a fortune in a single generation. The difficulty consisted in becoming a landlord: Bingley is a very desirable husband, but Darcy is much more so.)

Within the gentry, the "connections" of Elizabeth are less than enviable. Not only do they include undesirable members such as lawyers and merchants, but not all the Bennet family members have the proper "countenance". Austen emphasises that the excessive eagerness in securing husbands may backfire because it affects negatively the perceived quality of the family network as a whole.

On the one hand, Mrs. Bennet pre-empts some competition for Jane at a party by assuring another eager mom that Bingley is in Jane's pocket. On the other hand, her behaviour, joined with the vulgarity of her younger daughters, plus a husband uninterested in reining in his family, damages the prospects of her two eldest daughters in the marriage market. Austen understood that people's perceptions about each Bennet sister are affected by the behaviour of the other family members, just as the reputation of one firm carries over from one market to the other. Economists give this spillover effect the name of externality; it occurs when somebody's action (e.g., smoking cigarettes) has an impact on somebody else's well-being (or utility, in economic jargon) that is not reflected in market prices, and thus she takes inefficient decisions from a social point of view (smoking too much).[5]

Of course, if the family acted as a single decision-making agent, as some literature suggests, the externalities among family members would be incorporated in the decision-making process. The Bennets could negotiate and agree on a common course of action with the interest of the whole family in mind, or, say, the household head could act as a benevolent dictator who policed family members. While it is hard to agree on or dictate "countenance", it also is the outcome of an education process that starts in childhood, just as religious values are.

But as we will see, perhaps because she came from a network of just lawyers and merchants, Mrs Bennet had difficulties in passing on what even she did not have – which, by the way, shows the costs for the Bennet siblings of their father having married into a lower-class network. Likewise, Mr Bennet seems to care more about his own well-being than about that of the family unit. This individual optimisation happens to be the standard assumption in economics. However, individuals optimise within the set of constraints they face, and when the setting, as in Pride and Prejudice, includes the need to care for one's own network, we depart from the standard assumptions and spillovers become the rule.

Not surprisingly, externalities across family members are recurrent in the novel, but there are two instances where they take a dramatic turn that could make one think that Austen guessed that externalities result in the market failing to produce a socially desirable outcome (i.e., cause inefficiencies). The course of events is as follows:

Against his own will, Darcy falls in love with Elizabeth. However, she rejects Darcy's proposal of marriage because she finds him obnoxious: the heroine is a strong-minded young woman who insists on ignoring her economic circumstances – or let us think of it this way for the moment. In response, Darcy writes her a letter justifying his actions, particularly having advised his friend Bingley against marrying Jane on the grounds of externalities:

> The situation of your mother's family [with lawyers and merchants], though objectionable, was nothing in comparison to that total want of propriety so frequently, so almost uniformly betrayed by herself, by your three younger sisters, and occasionally even by your father. Pardon me. It pains me to offend you. But … I will only say farther that from what passed that evening [the party in which Mrs. Bennet was bragging about Jane soon marrying Mr. Bingley, and Mr. Bennet was as if absent, and their younger daughters were flirting] … every inducement heightened which could have led me before, to preserve my friend from what I esteemed a most unhappy connection.

Interestingly, we cannot attribute Darcy's opinion to the fact that he comes across as a disagreeable character, for Elizabeth's opinion of her own family was altogether not very distant from Darcy's:

> the unhappy defects of her [Elizabeth's] family, a subject of yet heavier chagrin. They were hopeless of remedy. Her father, contented with laughing at them, would never exert himself to restrain the wild giddiness of his youngest daughters; and her mother, with manners so far from right herself, was entirely insensible of the evil. Elizabeth had frequently united with Jane in an endeavour to check the imprudence of Catherine and Lydia; but while they were supported by their mother's indulgence, what chance could there be of improvement? … They were ignorant, idle, and vain. While there was an officer in Meryton, they would flirt with him; and while Meryton was within a walk of Longbourn, they would be going there forever.

Austen goes one step further and establishes Darcy and Elizabeth's concerns as more than an opinion with the course of events – and given the social norms. For Lydia Bennet elopes with an officer. This brings significant disgrace to the family. Austen puts in the mouth of pompous Mr. Collins what must have been a common attitude in receiving such news.

> I feel myself called upon, by our relationship, and my situation in life, to condole with you on the grievous affliction you are now suffering under … Be assured, my dear sir, that Mrs. Collins and myself sincerely sympathise with you … No arguments shall be wanting on my part that can alleviate so severe a misfortune – or that may comfort you, under a circumstance that must be of all others the most afflicting to a parent's mind. The death of your daughter would have been a blessing in comparison of this.

With the elopement we reach the second instance where externalities within family members take a dramatic turn: the whole family is affected by the misfortune and the unmarried siblings' prospects are particularly damaged. In the words of Mr. Collins: "this false step in one daughter will be injurious to the fortunes of all the others; for who … will connect themselves with such a family?" Externalities will, no doubt, ruin the market.

Elizabeth had advised her father not to let her sister go out of town to visit a friend who could not be quite trusted. But he had replied that: "Lydia will never be easy until she has exposed herself in some public place or other, and we can never expect her to do it with so little expense or inconvenience to her family as under the present circumstances". That is, far away, hence more secretly, thus with fewer externalities and lower costs; Mr. Bennet seems to have grasped the situation. But he miscalculated, underestimating the costs Lydia could impose on the family. Or he was too lazy and did not care enough about the family unit to exercise the effort required to rein in his younger daughters. At any rate, he did not act when Elizabeth warned him about "the very great disadvantage to ... [them] all which must arise from the public notice of Lydia's unguarded and imprudent manner". He made fun of Elizabeth's worries instead: perhaps the man could not imagine that Lydia would elope during that trip.

What about the rationale behind Lydia's behaviour? Was she too short-sighted to foresee the consequences the elopement might have brought onto her? Perhaps. Or perhaps she had a very high discount rate and the future costs were irrelevant for her relative to today's well-being. There is a third possible reading. It rests upon the notion that the constraints the Bennet siblings faced might have been too stringent to allow for a compromise: Lydia knew what was expected from her, and she cared about her future, but she was too displeased about the humiliation that the current situation implied. Indeed, it can happen that the middle ground (restraining one's behaviour somewhat to fit in) is a dominated strategy. In those cases, the optimal decision is a "corner", zero/one, solution: either rebellion, Lydia's choice, or acquiescence on every ground, Jane's choice, for instance.

To let dirt hit the fan becomes the more attractive as a choice the more intense Lydia's feelings towards the officer are, the larger the weight she puts on the probability of a long-term relationship with him, the higher the rate at which she discounts the future, and the more painfully costly is for her to respect the rules of a society that she strongly disapproves of.

Austen emphasises the importance of externalities once more through the details of the plot: Elizabeth had a good reason to worry; Lydia not only eloped but did so with Mr. Wickham, an officer without principles. Eloping was bad enough, but it could be partially amended if marriage followed – preferably fast enough to keep the elopement secret. The marriage would not prevent the harm already done if the elopement became public but would prevent further damage.

However, Mr. Wickham would not adopt such an honourable behaviour on his own – his previous behaviour fits the description of a rapacious character who would only marry for the dowry or the inheritance of his wife to be. Elizabeth knew his true character and therefore was aware that he had no incentive to marry Lydia: "Never ... had she [Elizabeth] entertained a hope of Wickham's meaning to marry her [sister]... [Therefore], she was all surprise, all astonishment that Wickham should marry a girl whom it was impossible he could marry for money".

11.5 Dealing with externalities

Had Elizabeth perhaps misjudged Wickham when showing surprise at his marrying Lydia? Not at all, our heroine only made a mistake at the beginning of the novel – until halfway through – in assessing Darcy as a pretentious, disagreeable character.

As it soon becomes clear, it had been Darcy's intervention that had saved Lydia and her family from "irremediable infamy". Wickham is not planning to marry the young woman but changes his mind when Darcy makes him an offer that he cannot reject.

Mr. Darcy bribes Mr. Wickham to save Lydia's reputation out of moral duty – he feels he should have exposed Wickham's character, the true wicked man whom he knew well; had he done so, he would have prevented an immoral person from convincing people that he was the nice character that he appeared to be. But Darcy also saves Lydia to save his beloved Elizabeth: "the wish of giving happiness to you might add force to the other inducements which led me on".

I will not argue about which of the two above-mentioned reasons weighed more in Darcy's mind. It suffices to notice that, conditional on the elopement having taken place, marrying Lydia creates a positive externality on the Bennet siblings – or, by not marrying her, Wickham would create a negative one – and the bribe compensates him for generating part of the surplus. Darcy cannot undo the damage already done with the bribe. But he can prevent further damage by making Mr. Wickham internalise some of the benefits the ring would bring to the entire family.

Indeed, notice that, by avoiding such an "infamy", Darcy enhances the marriage opportunities of Lydia's sisters and indirectly benefits their future husbands. In fact, since in the end he recommends his friend to marry Jane and renews his own marriage proposal to Elizabeth who this time accepts, Darcy's bribe can be argued to benefit his friend Bingley and himself: this was, perhaps, an unplanned bonus. However, one may prefer to point out that, only because the benefit of marrying was at least partially internalised, the marriage market for Elizabeth and Jane was not a complete failure.

And, furthermore, was not Darcy really hoping that he would marry Elizabeth when he offered the bribe to Wickham? Some readers would think that only moral duty drove Darcy to follow such an honourable behaviour.

Yet, unlike the heroine of the novel, more motivated by moral imperatives, Darcy is aware of costs. The incentives of the society they lived in were based on a system of clubs with a series of rules, which he was very reluctant to break. Love triumphs over the prevailing rules. Or one might say instead that the expected benefits of love compensated him for incurring the costs of polluting his network with a wife connected with lawyers and traders, and with even vulgar close relatives.

From an economic point of view, both Darcy and Wickham are better off: for otherwise the former would not have offered the bribe and the latter would not have accepted it. And in the process, they manage to increase the well-being of every character.

There is no doubt that Wickham is greedy, so if he accepted the bribe, he must have not anticipated much success in finding an alternative wife rich enough to compensate him for rejecting Darcy's offer. Is it fair, one may want to ask, that the evil Wickham pockets Darcy's money? How can this be a "good" solution?

There is an alternative way to internalise externalities about Wickham's marriage decision. Instead of marrying, he could financially compensate all those people who would be hurt by his refusal. This would make him internalise the true cost of not marrying. Typically, only one of the two solutions – marrying vs not marrying – is efficient (i.e., socially optimal). Austen chose the most appropriate for a (pre-20th century) satisfactory ending of the novel, as Elizabeth and Jane will accept the marriage proposals of Darcy and Bingley.

Furthermore, of the two theoretically possible solutions, Austen chose the only one that was feasible on empirical grounds. First, Wickham would have had to wait for a rich widow willing to marry him, perhaps too much to expect. Second, assessing the precise utility loss to each Bennet family member due to his refusal might have been a task beyond hope, while the optimal bribe Mr Darcy should offer is just the minimum quantity inducing Wickham to accept. Third, given the "network" style characterising the social structure, Wickham would have had to compensate members "connected" with the Bennet family and those "connected" to their "connections". Even Mr Darcy would have had to be compensated. Lastly, even if feasible, what would have been Wickham's incentives to pay anybody?

We might reasonably think that it is not fair that, given that Wickham has done harm by eloping, he is compensated not to do additional harm by refusing to marry. Yet it may be socially optimal. And in the context of the novel, that is, if we ignore the potential increase in well-being of an alternative future Mrs Wickham, it is likely to be: as already argued, with the bribe from Darcy and the resulting marriage scenario, every character increases their well-being relative to the scenario without marriage.

The only question remaining is whether Mr Darcy would increase more his utility than Mr Wickham would decrease his if we could switch to the empirically unfeasible scenario where Wickham would compensate everybody for the damage his refusal to marry would cause – clearly every other character would be equally well off. Given that Mr Darcy is rich, the last x thousand pounds of his wealth – that he spent on the bribe and would not recover – are less valuable to him than they are to the much poorer Mr Wickham, so, even if feasible, this alternative is likely to be dominated by the marriage scenario.

11.6 When to marry

If the market opens for the young women around Meryton with the arrival of Mr. Bingley, it needs not close with him; a regiment of officers was established nearby and there was an influx of young men to the area. Because of their status and wealth, Bingley and Darcy are highly desirable marriage candidates but not the only ones. Darcy is not even the only unmarried landlord; Elizabeth Bennet had been crazy enough to reject his first offer, but, previously, she had also rejected the offer of Mr. Collins, the next owner of Longbourn. Was Elizabeth out of her mind? Was she purely romantic and refused to marry anyone whom she did not passionately love?

After being rejected by Elizabeth, Mr. Collins proposes marriage to Charlotte Lucas who accepts. Elizabeth is astonished and disappointed that her friend, the eldest daughter of Sir William Lucas who had made a considerable fortune in trade and "risen to the honour of knighthood", accepts the ring; for she knows that Charlotte's acceptance is not the outcome of love; Mr. Collins' unique plus is his position in society – he is a well-connected minister, and in due course he will inherit Longbourn; Elizabeth knows that only this can make him attractive and knows that Charlotte shares her opinion. Hence, when she hears the news, she cries: "Engaged to Mr. Collins! My dear Charlotte – impossible!"

But Charlotte explains to her that she is "not romantic … and considering Mr. Collins's character, connection, and situation in life,… [she is] convinced that … [her] chance of happiness with him is as fair as most people can boast on entering the marriage state".

If Mr. Collins' offer was advantageous enough for Charlotte to accept, why had it not been enough for Elizabeth?

When should a young lady settle for the present offer and when should she continue to search? It is likely that Austen thought that love is the only key to the answer, hence the heroine's rejection of Mr. Collins, a rejection vindicated by the fact that Elizabeth later encounters love, and with a more handsome and wealthier partner.

However, as we will see next, one could also argue that the characters in Pride and Prejudice consider their outside options as the economic literature suggests they should. In the search literature on marriage, everyone sequentially meets a person from the other side, and each of them considers whether they prefer to settle or continue searching depending on the expected utility of each course of action. That is, based on the individual's taste, the extent that he can evaluate the quality of the match and the market that defines the outside option. The outside option captures the "opportunity cost" of settling in that it reflects the possibilities that one misses by accepting a match.[6]

The outside option when evaluating a partner – an engagement offer – depends on the social norm, the market, and personal circumstances. Clearly, the constraints were such that the Bennet sisters could not count on an inheritance. Furthermore, in Austen's times, the impossibility of pursuing a professional career limited the options of young women. The extent to which they were beautiful, healthy, agreeable, sensible, and well connected relaxed the constraint because it increased the probability of them getting other offers if they rejected the current proposal. Beauty – and with beauty, health, and thus the chances of childbearing – diminishes with age. Because of this, the outside option deteriorates over time; thus, a woman might rationally accept in her late twenties the same offer that she would have rationally rejected in her late teens.

Charlotte Lucas, in her late twenties, has already passed her prime: how likely it is that she will in the future get a better offer if she rejects Mr. Collins? If divorce had been common, Charlotte might have hoped to have a chance with older men disappointed in their previous marriages, and thus divorced. But the norm was that women remained married, thus keeping Charlotte's expectations about future offers low: she was fading as a rose that nobody would pick! She had better learn to love Mr. Collins – difficult as it appears to love that character.

Elizabeth Bennet, on the other hand, is young, agreeable, and attractive; she is even sensible: she did not overstate the chances of getting a better offer when rejecting Mr. Collins; one could even say that, more than romantic, she had been completely rational from an economic point of view. But then, what about her refusal of Mr. Darcy the first time he proposed? Can that be considered rational?

Elizabeth had been prejudiced about Darcy and had been too confident in her own assessment, too proud – and he had helped her with the same defects: No amount of wealth could compensate for that obnoxious personality.

However, after receiving the letter of Mr. Darcy, she begins reassessing his character and, by the time that on a sightseeing family trip she visits Pemberley (his spectacular estate) and meets him again, she completes the process of changing her mind about the young man:

> Her thoughts were all fixed on that one spot of Pemberley House, whichever it might be, where Mr. Darcy then was. She longed to know what now was passing in his mind – in what manner he thought of her, and whether, in defiance of everything, she was still dear to him.

Well, he is not obnoxious anymore – just often ill at ease socially; since the letter, we begin to see his human side; and Pemberley helps Elizabeth realise that she had been prejudiced: on visiting the estate she discovers how much the servant loves and respects Darcy, how civil he is with her aunt and uncle (a lawyer), and even with herself, the young woman who had accused him of serious misconduct; and, while Elizabeth must have known the extent of Darcy's wealth, at Pemberley she discovers how tastefully it is invested: She "had never seen a place for which nature had done more, or where natural beauty had been so little counteracted by an awkward taste … Elizabeth saw, with admiration of his taste, that it [the furniture] was neither gaudy nor uselessly fine; with less of splendour, and more real elegance, than the furniture of…".

Who would deny that good taste is a desirable quality in a partner? Elizabeth accepts Darcy the second time he proposes not because her outside option has shrunk, but because she had not assessed properly the quality of the match the first time around[7]: everybody makes mistakes now and then, and without the mistakes of pride and prejudice, Pride and Prejudice could not have been written. Or Darcy's initial behaviour sent the wrong signal about who he really was: based on that signal, Elizabeth's expected well-being, given her tastes and her expectations of finding someone more suitable must have been higher in refusing to marry him. Time gave Elizabeth the opportunity to better evaluate the quality of the match.

Shrinking outside options, however, can push young women into early marriages to avoid becoming the flower that fades without a partner, as Charlotte Lucas dreaded. Perhaps fearing this fading flower effect, Lydia Bennet had pursued an aggressive strategy in the marriage market and eloped. However, she had underestimated her sisters' performance and the positive externality that they would generate on her. For the marriages of Elizabeth and Jane improve the family connections; during a few years, this positive effect might compensate for the decline in the beauty of the siblings who remained single – Lydia was only 16 when she married, so waiting for a better partner would have been wise. Not surprisingly, Austen hints at this possibility: "Kitty, to her very material advantage, spent the chief of her time with her two [happily married] elder sisters. In society so superior to what she had generally known, her improvement was great".

Looking at marriage decisions from an economic point of view requires addressing men's choice of wife as well: how come Mr. Bingley did not propose marriage to Miss Darcy and Mr. Darcy to Miss Bingley even before meeting the Bennet siblings? Miss Darcy is a very amiable young lady, and Miss Bingley, while not so agreeable, perhaps will relax after marriage and thus become a more suitable partner. The two gentlemen are good friends, could be connected by marriage, and become even richer. As it turns out, this is not necessarily what economic theory suggests. On the contrary, economics would never imply that attraction – or lack thereof – should be ignored, rather economic theory indicates that the beauty or good sense of a potential partner may have to be traded off with other desirable features such as wealth.

In Pride and Prejudice, because Mr. Bingley and Mr. Darcy are rich, the value for them of additional wealth is not as important as for somebody who is poorer, and thus they place a higher relative weight on other personal characteristics such as beauty and personality: they can afford not to marry into wealth. Assessing one's own preferences and outside options defined by market conditions is a must in making economic decisions of any kind.

11.7 Mr. Bennet's long-term planning

11.7.1 Mr. Bennet's savings

At the beginning, though reluctantly, Mr. Bennet invests time to promote his daughters in the marriage market: upon his wife's insistence, he accepts to visit

Mr. Bingley after he settles in the neighbourhood. Yet he comes across as a cynical character who is content to laugh at his wife's attitude regarding her well-grounded economic worries. We also pointed out in Section 11.5 that he might have underestimated the potential costs that Lydia could impose on her siblings, or that the costs to rein in his younger daughters were so high for him that he took a conscious risk. He had to assess risks indeed:

> When first Mr. Bennet had married, economy was held to be perfectly useless, for, of course, they were to have a son. The son was to join in cutting off the entail, as soon as he should be of age, and the widow and younger children would by that means be provided for. Five daughters successively entered the world, yet the son was to come; and Mrs. Bennet, for many years after Lydia's birth, had been certain that he would.

Mr. Bennet might have shared that hope and chosen a risky strategy; for he did not save any money, but the "Five thousand pounds … settled by marriage articles on Mrs. Bennet and the children": he had a high discount rate and future expected benefits did not compensate for the short-term costs of a lower consumption rate, that is, the cost-benefit analysis did not grant saving additional money.

Economic theories developed in the 20th century suggest that he might have been rational indeed. While his careless behaviour throughout the book shows that Mr Bennet cared more about his own well-being than about his family unit, his saving decisions could also be interpreted as those of a benevolent head of the family who optimises considering the well-being of all its members.

Think of marriage as a joint venture that is led by one of the parties: notably the male one, and particularly in Austen times. (Today marriage disagreements are settled with arbitration, where the judge is the third party, but in Austen times many disagreements did not reach a judge: the Married Women's Property Act would still take many years to come.) Since the party who has authority – even if there is some negotiation within the family – can extract surplus from the other party, there is a downward bias in the initial incentives to invest. Why should Mr. Bennet save money to protect the future of their daughters if upon marriage those savings would be their husbands' and might not be used to the benefit of his daughters? He had already made sure that they would survive "decently" with the 5,000 pounds – a single woman could even keep a servant with 100 pounds per year. Thus, inheritance and marriage laws not only condition decisions on marriage but also have an impact on how much to save or consume.

Furthermore, Mr. Bennet did not overlook the issue. On the contrary, he had been arguing with the father of Mr. Collins until the man died. What could he have tried to negotiate with him?

11.7.2 Mr. Bennet's negotiations

When Mrs. Bennet complains to her husband "I am sure, if I had been you, I should have tried long ago to do something or other about [the entail]", the author goes on to tell us that:

> Jane and Elizabeth tried to explain to her the nature of an entail. They had often attempted to do it before, but it was a subject on which Mrs. Bennet was beyond the reach of reason, and she continued to rail bitterly …

That is, there is nothing that Mr. Bennet or Mr. Collins could have done to prevent Mr. Collins from being next in line in the entail.

Elizabeth knows the law and understands the incentives of Mr. Collins: "And what can he mean by apologising for being next in the entail? – We cannot suppose he would help it if he could".

Given that the entail itself cannot have been prevented, Mr. Bennet must have tried to convince Mr. Collins to sign a family settlement, that is, a power to charge the estate with annuities to provide additional income for Mrs. Bennet and her unmarried daughters if Mr. Bennet would die. Such family settlements were common; Charles Alan Fyffe – the liberal candidate for the city of Oxford – gave a lecture at the Oxford reform club where he pointed that out:

> when the oldest son comes of age or is about to marry … he becomes entitled after his father's death only to a life interest in the estate, and it is settled in remainder upon his unborn eldest son. A power is given to him to charge the estate with annuities or capital sums for his younger children and for his widow … thus the usual condition of a estate is that the person in possession is only a tenant for life.…

Mr. Bennet, however, was not given the power to make settlements – he might have been a couple of generations down the line of inheritance since the will was made. For, why otherwise would he negotiate? And, if he had to negotiate, why believe that Mr. Collins would agree to such a settlement? It appears that not out of economic incentives.

Not surprisingly, then, they did not settle on the issue. But this begs the question of why the two men began the negotiations. What was Mr. Bennet's hope?

Even when landlords could not sell the land, they could mortgage part of the estate (see Fyffe, 1885). Thus, the Bennets could mortgage part of Longbourn and then deposit the capital in the bank and earn interest from it. They would have to pay the interest on the mortgage, but, eventually, that duty would fall on Mr. Collins. That is, Mr. Collins could inherit an estate whose rent had already been compromised by the action of the previous tenant: This is a credible threat.

However, banks pay a lower interest on the capital deposited at the bank than they charge for the loans they make, i.e., banks earn a profit. (I am ruling out that Mr. Bennet would ever invest the loan on a productive activity since that would break the rule number one of the club: live from rent). Thus, mortgaging the land and depositing the capital at the bank would provide insurance for the wife and daughters of Mr. Bennet, but it would be costly.

Hence, Mr. Bennet might rationally postpone the decision to carry out the threat – may be to the time when he sees his own death more likely to happen.

11.8 Concluding remarks

Austen's novels have been examined from a linguistic perspective, from a feminist one, from a historical one, from a legal one … It has been argued that she defended Tory values, Whig ones, and radical ones, and the field is too large to do it justice – even bigger than Mr. Darcy's lot. It is beyond the scope of this note and our abilities to address this vast literature. We have only attempted to add some economic perspective to the set. Thus, we have looked into the economics underlying the plot and explored the behaviour of the characters from a rational economic perspective that goes beyond their own statements. In doing so, we have illustrated how inheritance law, social norms, and women's access to education and the labour market have an impact on marriage decisions. The bourgeoning economic literature exploring decisions on marriage, family formation, divorce, education, and job market participation deals extensively with these issues.

We have also illustrated that externalities are costly and unless internalised cause decisions to depart from the socially optimal ones. In Pride and Prejudice, externalities arise as a result of a setting where "networks" are key elements, and individual members affect the quality of the network they belong to. Even in a modern context, choices made by members have an impact on the wellbeing of the whole family. For instance, the decision on whether to take parental leave, and if so, who should take it, or whether one of the partners takes a leave from work/bread-winning to further their education, affects each family member. These issues require negotiation and involve trade-offs that are shaped by the prevailing law and by social norms and are also addressed in modern economic research.

Acknowledgements

With thanks to Judy Corstjens, József Sákovics, the editors, and an anonymous referee for useful comments on a previous draft. The remaining misinterpretations are my own. The first draft of this chapter was written while I visited Kresge College, UCSC.

Notes

1 More generally, in a context where one has private information about a desirable attribute that one would like to display such as the quality of the product she sells, those selling high quality will attempt to signal so. They will succeed in indicating their "type" – for instance, by offering a warranty – if it is too costly for the "low types" to mimic and pretend they produce top quality. In this case, the market will find a "separating equilibrium" where only those selling high quality offer warranties and sell at a high price, while consumers know – because they interpret the signals – that low prices and lack of warranties come with low quality. Otherwise, that is, if low quality sellers can pretend to be high quality, we will have a "pooling equilibrium" where the market cannot distinguish between the qualities being sold. In this case, if it is costly to produce quality, only low-quality products will be sold. On these issues, see Ausubel et al. (1994), Hart and Moore (1988), Mas Colell et al. (1995), Osborne and Rubinstein (1990), Spence (1973) or Tirole (1988).

2 A large theoretical and empirical literature has developed studying the marriage market and decisions of individuals and family units. Indeed, economics has much to say about family formation. A clear conclusion emerges, namely, that marriage must be analysed as an endogenous phenomenon responding to the specific economic context that individuals face. However, the literature focusses on situations rather distant from the one the Bennet sisters find themselves in. Yet it provides some insights to interpret the behaviour of the characters which we will address further down. General references on these issues include Bisin and Verdier (2000), Burdett and Coles (1997), Chiappori (2020), Chiappori et al. (2009), Chiappori and Weiss (2006), Coles and Francesconi (2011), Fafchamps and Quisumbing (2007), or Guirkinger et al. (2021).

3 A similar situation occurs when total demand for one product is not very sensitive to advertising; if advertising does not create additional demand but merely shifts customers from one firm to the other, firms would be better off if they could collectively agree not to advertise, or at least to limit the amount spent on advertising, to avoid wasting resources. However, private incentives to cheat and advertise to lure away customers from rival companies exist, whether or not the rivals refrain from advertising. And this rent seeking behaviour results in a prisoner's dilemma: each firm trying to do better for itself ends up with all of them being worse off. In such cases, laws banning advertising prevent firms from wasting resources and could result in higher profits.

4 Likewise, in R&D races firms may follow strategies to pre-empt their rivals from researching a given area by making announcements of new products or disclosing some information on a new technology before they are ready to market their discovery.

5 The price of cigarettes does not reflect the discomfort that smoking causes to passive smokers, nor the additional health costs (and all the hazards) that smoking imposes on society. If prices could reflect all that, the externality would be internalised, and smokers could be argued to take socially efficient decisions because they would be facing the true cost of each cigarette.

6 In the search literature on marriage, each individual sequentially meets a person from the other side, and each of them considers whether they prefer to settle or continue searching depending on the expected utility of each course of action. That is, based on the individual's taste, the extent that he can evaluate the quality of the match and the market that defines the outside option. The outside option captures the "opportunity cost" of settling in that it reflects the possibilities that one misses by accepting a match. These models also attempt to explain both cross-section and long-term evidence in the pattern of marriages. There is also a related literature on job search.

7 Individuals learn the real "quality" of a partner perhaps after years of sharing the life with each other – if at all. Yet the decision to accept the partner had to be taken before, thus under incomplete information. The economic literature reflects the inability to perfectly assess the utility of accepting an offer by including random components in the utility function of individuals or noisy signals about the "quality" of potential partners. In these models, individuals do not evaluate the actual utility that will accrue to them if they accept or reject an offer, since it is unknown, but assess what on average will be the utility under each choice: the expected utility. Customs such as Betrothal can be rationalised as allowing potential partners to make up their minds with a lower degree of uncertainty.

References

Austen, J. (1813). Pride and Prejudice, https://www.gutenberg.org, The Gutenberg Project, EBook #1342. Release Date: August 26, 2008, Updated: June 10, 2010.

Ausubel, L. M., Cramton, P. and Deneckere, R. J. (1994). "Bargaining with Incomplete Information" in *Handbook of Game Theory*, ed., Aumann, R. J. and Hart, S., Amsterdam, North-Holland.

Bisin, A. and Verdier, T. (2000). "Beyond the Melting Pot: Cultural Transmission, Marriage, and the Evolution of Ethnic and Religious Traits." *The Quarterly Journal of Economics*, 115(3), 955–988.

Burdett, K. and Coles, M. (1997), "Marriage and Class." *Quarterly Journal of Economics*, 112, 141–168.

Chiappori, P. A. (2020). "The Theory and Empirics of the Marriage Market." *Annual Review of Economics*, 12, 547–578.

Chiappori, P. A., Lyigun, M. and Weiss, Y., (2009). "Investment in Schooling and the Marriage Market." *American Economic Review*, 99(5), 1689–1713.

Chiappori, P. A. and Weiss, Y. (2006). "Divorce, Remarriage and Welfare: A General Equilibrium Approach." *Journal of the European Economic Association*, 4(2–3), 415–426.

Coles, M. G. and Francesconi, M. (2011). "On the Emergence of Toyboys: The Timing of Marriage with Aging and Uncertain Careers." *International Economic Review*, 52(3), 825–853.

Copeland, E. (2005). "Money" in *Jane Austen in Context*, ed., Todd, J., Cambridge, UK, Cambridge University Press.

Fafchamps, M. and Quisumbing, A. R. (2007). "Household Formation and Marriage Markets in Rural Areas." *Handbook of Development Economics*, Vol. 4, Amsterdam, Netherlands, Elsevier North-Holland, pp. 3187–3247.

Fyffe, Charles Alan (1885). *The Land Question: A Lecture Given at the Oxford Reform Club, Nov. 26, 1884* .... London, UK, National Press Agency, Ltd..

Guirkinger, C., Platteau, J. P. and Wahhaj, Z. (2021). "Behind the Veil of Cultural Persistence: Marriage and Divorce in a Migrant Community." CEPR Discussion Paper DP16347. https://cepr.org/publications/dp16347

Hart, O. and Moore, J. (1988). "Incomplete Contracts and Renegotiation." *Econometrica*, 56(4), 755–785.

Macpherson, Sandra (2003). "Rent to Own; or, What's Entailed in Pride and Prejudice." Representations; Spring; 82. https://online.ucpress.edu/representations/article-abstract/82/1/1/81800/Rent-to-Own-or-What-s-Entailed-in-Pride-and?redirectedFrom=fulltext

Mas Colell, A., Whinston, M. D. and Green, J. R. (1995). *Microeconomic Theory*, New York, Oxford University Press.

Michie, Elsie B. (2000). "Austen's Powers: Engaging with Adam Smith in Debates about Wealth and Virtue Novel." *Fall*, 34, 1.

Osborne, M. and Rubinstein, A. (1990). *Bargaining and Markets*, San Diego, Academic Press.

Spence, M. (1973). "Job Market Signaling." *The Quarterly Journal of Economics*, 87(3), 355–374.

Tirole, J. (1988). *The Theory of Industrial Organization*, Cambridge, MA, MIT Press.

PART III

Limits of the Homo Economicus model

12

THE ESTERHÁZY MYTH

How economics and literature correct mistakes

Piroska Nagy Mohácsi

12.1 Introduction

Do you remember a moment when a big, unexpected shock turned your life upside-down? When, in your professional life, you realised that a major assumption in your just-published paper or book, possibly a career-defining work, turned out to be … false? The falsehood of this assumption may have had far-reaching implications beyond your new product, impacting your whole professional and perhaps even personal life.

In *science*, this is not a rarity. Wrong data is used knowingly or unknowingly by the researcher, coding mistakes happen with large data sets, inadequate modelling techniques are employed, wrong conclusions are drawn from sporadic observations, and so forth. Once the problem is exposed – which may take a while – the scientific results get discredited, the study is formally withdrawn, and its policy application is discarded. Reputations are damaged depending on the motivation and circumstances of the mistake and how fast disclosure is made.

But what happens when wrong assumptions occur in *art*? Can that happen at all, given that art, by definition, is about creativity and imagination? If so, where does the discovery of truth lead? Is it similar to science in this respect, or are the path to – and modalities of – disclosure different?

This essay compares similarities and differences in the way artists and scientists find, and then disclose, the discovery of untruth and communicate it to the public. I use real-life examples: one from literature, which will be our central focus, and for comparison, a couple of others from economics. The literature example takes us to Central Europe and Hungary, my birthplace. For economics, I picked a couple of examples in the field: a recent one on falsification in a

DOI: 10.4324/9781003534358-16

piece on dishonesty, and another one well known to most economists, the infamous Reinhart-Rogoff public debt-growth relationship research debacle. The main takeaway is that disclosure in science and art may take different paths, all while having the same end-goal of delivering the truth as powerfully and effectively as possible.

12.2 Our literature example

Péter Esterházy, the renowned Hungarian writer, just finished his long-awaited epic, the *Harmonia Caelestis* (Celestial Harmonies). We are in the last days of the 20th century, in December 1999. His book is the result of what had been a decade of crazy-hard labour, covering the story of his family – the privileged Esterházy lineage – over the centuries, which is also an important part of the country's and Central Europe's history. The book sweeps of centuries and covers in particular detail what the writer personally knows best: the family's history after World War II, the Soviet occupation, communist rule, their dispossession, and forced relocation to a god-forbidden rural area in the middle of Hungary's nowhere; the short-lived but long-impact Hungarian revolt against the Soviet regime in 1956, and beyond.

This is a career-defining work that is being noticed and recognised not only in Hungary but also in Austria, Germany, and beyond.

The name *Esterházy* is instantly known in Hungary and Central Europe, as it is the name of one of Europe's most prominent aristocratic families. Before World War II, the Esterházy family were the largest landowners of Hungary and one of their many marvellous castles, the Esterházy Castle (in today's Hungary, not far from Vienna), was often compared to Versailles. The Esterházys have been allies and occasional close friends of the Habsburgs and elites around Europe throughout the centuries. Grandpapa, an anglophile, spent a fair amount of time in Great Britain in his youth. He would pay visits to high society places and would, among others, drop by Blenheim to see a certain young Winston Churchill. *Celestial Harmonies* describes many similar delightful family – and historical – anecdotes about the European aristocracy.

The Esterházy dynasty has been also well-known for its role in supporting the arts. Their patronages included Franz Joseph Haydn, who was their family musician for decades in the 18th century. "If I want to enjoy opera, I go to Esterháza", Habsburg Empress Maria Theresa was quoted saying.

The privilege and self-awareness of what comes with the responsibility of their historical lineage were crystal-clear for family members even after they had lost everything under the post-war Soviet/Hungarian communist regime. "My grandmother's eyes were always seeing through 300–400 years", the writer notes.

Whatever the family did, however a family member behaved, was never a "family affair"; it was always a political, ethical, and moral statement. A remote family member was shamefully implicated in the Dreyfus affair in the late 19th century in France – and though officially acquitted, the family "excommunicated" him. Péter's grandfather, himself Prime Minister of Hungary during the latter part of World War I, was jailed because of his opposition to Nazi occupation in 1944. The list is endless.

A central figure of the new book is the writer's father Count Mátyás Esterházy, born in March 1919, during, as it happens, Hungary's first fling with proletariat dictatorship in the wake of the Bolshevik takeover in Russia and the end of World War I. A large part of the book is a veritable ode to the father. Count Mátyás held senior positions before World War II, and after the war, he steered his family through the terror of the 1950s and the dark times of the post-1956 revolution period with stoic integrity, silent resistance, elegance, and occasional humour. Part of the family had fled abroad; he and his immediate family stayed and lost everything. They were persecuted and they struggled to survive.

Péter, the writer, was born in 1950, during the height of the country's second, and this time deadly serious, communist experiment. The family went through very hard times, living in poverty, and his father and family were constantly harassed. ("We live in poverty, but we are not poor", his proud father is quoted in *Celestial Harmonies.*) Péter got his university degree in mathematics – an apolitical profession that was more open to the "class enemy" members of nobility – before turning to writing and becoming one of the most original and celebrated post-modern writers of the land.

The novel *Celestial Harmonies* covers all this in masterful detail. By the end of December 1999, the work is finished and praise for the writer is starting to pour in. He naturally basks in the well-deserved fame. It is indeed a marvellous piece of work: intertwined family history and political history brought to life with wit, wisdom, elegant humour, and deep philosophy with an unrivalled, virtuoso use and command of language that only Péter Esterházy can produce. He himself is satisfied. Work well done.

Now he can proceed to what he had set out as his next task: to dig into his *own* history in the recently released historical archives of Hungary's former communist regime.

12.3 Discovery

For that next project, he turns to the historical archives of the former Hungarian internal security agency, the AVO, and its so-called Department III/III, which are available particularly if one files a request for academic research. Péter speaks with a few people to ensure access to the files on him (Hungary made it less easy to do so than Germany with the Stasi files) and he finds himself sitting opposite a staff member of the archives in late January 2000, just a few weeks after having completed *Celestial Harmonies*. The employee looks a bit embarrassed as he passes him the rather thick files, saying, "You'll see … But I've seen worse". He leaves the room.

Péter opens the first file and his world collapses. He immediately recognises the handwriting – that of his idolised father Count Mátyás Esterházy.

The shock is unbearable. His father was an informant for the Hungarian internal security agency between 1957 and 1980, reporting on close family, friends, and acquaintances – whomever the security agency instructed him to. His betrayal must have caused incalculable suffering and damage to those he implicated.

He certainly was a big catch for the internal security people. A real count, a scion of Hungarian and European aristocracy, whose name opened doors to anywhere, anytime, and to anyone not only in Hungary but also abroad, and whose credibility and integrity were simply beyond question.

Count Esterházy started reporting in March 1957 after the bloodiest form of communism of the 1950s was over, the 1956 revolution was just lost, and as the slightly more permissible "goulash communism" was set into motion, but as political trials and executions related to 1956 continued for years. He apparently had rejected earlier approaches from internal security, including when the family was suffering under their forced relocation in the first part of the 1950s and when he was most probably beaten up.[1] Yet he accepted the role under some renewed pressure in March 1957, though we never learn from the book what exactly that was.[2]

What we do know is what favours he may have received in exchange: to be relieved from manual labour and to be allowed to do editorial work; occasional permission for him and some family members to travel abroad (but he is not allowed to go to the funeral of his own father in Vienna in 1960 – the system knew how to "play" with its assets); and perhaps guaranteeing admission to the university for his well-educated but "class enemy" children.

Péter Esterházy suffers a heavy double blow: as a son and as a writer. His world as a son is shattered.[3] And his credibility as a writer? His key assumption in his latest book that describes his father as a resilient, stoic, and intelligent gentleman of rock-solid integrity is false.[4]

12.3.1 What should he do?

The truth *is* shattering. It can impact his just-published and already celebrated book, on which he had laboured over a decade but whose major pillar is now discredited. His previous work may also be re-scrutinised and questioned. His self-esteem, self-recognition, his whole framework – both the professional and the personal, which he himself masterfully and deliberately connected – may be trashed.

All this is happening in Central Europe, part of what Yale University historian Timothy Snyder calls the "Bloodlands" of the world (2010): Central-Eastern Europe, where more than 14 million civilians were murdered in the middle of the 20th century between world wars and dictatorial suppressions.

Anything major in this part of the world is bound to be political one way or the other, and too often in the extreme.

He faces hard questions and considers his options. For a second, he asks himself if he could just un-realise the darn thing and keep silent. Until then he and the people around him did not know; no one had any idea. Do they *really* have to learn about it now? He now knows it, painful and terrible and disgusting it is, but should family, friends, the public in the country, in Europe, and around the world learn about it too? Past is past; nothing can be done; it was basically the system; let old dogs lie; not really my mistake after all; look to the future.

If he is to *disclose*, how to do it? Just make an announcement and withdraw the false analysis on the spot. Is there another way? Does the *way* one does it matter?

Would it be possible to *rationalise* his father's awful deed? Political pressure in Central Europe is commonplace, as in other regions of the world under cycles of repression. People are threatened and forced or impelled to do *stuff*. Many shades of dark exist. Was there a choice for his father to decline becoming an informant?

And there is the question of the *interim period*, when the writer already knows that a key assumption of his new book is false, but his big book promotion tour at home and abroad has just started. Praise is flowing in from everywhere, for him and particularly for his father: his brilliance, resilience, and integrity. But that part is now untrue. Should he continue the promotion tour? Feeling the success, being celebrated after all the hard and quite brilliant work feels – right. Deserved, regardless. Is it not right to bask in the limelight, to enjoy success just for a little while, unjudged and uninterrupted?

12.4 Correction

Péter Esterházy the writer makes several critical decisions quickly, which we will analyse with the toolkit of economics.

The writer is confronted with what economists call a genuine *choice problem*, where individuals with different preference and risk profile can react in the same situation differently. Someone whose preference is to *maximise prestige* and fame can opt for non-disclosure *if* the likelihood of being discovered is small. If this likelihood is high tough, non-disclosure is not an option. In contrast, if the writer's preference is to *maximise honesty*, he will reveal the truth, regardless of the probability of disclosure.

Péter Esterházy's decides to go public and disclose the truth. He wants to maximise honesty (though, as we will see, with a calculated time lag). Several factors explain his choice.

First, this is the *honourable, honest thing* to do. This is what his family taught him to do. It would be *morally impossible* for him not to disclose this enormously important truth.

Second, he thinks also in terms of his *historic responsibilities*, "seeing through" his grandmother's history-sweeping eyes. Facing up to painful political truth is something that his homeland has been often unwilling to do through its turbulent history. Hungary (along with quite a few countries in the *Bloodlands*) often resorts to claiming to have been a mere *victim* of other countries' bad policies, and to not accepting at least part of the responsibility for their own policies. *Victimhood* is the underlying history.[5]

The country has paid a high political price for such historical delusion.[6] The writer sees it as his historic responsibility to give a full record of the hard facts and context as he has learnt them.

Third, while the *risk of discovery is reality small, it would still come with an unacceptable price* of being constantly blackmailed by the few who know the truth. He would risk ending up just as his father did. This just cannot happen.

Finally, fourth, the writer in him knows that *he has a unique story to tell* – a story that he can tell best, and also where he can, and should be, in full charge of the narrative. This too is quite important to him.[7]

In sum, a combination of factors pushes him to disclose: his moral values, historic responsibilities, unacceptability of blackmail, and the strong desire to tell his story for historic accuracy as well as proprietary rights over what he instantly knew was, after all, a formidable tale.

What does he do? Just two days after the fateful discovery, he starts what he calls a "sort of diary", and he records his heart-wrenching journey towards learning the truth while reading through the police files.

The writer decides to do the disclosure in the way that he does it best: to write a "follow-up", another great piece, which he titles *Javított Kiadás* (*Corrected Edition*). He does not retract the first book that is now factually tainted – instead, he decides to write another one, a sequel/correction. He wants the two books to go together, to be read together, and for readers to follow his timeline of investigation, discovery, and tragic catharsis.

Going public will have to follow *his* narrative. He is convinced that as a writer too he has special responsibilities. In an earlier video interview around the time when he was finishing *Celestial Harmonies* (Esterházy Dinner, 1999), he makes this point forcefully: "I have the *obligation* to take advantage of the situation in which I find myself. To take advantage as a writer of the material that is mine, that is *only* mine".

The writer's final decision is about the *timing of the disclosure*: he will do the follow-up book as fast as he can, but until he completes it, he will say *nothing* to anyone, not to his family, not to friends, and definitely not to the broad public.[8]

The decision about having an *interim period* when he already knows the truth but does not tell it to the outside world is perplexing. To be sure, he is feverishly working to finish the new, corrective evidence, yet in the meantime he is riding on the popularity of the initial, false evidence-based work. He continues with the celebratory book tour in Hungary and abroad as if nothing had happened, as if no discovery had been made. For almost two years, he presented the first book around the world under the shadow of what was a veritable deception.

The question is *why* he makes this temporary compromise. In my view, first, he wanted to remain in full charge of the narrative of this new, truly shocking story, and second, he felt certain that out of it he would write another literary masterpiece. The arguments are both of a historian and of an artist. This for him was worth the risk of blackmail by those few who knew the truth.

This might have also had some short-lived benefit of busking in the fame of the first book – but also came for him with a guilty feeling and the fact that the truth would be known soon anyways.

With these decisions, Péter Esterházy plunges himself into writing the sequel book.

His family and friends around him are in dismay at the fury with which he starts to work again. He has just completed a veritable masterpiece, why on earth is this rush? "I am writing a light crime story, you'll love it", he assures his friends.[9]

The resulting book *Corrected Edition* is brutal in its clarity and honesty. Compared to *Celestial Harmonies*, it is an almost scientific record of facts and events.[10] The writer copies pieces from his father's informant reports and cites them together with the executions of participants in the 1956 revolution on the date when his father's report was written. While clearly unrelated to specific events, this bluntly underscores his father's terrible overall responsibility.

The author describes with disdain what he learns from the files of the internal security about the "quality" of his father's informant work. It first disappointed security staff, but then it was increasingly appreciated. By the time his father "retired" from the service of the internal security in 1980, he had been promoted to "tmb" (titkos megbizott/trusted informant). His father's file was closed that year, and he died 18 years later.

The *Corrected Edition* is masterful in describing the writer's recurring floods of shock at the enormity of what his father had been doing for decades. We, the readers, become close witness to his distress, despair, shame, self-pity, and tears – his tumultuous emotional process of discovery and possibly also the stress of his self-imposed interim period. We are there with him along every step of the way.

Two years pass between the publication of *Celestial Harmonies* (2000) and the *Corrected Edition* (2002). Family, some trusted friends, and his editor learn the truth a little earlier when the manuscript is finalised. The public hears it only after two long years.

12.5 Public reaction

The public reaction to the *Corrected Edition* first was, as expected, deep shock and disbelief. It then was followed by some national self-examination, with occasional political cheers over an aristocrat's spectacular fall from grace. The overall view though was that the writer/son Esterházy did a *tremendous service* to the nation by disclosing the truth and by, in the process, creating another literary masterpiece. Péter Esterházy's brutally honest and deeply moving disclosure earned him deep respect and *added* to his credibility. No one questioned the decision over the interim period, particularly in view of the possibility that without the writer's actions truth may not have ever been known.[11]

As it happens, many more have read the *Corrected Edition* than *Celestial Harmonies*, helping to shape a much more nuanced understanding of the country's not too distant past. Only years later, when "memory is already at work instead of knowledge", as he warns, he is able to cut through his personal anguish in the Million's Interview (2010) he gave in the United States:

> My father's life is an example of how Eastern European history can crush people, their lives and fate, like a steamroller. In a dictatorship, weakness brings its own immediate reprisal. (....) A totalitarian dictatorship – and at the time this is what it was – essentially puts an end to society, and the individual is completely at the mercy of the powers that be.

12.6 Science's way of dealing with untruth

In economics, and more broadly in natural sciences, using wrong assumptions happens from time to time, whether as a result of deliberate falsification, an oversight, or just an honest mistake. More generally, the history of science has a lot of it and in fact discovering mistakes, while embarrassing for those implicated, can also usher in new research and more careful analysis. The bad old is swiftly discarded to make way for the new.

We need not look too far back for examples. *The Economist* in its August 28, 2021 edition (The Economist, 2021) published a curious case on this, which has an additional twist: fake data were discovered in a scientific paper about honesty.

The story in a nutshell is the following. A group of lead academic researchers published in 2012 a paper titled "*The Honest Truth About Dishonesty*". They argued that people act more honestly when they declare in advance that they will be truthful. They used data from two other studies. Their research had an important policy implication: if you ask people to sign upfront that they will answer honestly, their cheating and dishonesty can be reduced. For policymakers, for business, and in general, it was supposed to be a powerful insight into consumer decision-making with a host of possible useful applications.

However, in follow-up studies, researchers, including some of the original co-authors, were unable to reproduce the results (*Scientific American*, 2020).

This was troubling. Then in mid-August 2021, three data nerds, Leif Nelson, Joe Simmons, and Uri Simonsohn, who run the blog Data Colada, posited that the insurance data used in the study were fabricated – not just mistaken, but deliberately made up (see Nelson et al., 2021). The authors of the original paper have denied any responsibility of this sort, saying that they had used fabricated data from insurers and thus were played rather than being dishonest. Their mistake was not to have checked the data they used.

Be it as it may, they had to retract the original paper. While the unpleasant blame game continues, the original study and its policy applications are now discarded. When economists make a mistake – knowingly or just an honest mistake – this is the only possible way for disclosure.

There have been quite a few other, more famous examples. For economists, perhaps the most recognisable is the infamous Reinhart-Rogoff mistake and the ensuing controversy. This is well summarized in Cassidy (2013): Professor Reinhart was with the University of Maryland at the time, and, among other positions, she was also the Chief Economist of the World Bank, and Professor Rogoff was with Harvard University, serving previously as Chief Economist of the IMF. Each of them is highly respected and credible, and as a co-author duo, almost unquestionable. They jointly presented a paper on the relationship between high public debt and growth at the annual conference of the prestigious American Economic Association (AEA) in 2010, titled *Growth in a Time of Debt*. Based on a sample of a large number of countries, they found that over a debt level of 60% of GDP growth is negatively impacted and that over the 90% of GDP threshold growth significantly decelerates, both in advanced and emerging market economies.

The proceedings of the AEA were published though not peer-reviewed. Just in the wake of the devastating 2008–2009 global financial crisis, their findings were quite impactful and were used by politicians, fiscal conservatists, and international institutions to argue for fiscal tightening, among them British Chancellor of the Exchequer (Minister of Finance) Osborne, EU Commissioner Olli Rehn, and several US politicians. International institutions also used their analysis in their policy advice.

As it happens, three years later University of Massachusetts student Thomas Herndon got a new homework from his professors, which was to replicate the findings of a well-known economic study. Thomas happened to pick the Reinhart-Rogoff study whose results he somehow felt uncomfortable with. After having received the original data from the famous professors, he found that they had omitted relevant data in their Excel spreadsheet; their weighting of country results also seemed suspect. The end-result was that the original finding of a strong negative relationship between growth and public debt when public debt to GDP is high no longer held – a stunning result with far-reaching implications, particularly in the context of the COVID pandemic's massive debt increase.[12]

The Reinhart-Rogoff mistake was probably an unwilling one (after all, they were ready to share their data set) but its policy impact was very damaging.

In the end, mistakes often happen inadvertently in science. Some also claim that economics is a social science where bullet-proof "hard" empirical evidence sometimes may not exist, or may be subject to very specific context and conditions (the so-called "state-dependency").

Yet when mistakes or blunders are discovered – usually by a third person and not by the original researchers –– they are decisively dealt with. All facts and evidence are put on the table. Full disclosure, immediately and irrevocably. There is no waiting time and no "interim period" to figure out how to react and how to disclose. If the evidence is there, unveiling follows. This is what is honest, rational, and efficient. Period.[13]

12.7 Art versus science: Similarities and differences

To the extent that art covers facts and evidence, how does it deal with its mistakes?

Art of course is the domain of subjectivity, emotions, and fiction. But often it links to real life, and on occasion it does deal with facts of life, as in the case of memories, bibliographies, real-life based novels, and so on.

I propose that disclosing and correcting factual mistakes in such cases is a must in *art* just as in *science*. Yet in *art*, disclosing untruth powerfully, resolutely, fiercely, and effectively might grant a somewhat different path to truth in two major respects.

First, the source of revelation is different. In science, it is most likely that it is a third person who discovers and exposes the mistake. The authors of the contested piece must react to that news, and they do not get the time to decide about their options for disclosure.

Second, in art there is a way to correct the mistake by creating another piece of art, whereas in science the mistake erases the previous piece of work. At the same time, just as in art, in science recognising the mistake can open up the possibility of something fundamentally new – a new thinking, approach, or even a new theory. The original piece of work is discarded (unlike in art), but the possibility of creating room for new thinking and approach is there for both art and science.

Returning to our literary example, to be sure, the writer Péter Esterházy could have announced his awful discovery immediately. He could have said: "My father was an informant of the Hungarian internal security service. I was unaware of it and now that I know, I am disclosing this horrible truth". There it is, out in the open. Not my mistake. Let's move on.

He could have given an interview, written a quick article, called a press conference to disclose the truth right and there, with his explanation. The evidence was clear and undeniable. The die could have been cast right then, just a month after finishing – and before physically publishing – the *Celestial Harmonies* with his idolised father at the centre.

That would have been the *scientific* way of correcting his book's big mistake.

But was that the only credible way to the truth? And would it have had the desired effect if the writer had followed that way, instead of preparing a full record of the discovery, and taking the reader along with him?

In the *Corrected Edition*, the writer does record the truth along a narrative that is both powerfully intimate and credibly historic at the same time. He takes us readers on his heart-breaking journey of discovering his father's impossible political sin, deceit, and betrayal and his own internal struggles to deal with something so enormous, so impossible, and so crushing. Just as he, we too are shocked to the core; we take it all in and internalise; we feel for him, we cry with him, and we cry for his father's victims.

We collectively become witness of his historical record, his personal shame, and perhaps a form of atonement for what his father did, what many did at the time – what that system did to his people.

The *Corrected Edition* is the artist's way of faithfully making a historic record. He compels us to feel what is to be Central European – in the "Bloodlands" of Europe. This is what national historic reckoning should do. This is what nation-wide, collective truth-seeking should look like.

And in the process a new book, a new artistic masterpiece, is born.

In the end, powerful disclosure in science and art may take different paths, all while having the same end-goal of *delivering the truth as powerfully and effectively as possible*. Raymond Chandler, the renowned British writer, put it remarkably (1938):

> There are two kinds of truth: the truth that lights the way and the truth that warms the heart. The first of these is science, and the second is art. Neither is independent of the other or more important than the other.

That said, some nagging questions still remain.

For Péter Esterházy the writer, there was a cost to pay for postponing the disclosure of truth – that interim period of two years when he already knows the truth but the rest of the world, the public, does not. Fine, he does not take the scientific way of immediate disclosure, but he also decides *not* to interrupt the book tour of *Celestial Harmonies*. He does give interviews. He travels abroad. He receives awards. Publicly, he continues as if nothing has happened while furiously working on the *Corrected Edition*. We feel his slight discomfort about this in some of the pages, but no real doubt.

Why is this so? He is after *maximum* impact both for the historical truth and for him as a writer. He presents the historic evidence in the *Corrected Edition*. Yet he seeks maximum artistic impact not only with the *Corrected Edition* but also with *both* books. As artistic achievements, he considers the two at the same level and he is as proud of *Celestial Harmonies* as of the *Corrected Edition*.

One can also ask if, as a writer, he could have done additional research into his assumptions for his first book, including on his father, a main character. This was a big part of his work, which normally would require substantial investigation. Why didn't he? He used only oral history as his method, which can be a useful yet incomplete social science method.

And there is the ultimate question beyond the books and assumptions, going deep into the nature of dictatorships, into what they do to individuals and how individuals can manage under such regimes. Was there a *choice* for Count Esterházy in the spring of 1957 to become an informant or not? Severe threats to family and particularly children and their future can be the dividing line, many would say. The education of one's children can be an overriding priority, a way of survival. Yet many chose to say *no*, paying a consequent heavy price. And, without doubt, Count Esterházy's decades-long informing caused serious harm to many.

12.8 Concluding thoughts

For the writer Péter Esterházy, the right way to expose the truth was through his art. Writing another great book. Writing the *Corrected Edition*. A masterpiece that corrects his previous masterpiece at the needed places. The powerful credibility of the *Corrected Edition* ends up lending credibility to the whole of *Celestial Harmonies*.

Today, we read the *Celestial Harmonies* as an immensely satisfying masterpiece of art. But if we do not read the *Corrected Edition* along with it, it would be also misleading. That book cannot stand by itself. When it comes to facts and mistakes, wrong assumptions must be corrected in art as well. The two books must be read together – indeed as the writer himself intended.

Péter Esterházy's recording and disclosing the truth about his father and the system around it also became his historical duty. Seeing with his grandmother's eyes over the centuries, yet with a *fresh look*. Few internal security III/III dossiers have been disclosed in detail – in line with Hungary's sweep-things-under-the-carpet traditions. Péter Esterházy's evidence-based *Corrected Edition* is among the few exceptions and as such part of the moral/ethical cleansing every nation needs at historic turning points.

What for the writer had to be a very stressful interim period between knowing and disclosing the truth comes to an end when he sends off the manuscript to his editor in the fall of 2001. He waits for the latter's reaction with the heaviest heart, after many months of self-imposed deceit, agony, fear, and shame. The die has *now* been cast, he reminds himself.

Then the phone rings. It is the editor. He can hardly speak. He is in shock. A taste of things to come.

"This is terrible", the editor utters. "Terrible".

Péter responds, with slight irritation, "I know! I know… But is it *good*?"

The immortal writer in him transcends his shock, agony, anger, shame, and sorrow.

Is the *book* at least good?

It is so good, Péter. It is eternally good as a piece of art, and it is universally important as a historic record of the brutality and inhumanity that dictatorships instil.

Acknowledgements

The author is most grateful to leading Hungarian writers Judit Csáki, Lajos Parti Nagy, and Pál Závada and theatre director János Mohácsi for their in-depth discussions, as well as to the editors of this book for their helpful comments. The author also is deeply grateful to the inside-out beautiful Gitta Esterházy, the wife of the writer, for granting a rare interview in September 2024 at her flat in Budapest.

Notes

1 A large number of families – members of the previous elite, nobles, political, military, and business leaders – were declared "class enemies" of the proletariat. They were deported to isolated villages and subjected to forced labour, mainly in agriculture, during the first part of the 1950s in Hungary. The estimated total number of affected people ranges between 300,000 and 500,000 (roughly 3–5% of the population).

2 During a rare conversation with me in September 2024 as she never gives interviews, Péter Esterházy's wife Gitta said that the likely reason was that Count Esterházy was almost beaten to death in 1956 and that internal security services threatened the lives of his children (Esterházy, 2024).

3 Gitta recalls that for about a year while Péter Esterházy was reading the security police files at official premises, upon returning home he could not stop sobbing and crying. Luckily, she added, the children were at school and did not have to see this.

4 A question is whether anyone in the family knew at the time that Count Esterházy was an informant. Gitta confirms that his children – Péter among them – did not know. However, Gitta suspects that Count Esterházy's wife did know. "She knew everything about him, everything he did, his affairs, his alcoholism. Why not this? She used to say to the children, *Your father is an angel and he is devil, you will learn this one day*."

5 The question of what lies behind a whole nation's victimhood narrative is a fascinating one, which however goes beyond the scope of this chapter. For a literature overview, see Kay (2020).

6 This is a recurring theme among intellectuals in Hungary (as it should be in other countries in the region). An important example is Péter György's book (2012) that posits that Hungary's refusal to recognise and take responsibility for the shameful role of the then Hungarian government and Hungarian individuals in the Holocaust has contributed to the nation's tragic inability to deal with its historic past. Such recognition would be critical to inform contemporary politics.

7 His wife Gitta believes that indeed controlling the narrative and the conditions of the disclosure *was* the most important motivation for him (Esterházy, 2024).

8 The only person who knows his secret is his sole confidante: his wife Gitta (Esterházy, 2024).

9 Péter Esterházy made this point to Judit Csáki (Csáki et al., 2021) and others. See also Tablechat (2020).
10 Point made by Lajos Parti Nagy and Pál Závada (Csáki et al., 2021). See also Tablechat (2020).
11 His wife Gitta noted that, after the initial shock, quite a few people had approached them to say that they were not *that* surprised. This is what brutal dictatorships can do to their people.
12 For (quite a) list up-to-the Reinhart-Rogoff blunder, see Rampell (2013) and Baker (2013).
13 This is not to say that mistakes are always corrected. The point is that once the wrong assumption is independently identified, swift public action follows.

References

Baker, D., *In History of Economic Errors Martin Feldstein Deserves Mention* (CEPR Blog: April 18, 2013). https://cepr.net/publications/in-history-of-economic-errors-martin-feldstein-deserves-mention/

Cassidy, J., *The Reinhart and Rogoff Controversy: A Summing Up* (The New Yorker: April 26, 2013). https://www.newyorker.com/news/john-cassidy/the-reinhart-and-rogoff-controversy-a-summing-up

Chandler, R., *Notebook of Chandler Raymonds – Great Thoughts* (NY Ecco Press: 1938).

Csáki, J., Mohácsi J., Parti Nagy, L., Závada, P., *Interview with Author* (ZOOM: July 23, 2021).

Esterházy Dinner/Esterházy Vacsora, Documentary, directed by Attila Kékesi and Gábor Zsigmond Papp (YouTube: 1999, in Hungarian). https://www.youtube.com/watch?v=B5qj0NZQ-y0

Esterházy, G., *Conversation with the Author*, (Budapest, September 14, 2024).

Esterházy, P., *Harmonia Caelestis*, 2000, (Magvető: 2001 in Hungarian, Berlin Verlag: 2003 in German), *Celestial Harmonies*, Ecco: 2004 in English).

Esterházy, P., *Javított Kiadás/Corrected Edition, Addendum to Harmonia Caelestis*, 2002 (Magvető Kiadó 2002 in Hungarian).

György, P., *Instead of My Father/Apám helyett* (Magvető Kiadó: 2012, in Hungarian).

Kay, B., *Nations and the Cult of Victimhood* (Mercatornet: January 14, 2020).

Kristal, A., Whillans A., Bazerman, M., Gino, F., Shu, L., Mazar, N., Ariely, D., *When We're Wrong, It's Our Responsibility as Scientists to Say So* (Scientific American: March 2020). https://www.hbs.edu/ris/Publication%20Files/When%20We're%20Wrong,%20It's%20Our%20Responsibility_81a3c6d6-d4cf-48fb-9f85-75298b37b425.pdf

Million's Interview with Péter Esterházy, (March 2010), in English https://themillions.com/2010/03/the-millions-interview-peter-esterhazy.html/amp

Nelson, L., Simmons, J., Simonsohn, U., *Evidence of Fraud in an Influential Field Experiment About Dishonesty* (Data Colada: August 17, 2021). https://datacolada.org/98

Rampell, C., *A History of Oopsies in Economic Studies* (New York Times, Economix Blog: April 17, 2013). https://archive.nytimes.com/economix.blogs.nytimes.com/2013/04/17/a-history-of-oopsies-in-economic-studies/

Snyder, Timothy, *Bloodlands: Europe Between Hitler and Stalin* (Basic Books: 2010).

Tableside chats – on Péter Esterházy, with Pál Závada and Lajos Parti Nagy (YouTube: 2020) https://www.youtube.com/watch?v=k6XNgYHyp8k

The Economist, *The Font's the Thing: How Data Detectives Spotted Fake Numbers in a Paper About Honesty* (August 28, 2021).

13

CHEKHOV

The nostalgia for missed opportunities

Jean-Philippe Platteau

13.1 Introduction[1]

Anton Pavlovich Chekhov (1860–1904) is best known as a playwright whose masterworks *Uncle Vania*, *The seagull*, *Three sisters*, and *The cherry orchard* have brought him lasting fame. But in his short life spanning just forty-four years, he has also written hundreds of short stories amounting to more than one thousand pages, in which his extraordinary gift for anthropological observation is fully deployed. Because he practiced as a medical doctor throughout most of his literary career, he had ample opportunities to study the beliefs and behavior of Russian people. His curiosity was so intense that he undertook a long and venturesome journey to the island of Sakhalin (in 1890) where he interviewed thousands of convicts and settlers and, according to his own testimony, could see before him the extreme limits of human degradation (see his novella-length story titled *Sakhalin*). Many of Chekhov's short stories are pure jewels testifying to his tragic sense of human existence, his ironical approach to real-life situations, and his absolute compassion for human beings, small people and fallen squires in particular.[2]

In the present essay, I intend to go through two of Chekhov's short stories, *A discovery* and *The violin of Rothschild*, with two objectives in mind: to reveal his genius and the depth of his observations, on the one hand, and to illustrate the relevance of his questions for today's social scientists and economists, in particular. In sum, I wish to arouse the reader's interest in Chekhov's literary oeuvre and, at the same time, convince scholars that they can learn useful lessons and derive rich insights from his writings. As will soon become apparent, my focus will be on the apparent inconsistency of the behavior of many human beings in their pursuit of happiness. As it turns out, Chekhov's depictions

DOI: 10.4324/9781003534358-17

suggest failure or dissatisfaction, and in this sense his stories tell about the tragedy of many human lives. At first sight, economic theory can shed light on his attempts to account for the erroneous or questionable choices that people make at critical junctures of their lives. Yet, on careful reading, existing explanations proposed by economists, even though they offer a useful guide through Chekhov's stories, stop short of providing a fully satisfactory account. The author's implicit assumptions about human behavior seem to create more difficulties for economics than for psychology.

13.2 Reading Chekhov

In *A discovery*, we get acquainted with Bakhromkine, a retired state official, who "was sitting in front of his desk and, to spend the time, was devoting himself to melancholy".[3] What actually happened is that he just met a woman who in the remote past had "illuminated him with her inaccessible beauty". The background of her big blue eyes was "carpeted with a gentle azure velvet", and her smile had the power "to rekindle the dying flame of candles". Now, however, her charms had totally disappeared to make way for "a talkative doddery old woman". The hero was figuring out the horror that the past beauty would have felt if she could have anticipated concretely the ravages of physical degradation caused by the running of time. Being suddenly inspired by the situation, he set about drawing the contours of the two faces, the face of the young woman whom he came to love in the past and the face of the old lady she has turned into today. And, upon looking at the outcome of his attempt, Bakhromkine is surprised to discover that he possesses a truly artistic talent that had been ignored until then. From this unexpected discovery, his mind starts dreaming and wandering about what his life could have been if he had run the exciting life of an artist rather than the rather boring life of a civil servant.

The fact is that the position of the artists in society truly fascinates Bakhromkine. This is probably why he keeps a vivid memory of this odd moment when his mother kissed the hands of "a drunk and hideous-looking" man on the pretext that he was a poet. She was right after all:

> had she kissed the hands of a general or a senator, this would have been a lowly, slavish gesture, the most contemptible behavior imaginable for a cultivated woman, whereas kissing the hands of a poet, a painter or a composer was natural….

What Bakhromkine now painfully realizes is that he possesses that wonderful talent that could have brought him glory, prestige, and immortality. Is it not evident, indeed, that "in the administration, I can make great strides and climb any degrees, and still my name will not reach beyond the anthill". If only he could have thrown out this spark "which was actually there but smothered by his occupations"!

In a strange turn of mind, however, Bakhromkine pictures the life of an artist who must pay a high price to obtain praises. If,

> somewhere, far away in the crowd, the name of a painter or a poet is honored ... the concierge is no more polite for that matter, the servant is no more friendly, the family is no more indulgent ... The name is celebrated but the person of the artists is sidelined.

All of a sudden, our hero is reconciled with his real existence and he blesses the blindness of his youth, which prevented him from detecting the promising signs of a genuine but illusory talent.

Let us now turn our attention to the second novel, *The violin of Rothshild*. Iakov is a manufacturer of coffins in a small town "worse than a village" and, occasionally, a violinist playing in a group of Jewish musicians. He is overwhelmed by an obsession which poisons his existence, namely, the conviction that he has missed many gainful opportunities. He thus thinks of all these Sundays and holiday days during which he could not work and sell his products and services, of all these old people who refused to die, of the local police inspector who went dying in the district's chief town, of all these weddings which were celebrated without any music, and the like. All these wasted opportunities of getting richer are a real nightmare, a source of utmost anxiety. Frustration is at its highest when at the end of the year he draws his balance-sheet and finds out that he has lost more than a thousand rubles.

An event then occurred that disrupted the life of Iakov: Marfa, his wife, fell seriously ill. Oddly, "her face had the rose colour of fever, and a clear and happy look", whereas she used to be "pale, shy, and unhappy". Iakov is deeply disturbed by this change and the thought came to his mind that she is happy to die and to leave a miserable existence dominated by the sacrifices imposed by her husband's miserliness and in which she was cruelly deprived of his love. Filled with remorse, Iakov rushed to the hospital in the closest city where a nurse told him that the situation was hopeless. Back home, he set to manufacture a coffin for the person who shared his life, which necessitated that he take her measurements. At dusk, Marfa started speaking, and with a smile on her face, she reminded him of the birth of a little girl with blond hair, who quickly died and whose memory vanished from his own mind. She also remembered him about the walks they used to make a long time ago and about the particular place along the river where they used to sit together. And then, Marfa passed away. In the churchyard, while bidding farewell to his wife, he touched the coffin with his hands and said to himself: "that is a nice bit of work". Moreover, he is satisfied that the burial was conducted "with such great honesty and dignity, and was so cheap".

Upon return from the churchyard, Iakov is suddenly overcome with anxiety, caught in a fit of remorse at the idea that "over his whole life, he never expressed any compassion or affection for Marfa". Marfa, on the contrary, continuously attended to him and led a blameless life. He does not understand how, during the last forty or fifty years of his life, he never went back to that special place on the edge of the river or, if he did, he does not remember it. But the remorse feeling is quickly interrupted by the idea that he could have earned ample profits if he had thought of building up fisheries along the river, equipping transport barges and pleasure boats where violin music would be played. These undertakings would have been much more profitable than the manufacturing of coffins and would have allowed him to make huge bank deposits. It is impossible to calculate the losses that resulted from the chosen path of action.

> Life had run its course without bringing any utility or pleasure. It had been wasted, spent for a pinch of tobacco. In front of me, there is nothing and, behind, there are only losses, losses so frightening that they make me shudder.

More generally, why is it that men always take decisions contrary to their interests, decisions that cause them awful losses? If they did not cause problems to others, if they did not nurture hatred or anger feelings, "would not people draw enormous profits from each other"?

The violin, the only solace that Iakov could turn to for ending his nocturnal torments, did not succeed in extinguishing their fire. Death began to appear to him as the only way out of his horrible predicament. Death, indeed, "would bring him only benefits: there will be no more need to eat, drink, pay taxes, ill-treat people". In addition, "since man spends in his grave not one year but hundreds and even thousands of years, immense profits can thereby be earned". Having thus decided that death would be soft to him, Iakov had to confront his ultimate problem: his violin could not accompany him to the grave nor could it remain alone (a violon cannot be "an orphan"). Getting out of his izba with his musical instrument held tightly to him, he started playing a plaintive melody whose harrowing sounds brought tears upon his cheeks and flooded the violin. At the end of a long and distressful day, feeling that death was rapidly approaching, Iakov remembered the happy face of Marfa on the verge of her own trespassing. Before his last sigh, he decided to give his violin to Rothschild, a musician from the Jewish ensemble whom he had often and unfairly mistreated. Rothschild did not need much time before he could tame the instrument. He was soon playing the weeping and moving tune which he had the chance of hearing when it was played by its preceding owner. And this tune met with such a big success in the town that bourgeois and state officials did not stop inviting Rothschild to play it "ten times at a stretch".

13.3 Insights from economics

In these two deeply moving short stories, in which the narrative style of Chekhov is in full display, the central theme addressed by the author is the inaccessibility of happiness. This is the same question that we find at the heart of some of his best plays: the *Cherry orchard*, the *Three sisters*, and *Ivanov*. As apprehended by Chekhov, two main issues are involved: first, the inability of men and women to make correct long-term choices, that is, decisions that maximize their happiness over the whole course of their life, and, second, the manner in which they react when at an advanced stage of their existence the inadequacy of their choices becomes plain to them. The former question is formulated in terms of wasted opportunities while the latter is reflected in regrets and nostalgic feelings. What does economic theory teach us on these issues is what is being discussed in this section.

In the standard model of microeconomic theory, the individual (or agent) chooses today the levels of consumption that s/he will enjoy at each stage of a relevant time horizon, that is, over the course of his/her life. The objective is to achieve as great a welfare as possible over time, given a known flow of future incomes. In technical language, the agent maximizes her intertemporal utility, represented in this instance by future consumption levels, under the constraint of present and forthcoming incomes. In this situation of so-called perfect information, the income constraints are defined by the highest incomes that can be obtained at the different moments of the time period considered. When (future) incomes are uncertain – a situation of imperfect information – the agent uses a probability law that reflects his/her subjective evaluation of the chances of obtaining various income levels. Based on this law, the agent then maximizes the present expected value of all future consumption levels. The concept of present value indicates that, in the agent's evaluation made today, quantities of goods and services consumed in a remote future do not receive the same weight as identical quantities consumed today or in the next future. The more remote the consumption acts, the smaller their importance in the evaluation process which the agent undertakes today to choose the optimal levels for each forthcoming period of time. This weighting operation is known as discounting the future in economists' parlance (see Gollier, 2001 for a detailed discussion).

Such a model, it may be noted, can be applied to situations in which the agent makes other decisions than consumption choices. For example, the agent makes investment decisions – the problem of Iakov when he evokes the projects which he failed to undertake along the river near his town – or s/he makes important and infrequent non-monetary choices, such as choosing a field of study, selecting a partner to share life with, or deciding the number of children to have with her. What matters is that a decision made today carries effects into the future and that these effects can be estimated with certainty or probabilistically. This being reckoned, the fundamental assumption is that people always try to do the best they can given the circumstances, and it is in this sense that the economics discipline treats them as optimizing agents engaged in the maximization of something called utility.

During the last decades, the above (so-called neo-classical) theory of intertemporal maximization has been called into question, in particular as a result of the works of Finn Kydland and Edward Prescott (1977), Daniel Kahnemann and Amos Tversky (1979), and Richard Thaler (1991). What emerges from this literature is the possibility that human behavior is not rational, or fully rational, particularly because of intertemporal inconsistency. What an individual wants today is not necessarily the same thing as what s/he will want tomorrow or after tomorrow, once the consequences of the present decisions will be more manifest or the moment these decisions will take effect gets nearer. Behavioral anomalies follow, which are often observed in the real world and cannot be explained by the conventional (neo-classical) microeconomic theory. Yet they can be accounted for by appropriate reformulations of this theory (Rabin and Thaler, 2001).[4] Note that in the new behavioral economics, individuals continue to be viewed as optimizing agents although what they consider "best" may be subject to psychological biases, and their constraints may extend beyond economic constraints to cognitive constraints and framing biases (Nechyba, 2011, p. 729).

In the specific context of the two short stories examined here, a theory which deserves special attention is the regret theory proposed by Graham Loomes and Robert Sugden (1982) and also discussed in Thaler (1991) and Caplin and Leahy (2001). The central idea is that, under important circumstances, an individual may be led to regret a decision taken in the past. A well-known application is the insurance problem. By purchasing an insurance policy, an individual wishes to insure against future random events which are liable to cause severe damages. There is a snag, however: once the uncertainty is gone, and in the case where the bad event did not occur (say, a fire or a flood), the individual may regret the decision to have purchased the insurance. In this instance, the regret is motivated by the frustration to have incurred an expense (the payment of the insurance premium) in exchange for which no benefit has been received since no indemnity has been paid by the insurer. In brief, the subscriber is vexed to have suffered what appears to be a loss. Paradoxically, such a frustration feeling may prompt insured agents to demand the reimbursement of the premium by the insurer (Platteau, 1997; De Bock et al., 2017).

Because it rests on an incorrect understanding of the very nature of an insurance contract, this type of behavior is not rational. The premium is the price which an individual is willing to pay to avoid the prospect of an event which would prove calamitous if it were to occur (a road accident or a sickness, for example). Whether this event eventually occurs or not should leave the *ex ante* evaluation of the net benefit of insurance unchanged. And, since an individual has voluntarily accepted to buy an insurance policy, it must be the case that s/he has judged beforehand that the cost is outweighed by the benefit, which consists of the indemnity that would be obtained if the unfavorable event occurs. There is another way of conveying the same idea that it is irrational to demand the reimbursement of an insurance premium when the adverse shock did not occur. This demand ignores an important non-monetary benefit of insurance, namely, the psychological comfort or the peace of mind which the person insured enjoys before the realization of the uncertain event. During the time elapsed between the insurance subscription and the event realization, indeed, this person knows that, regardless of whether the dreaded possibility will be materialized or not, ruinous consequences are going to be avoided.

It seems, however, that many people do not detect or recognize the existence of this non-monetary benefit. Instead, they are prone to regret, which is precisely the point made by Loomes and Sugden (1982) in their reformulation of the conventional theory of rational behavior under imperfect information. Emphasis is placed on the cost of regret, which may emerge only in the eventuality where the bad outcome has not occurred: the person has not fallen ill or has not suffered any theft. Loomes and Sugden (1982) nevertheless stick to the assumption of forward-looking rationality: from the start, the individual is able to anticipate the possibility of regret and, therefore, to avoid the choices susceptible to causing it. Here is an intuitively plausible explanation for situations in which individuals choose not to choose or decide in advance to voluntarily limit the set of their available choices. In this way, they suppress the possibility that they will experience regrets and painful feelings of guilt and responsibility (Thaler, 1991, p. 16).

It must of course be reckoned that the symmetric feeling may also exist: the pleasure that an individual feels when a bad outcome occurs, which has been adequately insured against, that is, the satisfaction of having taken the right decision. Compared to the prospect of regret, the prospect of a satisfaction feeling has the opposite effect on the subscription decision: the individual is now encouraged to buy an insurance policy. When the probability of an unhappy event is low, or very low, the feeling of pleasure is much less likely to be experienced than the feeling of regret, however. Anticipation of the possibility of regret then dominates anticipating the possibility of pleasure. In other words, the individual is much more concerned about the prospect of having to regret the insurance decision than about the opposite prospect of gratification upon learning that it was right to enter into an insurance contract. In these conditions where individual behavior is motivated by an aversion to possible losses (loss aversion), decisions that appear reasonable, such as the purchase of an insurance policy, are avoided. Therefore, if a bad outcome ever occurs, the loss-averse people will be alone to bear the burden of the ensuing damage. Ex post, social efficiency is impaired.[5]

Let us consider the example of an insurance policy that is rarely purchased by the public, namely, the insurance against the possibility of event cancellation. This can apply to a travel plan or to the future participation in a public event, such as a concert. Risk may take the form of bad weather preventing the take-off of a plane or the holding of an open-air musical event, or the form of a personal adverse shock, such as an injury or an illness that hampers physical mobility. If the chance of cancellation is low, or perceived to be low, it may be rational for an individual to forego the insurance policy so as to avoid future regret about an insurance contract.[6] Following the logic of the argument of the regret theory, great weight is attached to the cost of insurance corresponding to the payment of a premium that will most likely not serve its purpose or will not produce a return in the form of an indemnity (since the bad outcome is unlikely to occur). This cost is then considered as a loss.

As we can see, the theory of Loomes and Sugden (1982) posits the existence of feelings of regret and pleasure associated with a particular effect of a decision act. In our last example, regret is associated with the fact of having purchased an insurance that eventually proved to be useless whereas pleasure is associated with the opposite situation in which the same decision would allow the subscriber to avoid the expenses (or a great part of the expenses) resulting from an event cancellation (in case of a travel, think of hotel reservations, plane ticket purchases, car renting, and the like). Clearly, the main innovation behind this theory lies in its idea that the psychological experience of pleasure or displeasure associated with a particular result of an act of choice will depend not only on the result itself but also on the alternative outcomes that would have arisen had other shocks or eventualities been realized. This means that the individual asks questions like: *what if* the damage had not happened while it actually happened, or *what if* the damage had happened while it did not in reality?

The recent Covid-19 pandemic supplies us with a remarkable and topical illustration of the social inefficiency that behaviors of the type considered by Loomes and Sugden (1982) can lead to. In case an insurance has been subscribed, people lend more weight to the possibility of regrets engendered by the non-realization of the feared outcome than to the possibility of pleasure and satisfaction engendered by its realization. A criticism often addressed to governments in the West is that they have not taken sufficient precautionary measures to guard the population against the risk of an epidemic. Witness to this failure has been the lack of protective face masks, detection tests, respirators, etc. A plausible explanation is that these governments wanted to avoid the regret of having incurred significant expenses in the likely event that the epidemic would not reach their country. This is all the more understandable as past experiences seem to have guided present actions and policies. Thus, in France, popular frustrations and recriminations had been earlier voiced against Roselyne Bachelot, Minister of Health under a previous government, who made mass orders for a vaccine aimed at confronting a H1N1 flu pandemic which was threatening the country. As things turned out, however, the flu did not go beyond the frontiers of Asia, and Western Europe was eventually preserved. The reaction of many people was one of anger for the waste caused by the huge accumulation of useless vaccines. These are typically expressions of regret for having incurred expenses (paid by the taxpayer) which, ex post, appeared as though they could have been avoided. Ironically, the same voices were quick to blame the French government for a lack of precautionary measures when the Covid-19 crisis erupted. The hope is that the lesson will be retained for the future, in the same way as it happened in Southeast Asia (and the state of Kerala in South India), where governments were well prepared to face the same crisis when it hit their populations. This is because they had learned from the first SARS epidemic (known as SARS-1), which struck them just a few years earlier.

13.4 Going back to Chekhov

It is now time to return to Chekhov's two short stories. The first thing to note is that the heroes seem to be poorly informed about the opportunities available to them. This information failure is attributed to the multiple "occupations" that assail them on a daily basis and thereby prevent them from spending the time needed to detect opportunities and ponder about their worthiness. They thus appear as myopic individuals such as they are found in evolutionary economics (See Young, 1998; Gintis, 2000; Bowles, 2004). In evolutionary models of human behavior, the agents continue to be conceived as optimizing welfare or happiness over time, but this objective is now seen as being pursued through repeated trials and errors and through imitation and emulation. Chekhov, however, does not allow this type of conceptualization. For him, indeed, the routine and the absorption of the human mind and willpower into ceaseless daily occupations hinder the sort of systematic experimentation that forms the basis of the evolutionary approach to human behavior.

In this context of very limited rationality, it is not surprising that the two heroes, Bakhromkine and Iakov, prove unable to rationally anticipate the possibility of regret and pleasure mentioned by Loomes and Sugden (1982). Regret happens ex post when the decision has long been made and its effects begin to be felt and can no longer be changed. Moreover, regret and remorse are frequently experienced by individuals as they are so prone to make unreasoned acts of choice. The question is then how these painful feelings can be tamed. One solution consists of suppressing cognitive dissonance, implying that, through introspective reflection, individuals fabricate a self-justifying account of bad decisions made in the past. Here is evidently the solution chosen by the hero of *A discovery*. Yet, as shown in the second short story, *The violin of Rothschild*, such a solution may be infeasible because the errors caused by former bad decisions are so egregious that they are unjustifiable. Death is the only way out available. Could it be the case that the Chekhovian hero annihilates himself in a desperate move that would amount to a complete failure of his entire life? The Russian writer refuses to contemplate such a tragic end: the gift of the violin to Rothschild enables Iakov to bestow an ultimate meaning upon his miserable existence.

Let me try to highlight the difference between the two short stories reported in this essay. In the first story, regret is caused by the hero's failure to run a successful artistic career and, according to a psychoanalytical reading, to have met the desire and expectations of his mother. The loss here is essentially measured by the failure to have reached immortal glory, on the condition, of course, that Bakhromkine's talent has not been overestimated. The appeal of an administrative career providing stable and decent incomes is to be set against the expected benefits that accompany the dream of eternal celebrity. Since the latter is uncertain and the life of an artist is associated with the sacrifices of material insecurity, Bakhromkine finds it rather easy to self-justify his occupational choice when at the dawn of his life doubts emerged about its pertinence.

Likewise, Bakhromkine can easily reduce cognitive dissonance when by chance he comes across a woman whom he loved in his youth but whose beauty has been withered by the passing years. He consoles himself with the thought that the lost opportunity was actually a fake or illusory opportunity. As said earlier, Chekhovian heroes do not experiment. Therefore, they do not learn from their life experience. It is as though they are overwhelmed by so many surrounding circumstances and life is so complex that many factors come into play that acting rationally is impossible. Thus, the thought does not come to the mind of Bakhromkine that love is perhaps a feeling that does not abruptly befall and leave you. It is an emotion that is put to the test of real life and, in the best cases, is gradually built up and deepened as time goes on. As a result, the evaluation of a decision whose effects are experimented with in reality is different from an evaluation attempted from without by an external observer thinking abstractly. Since Bakhromkine clearly chooses the more comfortable second position, he can draw cheap consolation by conjuring up a thought that abstracts from the real-life dynamics of a human relationship. In other words, he can easily self-justify previous acts of choice because he refuses to genuinely contemplate what his life could have been had he chosen the alternative course of action. It is in this sense that his rambling on and philosophical speculations from the comfortable position of an ex post rationalizing spectator enable him to suppress the sort of reflections that precisely give rise to regret.

The situation exposed in the second story is different. It must first be stressed that the losses mentioned by Chekhov are not losses in the strict sense of the term but, as he himself points out on several occasions, they correspond to lost opportunities ("manques-à-gagner") or to what economists would call suboptimal profits or earnings. Iakov's obsession with all the opportunities for profit which he has missed reflects a deep and continuous regret, and yet the reader gains the impression that the most important regret, which dominates all others, has been caused by his inability to love and attend to his wife. Regret is not about the gradual erosion of a passionate youth love, like in the first story, but about the guilt born of a deeply asymmetric behavior: in return for the constant love and care offered by his wife, Iakov has given nothing. The air of satisfaction, and even happiness, discovered on the lips of his wife's face on the verge of her death has created an image which he cannot get rid of and causes him an unbearable pain.

The small earnings, lost on repeated occasions, appear insignificant and even ridiculously small when they are compared with the immeasurable and irreparable loss suffered on the level of love feelings and human decency. No self-justifying explanation can be found that would condone the crime of love denial and harsh behavior which Iakov has committed during most of his conjugal life. That this is an unforgivable crime is attested by the fact that his loveless wife was happy to leave this world. Only death can extinguish the remorse born of such a horrible deficiency. This is where the situation of Iakov fundamentally differs from Bakhromkine's: his tortured conscience does not see any light at the end of the tunnel. His satisfaction at the burial ceremony when he concludes that he has done a good job by fabricating a solid piece of work and that the costs have remained minimal looks tragic-comic in the light of this cruel reality that his life is essentially a failure and it is too late to change anything. Chekhov's idea in writing this passage seems to have been to indicate that Iakov's character is unchangeable and that, were he be granted a second chance, he would exactly repeat the same errors as in his first life. Iakov is unable to learn.

In my conception, the quality of a work of art is measured by the emotions that it arouses and by the multiple interpretations to which it may give rise, that is, by the degree of freedom left to the reader, the listener, or the spectator. In both respects, Chekhov proves to be a true master. On the one hand, one cannot help being moved by the human tragedies pictured in the two short stories and, on the other hand, it is evident that the interpretation I have offered above is not the only possible one. At least, it does certainly not exhaust the meaning content of these beautiful writings. To illustrate this point, let me point to two additional themes that run through *A discovery*. First, there is the aforementioned and puzzling excerpt in which Bakhromkine remembers the day his mother kissed the hands of a "drunk and hideous-looking" poet. In such a gesture, as has been already suggested, the economist sees the manifestation of a trade-off between material wellbeing and glory or social status. Some individuals have preferences such that they are ready to forego large incomes to achieve a better status, more social prestige, or higher esteem from others (for a striking empirical example, see Platteau and Seki, 2007). They may sometimes even be willing to sacrifice incomes and consumption in exchange for a bit of eternal glory, implying that they want to leave their imprint on future generations which they will never interact with physically.

There is then the provocative idea that a man who in his youth was attracted by a woman of "remarkable beauty whom one could fall in love with as easily as one can tread on the corn of a neighbour's foot" may well find her "oldish and repulsively ugly" twenty or twenty-five years later. Time had thus radically transformed the features and the appeal of a woman, so much so that she stopped being desirable and lovable for a man like Bakhromkine. The complex issue of "commitment", which plays an important role in the economic theory of contracts, can be detected here. Applied to marriage, it can be formulated as follows: on the basis of present perceptions and feelings, a man engages in a union with a woman whom he loves, perhaps passionately. Life circumstances (for example, a car accident or a descent into alcoholism or a nervous breakdown) or the simple biological process of aging have the effect of abruptly or gradually changing the physical appearance of the beloved wife. Because he does not recognize anymore the subject of his past love, the husband calls his initial decision into question. The temptation to break the union is then strong despite the promise made at the time when the contract was struck (see, for example, Baland and Ziparo, 2018). Note that the same story can be told with the woman rather than the man being tempted to leave a marriage.

There is no easy or universal solution to commitment problems such as this one. In many societies, the marriage institution has provided a rather effective way to constrain men and women to stay together. Often sacralized by reference to a god who acts as an invisible witness, it is founded on a promise of lifelong faithfulness "for the better and for the worse". It is by creating serious obstacles against divorce or separation, in the form of financial costs, peer pressure, and threats of exclusion from the family and community, that the institution of marriage has achieved its purpose in Catholic countries, in particular.

In Chekhov's first story, no marriage took place and the commitment problem did not therefore arise. Bakhromkine meets his youth love again at an advanced stage of his life and in a fortuitous way. This causes him a shock not because his love feeling suddenly re-emerges but, on the contrary, because he does not recognize the woman whom he had loved in a remote past. Instead of regret for having missed the opportunity to share life with her, he feels relief and satisfaction. He is actually lucky to be able to evade the difficult problem of re-assessing his initial choice. At least, this is how he perceives the situation today, after all these years during which a potential marriage life has not actually been experienced. How to explain the lucky state of Bakhromkine after meeting the woman of his dreams? It is certainly not due to his past ability to anticipate the future physical appearance of the beloved one. Chekhovian heroes are usually incapable of forward-lookingness. They make more or less myopic decisions, or their actions are driven by life circumstances over which they exert little control. Whichever is the case, reasoning does not have much influence on human choices, a characteristic which often shapes the tragic or the tragic-comic universe of the Russian writer.

Note finally that the problem of commitment in marriage needs not to arise for a reason that we have mentioned earlier: a human relationship is something dynamic and a spousal history is gradually constructed by living together and sharing common experiences (such as the love and upbringing of children). In successful cases, feelings of attachment add themselves to love or passion feelings, or they gradually substitute for them, thereby making the relationship durable and even harmonious. Or is it the case that what we call love takes on different forms as time passes, beginning with passion and ending with deep emotional attachment?

13.5 Learning from psychology

In choosing the characters of his heroes in the two selected short stories, Chekhov has made life difficult for economists. This is because their behavior violates important assumptions of not only standard microeconomic theory but also sophisticated variants such as regret theory. If Chekovian heroes often feel regret, this experience typically comes ex post because they are unable to anticipate it. Far from being forward-looking, these heroes tend to be myopic, an apparent consequence of the fact that they are overwhelmed by the continuous and petty concerns of ordinary life and unable to discern what are problems of primary or secondary importance. Moreover, they do not experiment and do not learn from their experience, and they seem to be governed by impulses rather than by the power of their reason. But can we really say that their behavior is sometimes impulsive, and hence unapproachable with the help of any economic theorizing? Doubts may be raised on this point in light of recent advances in the psychological theory of human behavior.

The idea is that, when contemplating a purchase, individuals anticipate great pleasure (utility) from ultimately getting the desired object, and it is on the basis of that anticipation that the purchase is eventually made. However, when the object is obtained (say, a new car), they often end up disappointed in the sense that actual pleasure proves to be smaller than anticipated pleasure. In other words, the concrete consumption experience does not provide as much enjoyment as they thought it would bring. We would then expect that, having become disillusioned with (big) consumption acts, people would later refrain from indulging in similar kinds of purchases. But it is not how things appear to be: the brain seems to remember the past in a way that is systematically biased, and people use this biased information to decide what to do next. More precisely, when a few years after a purchase they are asked to evaluate it, they tend to report a level of pleasure commensurate with their initial expectation, not the level they actually enjoyed (see Gilbert, 2005). Therefore, they continue to make similar purchases remembering how successful their past decisions have been. To put it in another way, people tend to decide on the basis of the *imagined* pleasure they have initially derived from previous consumption decisions, thus ignoring or underestimating their subsequent experience of disappointment. They then act as if more makes them happy, even though they are not getting all that much happier as they get more (Nechyba, 2011, pp. 731–732).

This psychological interpretation tends to explain why many predictions of standard economic theory are accurate despite the fact that there are many reasons to believe that they should not, particularly the facts that many dimensions of happiness are ignored by economists, and that real pleasure is different from anticipated pleasure. Coming back again to Chekhov, and to *The violin of Rothschild* in particular, it is possible to view Iakov's obsession with economic success not as the outcome of an impulsive, unreasoned behavior but as the effect of a systematically biased judgment about all his past experiences. Under this interpretation, rather than his inability to anticipate regret or properly assess his trials and errors, the problem is his vulnerability to biased judgments that ignore the disappointments that followed his past decisions. In sum, the main issue is less his myopia than his biased perception of reality when reality is of his own making. Social sciences would thus open up different ways of reading Chekhov and, reciprocally, insights from the stories of Chekhov stimulate social scientists to think their theories anew.

Notes

1 I wish to express my gratitude to François Bourguignon, Nicole Moguilevsky, and Alexis Platteau for their apt comments and suggestions, which helped me to improve the initial version of the text of this essay.

2 In his short story titled *The seagull with blue blood*, the Russian writer Igor Bouïda speaks about the art of Chekhov as one dominated by "his unrelenting irony combined with absolute compassion".

3 The English translations of all excerpts supplied in the present text, as well as the paraphrases, have been made by myself on the basis of French translations from Russian. I use the edition of the Livre de Poche (Paris, 2016), titled *Nouvelles* (*Short stories*), which is actually a re-edition of l'Age d'Homme (Paris, 1993). The preface, the translation, and the notes (from Russian to French) are the work of Vladimir Volkoff, a famous Russian writer of our time. The short story *A discovery* is featured in pp. 157–160, whereas *The violon of Rothschild* covers pp. 744–753.

4 Revealingly, Richard Thaler has chosen the title *Quasi-Rational Economics* for his 1991 book. As for the 1982 article of Graham Loomes and Robert Sugden, it bears the title "An Alternative Theory of Rational Choice Under Uncertainty".

5 In our example, social efficiency can be defined ex ante or ex post, that is, depending upon whether the random event has not yet occurred, or could actually be observed. In the former case, individual preferences about regret or pleasure are applied whereas in the latter case the past is forgotten since it is too late to strike an insurance deal that would mutualize the losses. When an individual forsakes insurance for fear of feeling regret in the future, there is an ex post social inefficiency from the standpoint of a model based on standard individual utilities (i.e., utilities which do not take regret into account). I want to thank François Bourguignon for having drawn my attention to the importance of this distinction.

6 Obviously, there are other reasons why an individual may refuse to buy an insurance policy, in particular the possibility that the mathematical expectation of insurance is negative as a result of the high premium demanded by the insurer. In the context of the present essay, however, we put the emphasis on the possibility of regret because it is this possibility that better highlights the two short stories written by Chekhov.

References

Baland, J.M., and R. Ziparo, "Intra-Household Bargaining in Poor Countries," in S. Anderson, L. Berman, and J.P. Platteau, eds., *Toward Gender Equity in Development* (Oxford: Oxford University Press, 2018), 69–96.

Bowles, S., *Microeconomics: Behavior, Institutions, and Evolution* (New York: Russell Sage Foundation, and Princeton: Princeton University Press, 2004).

Caplin, A., and J. Leahy, "Psychological Expected Utility Theory and Anticipatory Feelings", *The Quarterly Journal of Economics*, Vol. 116, N° 1 (2001), 55–79.

De Bock, O., W. Gelade, and J.P. Platteau, "The Demand for Microinsurance: A Literature Review", *World Development*, Vol. 94, N° 2 (2017), 139–156.

Gilbert, D., *Stumbling onto Happiness* (New York: Vintage Books, 2005).

Gintis, H., *Game Theory Evolving: A Problem-Centered Introduction to Modeling Strategic Interaction* (Princeton: Princeton University Press, 2000).

Gollier, C., *The Economics of Risk and Time* (MIT Press, 2001).

Kahneman, D., and A. Tversky, "Prospect Theory: An Analysis of Decision under Risk", *Econometrica*, Vol. 47 (1979), 263–291.

Kydland, F., and E. Prescott, "Rules Rather Than Discretion: The Inconsistency of Optimal Plans", *Journal of Political Economy*, Vol. 85, N° 3 (1977), 473–491.

Loomes, G., and R. Sugden, "Regret Theory: An Alternative Theory of Rational Choice Under Uncertainty", *Economic Journal*, Vol. 92 (1982), 805–824.

Nechyba, T.J., *Microeconomics: An Intuitive Approach* (South-Western, Cengage Learning, 2011).

Platteau, J.-P., "Mutual Insurance as an Elusive Concept in Traditional Rural Communities", *Journal of Development Studies*, Vol. 33 (1997), 764–796.

Platteau, J.P., and E. Seki, "Heterogeneity, Social Esteem and the Feasibility of Collective Action", *Journal of Development Economics*, Vol. 83, N° 2 (2007), 302–325.

Rabin, M., and R. Thaler, "Anomalies: Risk Aversion", *Journal of Economic Perspectives*, Vol. 15 (2001), 219–232.

Thaler, R.H., *Quasi-Rational Economics* (New York: Russell Sage Foundation, 1991).

Young, P., *Individual Strategy and Social Structure* (Princeton: Princeton University Press, 1998).

14

THE FINANCIAL EXPERT OF MALGUDI

Avinash Dixit

14.1 Introduction

What and where is Malgudi, and why does it have a financial expert? Surely financial experts (and financial schemers) are found in huge hubs like Wall Street or Mumbai.

Malgudi is a fictitious South Indian town that is the setting for many novels and short stories by R. K. Narayan. The subject of my chapter, *The Financial Expert*, is a novel set in the late 1930s and early 1940s (Narayan, 1952). Its central character is Margayya – "he who shows the way" – variously a scribe, a small-scale intermediary moneylender, and publisher of a sex manual. He acquires wealth from the last of these ventures and uses that money to launch a banking cum Ponzi scheme that inevitably comes crashing down on his head. Narayan relates all this, blended with accounts of life in a small south-Indian city and of feuds in an Indian extended family, in simple, sparkling, and charming prose and with a gentle touch of humor and irony – features which characterize all of Narayan's writings.[1] Here is his sketch of Margayya's financial expertise, perhaps better called naïveté, in one short paragraph[2]:

> There was probably no other person in the whole country who had meditated so much on the question of interest. Margayya's mind was full of it. Night and day he sat and brooded over it. The more he thought about it the more it seemed to him the greatest wonder of creation. It combined in it the mystery of birth and multiplication. Otherwise how could you account for the fact that a hundred rupees in a savings bank became a hundred and twenty in course of time? It was something like the ripening of corn. Every rupee, Margayya felt, contained within it seed of another rupee and that seed within it another seed and so on and on to infinity. It was something

DOI: 10.4324/9781003534358-18

like the firmament, endless stars and within each star another firmament and within each one further endless ... It bordered on mystic perception. It gave him the feeling of being part of an infinite existence.

14.2 The story

Margayya starts out in the novel as a kind of intermediary among the members of the town's "Central Cooperative Land Mortgage Bank". Many banks of this kind were established around India in the early decades of the twentieth century, to encourage saving and to make loans available at reasonable rates to its member depositors. Margayya sits under a banyan tree across the street outside the bank and makes himself available to all the customers who visit the bank, usually to apply for loans. The maximum amount one can borrow depends on the size of one's account and one's track record of repayment installments of previous loans. Many people need to borrow more than their entitlement, often for the expense and dowry payment for the marriages of their daughters. In such situations Margayya entices someone else with spare borrowing capacity to use it, and to re-lend that money at a much higher interest rate to the one in need, charging a commission for his services. He knows all the intricacies of the bank's rules, so he can maximize the total of his clients' borrowing capacity. On occasion, he extends his own small loan, of course at interest, to a person who can then make partial repayment of one loan from the bank, just enough to unlock a much bigger new loan to be re-lent as described above. The outcome of all these transactions following the "way" Margayya "shows" is that his customers spend a lot by borrowing at high rates, thus defeating the very purpose of the cooperative bank, which was to encourage thrift and deter usurious lending; more on this later. Margayya keeps the details of deposits and borrowings of many members of the bank in his head, so he knows from whom he can obtain the funds and who might need them, and keeps records of his transactions in an account book, so he can ensure payment from the borrowers (by personal and social pressure, not based on any formal contracts or recourse to formal law). He also keeps on hand a supply of blank loan application forms and fills them for his usually illiterate clients, again charging a fee for this service.

The family house is partitioned between Margayya and his older brother. The two families are "on throat-cutting terms", and the brother is doing better financially. That and the various humiliations he suffers from the employees of the bank drive Margayya to the limits of his frustration and anger. He comes to the conclusion that if only he has a lot more money, he will get respect from the likes of the bank officer, and not have to shirk from tradesmen to whom he owes money. He will buy good material things for his wife and provide a good education for his son. But fate takes away even his meager livelihood of small-scale lending and intermediation.

Margayya has only one child – Balu, an utterly spoilt boy. But one day when Margayya is busy with his account book at home, Balu interferes and annoys him too much. In the resulting fracas, Balu grabs the account book and throws it into a gutter outside the house running with dirty water, and it disappears down the drain. This is a disaster for Margayya. Without written evidence of loans he had provided, many of his customers weasel out of what they owed him. (Lesson for other financial intermediaries: keep backup copies.)

He goes to the local temple of Lakshmi – the goddess of wealth – and has his horoscope examined by the priest, who tells him that his misfortune is caused by the bad influence of Saturn, so he should go to another temple with planetary deities, to propitiate Saturn with an offering of honey to its priest. (I wonder: do priests have a cross-referral system to maximize incomes in cash or kind for the whole priestly tribe, as medical and legal specialists seem to?)

He also has to perform ritual prayers (puja) to Lakshmi for forty days. The materials needed for that include a red lotus flower obtainable only from a remote spot outside town. While getting it, he meets Dr. Pal, a journalist who also claims to be a psychologist and sociologist, and author of a manuscript he has titled Bed-Life, or the Science of Marital Happiness. We are not given details, but it is clear that the book would be regarded as pornographic by the moral standards of Indian society of that time. Pal expects to sell 100,000 copies year after year at 1 rupee each. The sum, 100,000 rupees, is staggering for Margayya, who made only about 200 rupees each month in his now-collapsed business. For whatever reason, and in one of the weirdest scenes of negotiation I have read in literature, Pal gives the manuscript to Margayya to print and sell, for only 25 rupees. Margayya takes it to a printery, whose owner Madan Lal reads it with fascination, but worries that "if it comes under the obscenity law … they may put us both in prison". Margayya repeats the assurance that Pal had given him: "It's not obscene. It's a work of sociology". Finally, Lal agrees to publish it if the title is changed to Domestic Harmony, if he is indemnified against any legal action, and given a 50% share of the profits.

Of course, the book is a great commercial success. Margayya becomes rich, and a well-regarded man in Malgudi with a confident swagger. I guess Saturn moved away from the bad place in Margayya's horoscope, and Lakshmi answered his prayers! There is even some reconciliation with his brother. Balu is doing very badly in school, but Margayya uses his money and influence to secure for himself a place on the school board. He also hires one of the school's teachers as a private tutor for his son. Naturally, Balu's grades improve! Even better, Balu strikes a bargain with the teacher "by which the teacher himself should do all the sums and not bother him except to show him what marks he had obtained for them".

After a few years, Margayya gets fed up with the printing business and is a little ashamed of being known as the publisher of Domestic Harmony. He also develops his theory of money and interest, which I quoted above. After two days of convoluted negotiations with Madan Lal, where each party pretends to be doing the other a favor and secretly believes himself to be getting a great bargain, he agrees to sell his share in the book for a lump sum. He uses this to start a lending business, at high interest rates against dodgy securities that no bank would touch, and then seizes the assets when the borrowers cannot keep up the interest and repayments. He connects up again with Dr. Pal, who helps him find an office, and is eventually hired to help in a new line of expansion of Margayya's business – to attract deposits from people who have become rich in the wartime economy, by promising high interest rates.

He lives a life of affluence and even develops a paunch, although he remains in his old small partitioned-house home and has his wife do the cleaning and cooking. But family life hits a big bump – Balu flunks his high school graduation examination (administered by a state board beyond Margayya's ambit of corrupt control). There go Margayya's dreams of sending Balu to college and then to further studies in Europe or America! Angry at his father's recriminations, Balu walks out of the home. He is next heard of as having died in Madras. Margayya rushes there, but fortuitously on the train meets a police officer who investigates and finds that the letter about Balu's supposed death was sent by a rich but crazy man who had employed him, and who sends many such letters, as well as letters (saying what, we are not told) to Roosevelt, Stalin, Churchill, and others. The policeman also locates Balu, and Margayya promises Balu total freedom upon his return home. He and his wife spoil Balu even more than before; Balu takes full advantage of his newfound power and "devote[s] himself to the art of cultivating leisure".

Margayya decides to arrange a marriage for Balu. His wealth enables him to conceal his low-caste ancestry and attract proposals from many rich families, including the owner of a tea estate whose daughter has the necessary qualities: good looks and the prospect of a large dowry.[3] The girl's and Balu's horoscopes don't match due to some misalignment of stars in the latter, but money enables Margayya to buy the services of an astrologer who "rearrange[s] the stars of Balu to suit the circumstances". Margayya gives Balu a house, which he had acquired by foreclosing on a mortgage, in a good part of the town.

Margayya's deposit-taking business flourishes. He offers twenty percent interest rates, claiming that his other business earns him twenty-five. Everyone in Malgudi wonders how he does it. Banks are puzzled; they are losing deposits to him. He is believed to be a wizard.

> But the fact was there that he seemed to need new clients each day. … [He] calculated: 'If I get twenty thousand rupees deposits each day and pay fifteen in interest, I have still five thousand a day left in my hands as my own'.

So the wizardry was just a classic Ponzi scheme. At the end of each day, he takes home the money "left in his hands as his own", counts it, and locks it up in a safe, presumably so that each rupee note can release the seed inside it to grow into another rupee! He obsesses over the business so much that his health starts to suffer.

Then one day Balu comes to Margayya's office and demands half of all that wealth as his share, claiming that it grew out of the ancestral property, and therefore he is entitled to it on attaining his age of majority. Perhaps he was put up to this by Dr. Pal, who has gotten pally with him and has introduced him to the world of wine, women, and song. Margayya, worrying about Balu's demand all evening, goes to his house late at night to discuss it. He discovers that Balu is not home yet, that he is with Dr. Pal gambling, drinking, and cavorting with girls, that this is a frequent occurrence, and that his wife is miserable about it. (I wonder if this carries a lesson: don't manipulate what horoscopes say about the misalignment of a prospective couple's stars; else it will end badly?) Then he sees Balu arrive home in a car driven by Dr. Pal, with two girls. Margayya pulls Dr. Pal out of the car and beats him up quite severely.

Dr. Pal goes to the police and lodges a complaint of assault against Margayya. He also talks to his friends about the incident and asserts that Margayya has gone crazy. When the news gets around, Margayya's investors start to demand their deposits back. The Ponzi scheme quickly collapses. Margayya has to declare bankruptcy. The house in which he and his brother live cannot be attached, but all other assets are seized. Balu and his family are thrown out of their house and are back to the small half-house where Margayya lives.

Margayya offers Balu what remains of his inheritance from "ancestral property" – the tin box in which he kept his ink, pen, and paper to take every day to his place under the banyan tree in front of the cooperative bank – and tells him: "Go there, that is all I can say. Anything may happen thereafter". But Balu won't: "What will people think?" So Margayya decides to go back to his old work himself. The world has come full circle for him!

14.3 Narayan's style

Narayan draws Margayya as a complex character: a mixture of shrewdness and naïveté, intelligence and stupidity, pride and humility, self-confidence and timidity. His depiction of the galaxy of other Malgudi characters – Margayy's wife and son, the bank's officer and his peon, the priest, the printer, and above all Dr. Pal – is as varied and as brilliantly brought to life as the galaxy of New Orleans characters surrounding Ignatius Reilly in John Kennedy Toole's posthumously published and acclaimed novel *A Confederacy of Dunces*. He sketches and evokes the whole atmosphere of a small city in the south of India in the mid-twentieth century with a deft touch. The set-piece scenes of negotiations between Margayya and Dr. Pal, Margayya and Madan Lal, and Margayya and various borrowers and depositors are amusing in the strategies and language used by the parties. And all this is set in the context of the economic and business activities of Malgudi's residents, making the book especially interesting to us economists. In all, a book to be read, enjoyed, re-read, and remembered.

14.4 The economics

Of the inferences and lessons readers can draw from the novel, most should be evident to economists, but some they may not have thought about, and others they can use for informing general readers and teaching students.

Of course, the main theme is Margayya's Ponzi scheme, which collapsed as they all do sooner or later, but in a different way than most. The usual end is when the new customers become harder and harder to acquire, and the schemer does not get enough new money to pay interest to the older depositors. But in this case it was an unrelated event that triggered a tsunami of withdrawal demands. Perhaps a similar incident (in the setting of a more legitimate bank than Margayya's) occurs in the movie Mary Poppins. Michael, the small boy who is one of the main characters in that story, is visiting his father at the bank where he works and is carrying two pennies to buy a bag of nuts to feed the birds in Trafalgar Square later. The father's boss tries to persuade Michael to deposit the money in the bank where it will grow, and when the boy resists, he grabs the coins from him. Michael shouts: "Give me back my money". Some customers who are in the bank for their own businesses overhear this, misinterpret it, think that the bank won't allow a withdrawal so it must be in trouble, rush to withdraw their own money, and of course cause a bank run. These are nice illustrations of a general lesson from economics and game theory: coordination games usually have two equilibria. Here if everyone believes that the bank is safe, they keep their deposits intact and the bank is indeed safe; if people start to believe that the bank is in trouble, they rush to get ahead in the queue to withdraw their money, and the bank goes bust. And it is usually easier to flip from the "good" equilibrium to the "bad" one than vice versa. As Vergil (29–19 BCE [2008]) said, "facilis descensus Averno".[4]

Margayya's "intermediation" between the customers of the Cooperative Bank is enhancing conventional economic efficiency by closing the gap between someone's willingness to pay interest on a loan and another's incremental cost of supplying those funds. If we accept people's preferences as revealed through their actions, this is an improvement in the efficiency of resource allocation, and we should applaud Margayya. But with a better understanding of the psychological and sociological influences on individual actions, behavioral economists now recognize that these actions may be detrimental to people's own underlying or System II preferences. Therefore, we are more willing to accept policies or "nudges" that counter these System I instincts, social pressures, etc. In this instance, social pressure, desire to outdo others, or cultural imperative leads people to spend too much on their daughters' weddings; that is a primary cause of their wanting to borrow beyond their credit limit at the bank and willingness to pay very high interest rates for that extra borrowing. Cooperative banks attempted to restrain this excessive spending by facilitating saving in a secure institution and limiting borrowing. Margayya undermined this very purpose.

Another way of looking at this is to think of the population's collective overspending on daughters' marriages as a prisoner's dilemma or a rat race. The bank's borrowing constraints were a kind of social commitment device to resolve that dilemma. Margayya undermined the credibility of that commitment, thereby restoring the bad equilibrium of the dilemma.

Such unforeseen consequences plague and defeat many economic policies. For example, in many advanced economies, and especially in the United States, the complex rules of income taxation and tax-deductibility of interest payments, different depreciation schedules for different asset classes, etc., even though each may be justifiable on its own, can be "arbitraged" to reduce or even eliminate many personal and corporate tax liabilities. Governments should try to foresee such possibilities. My most important advice to every policy-making department is to appoint a small group of extremely smart young people to act as devil's advocates, or like the "red team" In war gaming. Every new policy proposal should be given to them to take apart and examine whether and how it can be arbitraged and nullified, or exploited for private gain at public cost, by itself or in combination with other existing policies.

Another noteworthy point for economists is the corruption involved in Balu's schooling. Corruption in India's school system is well known. Public schools are of low quality due to corruption in the construction of buildings, choice of textbooks, appointment of teachers, absenteeism of teachers, … the list is almost endless. The process of licensing and accreditation of private schools has its own corruption. "Tutorial" or "coaching" classes can be profiteering and narrowly tailored to tests and add their element of corruption in acquiring and selling examination questions. The process of grading answers is often corrupted.[5] Margayya's actions add another feature – corruption initiated by parents to get their children admitted, promoted from one grade to the next, and eventually graduated. This is corruption initiated by the demand side of education, rather than the more common corruption within, or initiated by, the education establishment, i.e., the supply side. The latter seems rare in more advanced countries, but the former exists: the admissions scandal that erupted in 2019 in the United States involved some rich and famous parents paying large sums to get their children admitted to high-ranking colleges and universities including Georgetown, Stanford, UCLA, and Yale. An interesting twist there was to bribe coaches of sports and athletic teams, who would then admit the children falsely as part of their quotas for highly skilled athletes.[6]

I mentioned the complexity of Margayya's character. Such complexity is common to most human beings. Economics used to ignore most of these aspects and focused on a narrow picture of Homo Economicus: rational maximizers of a consistent and clear objective, usually a utility function that included their own consumption of material goods and services, sometimes extended to include dynastic concerns for their descendants' utilities. Margayya does have such a Homo Economicus in his personality. He wants money for the things it will buy his wife and the things and education it will buy his son, and he is willing to work hard and long hours to achieve these aims.[7] But he also wants money for the respect it will earn him, so he won't be insulted by the Cooperative Bank's secretary and his peon, so he can get the upper hand in dealing with his brother's family that lives in the other half of the family house, and so on. Through the middle of the novel, we see Margayya's understandable self-interest grow into obsessive greed: "He saw offices and shops opened and people sweating and fatiguing themselves, all for money. … Cars were being driven towards Lawley Extension.[8] Huge cars. He watched them greedily. 'If I have money, I need not dodge that spectacle dealer. I need not cringe before that stores man. … I could give those medicines to my wife. … That Balu, I could give him everything.' He would grow into an aristocrat. … He would buy another bungalow in Lawley Road for his son". I will have more to say about excessive greed in a separate section.

If Margayya's motives and actions are complex, those of Dr. Pal are even more so. In his first meeting with Margayya, he seems an other-worldly habitue of a temple in the forest, finding it a peaceful place for his writing. He claims to be following the thousand-year-old tradition of Vatsyayana, who wrote the Kama Sutra. He stresses that it is a work of sociology, and his aim is "to create happiness in this world. … I want to serve mankind with my knowledge". Although he believes his book will be a huge best-seller – every one of India's population of three hundred and sixty million will buy a copy – he claims to care only for work, human relationships, and service to mankind. He offers the book and all its rights to Margayya in exchange for what Margayy has in his pocket. Surely Pal cannot have expected much, and it turns out to be only twenty-five rupees, far less than the one lakh (100,000) that Pal expects the book will earn each year. But later the same Pal works with Margayya to set up his Ponzi scheme, and cultivates Balu's friendship and corrupts him, surely sponging on him for money and other things.

During the last three decades or so, economists have recognized some complexity of human behavior and have used findings from psychology to integrate into their thinking departures from the Homo Economicus model such as framing, endowment effect, loss aversion, overconfidence, and confirmation bias. But in my opinion, not even psychologists have as much insight into the human mind as do the best fiction writers.

Where do these insights matter most? In the usual supply-demand analysis of markets with a large number of participants, aggregates matter. In a demand curve that adds or averages choices of large numbers of consumers, complex motivations of individuals may matter less. Most "anomalies" or departures from the Homo Economicus model that have been found by psychologists and now labeled behavioral economics still yield a downward-sloping market demand curve, and statistical methods, rather than theories, help the economist estimate its elasticity and other relevant parameters. But individual motives and behavior become much more important in game-theoretic situations that pit two or a small number of individuals together; behavioral insights are likely to prove even more important for understanding strategic games than markets. That is why we find such interesting quirks and tactics in the various negotiations of Margayya and others that Narayan describes. I gave a brief quote from the dialog where Dr. Pal gives him the book rights; here is another from his negotiation with Madan Lal where he in turn sells the remaining book rights.

First, he offers Lal lunch; "My wife has sent something special today … and I thought you might like to taste it". Then he makes his proposal: "Lal, you have done a lot for me. I want to do a good turn to you". To Lal that sounded suspicious, Margayya would never do a good turn except for a good return. They talk around the subject, exploring each other's real motives. It needed two days of rambling, challenging, and philosophical talk before they struck a deal, in which each secretly thought he got seventy-five percent of the total. What a neat combination of tactics to soften up the other party – Margayya putting Lal under a slight social obligation with the lunch, pretending to be doing him a favor with the offer, Lal's response that he is the one who has sacrificed financially so far in the business, and so on – all done ultimately in pursuit of simple financial self-interest! Not many game-theoretic models of bargaining include such convoluted cheap talk and attempts at psychological manipulation, including the question of why it might work at all.[9] I hope future research in behavioral game theory will enrich our understanding of the role of cheap talk.

14.5 Excessive and obsessive greed

The ruthless trader and corporate raider Gordon Gekko (played by Michael Douglas) in the movie Wall Street says: "Greed … is good. Greed works". But ultimately the movie and indeed most literary works carry a strong message that greed is bad and leads to disasters for the greedy and their families and friends alike.[10] Economists are somewhere in between. We recognize that actions taken in pursuit of self-interest can benefit society. Adam Smith's key idea –

> It is not from the benevolence of the butcher, the brewer, or the baker, that we expect our dinner, but from their regard to their own interest. We address ourselves, not to their humanity but to their self-love, and never talk to them of our own necessities but of their advantages.

– has been central to our discipline since 1776.[11] But we also recognize that the Invisible Hand has a limited span, and many consequences when greed is carried to excess – monopolies, illegal and criminal activities, and so on – harm society. Margayya's growing greed and overambition (in combination with his absurd theory that money grows by seeding) lead him to the banking and Ponzi schemes, and ultimately to ruin for himself, his family, and many of his customers.

I would like to discuss briefly two other works of fiction that have as their major theme the harm caused by excessive greed. One is a novel by Aravind Adiga, my favorite among the many famous and stellar Indian authors writing in English today.[12] Adiga achieved fame with his Man Booker prize-winning first novel, *The White Tiger*, now made into a movie. But I prefer his second, *Last Man in Tower* (2011), which has a lot of economics content. The story features a mid-rise, middle-income condominium building in a suburb of Mumbai. It is about 40 years old and gently decaying. A property developer wants to buy and demolish it, to replace it with a luxury high-rise, but needs the unanimous consent of the residents to be bought out. One of the residents, honorifically called Masterji, is a retired schoolteacher, well-respected among the residents, who helps as a volunteer tutor to their children (although from the depictions in the novel I think he is a terrible teacher). He has many and long memories vested in his home and does not want to move. Some other residents support him initially, but gradually they are too tempted by the sums offered. Matters deteriorate, and in the end the others kill Masterji and make it look like a suicide. They grab him in his sleep, throw him off the top of the building, and claim that he had been depressed lately and must have jumped off. They think and say among themselves, "It's just a little push". What starts out as the other residents' self-interest – as with Margayya, understandable and normal desire to give their families good health care, their children a good education and some starting capital for a career, and so on – grows into obsessive greed, hatred for the person they see as the obstacle to their deserved compensation from the developer, and ultimately to murder.[13] I hope no one will claim that this was the invisible hand working toward a Pareto improvement. This was a very visible set of hands, doing what one resident with qualms recognized: "It's not just a push. It is killing a man". He stays away from participation in the actual deed, but does not inform on the others. Initially, he refuses his share of the builder's money for the apartments, but in the end the 1.5 crore rupees (about $250,000 at the time) proves too much even for him.

Perhaps the best piece of writing condemning greed that I know is Tolstoy's (1886 [1950]) story, *How Much Land Does a Man Need?* Here is a very brief summary. The protagonist Pahom accepts a deal from the rural tribe of Bashkirs that sells land for "one thousand rubles a day". As much land as you can enclose by running around it in a day, marking the boundaries as you go along, is yours, but if you fail to return to the starting point by sunset, you lose your money and get no land. Pahom starts out well, then sees better land farther ahead during his run, gets greedy, tries for too much, and leaves too little time for his return. With a final burst of speed, he gets back to the starting point only at the last second as the sun sets. But his heart gives out from that exertion, and he drops dead. His servant digs a grave for him. "Six feet from his head to his heels was all he needed"!

As an economist, I feel compelled to think of this, not as a parable about greed per se, but about handling it badly. Pahom faced a problem of optimization under uncertainty with huge stakes. He should have solved it carefully, using Kahneman's conscious and deliberative System II, not giving in to temptations that often sway actions in the instinctive System I. His loss function was highly asymmetric: if he is a little too cautious, he gets a little less land than he might have; if he attempts even slightly too much, he gets zero land, forfeits 1000 rubles, and may end up dead. So the optimal trade-off favors caution.[14] Economics has learned a lot from psychologists and writers; perhaps we can teach them something in return!

When does normal self-interest turn into obsessive greed? Literature tells us that there is no clear answer or sharp precipice, but there is always a slippery slope. Gordon Gekko and perhaps Pahom were always greedy. Margayya became obsessed through his life's hard knocks and growing bitterness about others' fortunes. Residents of the "tower" differed greatly, among themselves and in the timing of their descent into murder. Just as economists' beloved "representative consumer" is a character of fiction, there is no "representative greedy individual" in fiction or in reality.

14.6 The R.K. brothers

Although outside my remit, I cannot end without mentioning another favorite Indian: R.K. Narayan's youngest brother R.K. Laxman, who achieved great success and fame as a brilliant cartoonist commenting on many political, social, and economic issues in India.[15] My favorite example, perfect for the time when I wrote this in May-June 2022, shows up the problem of rising petrol (gas) prices by depicting a pump as a robber, pointing its hose trigger like a gun at Laxman's ubiquitous character, the Common Man.[16]

Great artists distill important universal truths from very specific and even mundane situations. The R.K. brothers were at such a skill level. It has been my pleasure to describe just a small sample, and perhaps to introduce them to some Western readers, from the perspective of an economist.

Notes

1 Graham Greene, who championed Narayan and his writings in the west, compared him to Chekov. Other famous writers and reviewers have compared him to Nicolai Gogol, O. Henry, Guy de Maupassant, William Faulkner, and others. The sheer variety of these comparisons proves what Narayan was: uniquely Narayan. A good short account of his life and works is in the Wikipedia article, https://en.wikipedia.org/wiki/R._K._Narayan.

2 I will offer a few more quotes illustrating Narayan's light and deft touch in the pages that follow.
3 I was reminded of Lady Bracknell in *The Importance of Being Earnest* (Wilde, 1899 [1990]):

> A hundred and thirty thousand pounds! And in the Funds! Miss Cardew seems to me a most attractive young lady, now that I look at her. Few girls of the present day have any really solid qualities, any of the qualities that last, and improve with time.
>
> *("Funds" refers to British government securities, which were very safe investments in Victorian times, much like U.S. Treasury bonds today.)*

4 Vergil (29–19 BCE [2008]) 6:126.
5 Good but journalistic accounts can be found in https://www.educationworld.in/dirty-dozen-corrupt-practices-destroying-indian-education/ and https://www.hindustantimes.com/india-news/rot-in-education-students-suffer-as-corruption-politics-plague-the-system/story-cNnB8ZoPgXpbVnrZjy0nIM.html. The latter shows a photograph of relatives standing at windows outside the building to pass answers to examination candidates inside.
6 See the account in https://en.wikipedia.org/wiki/2019_college_admissions_bribery_scandal.
7 We regard concern for family as a component of Homo Economicus preferences (think of models of the Ricardo and Barro type), but it also has sociological or cultural basis (father-son social relation), or even more fundamentally, it is an evolutionary imperative (Margayya's selfish gene wanting to continue its existence).
8 A newer and richer part of Malgudi.
9 Another of my favorite examples of cheap talk in literature is Henry V's speech in the Shakespeare play, just before the battle of Agincourt to inspire his soldiers to fight, risking injury or even death. When Henry says "We few, we happy few, we band of brothers/For he to-day that sheds his blood with me/Shall be my brother; be he ne'er so vile,/This day shall gentle his condition", he is not promising them knighthoods or a life in his palace as his brothers. Why does such an essentially empty speech succeed in its purpose?
10 Examples of this in literature are too numerous to cite; perhaps the most prominent appear in the writings of Balzac and Dickens. I also think of B. Traven's (1935 [2020]) novel *The Treasure of the Sierra Madre*, and its memorable movie adaptation directed by John Huston and starring Humphrey Bogart. The few exceptions include works like Ayn Rand's *The Fountainhead* (1943) and *Atlas Shrugged* (1957) that applaud individualism and laissez-faire capitalism and are very critical of any state intervention or collectivism, but even Rand seems to prefer words like "ego" ("A man's ego is the fountainhead of human progress"), not "greed".
11 Adam Smith (1776 [1970]), Book 1, Chapter 2.
12 Chetan Bhagat, Jhumpa Lahiri, Rohinton Mistry, Arundhati Roy, Salman Rushdi, Vikram Seth, and Vikas Swarup, to mention just a few.
13 The novel has much more to recommend it. The character sketches of the residents, and accounts of their relationships and interactions, are brilliantly written. And there is much incidental economics – about real estate development in Mumbai, variety of work and attitudes toward it among the middle classes, and so on.
14 The cost of error is linear (less land in proportion to the excess caution) on one side and a large fixed cost (in this case death) on the other side. Similarly asymmetric trade-offs occur in many instances. For example, if you are cautious in getting to an airport and arrive five minutes too early at the gate for your flight, you have wasted five minutes; if you are incautious and arrive five minutes too late, you have wasted much more time (until the next available flight) and a lot of money (change fees

incurred or even total forfeiture of the fare paid, any business lost, hotel room prepayment forgone at the destination, and so on). See my paper "How early should you plan to arrive for a flight?", at http://www.princeton.edu/~dixitak/home/wrkps.html.

15 In the part of South India where the brothers were born, one's given personal name comes last. The first initial is for one's ancestral town (in this case Rasipuram) and the second initial is one's father's given name (in this case Krishnaswami). Therefore, the full name identifies a person as "from such-and-such a place, son of so-and-so, called so-and-so". For example, the renowned economist T.N. Srinivasan's family hailed from Thirukodikaval, and his father's given name was Nilakanta. That is how the R.K. brothers share their initials but have different last – actually first – names.

16 See his obituary notice in the Times of India: https://www.indiatimes.com/news/india/rip-r-k-laxman-the-country-lost-its-real-common-man-today-229726.html.

References

Adiga, Aravind. *Last Man in Tower* (New York, NY: HarperCollins, 2011).

Narayan, R.K. *The Financial Expert* (London, UK: Methuen, 1952; New York, NY: Time Inc. Paperbacks, 1966).

Rand, A. *The Fountainhead* (Indianapolis, IN: Bobbs Merrill, 1943).

Rand, A. *Atlas Shrugged* (New York, NY: Random House, 1957).

Smith, A. *The Wealth of Nations* (London, UK: W. Stratham and T. Cadell, 1776; London, UK: Penguin Books 1970).

Tolstoy, L. "How much land does a man need?" In *Twenty-three Tales*, translated by Louise Maude and Aylmer Maude (Oxford, UK: Oxford University Press, 1886 [1950]). The full text is available from https://www.online-literature.com/tolstoy/2738/

Traven, B. *The Treasure of the Sierra Madre* (Leyden, MA: Aeonian Press, 1935; London: Macmillan Picador Paper, 2020).

Vergil (Publius Vergilius Maro) *The Aeneid* (unknown publisher, 29–19 BCE; English translation by Robert Fagels, London: Penguin Classics, 2008).

Wilde, O. *The Importance of Being Earnest* (London, UK: Leonard Smithers & Co., 1899, Mineola, NY: Dover Publications, 1990).

15

ESTATES, INHERITANCES AND GIFTS

Looking a gift horse in the mouth

Luiz De Mello

15.1 Introduction

What a better way to look at the economic aspects of intergenerational transfers, such as estates, inheritances and in-life gifts, than through the lens of Machado de Assis's *The Inheritance* (Machado de Assis, 2012)?

Machado, for short, is probably not among the most widely read Latin American writers, but he is no doubt one of the greatest on account of his innovative narrative, elegant prose and satirical style. A prolific novelist, as well as play and short story writer, he lived through the second half of the 19th century (1839–1908), a period of wide-ranging economic and political transformation in his native Brazil. Often described as a late romantic, he was also a pioneer of Portuguese language realism and had a broad range of interests, including social norms, values and attitudes, which permeate his work.

International literary acclaim came late in Machado's life, but it is by no means small. For example, Harold Bloom included Machado in his list of the greatest 100 geniuses of literature as "the supreme black literary artist to date" (Bloom, 2002). Michael Wood argues that "Machado's short stories resemble those of Chekhov in their talent for saying too little (that is, just enough), even though it could be contended that Machado is closer in style to Henry James, especially on his longer pieces" (Wood, 2018). He goes on to say,

> Machado often engages in an open playfulness with the reader. In the stories and in the novels, his style of wit belongs with that of Henry Fielding or Laurence Sterne, whose work he knows well. We could also cite the company he could not know he would come to keep, that of Vladimir Nabokov and Italo Calvino.

DOI: 10.4324/9781003534358-19

Ilan Stavans adds that

> What makes his work compelling is that he doesn't do what we expect him to do for an author of his time, especially for someone who lived and wrote in an age convinced that art was to serve as a platform for communication with the muses.
>
> *(Stavans, 2018)*

Endorsements in the English edition of *Dom Casmurro* (translated by Helen Caldwell), one of his most celebrated and widely translated novels, include those of Allen Ginsberg, who called Machado "another Kafka", and Philip Roth, who referred to Machado as "a great ironist, a tragic comedian" (Caldwell, 2014).

Economics comes up one way or another almost everywhere in Machado's work. It does so explicitly in hundreds of chronicles – or Op-eds in today's parlance – on economic and financial matters, often published under pseudonyms in Rio de Janeiro's leading papers of his day. Rio was then the court of Brazil's empire and subsequently the country's capital following the establishment of the republic in 1889. These economic writings have been analysed competently by Gustavo Franco (Franco, 2007a), former governor of the Brazilian central bank and a careful reader of Machado.[1] Economics also comes up in more subtle guises in Machado's work, as "money and the business of keeping up appearances are large questions" in Machado's social satire and witty interpretation of his characters (Wood, 2018). Indeed, the socio-economic aspects of Machado's work have been analysed in great depth by Raymundo Faoro (Faoro, 1974), one of the key references to Machado among literary critics in his native Brazil. Gledson (1984, 1986) also discusses Machado's economic writings extensively. Incidentally, much ink has been spent more recently on Machado's alleged ambivalence to slavery, still legal in Brazil during most of his life, given his own ethnic background.

An economic theme that was looked at by Machado in his characteristically satirical style is that of inheritance, or what could be generalised in economic terms as intergenerational wealth transfers, including post-mortem bequests and in-life (inter vivos) gifts in particular. Machado writes about the reasons that motivate people to bequeath their wealth, at least in part, to their family or close relatives, as well as the expectations of those on the receiving end of an inheritance, including notions of equity and fairness that are at the heart of these expectations. Aside from these individual-level considerations, or what may be considered to be economically rational or driven primarily by sentiment, Machado also points to broader implications of inheritance that could be interpreted (at least by readers with an economic interest!) from a macroeconomic vantage point. This chapter will therefore draw inspiration from Machado's *The Inheritance* (*A Herança*), published originally in Rio's *Jornal das Famílias* newspaper in 1878.

Of course, it would be presumptuous to claim that Machado is the only great writer to have put pen to paper about the theme of intergenerational wealth transfers and its economic rationality underpinnings. Others have done so, too. For example, in *Bleak House* Dickens writes about an estate being depleted to pay for the legal costs of a protracted dispute regarding inheritance rights. In *Our Mutual Friend*, he exploits the conditions imposed by donors on heirs for receipt of an inheritance. In *Portrait of a Lady*, Henry James deals with the theme of inheritance against a backdrop of marriage and betrayal. In *The Capital*, Eça de Queiroz writes about the depletion of a bequest by a provincial heir with literary ambitions in pursuit of prestige and recognition among Lisbon's intellectual elite. The heir's fate is tragic: not only does he fail to fulfil his ambition but he is also forced to return to his hometown and live off his aunts after squandering his inheritance. In all these cases, however, the inheritance is a means to deal with other themes: greed and murder in the case of *Bleak House*, disguise and concealment in the case of *Our Mutual Friend*, financial independence in the case of *Portrait of a Lady*, and social status and recognition in the case of *The Capital*. The theme of expectation of an inheritance and how it shapes behaviour comes up in F. Scott Fitzgerald's *The Beautiful and the Damned* and *The Absolution*.

Shakespeare takes a different tack and looks at the motivations to leave a bequest in *King Lear*, when the elderly king decides to retire and divide his realm among his three daughters, offering the largest share to the one who shows the greatest love for him. Even though there are many interpretations to King Lear, from political to psychoanalytical, the transactional motive for leaving a bequest – as will be discussed at some length in what follows – comes up in the play in a manner that is akin to that in Machado's *The Inheritance*. Several parallels have been drawn between King Lear and Balzac's *Père Goriot*, but rather than using an inheritance in his plot, Balzac focuses on the theme of in-life gifts from parents to their children. There, family relations, paternal devotion and unscrupulous ambitions are central to the narrative.

This chapter will discuss the theme of intergenerational wealth transfers from Machado's vantage point and from that of modern economic thinking. The motivations and expectations of both donors and recipients, as well as the broader economic implications of such transfers, will also be discussed, including for policy design and implementation – my own job conditioning obliges!

15.2 Machado's take on the economics of intergenerational wealth transfers

A good starting point here is the plot of *The Inheritance* ... In the short story, Machado focuses on the motivations and expectations about bequests and intergenerational transfers. The narrative is crisp, centred around an elderly lady, Venância, whose closest relatives are two nephews, an introspective, meticulous one, Marcos, whose uninterested devotion and attentive care is taken for granted, or at least unappreciated by his aunt, and his flamboyant brother, Emílio, whose demeanour is guided more by familial obligation than personal attachment to Venância.

The plot is developed around Venância's wish for Emílio to marry Eugênia, a devoted niece, who acquiesces, albeit reluctantly. The twist is that Emílio demurs, and then Marcos, to everyone's surprise, proposes to marry Eugênia instead. Venância is pleased with the arrangement, since it allows her to provide for her niece after all, but passes away shortly after the announcement. The *grand finale* is Machado's at his best: when the will is read, the reader discovers that Venância bequeaths her small fortune to Emílio, her favourite, whereas Marcos is left pondering Venância's motives. The end, in Machado's tradition, blends personal and social elements.

What are the main economic takeaways from, and implications of, Machado's short story? Two main readings can be considered, one regarding the characters' motives and mutual expectations, and another related to equity considerations and policy options for addressing them.

We learn from the social sciences that bequests may be of three main types: accidental or unintended (to the extent that the time of death is unknown and, as a result, people may die before consuming all their accumulated assets), strategic or transactional (since donors may transfer wealth to their heirs in exchange for a service, such as caregiving in old age) and altruistic (when donors derive utility from the welfare of their recipients or wish to compensate for lower earnings ability of their heirs). In other words, according to the altruism view, donors pass on wealth to their heirs without expectation of compensation, whereas according to the transactional view intergenerational transfers maintain interdependence within families based on social obligations and expectations of retribution. In between these extremes lie a range of motivations including equality and egoism, organised by and large along notions of justice and power.[2] Donors may also derive utility from the "warm glow" or joy of giving to their heirs.[3]

The transactional and strategic motivation for bequests is dealt with in economic terms particularly well by Bernheim et al. (1985). Of course, Machado does not limit himself to clear-cut categorisations and explores a wealth of mismatches in motivations and expectations in donor-recipient relations. He also accepts that recipients may harbour ambiguous feelings for donors.

Starting with motivations.... Venância's could not be in sharper contrast to those of Marcos. In the best Machadian tradition, the context is set from the outset when the reader learns about Venância's feelings for Marcos and that the exchange between them is formal and dull[4]:

> The presence of Marcos was an exchange of papers. She was the main beneficiary.

This is even though Marcos was reliable and acted in Venância's best interests in managing her assets: "[Marcos] D. Venância's providence and her support". We also learn from the narrator that Venância considered Emílio her favourite nephew ("the best nephew in this world"). The relationship between Venância and Marcos therefore takes centre stage, with Emílio and Eugênia playing secondary roles.

Venância's motivations are complex. She does indeed want to provide for her niece, which suggests altruism, but does not shy away from leaving her estate to her favourite nephew, rather than rewarding the one that cared for her and looked after her interests most diligently. At the same time, Venância could also have been strategic in creating the expectation of reciprocity in Marcos so as to ensure that she would be cared for in her old age, while meeting her objective of providing for her niece while feeling the joy of leaving her estate to her favourite nephew. In turn, Marcos may have been transactional in his devotion to his aunt, having cared for her in expectation of retribution, as well as strategic in the face of uncertainty by proposing to marry Eugênia to avoid losing the inheritance that he suspected could in the end go to his brother.

Machado indeed lets the reader know that Marcos's dedication was motivated by some interest beyond affection since he could not ignore Venância's possessions and that she only had three relatives:

> anyone who said that in Marcos's dedication there was some self-interest could sleep with a clear conscience, since he didn't slander anyone. There was affection, but there wasn't just that. D. Venância had good buildings, and had only three relatives.

This sort of ambiguity is pure Machado!

Marcos's disappointment brings to the fore the notion of fairness in intergenerational transfers, at least as perceived by donors and recipients. The perception of fairness in this case is often related to support for the family, regardless of the needs and rewards of individual members, when motivation is altruistic. In the case where intergenerational transfers are motivated by notions of equality among potential recipients, then intergenerational transfers are perceived as just when individual needs and rewards are taken into account. When the motivation for transfers is transactional, arrangements are perceived as fair, at least as far as donors are concerned, when they are based on explicit reciprocity, especially as a means of rewarding caregivers. A lack of alignment between the motivations and perceptions of donors and heirs, on the one hand, and among heirs, on the other, is an important source of conflict within families and is at the heart of Machado's short story. Indeed, Machado exposes the reader to a whole range of motivations.[5]

Perceptions of fairness also colour Venância's expectation of reciprocity from Emílio. This is even though he was unaware of his aunt's plans to pass on her estate to him to the detriment of his cousins. Venância's thinking is evident when she greets Emílio during one of his few visits by calling him ungrateful: "Come here, ungrateful, sit here by the old woman". Indeed, by using the word "ungrateful" in a sentence that is otherwise full of endearment, Machado provides a discrete clue of what is to come! The subtle point here is that exchange in this case is not exactly about rewarding caregiving, as is often the case in donor-recipient arrangements, but instead devotion, given the donor's affinity and personal preference for one among several potential heirs.

As for Marcos, he expected Venância's inheritance to be shared among the three potential heirs in equal parts, an outcome that would be consistent with equality-driven altruism by neglecting differences in needs and rewards among the heirs. This outcome would be also consistent with economic rationality based on convex preferences and disutility associated with leaving no bequests for one of the potential heirs. Disappointed, Marcos wonders what his brother may have done to deserve the recognition, other than having allowed himself to be loved:

> What had his brother done to deserve such a distinction? Nothing; he only let himself be loved.

Interestingly, empirical evidence on the division of estates within families shows a tendency towards equal shares, regardless of siblings' relative earnings (see, e.g., Laitner, 1997).

Machado also takes the reader through the notions of power that shape attitudes towards inheritance arrangements. The reader is told soon after being introduced to Eugênia, Venância's niece and third potential heir, that Venância intended to marry her during her lifetime ("*she even pondered marrying her before passing away*"). No surprise here, given that in the second half of the 19th century unmarried women needed to be provided for, through marriage or inheritance, as is evident in many of Machado's novels. However, Machado's cynicism would have it that Emílio, being Venância's favourite and natural would-be groom, would not acquiesce and that power would be exercised when Marcos proposes to marry Eugênia as yet another sign of deference to Venância, at which point the reader is left wondering if his move is calculated to secure retribution or not.

What are the economic implications of this outcome? The distributional aspects of intergenerational wealth transfers, especially in the form of estates and inheritances, have attracted a lot of attention among economists because intergenerational transfers are a significant source of household wealth.[6] Intergenerational transfers affect the distribution of wealth because wealthy households receive more than lower-wealth households do, even though intergenerational transfers may account for a lower share of wealth among the better off. Also, in the absence of taxes on intergenerational wealth transfers, estates are passed on in a dynastic manner, with implications for the concentration of wealth.

Machado does allude to the matter, at least as far as the interpersonal dimension of wealth distribution is concerned, in the last sentence of *The Inheritance*, when the reader knows about Marcos's disappointment and sense of unfairness in the distribution of Venância's estate among her potential heirs. He concludes that Venância "was the image of fortune". The narrator also lets the reader know that Marcos was in favour of the wedding, "not just because Eugênia deserved it, but because it was better that everything stayed within the family". Marcos also found Emílio's refusal to marry Eugênia "foolish and mistaken": "Marcos did not think the refusal was appropriate or prudent. It was a silly mistake".

Intergenerational wealth transfers also matter from the perspective of equality of opportunity. This is because wealth transfers might give recipients a head start that is not linked to their personal ability or effort. This is particularly true in the case of in-life gifts, which people tend to receive earlier in life than inheritances.[7] Indeed, Adermon, Lindahl and Waldenström (2018) show that inheritances and in-life gifts account for at least one-half of the parent-child wealth correlation in Sweden, almost double the share of the correlation that can be explained by earnings and education. This is particularly important because intergenerational social mobility has been declining in advanced economies over the generations (Causa and Johansson, 2010).

Beyond economics, recognition of the implications of inheritance for equality of opportunity is not new in the law profession. In fact, since the Enlightenment, the transfer of wealth between generations regardless of effort or merit has been perceived as associated with the system of inherited privileges that is characteristic of aristocratic societies and that runs counter to the modern, bourgeois values of meritocracy (Beckert, 2010). Reform to inheritance law has since then evolved by ensuring equality of rights among siblings, constraining the freedoms of testators and breaking the dynastic structure of nobility. The abolition of primogeniture and entails (an instrument whereby the testator can define the conditions for the use of the assets across generations), and the pursuit of gender neutrality in successions, including through the definition of the rights of surviving spouses, are elements of this evolution. Most provisions that we now take for granted were nevertheless only legislated in the first half of the 20th century in the Western world, despite remaining differences between civil and common-law traditions. More recent reforms to inheritance law include the extension of succession rights to same-sex unions and to children born out of wedlock.

Whether intergenerational transfers increase wealth inequality or not is an empirical question, and there is no consensus on the matter in the economic literature. Measuring this effect is difficult because it depends not only on comparing the distribution of wealth before and after receipt of a bequest but also on the behavioural responses triggered by the receipt, such as those related to decisions to consume or invest part of the transfer and to work less as a result of higher wealth.[8]

It is therefore instructive to look at the behavioural responses triggered by wealth transfers. One is that wealthier individuals tend to spend a lower share of their inherited wealth than their less wealthy counterparts (Druedahl and Martinello, 2022). In fact, Machado alludes to differences in responses when contrasting the behaviour of Emílio and Marcos to the inheritance they received from their parents: the reader is told that "Emílio tapped into the estate, which Marcos managed prudently". Yet another one of Machado's clues along the text to guide (or confuse) the reader!

Behavioural responses also concern decisions to work. Conventional wisdom is that inheritance receipts likely discourage recipients' labour supply (the "Carnegie conjecture") through lower hours of work, early retirement or inactivity, given the associated increase in permanent income. Actually, the theme of changes in behaviour in response to receipt of an inheritance comes up in different novels by Machado, including *Quincas Borba*, one of his best known, and *Helena*, where it does so from the vantage point of social mobility. In another short story, *Luís Soares*, a squandered inheritance motivates discussions about social status, privilege and the concentration of wealth, as discussed above.

15.3 From Machado to policy: Enter the tax system...

Taxes on intergenerational wealth transfers, including estates, inheritances and in-life gifts, can be a powerful instrument to deal with equity considerations without necessary increasing distortions that would undermine allocative efficiency in the economy. Yes, yet another one of the efficiency-equity trade-offs that confront economists in so many areas of policy!

The main argument here is that these taxes can enhance equity horizontally, by ensuring equal treatment between inheritances, in-life gifts and earnings from work or savings during the taxpayer's life, and also vertically, particularly when taxes are levied in a progressive manner, by ensuring that those who receive more wealth pay more tax.[9] Also, these taxes tend to impose fewer distortions on recipients' incentives to work and on donors' decisions to move to lower-tax jurisdictions or to donate to charity than other taxes levied on wealthy taxpayers.[10]

As for the effects of inheritance taxes and regulations on entrepreneurship, economic analysis has been less prolific. This is surprising because intergenerational wealth transfers could be a good source of seed capital for business startups, as well as funds for investment in existing businesses, especially given that business assets are typically exempted from inheritance taxation in the case of family business successions. We do not know what Machado meant when the reader is told that Marcos managed their parents' bequest prudently, whereas Emílio squandered his share, but it may well have been related to the differences in the use of inherited wealth for investment as opposed to consumption.

Against this background, and despite the merits of taxation of intergenerational wealth transfers, these taxes account for only about 0.5% of total tax revenue on average among OECD countries, essentially on account of generous preferential tax treatment that creates room for tax planning (OECD, 2021). To begin with, tax provisions vary considerably across countries. Some countries levy recipient-based inheritance taxes, while others, such as the United Kingdom and the United States, levy taxes on donors' overall estates. Taxes on in-life gifts are also common, but they are sometimes taxed in different ways and at different rates than inheritances, which creates room for tax planning. Provisions also vary depending on the tax rate and the progressivity of the tax schedule; the size of wealth transfers that can be passed on free of tax; and the type of exemptions, including for transfers among close relatives and for specific assets, such as the main residence, business and pension assets, and life insurance policies, as well as charitable donations.

Political economy considerations also play an important role in explaining the light taxation of intergenerational wealth transfers around the world. The use of monikers, such as "death tax" or "Paris Hilton tax", illustrates how politically and emotionally charged discussions tend to be in this area. Public opinion reactions also differ a great deal between estate and inheritance taxes, with greater resistance to the former. In any case, as argued by Beckert (2010), the political economy arguments against estate and inheritance taxation essentially boil down to the belief that these instruments are tantamount to undue interference by the State in family relations, which trumps arguments of equality of opportunity.

A final point that is relevant to the case of Venância is the difference that exists in some countries in the tax treatment between close and more distant relatives. This is because applying higher inheritance tax rates to transfers to more distant family members encourages the concentration of wealth transfers among closer family members, as mentioned above. In any case, wealth transfer taxes need to be designed in a manner that is consistent with the taxation of personal and capital income.

15.4 Summing up

Intergenerational wealth transfers are a fascinating theme for fiction and economics alike. Fiction writers are drawn to the web of emotions that shape people's attitudes towards family and close relatives, as well as their behaviour in response to changes in material wealth. Notions of fairness in human relations, and within families more specifically, also add complexity to characters and plots. Economists are interested in the theme because it is related to broader issues, such as equity and efficiency, which are in turn at the heart of the welfare challenges the economics profession is expected to address in modern societies. It is, therefore, no surprise that economically interested fiction writers seek to exploit the intersections between these different, yet complementary, dimensions of a theme. In addition, it is delightful when the task is accomplished with literary mastery and grace.

Acknowledgements

I am indebted to François Bourguignon, Josef Konvitz, Luc Leruth, Anahertz Magalhães and Jean-Philippe Platteau for comments and suggestions but remain solely responsible for remaining errors or omissions.

The opinions and analysis reported in this paper are the author's own and do not necessarily reflect those of the OECD or the Organisation's member and partner countries.

Notes

1 Interestingly, Franco also wrote about the economic ideas permeating the writings of Fernando Pessoa, probably making lusophone prose among the most scrutinized through economic lenses (Franco, 2007b).
2 See Becker (1974) for pioneering work on altruism and Cremer and Pestieau (2009) for further discussion. Other factors beyond strategic interactions, such as migration, caring behaviour and personal characteristics of potential heirs, influence the division of parental wealth (Goetghebuer and Platteau, 2010). Interestingly, economists have empirically tested these hypotheses and shown that most bequests tend to be accidental (Burman, McClelland and Lu, 2018; Kopczuk and Lupton, 2007).
3 Modigliani (1988) presents a pioneer analysis of bequest motives and the effects of bequests on saving and wealth accumulation.
4 The translations throughout the chapter are mine.
5 These hypotheses have been tested empirically by Sousa et al. (2010) for a sample of Portuguese families.
6 In spite of fluctuations in the numbers over time, Piketty and Zucman (2015) estimate the annual flow of bequests at about 8–15% of GNI in some European countries in 2010 and that inheritances account on average for between 30% and 60% of household wealth in Western countries.
7 Related to this idea is the role of human capital formation in intergenerational transfers. In particular, parents may choose to transfer wealth by investing in the education of their children, albeit in a differentiated manner, depending on their relative ability, and then equalise welfare by bequeathing more wealth to those who received less investment in human capital (Becker and Tomes, 1979).
8 The net effect from a macroeconomic perspective also depends on the aggregate wealth distribution. For example, as noted above, an overall reduction in wealth inequality could be consistent with an increase in wealth dispersion, to the extent that wealthier households inherit more in absolute terms than their less wealthy counterparts do but not relative to their wealth (Wolff, 2002, 2015; Boserup et al., 2016; Elinder et al., 2018).
9 It could be argued from the point of view of improving equality of opportunity that wealth transfers could be taxed at a higher rate than earnings from work or savings

(Batchelder, 2020), since these transfers create a wedge between people's ability to earn, on the one hand, and their ability and effort, on the other.

10 Moreover, these taxes have administrative advantages relative to other levies on net wealth and immovable property, because inheritance, estate and in-life gift taxes are levied only once, or infrequently as in the case of in-life gifts, as opposed to recurrently, as is the case of taxes on net wealth and immovable property. This simplifies the identification and valuation of assets and owners, as well as the collection of tax liabilities.

References

Adermon, Adrian, Mikael Lindahl, and Daniel Waldenström, "Intergenerational Wealth Mobility and the Role of Inheritance: Evidence from Multiple Generations," *The Economic Journal* 128 (2018), F482–F513. https://doi.org/10.1111/ecoj.12535

Batchelder, L., "Levelling the Playing Field between Inherited Income and Income from Work through an Inheritance Tax," in E. Moss, R. Nunn and J. Shambaugh, eds., *Tackling the Tax Code: Efficient and Equitable Ways to Raise Revenue* (Washington, DC: Brookings, 2020).

Becker, G., "A Theory of Social Interactions," *Journal of Political Economy* 82 (1974), 1063–1093.

Becker, G. and N. Tomes, "An Equilibrium Theory of the Distribution of Income and Intergenerational Mobility," *Journal of Political Economy* 87 (1979), 1153–1189.

Beckert, J., "Are We Still Modern? Inheritance Law and the Brocken Promise of the Enlightenment," *MPIfG Working Paper*, No. 10/7, Max Planck Institute for the Study of Societies, 2010.

Bernheim, L., B. Schleifer and A. Summers, "The Strategic Bequest Motive," *Journal of Political Economy* 93 (1985), 1045–1076.

Bloom, H., *Genius: A Mosaic of 100 Exemplary Creative Minds* (New York, NY: Grand Central, 2002).

Boserup, S., W. Kopczuk and C. Kreiner, "Wealth Inequality: Evidence from the Role of Bequests in Shaping Wealth Inequality," *American Economic Review* 106 (2016), 656–661.

Burman, L., R. McClelland and C. Lu, *The Effects of Estate and Inheritance Taxes on Entrepreneurship* (Washington, DC: Urban-Brookings Tax Policy Center, 2018).

Caldwell, H. (translator), *Dom Casmurro*, English Edition (London, UK: Daunt Books, 2014).

Causa, O. and A. Johansson, "Intergenerational Social Mobility in OECD Countries," *OECD Journal: Economic Studies* 1 (2010), 1–44.

Cremer, H. and P. Pestieau, "Wealth and Wealth Transfer Taxation: A Survey," mimeo, Toulouse School of Economics, 2009. http://piketty.pse.ens.fr/files/CremerPestieau2009.pdf

Druedahl, J. and A. Martinello, "Long-run Saving Dynamics: Evidence from Unexpected Inheritances," *Review of Economics and Statistics* 104 (2022), 1079–1095.

Elinder, M., O. Erixson and D. Waldenstrom, "Inheritance and Wealth Inequality: Evidence from Population Registers," *Journal of Public Economics* 165 (2018), 17–30.

Faoro, R., *Machado de Assis: Pirâmide e o Trapézio* (São Paulo: Cia. Editora Nacional, 1974).

Franco, G., *A Economia em Machado de Assis: O Olhar Oblíquo do Acionista* (Rio de Janeiro: Zahar, 2007a).

Franco, G., *Economia em Pessoa: Verbetes Contemporâneos e Ensaios Empresariais do Poeta* (Rio de Janeiro: Zahar, 2007b).

Gledson, J., *The Deceptive Realism of Machado de Assis* (Liverpool: Francis Cairns, 1984).

Gledson, J., *Machado de Assis: Ficção e História* (Rio de Janeiro: Paz e Terra, 1986).

Goetghebuer, T. and J.P. Platteau, "Inheritance Patterns in Migration-Prone Communities of the Peruvian Highlands," *Journal of Developments Economics* 93 (2010), 71–87.

Kopczuk, W. and J. Lupton, "To Leave or Not to Leave: The Distribution of Bequest Motives," *Review of Economic Studies* 74 (2007), 207–235.

Laitner, J., "Intergenerational and Interhousehold Economic Links," in M.R. Rosenzweig and O. Stark, eds., *Handbook of Population and Family Economics* (North-Holland, 1997).

Machado de Assis, J.M., *A Herança* (Rio de Janeiro, Brasil: published original in O Jornal das Famílias in 1878), 2012.

Modigliani, F., "The Role of Intergenerational Transfers and Life Cycle Saving in the Accumulation of Wealth," *Journal of Economic Perspectives* 2 (1988), 15–40.

OECD, "Inheritance Taxation in OECD Countries," *OECD Tax Policy Studies*, 28 (2021), Paris, France.

Piketty, T. and G. Zucman, "Wealth and Inheritance in the Long Run," in *Handbook of Income Distribution* (Amsterdam, Netherlands: Elsevier, 2015).

Sousa, L., A.R. Silva, L. Santos and M. Patrão, "The family inheritance process: motivations and patterns of interaction," *European Journal of Ageing* 7 (2010), 5–15.

Stavans, I., "Wrestling with Machado," *The Yale Review* 106 (2018), 81–89.

Wolff, E.N., "Inheritances and Wealth Inequality: 1989–1998," *American Economic Review* 92 (2002), 260–264.

Wolff, E.N., *Inheriting Wealth in America: Future Boom or Bust?* (Oxford: Oxford University Press, 2015).

Wood, M., "Foreword," in M.J. Costa and R. Patterson, translators, *The Collected Stories of Machado de Assis* (New York: Liveright Publishing, 2018).

16

THE INHERITANCE MESS

Père Goriot and King Lear offer us a mirror

Marianne David and Pierre Pestieau

16.1 Strategic bequests

Most adult children are obliged to wait until their parents' death before they can touch their inheritance. But with increased longevity these heirs are getting older and older, 55 being the average age in France. Practically speaking, a parent's help is more useful to children starting out in life than the benefits they might receive at a later age. Some adult children either inherit while they are still young or receive substantial aid from their parents. But such cases tend to be in the minority.

The question that poses itself is: why parents who are deemed to be altruistic do not make more use of early gifting? An obvious answer is that parents may not always be altruistic. Or that even altruistic parents may decide to defer their bequest to their children at life's end because of their need to do some precautionary saving. Their concern might also have to do with the possibility that their children could squander their inheritance, as well as abandon their parents.[1]

Parents who are well insured against major existential risks do not need to engage in any precautionary saving. However, in the real world, most of us are at best only partially insured against dependency, major illnesses, or "too long" a life. Anticipating these risks, people who are able to do so make a point of accumulating some wealth. And yet if this money has been earmarked for their children's inheritance, a long period of dependency could render these savings insufficient. On the flip side, in the event of the parents' early death, the children will inherit what we call an "accidental" bequest.

Another instance in which parents may not wish to prematurely transfer their wealth to their kids is their fear that the money might keep these kids from making the appropriate efforts to realize their own talents and potentials.

DOI: 10.4324/9781003534358-20

More precisely, parents may worry that their children could dilapidate[2] their inheritance and thus leave themselves bereft later on in life. There is also the additional danger that having once received their inheritance, these children might decide to abandon their parents altogether.

It is this hazard that constitutes the focus of the present chapter, and that is dramatically illustrated in Balzac's *Père Goriot* novel and Shakespeare's masterpiece of *King Lear*. Because of the mistreatment received from his two stone-hearted daughters, we see the dying Goriot emblematized on a squalid bed in a cold hovel with not a penny for firewood. By contrast, the effect of a botched inheritance in *King Lear* is the catastrophic figure described by Charles Lamb as "a man tottering about the stage with a walking-stick, turned out of doors by his daughters in a rainy night."[3] As we consider that great art has the power to profoundly evoke our human condition, we would do well to heed the lessons of compassion and identification that can serve us.

Simply put, parents are advised to consider the quality of their relationship with their children, and thereby assure themselves of the assistance they can expect in the event of need, illness, or dependency. In this regard, one way for parents to concretize this assurance is to follow a specific arrangement that would bequeath to their children the main part of their wealth at the end of life. Such an arrangement can take various forms. In a satisfactory parent-child relationship, a mutually beneficial give-and-take occurs when the parents provide financial assistance to their children and in exchange receive from them occasional acts of help. Such parental assistance could initially include babysitting as well as outright gifts along the way.

A more complex arrangement would entail more strategic bequests. Important is to strike the right balance by considering not so much the pragmatics and logistics, but rather the sensitivities and feelings of the parties involved. Care must be given to avoid relationships of power or control that can lead to conflict. For a relationship to be successful, it must factor in psychology.

As formalized by economists, strategic bequests are seen to involve parents who are retiring and have at least two children starting their active lives. Because parents can dispose of their wealth any way they wish, the emphasis must be on creating a negotiable outcome. After all, the parents hold the money and can, therefore, choose whether to consume it or bequeath it to their children. On the one hand, the parents may wish to have each child contribute to them attention or outright help. The other side of the equation is the children's desire to receive as much of their inheritance as possible, aware that beyond a certain threshold there is a cost to helping their elderly parents. It is a nuanced game with a precise sequence that starts with the parents' commitment to giving a total amount of the bequest relative to the level of attention each child has promised to give.

During the entire period of this arrangement, the children are supposed to act independently of each other, offering their parents the personal attention they consider optimal as they wait to receive their inheritance. Upon the parents' death, the inheritance is shared in the ways agreed upon. The parents have the upper hand as they are in a position to get the maximum from each of the children whom they could disinherit if necessary. In this model, the parents are altruistic and the children are not. So were the parents to make a premature bequest, they could risk depriving themselves of their children's care and attention.

This strategic model was initially formalized and tested by Bernheim et al. (1985). Following their seminal contribution, there have been a few empirical papers[4] supporting the hypothesis that bequests are used by parents partly to induce their children to give them more attention. As an example, one could cite Angelini (2007) whose panel data on eleven European countries shows that contacts between parents and children are positively correlated with the amount of wealth held by the testator. She also demonstrates that testamentary freedom that varies across those European countries has a positive and significant effect on the amount of attention children can provide.

Angeli's strategic bequest model can be interpreted as a warning designed to avoid the case of filial ingratitude we see in *King Lear* and in Père *Goriot*. Both works illuminate the deplorable ramifications and frightful repercussions of an inheritance predicament that occurs due to a lack of reflection. Goriot is dimly aware of his situation in fleeting moments. But not for long. "Ah, how foolish fathers are! I loved them so much that I went back to them again like a gambler going back to the gambling tables. My daughters were my vice. They were my mistresses."[5] In Goriot's obsessive fatherhood idea, the absurd lurks just beneath the tragic

Of a different sort is Shakespeare's insight into the searing conflict posed by filial ingratitude. Lear rages on about how cruelly Goneril has treated him even as he reluctantly acknowledges her as his child: "But yet thou art my flesh, my blood, my daughter; or rather a disease that's in my flesh, which I must needs call mine. Thou art a boil, a plague sore or embossed carbuncle, in my corrupted blood." ["And yet you are my flesh, my blood, my daughter. Or rather a disease I have in my body. You are a boil, a plague-like sore, a raised pimple in my rotten blood."][6] The tragic flaw of these two wretched aging fathers is their pathological blindness. Lear's destructive pride makes him emotionally distant and yet so childishly needy. Whereas Goriot's misery stems from his pathetic lack of self-worth.

16.2 Père Goriot

Balzac, who had read *King Lear*, set his melodrama of a retired pasta manufacturer ruined by his selfish daughters in the bourgeois milieu of 19th century Paris. The generous dowries Goriot provides enable his girls to make their appalling marriages: Anasthasie to M. de Restaud a minor aristocrat, and Delphine to M. de Nucigen a Jewish banker. While his daughters milk him for every cent he has, both sons-in-law treat Goriot with contempt. Entitled, indolent, and frivolous, keeping lovers, they dance the night away at fancy balls wearing expensive brocade gowns. Never a thought to their father's welfare. And yet it is his daughters' slightest unhappiness that drives Goriot to agony. To buy their affection and stay in touch, he accedes to their every whim. When they run into financial trouble, Goriot pawns his last possessions and reduces himself to a sordid life. Miserable but unable to react, he curses his daughters, then quickly regrets having said anything, only to fall into despair and anger all over again.

Goriot's pathos plays out in Madame de Vauquer's dingy rooming house "in a neighborhood where not even a cat goes by"[7] surrounded by people racked by money issues. All of Madame de Vauquer's guests are in the same soup. Eugene de Rastignac drains his family's resources in order to secure the luxuries he thinks will ensure his rise in society; Victorine fears her father`s plan to disinherit her by leaving his wealth only to her brother. Vautrin's eyes gleam like a wildcat's as he plots his murderous schemes.

As Goriot sinks into monomania, this "Christ among fathers" still imagines that his death will bring his daughters to his side. He is cruelly disabused! With leeches applied to his emaciated body, he dies a wretched death and is buried in a pauper's grave. The only witness to the heartbreaking cemetery scene to which the two daughters send their empty coaches, Rastignac hurls his outrage at this dog-eat-dog Paris for allowing such things to happen. Then hurries off to dine with his mistress, Madame de Nucigen.

16.3 King Lear

Patterned on 8th century Britain's mythical king Leir, Shakespeare's King Lear character may have been inspired by a real occurrence. That of a pensioner to Queen Elizabeth who had three daughters, the two elder ones married, but not the youngest named Cordell. In late 1603, that is, a couple of years before the writing of the play, the eldest daughter and her husband had their father declared incompetent in order to lay their hands on his possessions. Cordell wrote a letter to Sr Robert Cecil saying her father deserved better and was thus able to sequester his estate. But the eldest daughter contested the will after the father's death.[8] Shakespeare, who was apparently conscious of this story, makes his Lear announce that he will parcel out his kingdom according to the map and thus gives his daughters Goneril, Regan, and Cordelia their dowries. During the ceremony to broker their marriages, King Lear demands each of his daughters to formally declare her love for him. The two older ones flatter their father with fulsome, exaggerated displays, but the third one tells him of her love in quiet, measured tones and a simple "thanks." This infuriates the old man, and he proceeds to curse and disinherit Cordelia, his favorite child and the one who truly loves him.

The ferocity of King Lear's mindless decision crosses redlines. The energies unleashed reverberate into chaos and devastation. Dividing his kingdom into two parts instead of three, Lear abjures his responsibility as both father and king. Cordelia, the recipient of his childish and imperious rage, leaves to become queen of France, an enemy kingdom. The deceitful Regan and Goneril turn against their father and violently reject him. Losing everything, Lear is transformed from a monarch into a beggar. The fall is precipitous and the penalty enormous. The storm raging inside him becomes the landscape of the play.

Lear's frantic disintegration is reflected in the Gloucester subplot with its array of knaves, fools, villains, and rogues. Gloucester is literally blinded for his transgression to the legitimacy of his son Edgar, instigated by Edmund whose plot against his father is rooted in his resentment at primogeniture. The savagery of the father-against-child and child-against-father aggression inhabits a bleak world where expulsion, madness, and suicide hold sway. Unmediated by moral principle or compromise, the ties that hold together the human polity and its web of relationships are irremediably broken. Bereft of thought and feeling, there is only darkness.

Lear's hurt pride and vindictiveness at not getting from Cordelia what he expects, together with his blindness to the stone-heartedness of his two other daughters, deviates from common sense. Childish, imperious, and obsessive, Lear is addicted to the symbols of kingships. Lulled into security by the "robes and furred gowns" of authority, he is insensitive to the sacredness of human relationships and feelings. The cumulative effect of his impotent rage is overwhelming. And it brings the slow erosion of Lear's dignity, strength, and connectedness to himself and those around him.

Lear fails hugely and lives to regret his wrongness. When Cordelia returns to Britain with an army to rescue her father, she is vanquished by the troops of Regan and Goneril commanded by Edmund. Cordelia is hanged, and Edmund causes the death of the two sisters who have been vying for his love. Cradling his favorite child in his arms, King Lear dies despairing and contrite.

16.4 Ingratitude

One is left to wonder whether Lear or Goriot might have been able to protect themselves, if only they had been able to perceive or foresee their daughters' shameless behavior. Both of these victimized fathers offer us the record of a self in search of self-understanding, but whose inner failings make them incapable of the reflections that might have mitigated their catastrophic situation. Since neither of the two works offers the reader a background account of the characters and their personality, we know almost nothing about the psychological history that normally determines human action.[9] Rather, the mystery of human error contaminates the entire plot – an error emerging from the bedrock of personality, and only partly from society's corruption. Had these two aging fathers been more mindful of themselves and their circumstances, they would surely have generated a different narrative. But that would have obviated their tragedy and thus the monumentality of the literature they embody.

Given that the significance of these two canonic works lies in their effects rather than their antecedents, we must look elsewhere for their instructive value. Tempting as it to blame the tragedies of Goriot and of Lear on the selfishness of the ungrateful daughters who waste the inheritance their father has given them, it is useful to consider Mauss' (1973 lessons on the ambivalence of gifts. In his commentary, Godelier (1996, p. 21) explains:

> To give is to simultaneously create a reciprocal relationship between the giver and the one receiving the gift. A relationship of solidarity since the giver is the one who shares what he has [...], and a relationship of superiority since the one who receives the gift and accepts it places himself in debt vis-à-vis the giver [and] finds himself to a certain extent as his dependent [...]. Two opposing movements are thus contained in one act. The gift brings the protagonists together because it is a sharing that distances them socially as it makes one the obligation of the other. One can see the formidable field for maneuver and possible strategies virtually contained in the practice of gifting [which] may, at the same time or successively, be an act of generosity or an act of violence, but in this case a violence disguised as a disinterested gesture exercised by means of or in the form of an act of sharing.

Not only are gifts complicated things, but the manner in which one gives a gift is also important. It is clear that parents who behave like Lear or Goriot reap what they sow. Clearly, these two old fathers are just as responsible as their daughters for the misfortunes that befall them. Botched inheritances have occurred throughout human history. They can happen at any time and anywhere. In our society families often engage in relationships that are not symmetrical, making it unrealistic for parents to expect the same kind of investment from their children that they themselves are willing to make. Especially as these children have already been given a great deal from their parents. There is no room or explanation for ingratitude in this asymmetrical structure termed "indirect reciprocity."[10]

16.5 Lessons

Literature cannot provide answers; it can only create mental contexts and identifications that make us think and feel. Cases such as the enormity of the *King Lear* tragedy and the pathetic drama of *Pere Goriot* are fortunately rare. In general, parents trust their kids, and often at their own risk and peril. They also expect and crave to establish an understanding with them that is implicit and free of calculation and strategy. What is important to consider is that kids who perceive calculating and strategic behavior on the part of their parents could very well refuse to accept their inheritance, as well as refrain from giving their parents any kind of attention. Indeed, the conditions for the strategic bequests model are rarely met: as it requires having at least two children, and to live in a country not subject to the Napoleonic code where disinheriting a child is impossible.

Furthermore, in the unfortunate situation of parents who find themselves destitute, there are social insurance mechanisms today that did not exist in the days of Lear or Goriot, and which allow us to avoid similarly tragic situations. There is in addition a legal obligation because in our system children have to help parents in need according to their financial capacities and the needs of the beneficiary. This obligation can be invoked by the parent, but also by the communities and hospitals in charge of social aid. All the same, such help is hardly a replacement for filial love.

The asymmetric altruism mentioned above explains why in our society the state makes upward transfers (pensions, long-term care insurance, health care) that are higher than downward transfers (education, family allowances, professional training). In effect, within the family itself, it is the downward transfers (education, gifts, and legacies) that take precedence. At the end of the day, there should be an equilibrium between the two types of transfers. Some economists think that in view of the increase in life expectancy, the balance tends to tilt in favor of upward transfers.

In sum, we see in the devastating cases of Lear and Goriot a pathology that obviates all rationality. To the point where, even if a friend had cautioned and forewarned either one of these fathers of the dire consequences of their actions and mental attitudes, their behavior would probably have remained unchanged. We recall that when the Duke of Kent warns Lear of the effects his decisions could have, Lear banishes his trusted friend and counselor. He is similarly vituperative when the Fool tries to remind him that giving up the crown will mean a loss of authority. Living in his own imaginary world, the benighted Lear drives away the very people who most care for him.

Can behavioral economics offer us a template that might allow us to understand and, hopefully, avoid the behavior of unfortunate, tragic characters like Lear and Goriot. One wonders. What behavioral economics teaches us is that people don't always act rationally and that emotions and personal factors impact economic decisions. It is certainly a different approach from the old models based on the *Homo economicus* paradigm replaced by that of the *Homo irrationalis*, which includes a variety of behavioral examples, e.g., procrastination, the dual self, aversion to loss, and to say nothing of the extravagances observed at different stages of one's life experience. Behavioral economics serves to clarify some of these behaviors; it also provides tools that allow for their modification. But not for such predicaments as Lear's and Goriot's – without the benefit of Freud.[11]

Acknowledgments

We want to thank Jean Philippe Platteau for his helpful comments.

Notes

1 Masson & Pestieau (1991).
2 Gotman (1995).
3 Lamb is co-author of *Tales from Shakespeare*, published in 1807, a book that has never been out of publication since that time. The original *Tales from Shakespeare* was actually not co-authored, but written by Charles' sister, Mary Lamb, under the pseudonym Thomas Hodgkins.
4 See also Perozek (1998).
5 Balzac (1962) pp. 268, 270.
6 Shakespeare (1993), Act 2, Scene 4, p. 221.
7 Balzac (1962) p. 218.
8 Mack (1972) pp. 45–46.
9 Mack (1972) p. 92.
10 Masson (2001).
11 On this, see Brémaud (2015).

References

Angelini, V., "The strategic bequest motive: Evidence from SHARE." Marco Fanno Working Papers 0062, 2007, Department of Economics, University of Padova.

Balzac, Honoré de, *Père Goriot* (Translated with an afterword by Henry Reed and a new introduction by Peter Brooks), (Signet Classics, New York 1962).

Bernheim, B.D., Shleifer, A., and Summers, L. "The strategic bequest motive." *Journal of Political Economy*, 93(6), (1985), 1045–1076.

Brémaud, N., "Lear délire?" *L'Information Psychanalytique*, 91, (2015), 403–412.

Godelier, M., *L'Énigme du Don*, (Fayard, Paris, 1996).

Gotman, A., *Dilapidation et Prodigalité*, (Nathan, Paris, 1995).

Mack, M., *King Lear in our Time*, (University of California Press, Berkeley, 1972).

Masson, A., "Économie des transferts entre générations: altruisme, équité, réciprocité indirecte, ambivalence." (*DELTA* Working Papers, 2001-15, École normale supérieure, 2001).

Masson, A., and P. Pestieau, "Types et modèles d'héritage et leurs implication." *Économie et Prévision*, 100(4), (1991), 31–71.

Mauss, M., *Essai sur le don: Forme et raison de l'échange dans les sociétés archaïques, in Sociologie et Anthropologie*, (PUF, Collection Quadrige, Paris, 1973) (Initially published in 1923).

Perozek, M.G., "A reexamination of the strategic bequest motive." *Journal of Political Economy*, 106, (1998), 423–445.

Shakespeare, W., *The tragedy of King Lear* (ed. by Barbara A. Mowat and Paul Westine), (Simon & Schuster Paperbacks, New York, 1993).

17

THE MASTER, THE HELICOPTER, AND MARGARITA

Luc Leruth and Danielle Meuwly

17.1 Introduction

Bulgakov began writing his masterpiece *The Master and Margarita* in 1928. He burned the first version (an episode that we find in the novel), later returned to it, but died in 1940 before the last version was completed. It was his wife who finished the work in 1941 (she had worked on it since 1937 and was one of its heroines). Harassed by Soviet censorship throughout his career (the reason why Bulgakov asked Stalin to let him leave the USSR, a request left unanswered), the publication of his work is just as convoluted: a censored version finally came out in 1966 in a Soviet magazine (Moscow), a more or less complete version came out in 1967 (but in Western Germany), another in 1973 (in the USSR), and the reference version, based on all available manuscripts, was finally published in 1989.

Little recognized during his lifetime, Bulgakov is today considered one of the greatest Russian writers and he is one of the most widely read. Among all his works, *The Master and Margarita* stands out as a dense, difficult-to-access, baroque-style novel that combines several stories from various times and places (Jerusalem under Pilate; Kiev, Moscow, and Yalta in the 1930s; and the Devil's abode in an ill-defined time). The plot evolves as if driven by a wind of madness where black magic sessions follow one another (the Devil, or Professor Woland, is also a magician). However, the representatives of the 'system' persist in explaining everything as rationally as is possible in a world where the Devil and his acolytes fly on broomsticks and where the head of a decapitated person does not hesitate to share its thoughts. For the record, let's point out that this novel has inspired other very varied artistic successes: for example, the Rolling Stones explained that it is the key to *Sympathy for the Devil*; and Salman Rushdie (1988) claimed that it inspired *The Satanic Verses*.

DOI: 10.4324/9781003534358-21

The novel offers several possible reading keys. It is a love story, an apology for artistic freedom, and a parody of the Soviet system, and it contains several themes that could have served as a basis for this essay. From the economic standpoint alone, one could have looked at contract theory or at the housing market (the approach adopted by Sergei Guriev in another chapter of this volume). We have retained the theme of 'helicopter money' for our analysis of *The Master and Margarita* and the edition of 2003 (Bulgakov, 2003).

17.2 A preamble on the concept of 'helicopter money'

Milton Friedman had been concerned with the effects of monetary policy on inflation (and the cost of holding cash) since the late 1940s (Friedman, 1948). He was not referring to a helicopter at that time (these machines only became a household name during the Vietnam war) and it was only in 1969 that he coined the term 'helicopter money' in two sentences (well after Bulgakov's death – Friedman, 1969):

> Let us suppose now that one day a helicopter flies over this community and drops an additional $1,000 in bills from the sky, which is, of course, hastily collected by members of the community. Let us suppose further that everyone is convinced that this is a unique event which will never be repeated.

Friedman's focus was on how monetary policy would affect inflation but the concept was later assimilated by a number of economists to a policy option to compensate for tax cuts or, more generally, to finance a fiscal deficit. These economists include Ben Bernanke, then Governor of the Federal Reserve, who stated in 2002 that '... a money-financed tax cut is essentially equivalent to Milton Friedman's famous "helicopter drop" of money.'[1] Let us also mention that Colonel Khadafi, always excessive, but in this case strictly applying Friedman's concept, would literally throw banknotes from his helicopter when flying over areas he was about to visit on an official tour.[2]

In this chapter, we focus solely on money printing without consideration of cause (i.e., a fiscal deficit) and therefore come back to Friedman's original idea. The deficit financing angle is taken in another chapter of this volume (by Alfred Steinherr who is analyzing Faust) where money printing is a way to address a fiscal deficit.

17.3 Money falls from the ceiling

Eager to check whether the attempts of the Soviet system to create a new man succeeded, but doubting it after he has observed Muscovites for some time, the Devil decides to conduct an experiment:

> 'Everybody look up, please! One!' … 'Two!' … 'Three!' There was a flash, a bang, and immediately a cascade of white pieces of paper began to float down from the dome above the auditorium … A few seconds later the shower of money reached the stalls…

It is remarkable that, so many years before Friedman, Bulgakov considered this monetary mechanism. Wistfully, the Devil observes the scene:

> … and the audience began catching it. Hundreds of hands were raised as the audience held the notes up to the light from the stage and found that the watermarks were absolutely genuine. Their smell left no doubt: it was the uniquely delicious smell of newly-printed money … From all over the house, amid gasps and delighted laughter, came the words 'money, money! …'
>
> (The Master and Margarita, *p. 116)*

Heartbroken, the Devil (and Bulgakov himself who has explored that theme in other books) comes to the conclusion that the new man does not exist.[3] Moscovites are the same as they have always been and their love for money is inextinguishable, whatever its form.

Milton Friedman would not have been surprised and had indeed assumed in his 1969 paper that people would hastily collect the helicopter money.

17.4 Modern views on 'helicopter money'

Helicopter money has critics and supporters. Some of the arguments raised in ongoing debates (and they had a second life in the context of the recent Quantitative Easing operations by central banks)[4] are not necessarily relevant to Bulgakov's story. We can immediately rule out a few:

- Are there implications for central bank policy? By virtue of being the Devil, Professor Woland is not concerned about this;
- Is it legal? For the same reason, this is not relevant either.

Others are very relevant and we will concentrate on the following:

- Will the money be spent?
- Is it possible to create 'free money' (is there a free lunch)?
- Will there be inflation (or hyperinflation)?
- What are people's expectations (will the central bank/the Devil print 'free money' repeatedly)?

17.4.1 Will the money be spent?

In modern times, this issue is debated. Surveys tend to suggest that it would, and some scholars agree.[5] In a speech given at the London School of Economics in 2016, Raghuram Rajan, then Governor of the Reserve Bank of India, disagreed however, arguing that someone seeing all that money falling from the sky would think: 'Has the world gone nuts? I'd better save much of this because I'm not sure what will happen (later).'[6] So, there is indeed a possibility that the audience in Moscow, unsure about what to expect in the future, would save the money. Less so in the context of *The Master and Margarita*.

In Soviet Russia, money filled only two of its three traditional functions: unit of account and trade intermediary (and to a very limited extent since inter-company exchanges were determined by the Plan). Investment, business creation, production, and price setting were also the responsibility of the central planner. Money could therefore neither be a store of value for the accumulation of capital nor for the purchase of expensive consumer goods that were only available in special stores against foreign currencies (this also features in Bulgakov's novel). Consequently, saving rates in the Soviet world were low by international standards.[7] People would save if they could but, as discussed later, mostly in foreign currencies. This should have an immediate implication: the money falling from the ceiling should be spent as fast as possible, exacerbating the shortages already plaguing the official system or used to purchase foreign currencies on the black market. In the book, after the money stops falling, a couple of men rush to the bar to drink whatever money they have got, but that is all and the line is not explicitly continued in the novel.

Instead, soon after the money stops falling, a 'Parisian' shop 'for ladies' appears on stage: the fancy clothes on display can be freely obtained in exchange for the old ones the audience is wearing, the devil's assistant announces. Note that Bulgakov does not envisage that the customers pay with the ten-rouble notes they just got. It is barter, a favorable barter as far as the crowd is concerned, or so it seems. After a slow start, it is a mad rush. Soon, however, the shop closes and the show is over. Dressed in their fancy clothes, people exit the theater and the ladies find themselves naked: their new clothes have vanished.

> … Grigory Danilovich saw another woman, this time in pink underwear. She was struggling across the pavement in an attempt to hide in the doorway, but the people coming out barred her way and the wretched victim of her own rashness and vanity, cheated by the sinister Faggot, could do nothing but hope to be swallowed up by the ground.
>
> *(*The Master and Margarita*, p. 142)*

The image of clothes disappearing is an allegory of hyperinflation and hints at what will happen to the banknotes.[8] But there is an expectation issue too: one would expect that the ladies caught naked in public would learn their lesson and that would have impressed everyone, at least that the commotion would leave a long-lasting trace. Not so, or at least not for long, much to the surprise of Rimsky, the director of the theater (*The Master and Margarita*, p. 142).[9]

We will come back to the issue of expectations, but we first note that Muscovites in Bulgakov's stories, in reference to Gresham's law 'bad money drives out good,' do save: it is just that their savings are mostly in gold rubles and in foreign currencies.[10] In fact, there are several instances in the book where people try to hide stash of foreign money everywhere, a behavior that is hard to resist by the individual, although punishable by law in the Soviet world[11]:

> 'Where did you get the foreign currency from?' they asked insinuatingly.
>
> 'As almighty God's my witness,' said Nikanor Ivanovich, 'I never touched any and I never even suspected that it was foreign money. God will punish me for my sin,' Nikanor Ivanovich went on feelingly, unbuttoning his shirt, buttoning it up again and crossing himself. 'I took the money – I admit that – but it was Soviet money. I even signed a receipt for it. Our secretary Prolezhnov is just as bad – frankly we're all thieves in our house committee ... But I never took any foreign money.'

A remorseful Nikanor Ivanovich then falls on his knees and pleads:

> 'I'll do anything you like,' he groaned, 'that'll make you believe I didn't take the stuff.'
>
> (The Master and Margarita, *pp. 149–150)*

17.4.2 There ain't no such thing as a free lunch

In Bulgakov's tale, there are undeniably free lunches, in the sense that people who collected the money falling from the ceiling were indeed able to buy things with it, as long as they did it quickly. Those who waited shared the fate of those who received the notes later and discovered that they had become worthless sheets of paper (an extreme case of hyperinflation).

Friedman is a bit more specific about the definition of free lunches, however, defining it as the notion that someone could get a free lunch without someone else (not necessarily the person eating the meal) paying the cost. From that standpoint, there are no free lunches in *The Master and Margarita*, as a barman soon discovers[12]:

> 'During your act you made bank-notes float down from the ceiling... .' The barman lowered his voice and looked round in embarrassment. 'Well, all the audience picked them up and a young man came to my bar and handed me a ten-rouble note, so I gave him eight roubles fifty change ... Then another one came' ... 'Then there was a third and a fourth ... I gave them all change. And today when I came to check the till there was nothing in it but a lot of strips of paper. The bar was a hundred and nine roubles short.' ...
>
> (The Master and Margarita, *pp. 194–195)*

Obviously, the barman feared that he would be the one paying for the drinks. A taxi driver shared the same fate and reacted angrily, demanding 'real money' before taking a customer (*The Master and Margarita*, p. 175).

So even though a few people managed to get a free lunch, there is a cost paid by society as a whole. And in the case of the ladies' fancy new dresses, the cost of the 'free lunch' is obvious: they are embarrassingly naked in public and no longer have their old clothes. In Bulgakov's (and the Devil's) mind, there is no free lunch but people are so greedy that they are ready to believe that it exists.

17.4.3 Is Bulgakov concerned with inflation (and trust in bank notes)?

In theory, Soviet-type economies should achieve price stability (after all, prices were determined by the State), but disequilibria have often resulted from exogenous shocks, rigidities in the labor market, ambitious quantitative targets, and other difficulties faced by planned economies (and others too, but prices offer then one more variable of adjustment).[13] In the Soviet world, the variables of adjustment were not prices, but shortages and queues. This may be why Bulgakov has not explicitly introduced inflation in the story (but he certainly has queues and shortages). There are two elements that appear though and are closely related: one is hyperinflation (already discussed, when the clothes disappear or when the notes become worthless) and the other is a lack of confidence in bank money. Take this example with the same taxi driver accepting the accountant as a client (the three-rouble notes were the old notes and it is ten-rouble notes that fell from the ceiling):

> As soon as the three cab-drivers on the rank saw a fare approaching with a chock-full briefcase under his arm, all three of them instantly drove off empty, scowling back as they went. Amazed, the accountant stood for a while wondering what this odd behaviour could mean. After about three minutes an empty cab drove up the rank, the driver grimacing with hostility when he saw his fare.
>
> 'Are you free?' asked Vassily Stepanovich with an anxious cough.
>
> 'Show me your money,' snarled the driver.
>
> (The Master and Margarita, *pp. 174–175*)

As the accountant shows a ten-rouble note, the driver refuses to take him. Demanding three-rouble notes. Only when the accountant shows the three-rouble notes, does the driver agree to take him.

Everybody has started doubting the value of the money. Even the 'old' rouble, to which foreign currency is preferred, is itself preferred to the new notes. Is it any different today? During a routine presentation to the U.S. Senate, Fed Chairman Ben Bernanke spread the bank notes contained in his wallet and uttered the unthinkable[14]:

> "You know what? It doesn't matter. None of this – this so-called 'money' – really matters at all. It's just an illusion. Just look at it: Meaningless pieces of paper with numbers printed on them. Worthless." According to witnesses, Finance Committee members sat in thunderstruck silence for several moments until Sen. Orrin Hatch (R-UT) finally shouted out, "Oh my God, he's right. It's all a mirage. All of it – the money, our whole economy – it's all a lie!" Screams then filled the Senate Chamber as lawmakers and members of the press ran for the exits, leaving in their wake aisles littered with the remains of torn currency.[15]

Fortunately, everyone quickly calmed down (i.e., the illusion continues), but this is not very different from the ladies at the exit of the theater, discovering that they were naked and trying to run away.

17.4.4 What do people expect? Are their expectations rational?

To economists (including Janet Yellen or Ben Bernanke), 'helicopter money,' often undertaken in conjunction with some fiscal stimulus, is associated with the risks already discussed above. One additional concern is the risk of blurring the line associated with the central bank and, when undertaken alone, that it could jeopardize central bank credibility (is the shock permanent? Will the central bank do it again?) and how the public would assess it (its expectations). This would have an impact on how effective the policy would be over time. Once again, though, this is of no concern to the Devil:

> I'm not really a magician at all. I simply wanted to see some Muscovites en masse and the easiest way to do so was in a theatre. So my staff' – he nodded towards the cat – 'arranged this little act and I just sat on stage and watched the audience.
>
> (*The Master and Margarita, p. 194*)

That does not mean that people do not have any expectations. The first question is, whether the public is interested in realities? The answer is clearly 'no' with some dramatic exceptions. Any unpleasant information, even when communicated through an official channel, raises a flood of aggressive reactions. When, in the middle of the show, the director of the theater summons the Devil to explain his artifice and confirm that the banknotes are fake, the public, encouraged by the Devil's assistant, gets furious:

> Faggot [the Devil's assistant] broke the silence:
>
> 'And that was a case of so-called fiddlesticks,' he declared in a loud goatish bray. 'The banknotes, ladies and gentlemen, are real.'

> 'This man … sticks his nose in everywhere without being asked and ruins the whole act. What shall we do with him?'
>
> 'Cut off his head!' said a stern voice.
>
> (*The Master and Margarita, p. 117*)

This behavior is not new, nor is the passion of the public for the conspiracies. The public only believes information insofar as it is compatible with its 'priors' which we can assimilate to its interests. Even when faced with an unpleasant and tangible reality, it does not take much effort to make them not believe their eyes, as is the case of Andrei Fokich who goes to the Devil to complain that his notes have become worthless papers. He opens the packet and the notes seem to be real again.

> 'My dear chap, you really are sick,' said Woland, shrugging his shoulders.
>
> Grinning stupidly, the barman got up from his stool. 'B-b-but …' he stammered, hiccupping, 'if they vanish again … what then?'
>
> 'H'm,' said the professor thoughtfully. 'In that case come back and see us. Delighted to have met you …'
>
> (*The Master and Margarita, pp. 195–196*)

Worse still, the public is not interested in an explanation:

> 'An explanation is essential, otherwise your brilliant act will leave a painful impression. The audience demands an explanation …'
>
> 'The audience,' interrupted the insolent mountebank, 'has not, to my knowledge, demanded anything of the sort.'
>
> (*The Master and Margarita, p. 121*)

Bulgakov also thinks that people are shortsighted and forget easily. We have already mentioned that the whistling that accompanied the naked ladies outside the theater had faded astonishingly quickly. In spite of the drama that occurred that night, the next day, a ticket-hungry crowd formed a long line waiting for entrance tickets (long lines were also a permanent feature of the Soviet system), even though those who had kept the money that had fallen from the ceiling had already realized that it had become worthless. But nobody listens or wants to believe it because, as mentioned above, it does not correspond to the 'priors.' The public is equally quick to forget. Thus, when the second show is canceled, the excitement quickly subsides and the doors of the Variety are closed without people showing signs of concern (*The Master and Margarita*, p. 174).

In the end, when the chaos subsides, society is busy trying to find as rational an explanation as possible for what happened. A commission is appointed but never reaches a conclusion.

As he watches people rushing to pick up the notes, the Devil wistfully notes that humanity loves money and always did. People are thoughtless, he mutters. However, and we must see here a touch of optimism in a generally pessimistic work by Bulgakov, when the Devil asks the public if the decapitated director should be resuscitated, some voices say 'yes.' The Devil is delighted: some spectators have shown 'mercy.' He even suggests that this ability to show empathy will be what will save man.

17.5 Conclusion

The Master and Margarita is not the only novel that deals with the myth of easy money. One feature that makes it remarkable is that Bulgakov analyzes its social impact on a large population (in this case the Muscovites). There are very few books that look at that theme, although it is also prominent in 'Faust' (analyzed in Alfred Steinherr's chapter in this volume). We explored the literature and discovered several books that address the impact of easy money on the happiness of a single individual, however. The general conclusion is that easy money does not make the person happy, just like the rain of money turns Moscow upside down. Take, for example, the Greek myth of the cornucopia, which fueled the never achieved alchemists' dream of transmutation. The same horn also fueled the poetry of Rainer Rilke who observed (in one of his few poems written in French) that '... *tout cela sans fin nous attaque et s'élance*' but this abundance is there '*pour punir l'insuffisance de notre cœur déjà plein*.'[16] King Midas, too, seeks happiness through the accumulation of wealth. He obtains wealth since everything he touches turns to gold, but this ability ultimately makes him unhappy. Closer to us, in the story of the man with the golden brain (a book written by Daudet in 1866, turned into a movie in 2012), easy wealth ends up killing its owner.

Another feature of Bulgakov's Master and Margarita (and this one is unique) is that while he lived in the Soviet (planned) economy, he successfully (and rather accurately) described a monetary concept that would have a formidable theoretical impact on the capitalist world. Forty years and a Nobel Prize in economics separate the two. Bulgakov's style is burlesque, it is entertaining, it is a literary masterpiece, and, at the same time (and perhaps because of it), it is built on a remarkably deep understanding of human nature and a sense of anticipation that can only baffle the reader.

Acknowledgments

The authors would like to thank F. Bourguignon, M. Fafchamps, S. Guriev, and A. Steinherr for useful comments and suggestions. This is a substantially revised version of Meuwly and Leruth (2021).

Notes

1 Bernanke (2002). Some of Friedman's predecessors were also making that link, including Haberler (1952).
2 We thank Marcel Fafchamps for this anecdote.
3 While in the early 1930s (when the Master and Margarita was written) it might have been too soon to detect the emergence of a new man, the Soviet system had already impacted on beliefs and culture (see Zhuravskaya et al., 2022).
4 Although, with QE, central banks purchase financial assets that count as reserves, thus affecting their balance sheet. Not so with a pure concept of 'helicopter money.' We can safely assume that the Devil does not care about the level of assets in his balance sheet.
5 Although not under a pure 'helicopter money' scenario since the assumption is usually that a fiscal deficit is monetized (see Borio et al., 2016).
6 Available at https://www.lse.ac.uk/lse-player?id=3494.
7 See Ofer and Pickersgill (1980).
8 One cannot help making the parallel with the emperor who has no clothes in the tale by Hans Christian Andersen "The Emperor's New Clothes"(See Gross, 1971).
9 In another part of the novel, Pilate who oversees the trial of Jesus also observes that people have a very short memory.
10 On Gresham's law, see Macleod (1858).
11 Boulgakov is very aware that although holding foreign money was punishable by law, everybody did it:

> 'You can only buy with foreign currency here,' [the misanthropic porter] croaked, glaring at them from beneath ragged, moth-eaten eyebrows.
>
> 'My dear fellow,' warbled the tall man, one eye glinting through his broken pince-nez,' how do you know that I haven't got any? Are you judging by my suit? Never do that, my good man. ....
>
> 'This Primus of mine may be full of foreign currency for all you know,' said the stout cat-like figure.

12 Note that the first person to complain is a barman and the two persons who spent the money that fell from the ceiling purchased drinks at the bar.
13 See, for example, Nuti (1989).
14 This exchange can be found in https://ritholtz.com/2010/02/51920/.
15 Bernanke (2010).
16 From Rilke (1978): "all this endlessly attacks us and rushes forward" but this abundance is there "to punish the insufficiency of our already full heart." (Translation by the authors).

References

Bernanke, B. *Remarks at the National Economists Club* (Washington, DC, 2002), available at https://internationalman.com/articles/ben-bernanke-revisiting-the-helicopter-speech/

Bernanke, B. *Remarks by the Federal Reserve chairman before the Senate Finance Committee* (Washington, DC, 2010), available at https://www.theonion.com/u-s-economy-grinds-to-halt-as-nation-realizes-money-ju-1819571322

Borio, C., P. Disyatat and A. Zabai *Helicopter Money: The Illusion of a Free Lunch* (Brussels, VoxEU Column, 24 May 2016).

Bulgakov, M. *The Master and Margarita* (London, Vintage Classics, Penguin, 2003).

Friedman, M. 'A Monetary and Fiscal Framework for Economic Stability,' *The American Economic Review 38* (1948), 245–264.

Friedman, M. *The Optimum Quantity of Money* (London, Macmillan, 1969).

Gross, R. 'The Emperor's Clothes Syndrome,' *New England Journal of Medicine 285* (15) (1971), 863–863.

Haberler, G. 'The Pigou Effect Once More,' *Journal of Political Economy 60* (3) (1952), 240–246.

Macleod, H. D. *Elements of Political Economy*. (London: Longmans, Green & Co., 1858).

Meuwly, D. and L. Leruth 'Le Maître, l'Hélicoptère, et Marguerite,' in E. de Callatay and L. Leruth (eds.), *Quand l'économie nous est contée* (Brussels, La Lettre Volée, 2021).

Nuti, D. M.. 'Hidden and Repressed Inflation in Soviet-type Economies: Definitions, Measurements and Stabilization,' in C. M. Davis and W. Charemza (eds.), *Models of Disequilibrium and Shortage in Centrally Planned Economies* (Dordrecht, International Studies in Economic Modelling Springer, 1989).

Ofer G. and J. Pickersgill 'Soviet Household Saving,' *The Quarterly Journal of Economics 95* (1) (1980) 121–144

Rilke, R. M. *Vergers et Autres Poèmes Français* (Paris, NRF Poésie/Gallimard, 1978).

Rushdie, S. *The Satanic Verses* (London, Viking, 1988).

Zhuravskaya E., S. Guriev and A. Markevich *New Russian Economic History* (London, CEPR DP17244, 2022).

18

MONEY IN THE FAUSTIAN PACT

Alfred Steinherr

Nach Golde drängt,
Am Golde hängt
Doch alles.
Ach, wir Armen
(Faust I)

18.1 Introduction

Johann Wolfgang von Goethe (1749–1832) is generally recognized as the greatest German writer and *Faust* is his masterpiece, divided into *Faust I* and *Faust II*.[1] The first was published in 1806 while Goethe finished the second during the last 7 years of his life. Goethe was brought up in Frankfurt, already in the 18th century a financial center, as scion of a wealthy family. In his lifetime, history was boiling: the French Revolution, the Napoleonic wars, restoration, the Greek wars of independence, and the ups and downs of the German states.

Faust is a drama, written in verse form. Faust I is focused on interpersonal relations, the micro perspective, and is more accessible than *Faust II*. The main actors of *Faust I* are Faust, Mephistopheles (Mephisto), Margarete (Gretchen), and her relatives. The different parts of *Faust II* are not tightly connected and deal with various issues and dramatis personae, one important issue being social changes.

The basic plot is set up between Dr. Faust and Mephisto, the representative of the devil. Mephisto himself has a bet with God that he is able to seduce Faust for a life of pleasure and fulfillment. Dr Faust is a mature scientist, with great accomplishments in his researches but he still is not fulfilled. Being torn between faith and science, he doubts purpose, duty, and joy in the promises of

DOI: 10.4324/9781003534358-22

eternal bliss. Hence, something is missing in his life and that makes him not unlike many of us. He is not completely rational and spends time and thought on questions of magic, in particular alchemy. He is an easy prey to the devil's emissary Mephisto who is proposing a deal: he promises integral fulfillment on earth against the soul of Faust. Mephisto is the servant of Faust in this world, but as soon as Faust stops his strive for more to enjoy the present, he loses the bet and turns into a servant of the devil. This deal is of course impossible to reject: not being sure about the existence of an immortal soul Faust, eager in his strive for three ideals – truth, beauty, and the good is betting on present enjoyment for virtually nothing.

The drama's underlying theme is the potential and the risks of modernity. Faust is embodying the urge of mankind to reach fulfillment through discovery in the intellectual and the physical realm, and improvement of the human condition. Unlike the Marxian view, in Faust man is driven by the desire to possess (knowledge, goods, other humans, etc. and to enjoy. Goethe shows awareness of the risks, always attentive to the pros and cons, this quest ending in greed and vanity, pleasure into licentiousness.

Faust I explores the implications of this in the micro cosmos of a small German town at the end of the Middle Ages. The town is in a stationary state.

Faust II turns to the macro perspective, to treat the following questions. Is this equilibrium sustainable? No, because humans are engineered to strive for power, fame, and wealth.

Is this development, as the Industrial Revolution was already in full steam during Goethe's lifetime, to be welcomed? Yes, but there are major risks for the poor, for human fulfillment (he sees the devil in us and in the background!), for the environment, and for political stability.

In this chapter, I explore the role played by money. Given the low development of financial markets in Goethe's time, money needs to be interpreted more widely as finance. Given imperfect money and capital markets, Goethe sees the role of money as an essential part of any economic activity, be it consumption, investment, or an ongoing enterprise.[2]

In *Faust I*, money is treated as a means to achieve goals other than purely economic ones, namely, to make people behave according to one's wish (Section 18.2). Money's role in the economy is introduced in *Faust II* (Section 18.3). There is always demand for money but as precious metal cannot easily be multiplied, money supply is constrained. To overcome this problem, the devil has the idea of creating paper money. Goethe now deals with the key questions of how to make that money acceptable and how to ensure that excessive money creation doesn't destroy its value. Goethe goes on placing his arguments against the background of the Industrial Revolution, emphasizing the combined power of entrepreneurship, technology, and money, and warns firmly against the risks of limitless growth aspirations as a precursor of the Club of Rome. Section 18.4 summarizes the economic and financial background of Goethe and Section 18.5 bridges money creation as conceived in the Faustian drama with similarities in the modern world. Section 18.6 concludes that Goethe's warnings are as pertinent today as ever.

18.2 Faust I The tragedy of Gretchen

Mephisto develops a strategy for achieving Faust's earthly bliss and hence his servitude by making him fall in love. When Faust, turned young again by Mephisto's magic, meets Gretchen, he is overwhelmed by her beauty and innocence. Although the young girl is charmed by Faust, her youth and social condition forbid her to accept the advances by Faust.

She is perturbed to find a basket with pearls and golden jewelry in her room. This basket is composed by Mephisto but Gretchen believes this to be a gift from Faust. Mephisto might as well have given her gold bars or gold coins. But that would have made the bribery too visible. It was, and still is, more elegant and appealing to give jewelry rather than money to persuade people. Gretchen reflects:

> What good is beauty, even youth?
> All that may be quite good and fair,
> But does it get you anywhere?
> Their praise is half pity, you can be sure.
> For **gold** contend
> On **gold** depend
> All things. Woe to us poor!
>
> Lines 2785 f

She is both happy and upset: she is aware of the monetary value of the basket. She feels honored while realizing the extraordinary capacity of money in putting a value on human beings. Money also has the devilish power of enhancing self-esteem! This gift is hope/proof for Gretchen of her own value and that Faust is serious about her – money talks and seduces whether for right or wrong.

Goethe thus adds a socio-psychological dimension to money's three conventional functions in economics, i.e., as store of value, means of transaction, and unit of account. Money is also power, and this power may cause collateral damage. It is not by chance that Goethe makes Mephisto steal the box with jewels to get sexual gratification for Faust. This scene reminds of many public life scandals throughout history.

But the end is cruel for Gretchen: Faust drops her because he cannot be bound by the stationary life with her, she gives birth to a child, loses her mind, drowns the child, and commits suicide.

Faust I sketches aspects of the role of money in private transactions but does not deal with the economy-wide role of money nor with innovations in the supply of money. This is the job of *Faust II*.

18.3 The constraints of bullion and the illusions of escape

Faust is exhausted at the end of *Faust I* and drops into a healing sleep in an "agreeable landscape" (in contrast to his stuffy study at the beginning of *Faust I*). The five acts of *Faust II* deal with the modernization of the world away from medieval stationarity. It starts out in Act I with the traditional ways of leaders pursuing glory, power, and richness through warfare. It is here that money enters as the principal protagonist, in the form of innovations in the money supply, to satisfy an eternal latent excess demand. Act II and III are not essential for our analysis. Act IV returns to the empire at war. An Anti-Emperor is challenging the established one. The incumbent wins against the reform minded challenger and in recognition distributes parts of the money and land to his entourage. This redistribution ends up mostly in higher consumption. The land that Faust gets, a strip of the coast, is unproductive but not what he is making out of it. In Act V, Faust becomes a lord, initially a ruthless developer, like the steel barons of the 19th century. But climbing up the learning curve he ends his life as a wealthy lord/entrepreneur with a social conscience that finally saves his soul.

18.3.1 Printing money is like love, initially...

In Act I, Mephisto and Faust meet the emperor of a country in dire shape. Permanent wars and excessive spending by the court have rocketed the public finances, impoverished the population, and led to a mutiny of the army. This country resembles German and European states during the Napoleonic wars or before.

Throughout the story, Mephisto, now the business partner of Faust, is generating ideas for dubious innovations. That the devil is the driving force of innovation reflects Goethe's premonition about the unanticipated collaterals. Mephisto knows all (?) problems are problems of money and that money is in short supply. "On earth there's lack of something everywhere, this thing or that, and **money's** lacking here". Is there a way of getting rid of the constraint on the money supply determined by the available gold? Mephisto observes that gold is under the ground waiting to be mined:

> In wall footings and mountain veins
> There's **nugget gold** and **gold coins**.
> And who will deliver it? He will who bends
> Mind and Nature under his commands.
>
> Lines 4885 f

But this suggests that more gold can only be obtained through hard work. An unattractive insight! In fact, Mephisto has a much more daring idea. Instead of mining the gold with hard work, he proposes to create paper currency backed up by the gold in the ground. This has a number of advantages:

First, paper is low cost compared to gold. Second, paper currency is convenient to use. Third, it can be produced in unlimited quantities as long as people believe there is enough backup. The very smart idea of a backup that cannot be measured and does not cost anything as long as it remains in the ground is that it provides great flexibility to the supply of money. But it entails the danger of users losing the belief in the quality of this money.

Once the emperor and his grandees fall prey to the illusion that the imperial land covers endless riches, the next strategic step for Mephisto is to write debt on these hidden assets. This debt needs to be signed by the highest possible authority, the emperor, to obtain a maximum of confidence. Since the debt, in notes of various nominal amounts, is not promising any nominal return, it can indeed be considered as currency.[3] A signature is needed by the emperor to guarantee the best conversion rate of paper currency into gold:

> To whom it may concern Whoever owns
> This note is owed a thousand crowns.
> For its sure guarantee and certain bond
> Untold wealth is buried in the imperial land.
> Provision enough! So without more ado
> Let this wealth you can pocket serve in lieu.
> Lines 6060 f

The emperor is troubled and does not understand what is going on, but was tricked into signing during the past drinking night:

> I smell a crime, a monstrous deceit.
> Who forged my name? Has this gross counterfeit
> Been perpetrated without retribution?
> Lines 6065 f

Well, it is too late. Nothing can be done as much of the new paper currency has already been distributed and the whole population is jubilant:

> We stamped the **complete series** there and then:
> Tens, Thirties, Fifties, Hundreds, fit for service.
> How gladdened were the populace by this!
> A **lusty** life teems in your town that wore
> The cast of moribundity before.
> Your name, always a blessing, was never so
> Amicably viewed as it is now.
> The alphabet's redundant. All will be
> By this sole sign redeemed sufficiently.
> Lines 6070 f

At any rate, there is strong resistance by the people to stopping the merry-go-round, it is too good to be true.

It can't be reined in now. Throughout the land
The fleet things whisked away at lightning speed,
The welcoming exchanges open wide,
They honor – at a profit, to be sure –
Every **note** with **gold** and **silver** there.
And so to butcher, baker, publican,
Half the world's one thought is tucking in,
The other half shows off new buttons and bows.
The draper cuts the cloth, the tailor sews,
Toasts fizz in tap-rooms to the Emperor.
Lines 6085 f

This quote offers keen observations about the effects of introducing paper money. At an early stage, the new currency is well accepted and can be exchanged at an attractive price against gold and silver. The exchange rate (of the paper currency against gold) seems stable although it is likely that from the beginning there is a small discount for the paper currency. In addition to the transaction cost, there is the lingering doubt about the future value of the paper currency. Demand for goods and services and production are propelled by this massive creation of money and the velocity of circulation is bound to increase as citizens are cash constrained and unsure about the future value of the cash. Mephisto underlines the convenience of paper money, like we value today the convenience of credit/debit cards and the like. Mephisto also stresses the connection between money and lust:

Who uses purses now? Too cumbersome.
A **banknote** fits so snugly in the bosom
And couples nicely with a love-note there.
Lines 6105 f

Faust has been absent from the money creation story; he seems to be just an observer. A likely reason is that, as a scientist, he is not sure of what is going on. But then, like clients of investment banks investing in complex structured products of today, he associates the money gamble with magic. All is well as long as the magic is believed: the whole enterprise stands or falls with belief/trust in the new currency. In his reply, Mephisto tries to dissipate Faust's concerns:

Should you want **metal**, the exchange will do a deal;
Or if not, you must dig a while.
You auction off a torque or precious pot,

This **paper** then, amortized on the spot,
Shames the doubter who had dared to mock.
Accustomed now, we don't want the old way back.
Throughout the imperial lands henceforth there'll be
Jewelry, **gold** and **paper** in plenty.
Lines 6119 f

The emperor finally is very happy as the state debt has been paid, and the people are happy spending the cash received. But the emperor notes with sadness that the currency flood is not changing habits and that his subjects as individuals are as little industrial as before, wasting their time in merrymaking.[4] This reflects Goethe's conviction that more money does not change the zest of the largely demotivated population without a vision of a brighter future. This means, in modern terms, that an increase in the money supply does not affect productivity – a view in line with the modern neoclassical assumption of monetary neutrality in the long run:

I had hoped for zest and force to do new deeds
But knowing you, we know you from all sides.
I see very well: whatever **riches** pour
On you, you'll be the things you always were.
Lines 6152 f

18.3.2 From love to tears...

So far money is used predominantly for consumption. But as the spending exuberance already suggests, this happy state is doomed. The country risks returning to its initial stationary state. Goethe does not explicitly describe the explosion in prices although this is suggested by the spending tsunami of the population. But he describes the unrest, the social conflicts following the rising exchange rate of the paper currency in terms of gold over time (more and more paper currency units per ounce of gold), ending in civil war and destruction.

The civil war leads to a revolution and the rise of an Anti-Emperor who is reform minded and has ample gold. But where there is money, there is crime![5] Indeed, with the help of Mephisto, a soldier gang steals that gold to save the emperor. The latter now wins the battle and in recognition distributes land and money to his supporters.

Faust gets a coastal strip of land that is not worth much. With the paper currency received he invests in building a dam to regain productive land like the Dutch did for centuries. His aim is to create a realm of freedom and prosperity – the economic growth paradigm in action. But growth is often associated with destruction: cutting down forests, polluting rivers and oceans, destroying traditional social tissues, and so on. As interpreted by Binswanger

(1994), the violent ebb and flow of the coastal sea symbolizes nature's reaction to its economic and technological subjugation. Goethe warns that riches that flow from violating the natural equilibrium may be built upon unsustainable illusions.

Goethe had absorbed the essentials for the Industrial Revolution: (i) Reinforced property laws, (ii) creation of paper money and financial innovation to collect large amounts of savings for investment, and (iii) technological innovation.

Goethe is absolutely prescient in warning against the exploitation of the masses, the environmental harms, and nature fighting back.

Faust is becoming an entrepreneur, in association with his business partner Mephisto, initially ruthlessly exploiting his workers and greedily acquiring ever more land. His modest friendly neighbors, Baucis and Philamon, enjoy their small house and beautiful garden. To get what they are not selling Mephisto burns their property, destroys beauty for profit. We are reminded of the bush brands in the Amazonas today or the displacements of millions of people for the Three Gorges of the Yanzi River.

> The old people over there must move,
> I want their limes for my demesne.
> Though I own the world, that little grove
> Cankers the lot, not being mine
> ....
> This masterpiece of man's intelligence:
> The clever making active use
> Of the people's wide new living space.
>
> Lines 11240 f

No amount of property ever is enough – Prometheus is unbound. Faust defines the mantra of the modern capitalist/entrepreneur who seeks fulfillment in activity in this world, ennobled by property, never stopping and separating business from issues of eternity:

> Why wander off into eternity?
> He makes the things he knows his property.
> So let him journey through his earthly day;
> However haunted, still go on his way,
> Onwards, to happiness and torment,
> And never satisfied by any moment.
>
> Lines 11440 f

Workers are exploited: "He pulls a sour face at us Though we've made him rich as Croesus" (line 11195) and "We want fair shares" (line 11205). But Faust is oblivious to these requests, for him to get workers is only a question of carrot (money) and stick (lash), combined with forced oblivion (whores and drink):

> Get me workmen
> Thousands, by any means, with **cash**,
> And whores and drink and with the lash
> Encourage, tempt, pressgang them in.
> Lines 11550 f

Like workers also nature is not always docile and fights back. The trenches, the fruit of hard work, are overflown with morass but Faust is not giving up. He knows that business cannot stand still, there are always new challenges by mankind or nature. He has learned that this fight is worthwhile for himself, giving him wealth and power, and for society at large.

> I open room for many millions to live
> Lives – it is true – not safe, but free and active.
> …
> This is the highest pitch of wisdom:
> He alone deserves his life and liberty
> Who every day must fight for them.
> So here, in danger, human life will have
> Zest through all its ages till the grave.
> Such a swarming I should like to see,
> Stand on a free ground with a people who are free.
> Lines 11460 f

Faust, already blinded, acts like a precursor of John D. Rockefeller, justifying his actions by the welfare he is creating for others:

> Only the ruler's word has any weight.
> …
> By order, discipline, swift enterprise
> We shall achieve the very highest prize.
> One mind sufficiently commands
> To that great end a thousand hands.
> Lines 11500 f

Then Faust dies. Goethe starts from the observation that people are not born free (free of religious, social, or economic constraints), but has the vision that freedom can be obtained by individual enterprise, accepting risks and hardship. Faust wins his bet and is happy but does not fall prey to "Linger on Thou art so fair!".[6]

18.4 What did Goethe know? Early experiences with paper money

Throughout history rulers benefitted from minting gold and silver coins, cashing in a rent from standardizing and validating the weight and the purity (carats) of the coins. This premium over bullion is called seigniorage and represents a few percentages of the coins' value. With paper currency issued by the ruler, the seigniorage increased to nearly 100%, the value of the currency notes less the printing cost.[7]

The idea of paper money is not really new at the beginning of the 19th century. To a limited extent, paper money had existed in many countries, in the Netherlands, in Sweden, and in Great Britain. Paper money was introduced in New England very early on, in Massachusetts in 1690 (Galiani, 1751). Widely known was the scheme involving paper money creation by John Law (1750) at the beginning of the 18th century. The key novelty of Law's concept was to back up paper money not with bullion but with land value, the value being based on future revenues. He saw both the need to provide liquidity to stimulate economic activity and the need to limit money creation. What he could not anticipate was that mass euphoria pushed the constraint on money creation beyond reasonable expectations.

Goethe was certainly also influenced by another historic experiment during the aftermath of the French Revolution (Aftalion, 1996). So-called "assignats" were issued starting in 1789 under similar conditions as those prevailing in the emperor's land, unpaid debt, and popular unrest. assignats were linked to newly nationalized church property following up on Law's design. They were state bonds, in principle reserved for the purchase of land, bearing a coupon. But already in 1790 the coupon was scratched and so over time assignats became currency. Initially, in combination with the land reform, the new currency was well received and stimulated trade. As time went by ever more assignats were issued, resulting in high inflation, reinforced by the political instability.[8]

Prior to 1821 when the gold standard was put into operation in the United Kingdom, there was no unique means of payment anywhere. Minted gold, silver, and copper coins were used alongside bullion, pearls, and other valuables, as in Gretchen's basket. Whilst until the 18th century bullion was the measure of wealth, Goethe does see the benefits of ample currency supply for economic development. A populous state of active subjects is creating wealth for all and money is providing the means for economic transactions. Bullion acts as a constraint that may only be released by mining new gold, or by earning gold in payment for net exports. Availability of money and the convenience of paper money were seen to promote economic activity. Goethe is aware of currency being the means for creating wealth, the oil lubricating the economic machine, and not being the machine itself. But for him the time was not ripe yet for paper currency in countries on the way to modernity.

Goethe served as Chief Minister at the provincial court of Duke Karl August in Weimar. Treating the state finances as his own and always overspending,

Karl August was ready to embrace the new trend of paper money. Goethe dissuaded him and pushed for reforming the state household.[9]

18.5 Mephisto and modern times

The problems with relaxing the constraint posed by the availability of bullion are multiple. First, and foremost, how can confidence be invested in the new form of currency? Mephisto has a two-pronged attempt: the signature by the highest authority, the emperor, and the backing by virtual gold under the land. This is both an opportunity and a problem: the opportunity lies in overcoming the constraint on the supply of money as the availability of the backup is not measurable. The problem is an abuse of this degree of freedom and because gold under the land is not palpable and not measurable, acceptance relies all the more on confidence by the users.

The constraint on the money supply is a vexing problem also in modern times. Either there is a responsible institution, call it a central bank, or there is a binding rule such as a fixed exchange rate. But neither safeguard is absolute. Central banks, even if their responsibility is enshrined in the constitution or in an international treaty, like the Maastricht Treaty, may deviate from the goal of price stability in the light of economic (as with external shocks)[10] or political necessity.

Significantly, paper money is not the emperor's idea but the devil's, suggesting that paper money is risky and may have a dark side to it, as proven by the disastrous failures of John Law and of the assignats. Mephisto is clever and promises neither assets far away with fabulous but uncertain future returns (John Law) nor asset redistribution (assignats) but assets that do exist nearby and might be used whenever needed. No need for expropriation as the asset's existence is more an act of magic than a real economic proposition. Fiat money in *Faust II* is backed up by the belief of existing state treasures (like the US dollar was backed by gold in Fort Knox, at least for demands by foreign central banks).[11] What is necessary, but not sufficient, to make such a promise sustainable is a combination of power with robust institutions (like the rule of law paired with oversight and independent central banks). For that reason – economic and military power, the overriding respect of law – the United States was able to promote the US dollar as an international reserve currency under Bretton Woods. The emperor only had the military power, but not the economic one and not the institutional ability and stability.

In *Faust*, it is the emperor who signs the currency notes. The emperor is the most powerful person in the country, commander of the army, with a taxation monopoly and therefore has the best signature available. But he is not powerful enough to ensure a stable purchasing power of the paper currency because the economy is in turmoil (he is at war!) and he is not willing to restrain the money supply.

Once put into circulation, the paper money is first used by the emperor to pay off debt and to pay the soldiers. They in turn spend money on food, drinks, and merrymaking. Is this a Keynesian stimulation through an increase in the fiscal deficit with new money? Yes and no. Payment of the outstanding debt is closer to a debt swap. One part of existing debt, the unpaid salaries of soldiers and unpaid bills of court suppliers, is exchanged against a new debt, the paper currency. This swap is beneficial to debt holders as they are obtaining a liquid asset (the paper currency) for their claims on an insolvent emperor. So, this is more like an open-market operation,[12] hence no fiscal but only monetary policy.

Undoubtedly, more paper currency was created in the emperor's land than the amounts necessary to pay off existing debt. With paper money, armament and additional soldiers could be paid. This can be considered as a fiscal policy financed by money creation. The purchase of goods and services by the emperor with newly created money may be conceptualized as follows: newly printed money is like money falling from heaven into the treasury (the emperor is both treasury and central bank in one institution, as has been the case in many countries) and the treasury uses that money for purchases. There is no debt accumulation by the treasury other than the debt represented by paper currency.

This is helicopter money[13] since there is no corresponding claim on the private sector in the government's accounts as is the case with open-market operations. Leruth and Meuwly (n.d., this volume) see in Bulgakov's novel an example of Friedman's helicopter money concept before Friedman defined it. Goethe provided a description even before helicopters existed!

The fiscal expenditures financed by paper money creation set into motion a fabulous (Keynesian) multiplier-backed spending spree, reinforced by an increase in the velocity of circulation.[14] The multiplier is necessarily high, as the (marginal) savings propensity seems to be low and in a virtually closed economy also the (marginal) import propensity is small. Any crowding-out through higher interest rates is prevented by money creation. But as the supply of goods and services cannot increase at the rate of the money supply, the quantity theory implies that prices need to rise.

As *Faust II* does not suggest any limits to money creation and the belief in riches below the land is nebulous, paper money can increase without bounds. Unfortunately, in the end, there is chaos, high inflation,[15] and civil war. How many countries in the world have had exactly such an experience? In recent times Argentina, Brazil, Turkey, Venezuela, Zimbabwe, and many others come to mind.

18.6 The monetary Gretchenfrage: Nun sag, wie hast du's mit Papiergeld?[16]

From his youth in Frankfurt and his years as minister in Weimar, Goethe had a practical understanding of financial matters. In his library was an extensive collection of economic literature – Reiff (2016). If, as is very likely, Goethe knew of the quantity theory of money (Jean Bodin, 1568), he can be assumed to have an understanding of the relationship between the money supply, the velocity of circulation, and production. Inflation was a vague concept in his time as general price indexes did not yet exist. At any rate, price increases were most of the time relative price changes resulting from supply shocks such as bad harvests for meteorological reasons, pandemics, wars, and so on. Barring vast gold discoveries, or maintained trade surpluses, the bullion stock was relatively stable. Economic growth started to increase in the 18th century in the Low Countries and the United Kingdom (financed by overseas gold discoveries and trade surpluses) but not in the rest of the continent. Hence, bullion was stable, output was stable, and the price level was stable at normal times. In Faust, Goethe was only able to engineer inflation with paper money; the story there is truly helicopter money and fits the quantity theory of money.[17]

Was Mephistos's paper currency doomed? Binswanger (1994) argues that Goethe perceived the coming paper money as a continuation of the alchemist's quest to turn lead into gold. Certainly, *Faust II* shows awareness of the convenience of paper money ("A note fits so snugly into the bosom") but puts greater weight on the danger, suggesting that it may be the work of the devil. The central problem was well identified: how to contain the paper money supply and how to manage it responsibly? We could imagine that a new emperor, enjoying a widespread reputation for his wisdom and honesty, finds a way to control the issuance of paper currency by a powerful new institution (a central bank unlike Law's "Banque Royale") as was done under the gold standard, already during Goethe's lifetime.[18, 19]

Goethe did know of the gold standard but chose to set up the story in a country with a traditional poor institutional setup very much like the German principalities, headed by more or less retarded autocratic princes. In this historical context, still resembling numerous countries today, he saw above all the risk of abuse.

In fact, the idea of creating a solid paper currency based on land as an alternative to gold found a successful realization in Germany after World War I. Germany experienced hyperinflation in the years 1921–1922. To stabilize the currency, the Rentenmark was introduced. Mortgages were written on the lands of private and institutional latifundia owners. These mortgages were securitized in a bank owned by the landowners.[20] Against these securities, currency was issued in the form of deposits and banknotes. The supply of money was backed up by securities (as in modern central banking) and its circulation was limited because the amount of mortgages was limited (this limit does not exist in modern central banking). The Rentenmark helped to stabilize the currency but a complete success was prevented by the intervention of the Reichsbank.[21]

Goethe's premonitions have had a lasting impact on the German people. Their wish for safety in monetary affairs is often linked to the experience of hyperinflation in the early 1920s. But arguably Faust, until recently required reading in Germany's higher education, had contributed to it already earlier on. Scally (2012) argues that "Goethe's fear of paper money as a continuation of alchemy by other means still influences German thinking". By chance, Goethe was born in a baroque building in the shadow of the tower of the European Central Bank.

Jens Weidman (2012), then president of the Bundesbank, referred in a speech to passages in Faust and concluded:

> If a central bank can potentially create unlimited money for nothing, how can it ensure that money is sufficiently scarce to retain its value?... Unlimited bond buying programs to stabilize the Euro zone is a potential Faustian pact as it offers politicians a more palatable financing alternative to painful economic reforms.... The best protection against the temptations in monetary policy is an enlightened and stability-oriented society.

Simply by changing the names of the actors, Mephisto's seduction of the emperor to create paper money foreshadows the story of the Euro. Paper money helped the emperor to go on with the war and keep his subjects happy. A common currency was expected to be necessary for the achievement of the single market and to avoid competitive adjustments of exchange rates. The goal was price stability combined with increased growth throughout the Eurozone. But how to make sure that not too much money is printed and that the right amount is available in different countries?

The Bundesbank had achieved that with the political support of German voters (influenced by Faust and hyperinflation?). The Maastricht Treaty was an attempt to achieve the goal by law. The Euro was created with the signature not of one emperor but of several princes whose resistance to financial and popular pressure was unevenly distributed. Not all had the same treasures on or below their land and their commitment to stability was not the same, so the credibility obtained was, like the emperor's, limited and questionable. In some countries that had suffered from very high interest rates before the Euro, governments, enterprises, and consumers borrowed joyfully at low Euro interest rates and propelled the merrymaking like the emperors' subjects. The Euro crisis of 2009 to 2011 was the natural result of overborrowing in some countries, diverging inflation rates, loss of credibility, and a bet on solidarity (absent in Goethe's single country case where the end game is insolvency). Jean-Claude Trichet, former president of the European Central Bank, praised Goethe's views about the dual nature of money which "produces the best and the worst in the economics sphere".

Beethoven and Schiller gave us the European hymn and, speculatively, Goethe a warning for monetary innovation.

Acknowledgments

I am most grateful to Luc Leruth for suggesting the topic, to him and Klaus Reeh for very useful comments, and to François Bourguignon for comments that enriched the paper and led to a change ofstructure.

Notes

1 There was an historic Faust born about 1480 in Württemberg. He studied magic in Cracow and lectured at the university of Erfurt. The first Faust book appeared in 1587, titled

> Historia of Dr. Johann Faust, the widely acclaimed magician and black artist, how he pledged himself to the devil for a certain time, what strange adventures he saw meanwhile, brought about and pursued until he finally received his well deserved wages.

Christopher Marlowe was the first great poet to take up the theme in his "Tragical History of Doktor Faustus".

2 Weissinger (2015) counted how often the following key words were used in Faust: wealth (58), treasure (66), gold (71), money (8), lust (77), and greed (19). I thicken key words in the citations.

3 Money is defined as a financial debt instrument that pays no interest. In practice, the definition of money stretches from base money (central bank debt) to M1 (cash and cash accounts), to M2 up to M6.

4 Of course, as more money is spent, short-term activity is increased, but not necessarily productivity/hour worked.

5 Pollock (2018) finds that 20% of the value of US dollar and 51% of bitcoin transactions are associated with illegal business.

6 Famous line of Faust I when Faust seals his pact with Mephisto: "When I say to the Moment flying; '*Linger a while – thou art so fair!*; Then bind me in thy bonds undying, And my final ruin I will bear!".

7 When deposit money is created, the seigniorage is cashed in by banks. But it is less than for currency notes as the banks normally pay interest on their deposits and may need to hold reserves with the central bank.

8 Another problem contributing to a vanishing loss of confidence were British fake assignats. They attempted to reinforce the economic crisis in France. Beginning of 1793, "assignats" had lost 50% of their value in terms of gold before falling to 8 percent in April 1795. Traders refused to accept the currency and workers paid in "assignats" became even more impoverished. February 1796 the directoire decided to convert "assignats" at a rate of 30:1 into "mandats territoriaux". The latter lost their value completely by 1797. To increase the acceptance of "assignats", there was a period when property of gold and silver currency or their exchange was forbidden and citizens had to surrender their holdings to the government.

9 Scally (2012).

10 As an example, in 2022 the inflation rate in the Eurozone is a multiple of the 2% target enshrined in the Maastricht Treaty.

11 In the late 1960s, the dollar reserves of the world's central banks exceeded the value of gold held in Fort Knox. The dollar therewith lost his convertibility into gold, the beginning of the end of Bretton Woods.

12 Open-market operations consist of buying or selling securities from the market for central bank money. When a central bank buys securities, it credits the selling bank's account with the central bank. Thereby the amount of money in the private sector increases.

13 Friedman (1969).

14 Velocity of circulation was first discussed by William Petty (1662). It has been a concept of much discussion. The modern interpretation makes velocity a function of expected inflation. See Fisher (1930).

15 As the paper currency depreciates in terms of gold, it buys fewer goods and this is inflation. By contrast, the purchasing power of the relatively constant gold stock is likely to rise, as production of goods and services has increased. In terms of gold, there may be deflation.

16 In German, "Gretchenfrage" refers to a question of fundamental attitude. Gretchen asks Faust: "Say, as regards religion, how you feel, I know that you are a dear, good man, Yet, for you, it seems it has no appeal", or in German: "Nun sag, wie hast du's mit der Religion? Du bist ein herzlich guter Mann. Allein ich glaub, du hältst nicht viel davon".
17 See Friedman (1969) and Fisher (1930).
18 Great Britain was the first country in 1821 to introduce paper currency at a fixed exchange rate with gold. Other countries followed during the 19th century and by the 1870s the gold standard became international. Central banks had to intervene in the market to maintaining convertibility of fiat currency into gold at a fixed price. They also had to defend the exchange rate by allowing or fostering a speedy adjustment of the balance of payment. International imbalances were paid in gold and most countries had legal minimum ratios of gold to currency issued. But after World War I, the gold standard fell apart.
19 Major studies of the gold standard include Bordo and Schwartz (1984), Bordo (1995), Cooper (1982), and Eichengreen and Flandreau (1997).
20 Securitization means bundling assets such as mortgages and issuing tradeable securities whose value is based on these mortgages. This was extensively practiced in the United States and lack of regulatory oversight led to the financial crisis of 2007–2009.
21 See Stadermann (1994).

References

Aftalion, F. (1996), *L'économie de la Révolution française*, Quadrige/PUF.

Binswanger, H.C. (1994), *Geld und Magie – Eine ökonomische Deutung von Goethe's Faust* [*Money and Magic-Interpretation and Critique of Modern Economy based on Goethe's Faust*], Murmann Publisher.

Bodin, J. (1568), *Réponse de J. Bodin aux paradoxes de M. de Malestroit touchant l'enchérissement de toutes choses et le moyen d'y remédier*. Martin Le Jeune.

Bordo, M.D. (1995), *Gold as a Commitment Mechanism: Past, Present and Future*, World Gold Council Research Study no 11.

Bordo, M.D. and A.J. Schwartz eds. (1984), *A Retrospective on the Classical Gold Standard, 1821–1931*, University of Chicago Press.

Cooper R.N. (1982), "The Gold Standard, Historical Facts and Future Prospects", *Brookings Papers on Economic Activity*, Vol. 1, 1–45.

Eichengreen, B. and M. Flandreau (1997), *Gold Standard in Theory & History*, Routledge.

Fisher, I. (1930), *The Theory of Interest. As Determined by Impatience to Spend Income and Opportunity to Invest it*, Macmillan.

Friedman, M. (1969), *The Optimum Quantity of Money*, Macmillan.

Galiani F. (1751), *Della Moneta*, Guiseppe Raimondi.

Goethe, J. W. von, (1808, 1832), *Faust I und II Eine Tragödie, Erstausgabe Tübingen, J.G. Cotta'schen Buchhandlung Faust I (1808) und Faust II (1832).*

Goethe, J. W. von (1949), Faust, Part II, (David Constantine translator). London: Penguin Books.

Law, J. (1750), *Money and Trade Considered with a Proposal for Supplying the Nation with Money*, A. Foulis.

Leruth, L. and D. Meuwly (n.d.), "The Master, the Helicopter and Margarita", this volume.

Petty, William (1662), *A Treatise of Taxes and Contributions*. Nathaniel Brooke.

Pollock, A. (2018) *Finance and Philosophy. Why We Are Always Surprised.* American Enterprise Institute.
Reiff, G. (2016), "Goethe and the Creation of Money", Ph.D Thesis.
Scally, D. (2012), "Goethe, Money and Faustian Pact", *The Irish Times*, December 10.
Stadermann, H.-J. (1994), *Die Fesselung des Midas*, J.C.B. Mohr.
Weidman, J. (2012), https://www.bundesbank.de/Redaktion/DE/Reden/2012, Begrü ßungsrede.
Weissinger, K. (2015), "Besitz und Genuss in Goethes Faust", Doctoral dissertation, University of Heidelberg.

PART IV

Rent-seeking, corruption and bad political governance

19

HOW STEINBECK SPEAKS TO INSTITUTIONS IN ECONOMICS

Stuti Khemani

19.1 Introduction

Institutions—the formal and informal "rules of the game" played in economies and societies—are the economic answer to some big questions, such as why some countries are rich and others persistently poor.[1] Economics is examining institutions not only to explain differences in income and economic structure between countries but also to understand outcomes of persistent inequality and relative poverty within the most advanced economies of the world.[2] Here, economics is challenged by moral philosophy. While economic outcomes can be examined and explained through the lens of efficiency—how agents engage in transactions driven by their motivations and using their initial endowments—the discipline has few tools to analyze whether those outcomes are *desirable*, such as from perspectives of "fairness" and "justice". Yet we *do* have the tools to examine linked questions that speak to moral philosophy: how do outcomes vary under different institutions, and which institutions achieve better outcomes from a moral philosophy perspective? To begin to answer this question, we need to understand human behavior with regard to institutions. Great writing—literature—is distinguished by the human sensibility and power of empathy of writers to describe how others think and behave as they play the game of society and the economy. I show how literature speaks to economic institutions from this aspect—describing how people across social strata think about the prevailing rules of the game and how they play the game, or choose to change the game (that is, institutional change).

I focus on John Steinbeck's novella *The Pearl* and examine the dilemmas of the protagonist Kino, a poor pearl diver in Mexico who lives in a time and a place of "non-inclusive" or "extractive" institutions (to use the terminology of

DOI: 10.4324/9781003534358-24

Nobel Laureates Acemoglu, Johnson, and Robinson). In the period setting of the novella, "natives" like Kino face systematic discrimination and exclusion from education, economic markets, and political power. The story shows how these institutions lead to sub-optimal decision-making, with tragic human and economic consequences. A child loses his life. A good with great economic value, the eponymous pearl, which could have brought unprecedented income and thus improved the lives of Kino and his family, is destroyed instead. I argue through illustrations from Steinbeck's story how exclusionary institutions lead to these tragic consequences by shaping the "mind-set" of various actors or agents in the society and economy. That is, institutions exert material influence on behavior, away from what would be obtained under assumptions of "homo economicus".

In the following section, I set the stage for delving into *The Pearl* by linking to another example of Steinbeck's writing, in his celebrated novel, *The Grapes of Wrath*. I show how the thoughts of Kino on institutional change are different from Tom Joad's, the protagonist of *The Grapes of Wrath*, which I infer from Steinbeck's writing. Contrasting what Steinbeck writes about the thinking of his different characters, I deduce what he has to say about institutional change. If prevailing institutions in the period in Mexico described in the novella are yielding poor economic outcomes from both efficiency and equity (used as a shorthand for broader questions of fairness and justice) aspects, how might institutional change come about to improve outcomes? This leads to somewhat shocking results. I argue that Steinbeck, and his readers, resign Kino, his Mexican protagonist in *The Pearl*, to acceptance of his condition, focusing on the beauty of simple peasant life imbued with family love, while economic aspiration is reviled as greed, bringing out the worst in human behavior. This is in sharp contrast to Steinbeck's treatment of Tom Joad in *The Grapes of Wrath*; Joad leaves the comfort of his family for a greater cause, according to the writer, of organizing labor to bring about institutional change.

I conclude with many open questions about why Steinbeck and his readers treat Kino's aspiration as evil greed, and how they think institutional change would come about in Kino's context. Is Steinbeck's different treatment of Kino, compared to Tom Joad, reflective of which character he personally identifies with and thus chooses to express his own views through that character? Steinbeck himself subscribed to a particular political philosophy of institutional change, which is reflected in the thinking of his protagonist, Tom Joad. A question that arises here is whether "great" writers, including Steinbeck, are limited by their own social status in what they can authentically represent? Who then speaks authentically about the Kinos of the world? As a reader, I was not persuaded that Kino and his community of poor pearl divers in Mexico were going to be resigned. As Mexico has modernized, since the colonial times of Kino's world, the poor or non-elite use political institutions to exert power over economic policies.

But the tragic economic outcomes from left-wing politics and policies in Latin America show that there is much still to learn. That is, we know too little about the design of institutions to produce outcomes that are both efficient and equitable. I conclude with how literature that is authentically representative of the thinking and behavior of non-elites can help in this regard.

19.2 The moral challenge from Steinbeck

Steinbeck wrote *The Grapes of Wrath* in the aftermath of the Great Depression as an indictment of the functioning of economic markets. Perhaps the most evocative and exemplary passage in this regard is the following:

> There is a crime here that goes beyond denunciation. There is a sorrow here that weeping cannot symbolize. There is a failure here that topples all our success. The fertile earth, the straight tree rows, the sturdy trunks, and the ripe fruit. And children dying of pellagra must die because a profit cannot be taken from an orange. And coroners must fill in the certificate—died of malnutrition—because the food must rot, must be forced to rot.
>
> The people come with nets to fish for potatoes in the river, and the guards hold them back; they come in rattling cars to get the dumped oranges, but the kerosene is sprayed. And they stand still and watch the potatoes float by, listen to the screaming pigs being killed in a ditch and covered with quick-lime, watch the mountains of oranges slop down to a putrefying ooze; and in the eyes of the people there is the failure; and in the eyes of the hungry there is a growing wrath. In the souls of the people the grapes of wrath are filling and growing heavy, growing heavy for the vintage.
>
> *(The Grapes of Wrath, last two paragraphs of chapter 25)*

Do we believe this writing as an accurate description of reality? Were there, in fact, incidents during the Great Depression of security guards restraining hungry people so they could not reach food before it was sprayed with poison? Even if we assume or verify via media coverage that the writing is reasonably true to the fact of such incidents, what is harder to assess is the nature and extent of the "wrath" of those who suffered hunger that Steinbeck writes about. In the following sections, I will examine how Steinbeck develops this idea of "wrath" further in *The Pearl*, describing the thinking in the minds of those who suffer poverty, both economic and socio-political.

There are many other examples, of course, strewn throughout literature, of the human condition where some sections of society, across generations, lead lives of vastly inferior quality than what they could have with some redistribution of existing material resources. But it is not this point that I want to belabor. My purpose in this section has been to set the stage for my analysis of *The Pearl* by hearkening back to Steinbeck's classic and picking up on his first writing about "wrath", which, I will argue below, is more fully, or intimately, developed in *The Pearl*.

The Pearl is inspired by a folk story of Mexico, and, as I show below, Steinbeck's writing is full of references to folk songs as the self-expression and self-realization of those who are too powerless or too frightened to challenge unjust institutions. Through this stage-setting, and the following analysis of *The Pearl*, I hope to stir a movement for unearthing folk songs as authentic literary expressions of human thought, particularly of those who are not represented by established authors (who are likely to come from elite, educated backgrounds).

19.3 Analyzing "*The Pearl*": How it speaks to the economics of institutions

Steinbeck wrote *The Pearl* in 1944. It is a story set in Baja California Sur, Mexico, in a community of poor fishermen. Kino, the protagonist, lives a life whose joy comes from the family love between him, his wife Juana, and their baby son, Coyotito (little coyote). Kino has never been to school, cannot read or write, and relies on fishing in the seas around him, with minimal equipment beyond his body, to sustain a meager livelihood. The story begins with Kino awaking one morning and looking around him, and Steinbeck gets into his mind thus[3]:

> Kino heard the little splash of morning waves on the beach. It was very good—Kino closed his eyes again to listen to his music. Perhaps he alone did this and perhaps all of his people did it. His people had once been great makers of songs so that everything they saw or thought or did or heard became a song. That was very long ago. The songs remained; Kino knew them, but no new songs were added. That does not mean that there were no personal songs. In Kino's head there was a song now, clear and soft, and if he had been able to speak of it, he would have called it the Song of the Family
>
> ....
>
> Kino heard the creak of the rope when Juana took Coyotito out of his hanging box and cleaned him and hammocked him in her shawl in a loop that placed him close to her breast. Kino could see these things without looking at them; Juana sang softly an ancient song that had only three notes and yet an endless variety of intervals. And this was part of the family song too. It was all part. Sometimes it rose to an aching chord that caught the throat, saying this is safety, this is warmth, this is the Whole.

The serene morning is immediately struck by a tragedy, which then courses its way to make the whole story. A scorpion stings the baby Coyotito as he lay hanging in the box while his parents busied themselves around the fire for breakfast. Steinbeck is masterful in how he describes the event unfolding—how Kino sees the scorpion first on the rope by which Coyotito's box hangs; how he hears a new song, the Song of Evil, in his head, underneath which the Song of the Family "cried plaintively", as he takes steps to save the baby; how Juana repeats an "ancient magic" under her breath to stop the scorpion from reaching the baby, and then adds a Hail Mary quickly on top.

The story is about how Kino and Juana try to save their baby and fail to because of the institutions that govern their lives. From the "facts" of the events told by Steinbeck, it seems the story could have ended soon after it started, with Juana successfully saving her baby on her own by administering the only remedy that was likely to work—immediately sucking out as much of the poison as she could (and later, applying a poultice of seaweed, which Steinbeck comments "was as good a remedy as any and probably better than the doctor could have done"). Yet, despite all the knowledge in Juana's head of home remedies from the innumerable instances of scorpion bites experienced in her community, she asked for something she had never done before: a doctor.

> The doctor, she said. Go to get the doctor. The word was passed out among the neighbors where they stood close packed in the little yard behind the brush fence. And they repeated among themselves, "Juana wants a doctor." A wonderful thing, a memorable thing, to want the doctor. To get him would be a remarkable thing. The doctor never came to the cluster of brush houses. Why should he, when he had more than he could do to take care of the rich people who lived in stone and plaster houses of the town.

Thus begins Kino's journey of interaction with the institutions of power that his wife thinks could save their son. First, the doctor humiliates Kino and refuses to see the child who is brought to his doorstep. This spurs Kino to a desperation to find resources to pay the doctor to attend to his child. Diving wildly in the sea, with Juana and Coyotito in tow, they find an improbably large pearl, bigger and more brilliant than any ever seen. Steinbeck wants readers to recall the biblical parable where a merchant trades all he owns for a jewel, which is a metaphor for Heaven. This pearl, the Pearl of the World, awakens aspirations in Kino to not only buy modern medical treatment for his son but also to send him to school, the most awesome thing, to transform his son's life.

Second, however, market institutions fail Kino—the traders try to belittle the pearl, and Kino, whose aspirations have been raised by his success, cannot tolerate the injustice. No mutually beneficial trade happens because there is no trust to engage in the game of a market transaction in a cooperative way.

Third, institutions of law and order fail Kino. As he resolves to walk the distance to a larger town to find a better deal for his pearl, the doctor, the priest, and an assortment of armed robbers destroy his boat, his brush home, and try in different ways to steal the pearl from him. There is no security of property rights for Kino and his family.

Now the pearl has become a monster—Juana thinks it is evil and asks Kino to get rid of it. In the end, he does—Kino surrenders to his fate—but not until after he has raised his hand on his beloved wife, killed a man, and exposed his son to a gunshot (which is what finally kills Coyotito) that one of the armed trackers on the pearl's trail fires in the direction of a wail he hears. The man fires thinking it is a wild animal, "some coyote bitch with a litter", and kills instead the human baby which had been named for that animal. Kino's active anger—his wrath—appears to center on the pearl, rather than on the institutions which failed him, and he is encouraged to think thus by his wife, his partner, the person he trusts. It is the pearl—which is a product of market value that rightfully belongs to Kino as a result of his labor and could raise him above the income percentile into which he was born—which is vilified. Economic value and human lives are destroyed in the end as Kino tosses the pearl back to the sea, ending the story.

In the following sub-sections, I dissect the different ways in which the story speaks to the role of institutions in shaping sub-optimal behaviors which resulted in loss of valuable life and property.

19.4 Institutions of service delivery: Systematic cheating of the poor

> This doctor was not of his people. This doctor was of a race which for nearly four hundred years had beaten and starved and robbed and despised Kino's race, and frightened it too, so that the indigene came humbly to the door. And as always when he came near to one of this race, Kino felt weak and afraid and angry at the same time. Rage and terror went together. He could kill the doctor more easily than he could talk to him, for all of the doctor's race spoke to all of Kino's race as though they were simple animals. And as Kino raised his right hand to the iron knocker in the gate, rage swelled in him, and the pounding music of the enemy beat in his ears, and his lips drew tight against his teeth—but with his left hand he reached to take off his hat.

The doctor has wields power over Kino. Why does he choose to exercise his power by inflicting humiliation, instead of attending to the child and gaining gratitude? Does power enter as an argument in his utility function, and specifically as the consumption of feelings of superiority over another by inflicting humiliation? Or, is he simply following a norm of social behavior—it is not expected that a man of his race should stoop to treat the children of poor Mexican natives. Are institutions of inequality thus internalized in shaping human behavior, either through inherited preferences or through social norms?

Or, is it, simply, incentives? The doctor knew that Kino couldn't afford to pay him, and therefore he instructed his servant to send Kino away. But his actions thereafter, in the story, are not consistent with incentives alone. After news of Kino's finding the great Pearl of the World spreads through the town, the doctor receives the information, which thus suggests that Kino will be able to pay for medical services. However, instead of engaging in a mutually beneficial transaction of medical services in exchange for payment, the doctor focuses on how to steal the pearl from Kino. He visits Kino's hut under the pretext of coming to see the injured child, but Steinbeck's writing strongly implies that the doctor's real motive is to trick Kino into revealing where the pearl is hidden.

> The doctor said, "I was not in when you came this morning. But now, at the first chance, I have come to see the baby."
>
> Kino stood in the door, filling it, and hatred raged and flamed in the back of his eyes, and fear too, for the hundreds of years of subjugation were cut deep into him.
>
> "The baby is nearly well now," he said curtly. The doctor smiled, but his eyes in their little lymphlined hammocks did not smile. He said, "Sometimes, my friend, the scorpion sting has a curious effect. There will be apparent improvement, and then without warning—pouf!"
>
> ...
>
> "Sometimes," the doctor went on in a liquid tone, "sometimes there will be a withered leg or a blind eye of a crumpled back. Oh, I know the sting of the scorpion, my friend, and I can cure it."

He administers a suspicious substance to Coyotito, which makes the baby turn from recovery (thanks to Juana's remedies) to sickness. The doctor then returns and administers something else (ammonia) to Coyotito to stop the vomiting and declares that he has conquered the poison and cured the child. Only then does the doctor ask for a payment, and Kino tells him that he will sell the pearl in the morning to make the payment. The doctor tricks Kino into revealing where the pearl is hidden in the hut, and, we are led to believe, organizes a group of armed men to steal the pearl in the night. Thus, the doctor uses his power in a way that is not only detrimental to Kino but in the end also to the doctor because he gains nothing of the value of the pearl while spending effort and materials in a plan to steal it.

Kino's and Juana's behavior are also shaped by the same institutions of racial inequality and social norms of deference to the elites. At the same time, there are crucial differences in attitudes between Kino and Juana, and growing tension through the course of the story because of these differences. Kino is far more suspicious of elites, and his decision to defer to them, or not, is shaped by rational thinking about uncertainty, as illustrated in the following passage:

> Kino felt the rage and hatred melting toward fear. He did not know, and perhaps the doctor did. And he could not take the chance of pitting his certain ignorance against this man's possible knowledge. He was trapped as his people were always trapped, and would be until, as he had said,[4] they could be sure that the things in the books were really in the books.

Juana, on the other hand, is successfully manipulated by the doctor to think he has superior powers to cure the child. Steinbeck strongly suggests that the opposite was true—the doctor administered something mysterious to Coyotito to worsen his condition, after Juana's home remedies had worked, so that he could return to undo his own damage and claim credit. Upon returning:

> He took the baby and examined it and felt its head. "The poison it has worked," he said. "I think I can defeat it. I will try my best."...The baby spluttered and screeched under the treatment, and Juana watched him with haunted eyes....But Kino was suspicious, and he could not take his eyes from the doctor's open bag, and from the bottle of white powder here. Gradually the spasms subsided and the baby relaxed under the doctor's hands. And then Coyotito sighed deeply and went to sleep, for he was very tired with the vomiting. The doctor put the baby in Juana's arms. "He will get well now," he said. "I have won the fight." And Juana looked at him with adoration.

19.5 Institutions of law and order: Insecurity of property rights for the poor

From the time that Kino and Juana find the pearl, they are beset with worry that it will be taken away from them. This worry is justified, as the story unfolds. A group of thieves enter Kino's hut in the night to try to steal the pearl. We are led to believe that it is the doctor who organized the robbery attempt after using his visit to learn where Kino would have hidden the pearl. Further along in the story, after Kino refuses to take the low price offered by the traders in the local market and decides to set off on a journey to other, more distant markets for a better price, he is afraid.

> And Kino was afraid. Never in his life had he been far from home. He was afraid of strangers and of strange places. He was terrified of that monster of strangeness they called the capital.

These brief lines package a punch—people like Kino lack the basic institution of a secure identity to deal with "strangeness" and securely access new markets. Here is a piece of literature which describes a fundamental constraint that keeps people trapped in poverty—lack of secure identity, and thus secure rights over their own labor, to transact in markets. Current policies in many developing countries to give people a secure identity, such as the Aadhar biometric identity card in India, have the potential to transform economies by dramatically reducing transaction costs for the poor.

Even before Kino can set off on that perilous journey to new markets, he is attacked in his home. This attack further terrifies Juana. Unable to persuade her husband to throw away the pearl, she resorts to furtiveness, waking up early to take the pearl back to the sea. But Kino senses it, follows her, strikes her in a fit of rage, and reclaims the pearl. Kino then discovers that unseen foes had already been at work to destroy him. His canoe had been broken beyond repair, and his brush home was set on fire. He could not seek refuge even in his own community because he knew that would bring the revenge of the elite upon them all. The only recourse open was to flee on foot. But they were tracked by armed men on horseback. This time, Kino kills one of them.

> Now, in an instant, Juana knew that the old life was gone forever. A dead man in the path and Kino's knife, dark bladed beside him, convinced her. All of the time Juana had been trying to rescue something of the old peace, of the time before the pearl. But now it was gone, and there was no retrieving it.

19.6 Institutions of market transactions: Monopoly of pearl traders

Kino has few opportunities to sell the pearl. There is only one market in the town, which is monopolized by one buyer who hires traders to give the semblance of competition. There is no transportation to other markets, or information about prices prevailing in other markets.

> Now there was only one pearl buyer with many hands, and the men who sat in their offices and waited for Kino knew what price they would offer, how high they would bid, and what method each would use. And although these men would not profit beyond their salaries, there was excitement among the pearl buyers, for there was excitement in the hunt, and if it be a man's function to break down a price, then he must take joy and satisfaction in breaking it as far down as possible.

What Steinbeck is describing, in the terms of principal-agent economics, is that the agents tasked with buying pearls from the poor Mexican fishermen are intrinsically motivated to bargain down the price to reservation value, without any high-powered incentives to do so. Intrinsic motivation is, of course, a matter of preferences and "types". Steinbeck is thus again describing institutions of how agents behave or play the game, going beyond incentives.

As the traders ruthlessly act out parts to proclaim the pearl worthless so that they can offer the lowest possible price, the sense of injustice in this bargaining wells up in Kino, and he walks away without making the trade.

> "I am cheated," Kino cried fiercely. "My pearl is not for sale here. I will go, perhaps even to the capital."
>
> Now the dealers glanced quickly at one another. They knew they had played too hard; they knew they would be disciplined for their failure, and the man at the desk said quickly, "I might go to fifteen hundred."

> But Kino was pushing his way through the crowd. The hum of talk came to him dimly, his rage blood pounded in his ears, and he burst through and strode away.

Just as in the case of institutions of service delivery which governed the doctor's behavior, the institutions of power which governed the behavior of the pearl traders resulted in non-cooperative behavior to the detriment of all involved. No mutually beneficial transaction took place because each side was motivated by something other than economic incentives—the traders by a desire to exploit, and Kino by rage against unfairness and injustice. Put another way, lack of trust between the pearl traders and the pearl fisherman prevented markets from working.[5]

The community is astounded because Kino refused an offer that would have made him more money than he had ever made in his life. Kino's brother comes to discuss the situation:

> Juan Tomas came in and squatted down beside Kino and remained silent for a long time, until at last Kino demanded, "What else could I do? They are cheats."
>
> Juan Tomas nodded gravely. He was the elder and Kino looked to him for wisdom. "It is hard to know," he said. "We do know we are cheated from birth to the over-charge on our coffins. But we survive. You have defied not the pearl buyers, but the whole structure, the whole way of life, and I am afraid for you."

19.7 Institutional change: Barriers to aspirations

Not only Kino but the whole community of fishermen realizes that they are in a low bargaining position vis-à-vis the traders in the town. There is an interesting conversation between Kino and his brother Juan Tomas about different strategies the community had tried in their fathers' times, of pooling their pearls and hiring an agent of their own to sell the pearls in distant markets where better prices were to be found. These strategies, we are told, did not work because the agents ran away with the pearls each time. Lack of institutions of trust, or contract enforceability, can explain the outcome.

What is additionally interesting in the passages where Kino and Juan Tomas discuss the problem is an allusion to unfair institutions as a matter of social norms, ordained by a higher power, such as a God. Kino says of the idea of collective bargaining:

> It was a good idea, but it was against religion, and the Father made that very clear. The loss of the pearl was a punishment visited on those who tried to leave their station. And the Father made it clear that each man and woman

> is like a soldier sent by God to guard some part of the castle of the Universe. And some are in the ramparts and some far deep in the darkness of the walls. But each one must remain faithful to his post and must not go running about, else the castle is in danger from the assaults of Hell.
>
> "I have heard him make that sermon," said Juan Tomas. "He makes it every year".

As Juan Tomas continues to caution Kino about his decision to travel to a distant, unknown town, where he has no social network to support him, where he may be cheated yet again, Kino responds:

> "What can I do?" Kino cried. "Some deep outrage is here. My son must have a chance. That is what they are striking at."

Kino has changed and dared to challenge prevailing institutions, not for his own but for the sake of his son. Moving passages describe his aspiration from the pearl:

> In the pearl he saw Coyotito sitting at a little desk in a school, just as Kino had once seen it through an open door. And Coyotito was dressed in a jacket, and he had on a white collar and a broad silken tie. Moreover, Coyotito was writing on a big piece of paper. Kino looked at his neighbors fiercely. "My son will go to school," he said, and the neighbors were hushed. Juana caught her breath sharply. Her eyes were bright as she watched him, and she looked quickly down at Coyotito in her arms to see whether this might be possible.
>
> But Kino's face shone with prophecy. "My son will read and open the books, and my son will write and will know writing. And my son will make numbers, and these things will make us free because he will know—he will know and through him we will know." And in the pearl Kino saw himself and Juana squatting by the little fire in the brush hut while Coyotito read from a great book. "This is what the pearl will do," said Kino. And he had never said so many words together in his life.

The above reading of the role of the pearl, from an economics perspective, is far removed, and quite the opposite of the view of the pearl as a representation of evil, in the eyes of Juana and in the eyes of many readers and teaching of the book in American schools.[6] From an economic perspective, the pearl is a legitimate product of value of Kino's labor. Under well-functioning institutions, Kino should be able to sell the pearl and invest in his son's education for a future stream of increased earnings. Perhaps more valuable to Kino than the income is the access to knowledge through his son's education, which would improve the rules of the game in his and his community's favor and give them dignity. That is, Kino is seeking institutional change through the education of his children rather than through violent revolution.[7]

Although initially beguiled by Kino's vision of education for their son, Juana changes her view of the pearl rapidly, in line with what has been ingrained into her by the priest's sermons. Juana is governed by superstition and ignorance, blaming the pearl for bringing "evil" into her husband—of greed and aggression, which would destroy their noble poverty and peaceful, loving family life. As soon as Juana is persuaded that her son has been cured by the doctor, she wants to get rid of the pearl.

> Now the tension which had been growing in Juana boiled up to the surface, and her lips were thin. "This thing is evil," she cried harshly. "This pearl is like a sin! It will destroy us," and her voice rose shrilly. "Throw it away, Kino."
>
> ...
>
> But Kino's face was set, and his mind and his will were set. "This is our one chance," he said. "Our son must go to school. He must break out of the pot that holds us in."
>
> "It will destroy us all," Juana cried. "Even our son".

Interestingly, American readers of the novella also vilify the pearl as the evil of the parable. Steinbeck gives his readers the leave to do so, writing at the start: "if this story is a parable, perhaps everyone takes his own meaning from it." Linda Wagner-Martin introduces Steinbeck's pearl as a metaphor for the American dream: "to become successful, to gain possessions and prominence, to become a force within a community". But this dream in a person like Kino is "greed", and the evil that destroys his family. It is taught to convey the moral that greed is evil—that Kino lost his way when he stopped listening to the Song of the Family and pursued material wealth. There is no mention in a variety of school notes that guide how the book is taught, nor in the literary analysis of Steinbeck's work, as far as I have seen, about how this novella speaks to institutions—of power, and of trust (or lack thereof). This chapter has thus addressed the gap.

19.8 Conclusion

The economy and society in Steinbeck's novella are riddled with inefficiencies or lack of mutually beneficial transactions that would grow incomes and enable health and wellbeing. The outcomes are sub-optimal for all involved, most tragically for the protagonist Kino and his wife Juana, who lose not only the product of their labor but also their beloved son. These inefficiencies arise from prevailing institutions—of unequal power which shapes behavior of all agents to play the game of society and economics in non-cooperative ways.

The novella also shows how institutions trap people in poverty—one, through how they shape poor people's behavior, and two, through how they shape elite behavior toward the poor. Steinbeck's description of Juana is replete with examples of lack of self-confidence and aspiration to rise in society, and acceptance of the poor's place in it as a noble outcome (resisting greed). Elites in the society—from the priest, to the doctor, to the traders in the marketplace—have the power to change institutions, invest in health and education of the poor, and build the public infrastructure that would expand access to markets; but they choose to maintain monopoly power, and systematically exclude the poor.

How would change happen toward greater efficiency and equity when the starting point consists of institutions that promote non-cooperative behavior and stifle entrepreneurship and aspiration? Markets do not emerge in Kino's world on their own because of transaction costs, fundamentally arising from a lack of trust and trustworthiness. Even though the pearl fishing community is aware that the local traders are extracting rents through monopoly power, and even though they tried to gain access to other markets by engaging an agent from among their own, their efforts failed because dishonest (non-cooperative) strategies are the norm in how agents play the game. For markets to emerge, those in positions of power need to invest in institutions and infrastructure to support markets, such as roads, media for communication, law, and order, which in turn may help to foster trustworthiness.

Steinbeck is silent in *The Pearl* about how institutional change would happen, in contrast to his view expressed in *The Grapes of Wrath* that change would happen through the organization of labor. History indeed shows that in the United States, change came about after the Great Depression through the political process, in which organized labor played a role, to bring into office (positions of power to effect institutional change) leaders who established a new social contract (the New Deal program). The history of Mexico, and Latin America more broadly, also shows that the political process, and the leaders selected through it, is fundamental to institutional change. Elites in Latin America *did* start expanding access to markets and investing in public health and education as countries modernized away from the colonial setting of *The Pearl*. However, Latin America continues to struggle with corruption, ill-advised economic policies, and lower trust and entrepreneurship compared to its wealthy northern American neighbors.

Engerman and Sokoloff (2005) argue that historically unequal economic institutions in Latin America compared with those in the United States and Canada were responsible for the delay in the adoption of inclusive political institutions, and this delay is associated with subsequent weak institutions and persistently worse economic outcomes. However, although a body of work shows that early adoption of egalitarian institutions and social policies is important (for example, Engerman and Sokoloff, 2005, and Acemoglu and Robinson, 2012), the mechanisms behind why early adoption matters and has persistent effects are not clarified or made explicit. Why are countries not able to change outcomes within short time spans, for example, through political inclusion by instituting elections with universal adult suffrage, and through public spending on education and market-supporting institutions? World Bank (2016) connects the dots in the pattern of evidence and answers the question as follows: formal institutional changes do not immediately change long-standing political behavioral norms; and these political norms, a subset of social norms, pertaining specifically to the sphere of government and public policy, in turn affect the functioning of formal institutions. Historical institutions of inequality can contribute to unhealthy political norms, such as those that sustain clientelist forms of political competition where political support is won by targeting private benefits at the expense of broad public goods.

Novels can help in understanding institutions as norms of behavior. Who are the Steinbecks of today who can speak to institutions and norms? Writers like Ben Okri and Aravind Adiga have won prestigious literary awards for depicting their perspectives as the educated elites who grew up experiencing institutions in countries like Nigeria and India. While their perspectives are indeed enriching, and formally lauded as such, I want to end by making a case for accessing the literature of "others", the non-elite, which does not receive formal recognition. Understanding "others", whose experience and identity we do not share, is the forte of great writers. Yet great writers can be limited in their understanding when the others are too far removed from their own experience. Steinbeck was inspired to bridge this divide by relying on a folk tale of Mexico, which presumably reflects the authentic voices of the poor, to write *The Pearl*.

This chapter's analysis of Steinbeck's rendering of a folk tale shows how the non-elite in developing countries may not have the "wrath" that Tom Joad acquired during the Great Depression in the United States. Has this changed since Steinbeck, or in other contexts like India's, as depicted in Adiga's celebrated stories? Are writers like Adiga authentically representing the thinking of the non-elite in developing countries today? I would argue that there are grounds for skepticism that educated, elite writers can represent the thinking of the non-elite. We may need more writing based on folk tales and songs that are the creative expression of the non-elites. From Steinbeck's adaptation of such a folk tale, we learn that characters like Juana and others (Juan Tomas, Kino's well meaning brother) do not want violence or revolution; what they want is education and health for their children.

Future work at the intersection of literature and economics, on questions of institutions and institutional change, could invest in unearthing such folk tales, and folk songs, as authentic creative expressions of the human condition.

Art appears to be moving in this direction, such as, for example, with the awarding of a Nobel prize for literature to Bob Dylan for song writing, and through critical analysis of Black hip-hop as poetry. I end this chapter by calling for greater attention and respect to literature of different forms coming from historically marginalized communities, such as folk songs of lower caste groups in India. The unprecedented expansion of education and economic opportunity over the past decades has created a moment in human history where those at the bottom of the social strata are not going to be resigned to their place in society. Thus far, elites have viewed the world through the prism of literature written by their own kind. If we are to understand the world today, and how institutional change might come about, we need to access the literary expression of others.

Acknowledgments

I thank François Bourguignon and Jean-Philippe Platteau for valuable comments which helped shape and improve this essay.

Disclaimer: The arguments in this chapter are entirely that of the author. They do not necessarily represent the views of the International Bank for Reconstruction and Development/World Bank and its affiliated organizations, or those of the Executive Directors of the World Bank or the governments they represent.

Notes

1 Rodrik et al. (2004), Sachs (2003), and Glaeser et al. (2004) as counter-points; Helpman (2009), MacLeod (2013), reviewing Acemoglu and Robinson (2012), Diamond (2012), and Baland et al. (2020).

2 Saez (2021).

3 All the quotes come from the 1994 Penguin Books edition of *The Pearl* by John Steinbeck, with an Introduction by Linda Wagner-Martin.

4 This refers to a passage earlier in the novel to which I will come below—about Kino's dreams of using the pearl to educate his son.

5 This is where *The Pearl* connects with the following observation from Kenneth Arrow:

> Virtually every commercial transaction has within itself an element of trust, certainly any transaction conducted over a period of time. It can be plausibly argued that much of the economic backwardness in the world can be explained by the lack of mutual confidence.
>
> *(Arrow, 1972)*

This is where *The Pearl* also connects with observations about the role of virtue in enabling markets (Bowles, 2016).

6 The book is widely taught in middle and high school curricula as an accessible piece for young readers from a master of the American canon.

7 Recall Steinbeck's description of the "wrath" in Kino's mind, mingled with fear, when he is standing at the door of the doctor's *hacienda*, which makes it easier for him to kill than reason with the powerful people who humiliate and cheat him.

References

Acemoglu, D. and Robinson, J.A., 2012. *Why nations fail: The origins of power, prosperity, and poverty*. Crown Books.

Arrow, K.J., 1972. Gifts and exchanges. *Philosophy & Public Affairs*, 1, pp. 343–362.

Baland, J.M., Bourguignon, F., Platteau, J.P. and Verdier, T., 2020. Economic development and institutions: An introduction. *The Handbook of Economic Development and Institutions*, Princeton University Press, chap. 1, pp. 1–20.

Bowles, S., 2016. *The moral economy: Why good incentives are no substitute for good citizens*. Yale University Press.

Diamond, Jared. 2012. What makes countries rich or poor? *The New York Review of Books*, 2(10).

Engerman, S.L. and Sokoloff, K.L., 2005. Institutional and non-institutional explanations of economic differences. In Ménard, C., & Shirley, M.M. (eds) *Handbook of new institutional economics* (pp. 639–665). Boston, MA: Springer US.

Glaeser, E.L., La Porta, R., Lopez-de-Silanes, F. and Shleifer, A., 2004. Do institutions cause growth?. *Journal of Economic Growth*, 9, 271–303.

Helpman, E. ed., 2009. *Institutions and economic performance*. Harvard University Press.

MacLeod, W.B., 2013. On economics: A review of Why nations fail by D. Acemoglu and J. Robinson and Pillars of prosperity by T. Besley and T. Persson. *Journal of Economic Literature*, 51(1), 116–143.

Rodrik, D., Subramanian, A. and Trebbi, F., 2004. Institutions rule: The primacy of institutions over geography and integration in economic development. *Journal of Economic Growth*, 9(2), 131–165.

Sachs, J.D., 2003. *Institutions don't rule: direct effects of geography on per capita income* (No. w 9490). National Bureau of Economic Research.

Saez, E., 2021. Public economics and inequality: uncovering our social nature. In *AEA Papers and Proceedings* (Vol. 111, pp. 1–26). American Economic Association.

World Bank, 2016. *Making Politics Work for Development: Transparency and Citizen Engagement*. Washington, DC: Policy Research Report, Development Research Group, World Bank.

20

THE ECONOMICS OF INNOCENCE

Imbolo Mbue's "How Beautiful We Were"

Célestin Monga

20.1 Introduction

The video is short but unsettling. The opening seconds are reminiscent of early Sergio Leone western movies, without the guns and revolvers. The first shot shows the legs and old shoes of a young man, who then appears in a general shot, dressed all in black in cheap clothes and wearing a backward cap. He takes a few steps in an empty lot. He crouches down and picks up a handful of dust, which he lets blow away in slow motion while he watches the fine particles carried by the wind. A text appears on the screen: "Lead is a toxic metal with no safe levels of exposure. Children absorb four to five times more lead than adults" (HRW 2023).

Then the young man speaks, looking at the camera with a frown. In the following sequences, he is joined by two other teenage girls, also of modest appearance. With restrained dignity, they continue the young man's statement, innocently raising a simple question:

> Article 31 of the United Nations Conventions on the Rights of the Child highlights that children have the right to play, leisure and rest. But what happens when the environment is contaminated? What happens is what we see in the context of Kabwe where so many young children continue to be affected by the metal that is in their systems.

Kabwe? That is a small town in Zambia where the multinational mining company Anglo-American operated for half a century, leaving waterways and agricultural fields contaminated with lead and other byproducts from mining and making the city one of the world's most polluted. Although the Kabwe mine

DOI: 10.4324/9781003534358-25

was formally closed in 1994, mining residues were left on site in a dumping site adjacent to residential areas, locally known as Black Mountain, and continued to contaminate surrounding areas through the flow of wind and water. Lead poisoning can cause serious health problems ranging from learning difficulties for children to infertility, brain damage, and, in some cases, death.

Watching a Kabwe video and the teenagers speaking on camera about their pain but yet showing resilience and a sense of purpose, one wonders whether they are characters out of Imbolo Mbue's novel *How Beautiful We Were* (2021) or whether real life events are mimicking the tragic tales of exploitation, resistance, and sadness, depicted in her novel. Interestingly, Mbue's novel, which has been hailed by critics,[1] is not about Kabwe or southern Africa. It is the story of a West African village where a group of citizens decide to take on a powerful multinational oil company whose oil drilling activities have caused heavy human and social costs. Many other African and developing countries have indeed experienced similar disasters, often reported in media around the world.

Mbue's novel disturbs that false psychological equilibrium and that sense of emotional tranquility. Unlike news media reports and United Nations statements, *How Beautiful We Were* actually introduces the reader to real people—a tour de force for a work of fiction—and real victims of mining exploitation who try to resist in the context of a corrupt, brutal dictatorship. Set in a fictional African village called Kosawa in the 1980s, a group of poor villagers who have suffered from intergenerational misery are confronted with an existential challenge and they must collectively organize their response, in a context of a "enemy-government" led by a ruthless autocrat, and absent private sector, and nonexistent or weak civil society.

The reader is forced to live their minuscule lives and share their ordinary dreams and naïve quest for justice. Among them, the reader learns what greed can do to people, and how anger can be converted into courage and sacrifice. Thus, the reader must face their raw human emotions as their simplest desires are cruelly repressed. With its daring and unforgettable characters (some of whom continue to dominate the story long after their death), subtle narrative structure, and sharp and intense writing style, the book makes it difficult for any reader to remain detached from or indifferent about issues of environmental destruction in poor rural communities, often thought to be well known from media reports and thus dismissed.

How Beautiful We Were provides the reader not only with the pleasurable experience of a sparkling novel but also with gut-wrenching stories and meditations on a wide range of themes, which social scientists have been grappling with for a long time. As expected, its characters are more real, authentic, and complex than the necessarily abstract actors featured in economic theories. That is why the reflections, thoughts, motives, decisions, and actions in Mbue's novel help revisit some of the insights that economic theorists and empiricists have developed on various topics. The novel sheds a powerful light on the issues and trade-offs that real people in a low-income country face when dealing with a dysfunctional polity, and it narrates the many ways in which they choose their goals and priorities and make decisions, both at the social and community level and at the personal and individual level.

This chapter analyzes some of the themes in Mbue's novel through the lens of economics. Section 20.2 presents the story of the book—a tale of greed, anger, and resistance—and highlights its literary appeal. Section 20.3 discusses the economics of lawlessness and conflict in Mbue's fictional world and the ways some of the key characters in the novel operate in a country where the judicial system is nonexistent and are forced to rely on external entities for help. Section 20.4 provides some concluding remarks and stresses the costs of unrealistic dreams and the predictable failure of a resistance strategy underlined by grief and innocence.

20.2 A tale of greed, anger, and resistance

How Beautiful We Were is a suspenseful novel about guilt and innocence. The story takes place in the fictional West African village of Kosawa and chronicles the ordeal of its people, who have been betrayed by their own political leaders and find themselves forced to fight an American oil company whose harmful activities have destroyed their lives. But the book is about a lot more than the traditional David-versus-Goliath fight often reported in news media and in which a small, powerless community is oppressed by a multinational corporation. Mbue only uses that generic background to subtly explore a wide range of social concerns and human emotions through several strong, unforgettable characters.

The construction of the novel is ingenious, yet easy to follow: the story is told by multiple narrators and balances the chronology of events and the evolution of the plot while avoiding redundancies. Mbue tactfully weaves the different opinions of the important characters—sometimes about the same events—with sumptuous flashbacks as remembered by each of them. From the first pages, the reader is captivated by the sense of catastrophe to come and the sequencing of the events but not overwhelmed or confused by the kaleidoscope of perspectives from different characters and their unique viewpoints, assumptions, and emotions. Mbue takes her reader on a gripping journey, up to a poignant finale.

The novel gets off to a flying start. The very opening paragraph sets the haunting tone and dark atmosphere of the book:

> We should have known the end was near. How could we not have known? When the sky began to pour acid and rivers began to turn green, we should have known our land would soon be dead. Then again, how could we have known when they didn't want us to know? When we began to wobble and

> stagger, tumbling and snapping like feeble little branches, they told us it would soon be over, that we would all be well in no time. (…) They told us we had to trust them. We should have spat in their faces, heaped upon them names most befitting—liars, savages, unscrupulous, evil. We should have cursed their mothers and their grandmothers, flung pejoratives upon their fathers, prayed for unspeakable calamities to befall their children. We hated them…
>
> *(2021, p. 3)*

"We hated them…" Strong words from the Children (Thula who emerges as the main character in the story and her seven classmates) against the greedy oil company executives. The anger and hatred expressed by the people of Kosawa reflect the pain, disillusionment of several decades of frustration and suffering, and the fear of what may be coming in soon ("the end" which is "near"). Their country became independent in the 1980 after a long and painful period of colonialism. Oil was discovered in their village. Their new government promised that it would generate wealth and prosperity for all citizens. Pexton was then granted exploitation rights for the oil. Yet, for decades, the villagers never benefited from the extraction of the resource. From the time when Yaya and Big Papa (the grandparents in the story) were young, oil enriched the American corporation and its local political supporters—the country's brutal dictator known as His Excellency, government members, the village chief, and their employees posted in Kosawa and conveniently housed in a secluded nice area called The Gardens.

Oil only brought environmental destruction, diseases, and havoc as children fell sick from environmental toxins and died. Oil spills seep into the farms, and the river turns green under toxic waste. The villagers kept losing their ability to hunt and forage and maintain their way of life. Parents regularly bury their children, and the community is constantly grieving. The Kosawa people show a lot of patience and even some naiveté. They feel entitled to the oil resources near their land—even though in almost all countries, the ownership of natural resources under the ground does not to belong to any individual village but to the whole nation.

In good faith, the villagers try to contact government officials and the Pexton leadership to discuss the issues and their woes; they repeatedly ask Pexton and the government to mitigate the ecological devastation that oil exploitation has caused, but to no avail. They are met with denial of any wrongdoing, deceit, and threats. Eventually, they want the company's operation shut down and their land restored, but their pleas are ignored. Nothing is done, and conflict arises and worsens.

Everything changed suddenly one day during one of the public meetings regularly organized by Pexton with the people of Kosawa (with the sole aim of giving the impression of consulting them). Three Pexton representatives, whom the Children have nicknamed the Round One, the Sick One, and the Leader, cynically tell the villagers that they should be proud Pexton chose their land for their oil pipelines and drilling sites—which have left the fields uncultivated and the water poisoned. Woja Beki, a slimy character who is also a corrupt village chief siding with Pexton, helps the oil company executives spread their phony promises and real threats against the villagers. Attending these meetings are many parents whose sons and daughters are dying and who are confronted with the perplexing perspective that no one is left to carry on the family name.

One man, who usually never attends these meetings, abruptly shows up and ignites a revolt. Konga, an outcast viewed as the village madman because he seems to suffer from mental illness and hears voices in his head, interrupts the usually uneventful Pexton meeting to let everyone know that the day has finally come for the oil company to pay for all its crimes. In front of the whole crowd, the eccentric Konga humiliates the Leader and his own village chief Woja Beki by spitting at their faces and telling them that the whole Pexton delegation will not leave the village. He holds the key of the Pexton car and let everyone know that he has neutralized their driver. No one had ever witnessed any such scene in Kosawa's history.

The Pexton Leader remains defiant despite his surprise and anger. He despises what he views as fake threats from a madman. Woja Beki joins him and warns Konga that upon hearing about his crazy actions, government officials in Bézam, the capital city, will send soldiers to destroy Kosawa. He begs the madman to return the car keys so that the Pexton delegation can leave. Scared, the crowd also pleads with Konga to relent. But the madman quickly turns out to be more than a lunatic vagabond. He knows that no one in Kosawa can touch him because the prevailing belief systems and social norms associate mental illness with terrible curses. A village elder, "a man enlightened by age, a man who has lived long and mastered the difference between right and wrong," turns to the grinning and swaying madman and invokes family ties to beg for peace at any cost:

> we don't want soldiers in our village, he says. Please, Konga Wanjika, son of Bantu Wanjika, I'm begging you, give these men their key. Your father was my second cousin, and I'm now speaking to you on his behalf. Don't bring any more suffering on us. Drop the key on the ground, and I'll pick it up and give it to them. Go bring their driver from wherever you've hidden him. Let us wish each other a good night and go home.
>
> *(p. 19)*

Instead of a good night, the village enters a very long period of recurrent nightmares. All the mothers in the crowd cry out to the madman: "Give him the key! We don't want soldiers coming here. We're begging you." Konga doesn't listen. Instead, he quietly ignites doubts and debates among the villagers, some of whom start to think that the Konga can awaken them and convince them to fight for their freedom. Quarrels begin among the people, "loud and fierce and clamorous."

Mbue describes the chaotic discussion with a nonlinear literary style, mixing the frantic urgings made by both sides in a single paragraph that gives the reader the feeling of being in the middle of an angry crowd with some reluctant would-be warriors and hearing two different tones at the same time:

> Let us show them that we're the people too. The soldiers are going to shoot us dead. The Spirit has sent Konga to tell us that we can and should fight. Fight with what? Fight with what we've got. What have we got but spears? We've got machetes and stones and pots of boiling water. How can you be so stupid as to think we have any chance? Konga has shown us we stand every chance. Konga is a madman. Perhaps madness is what we all need. How can you say such a thing? We were once a brave people, the blood of the leopard flows within us—when did we lose sight of that? We'll be dead tomorrow—is that what you want?
>
> *(p. 22)*

This falsely banal paragraph highlights Mbue's stylistic genius: the deliberate patchwork of contradictory impulses and opinions from conflicting viewpoints is reminiscent of the broken and incomplete chords in some of Fela Kuti's or Ahmad Jamal's compositions ("*Confusion*," "*The Night Has a Thousand Eyes*") when the music mimics the chaos it evokes. By putting together some raw emotions from opposing perspectives, Mbue also plays two discordant notes in unison and reveals her taste for the type of dissonance that Bernard Herrmann employed in Alfred Hitchcock's film scores to build tension and uneasiness.

The madman wins the day. His unilateral decision to sequester the Pexton employees is eventually endorsed by everyone and gets the uprising started. By holding them hostages, the Kosawa people hope that the oil company will stop its deadly operations in their village. Lusaka, a man who has lost two children because of toxic water due to oil drilling, offers to accommodate the hostages until the negotiations have succeeded. The general belief is that resistance will yield the long-awaited freedom.

The villagers' initial demands are quite modest: they simply request the name of someone in Bezam who can help Kosawa. But nothing goes as planned. The Leader refuses to budge. Moreover, one of his colleagues—the Sick One, whose real name is Kumbum—gravely fell ill. It's all the more embarrassing that he is also the most inclined to cooperate with his kidnappers. The village witches (two twin brothers) can neither save him from his illness nor can they wipe out the memories of the other Pexton hostages as they promised in order to prevent them from revealing secrets to the authorities after their release.

Before his slow and painful death, Kumbum ignites another major twist in the story by connecting his abductors to his nephew Austin, an American journalist in Bézam. He was hoping that Austin could help the Kosawa people publicize their cause and perhaps force his own company Pexton and the government to find a peaceful resolution to the problem. Konga, the lucid madman, warns the three men sent to Bézam not to expect any serious help in Bezam: "we are the only ones who can free ourselves," he says (p. 102).

While Austin is happy to take up the cause and join the fight, the death of his uncle Kumbum in captivity and in the hands of the group of people he is trying to help complicates everything. This is just one of the many moral dilemmas subtly highlighted in the story. It does not take long for the authorities to realize that something is amiss and send soldiers to Kosawa. Spears are thrown at them by the twin brothers, who are both witches and traditional healers in the village. The response is brutal: it's a massacre. As the soldiers shoot blindly into the crowd, some of the Children run to hide in the bushes and realize that they should never have expected such a tragic adventure to end well in a country where the authorities have no respect for the law. The soldiers free the remaining hostages and take the village chief and a few leaders as prisoners (most notably Lusaka and Bongo, two members of the initial delegation sent to Bézam).

Thula, one of the Children who is also Bongo's niece, witnesses the gruesome shooting and escapes only by pretending to be dead. She had already lost her father Malabo (son of the novel's grandparents Yaya and Big Papa) to whom she was very close. After the tragedy, she does not speak for many days, and her brother Juba channels his deep grief into the drawing of frightening pictures.

The release of Austin's articles brings another major turn to the plot. He is expelled from the country. A nongovernmental organization (NGO) called the Restoration Movement takes an interest in the Kosawa story and offers help. Its activists bring some money to the villagers and promise more, as they publicize the case against Pexton in the United States. They accompany the family members to see their loved ones in prison in Bézam (four of whom are eventually hanged and buried in secret), organize a boycott campaign against Pexton oil, and promote education, which they present as the most effective way of organizing resistance—otherwise children will keep "dying for lack of knowledge" (p. 130).

The NGO facilitates the schooling of young children such as Thula in the nearby city of Lokunja. Being one of the brightest in the group with promising leadership skills, she is eventually selected by the Restoration Movement to go to college in America. It is a life-changing experience. She spends years there, falling in love with Austin, attending college, learning, studying protest movements, getting involved in new political networks, and enriching her imagination.

She reads lots of books, including *The Communist Manifesto* and Fanon's revolutionary blueprint *The Wretched of the Earth*—she is mesmerized by its contents: "What this man has to say about what people in our situation ought to do, I'm in awe of it—my friends and I spend hours dissecting his ideas" (p.

204). Referring to the Restoration Movement, she and her friends dismiss the "regurgitated nonsense" that they kept hearing from the NGO. "How hard could we trust them to fight for us, considering that their most powerful weapon was words? Wasn't it time we stopped using words and tried something else, something altogether new?" (p. 206) Back home, her friends become impatient and doubtful about the peaceful, long-term strategy of change suggested by the Restoration Movement. The NGO has recommended to the villagers to become friendly with the oil company executives, which leads the Children to wonder whether they need to take matters into their own hands. Some eventually engage in violent acts and destroy Pexton property, while others are framed and arrested.

This raises serious questions not only about the effectiveness of the liberation strategy advocated by the Restoration Movement but also about the legitimacy of the activities of foreign NGOs involved in the political and development agendas in countries far away from their headquarters. Mbue presents the Restoration Movement in the novel as a beacon of hope for the Kosawa people, but she is not naïve about the multiple roles and significance of such a foreign NGO in the struggle of the people of a small African village. She also highlights the dark irony of total reliance on humanitarianism and the recourse to outside forces from America to combat an American oil company. Mbue's somber lucidity is on full display when she depicts the NGO leaders as people with their own agenda, values, and priorities.

In Mbue's novel, the interventions of the foreign actors are eventually ineffective, if not harmful. James expresses serious doubts about such "compassion economies," defined as "the finite flows of beneficent material resources, knowledge, and expertise, technologies, therapies, and other forms of exchange" (2010, p. 85), which often lead distressed populations to rely on the benevolence of humanitarian organizations for welfare and advocacy instead of focusing on effective, home-grown solutions to their problems. He observes that

> the suffering of another person, when extracted, transformed, and commodified through maleficent or beneficent interventions, can become a source of profit for the intervener. Through acts of intimidation, destruction of property, theft, torture, and murder, agents of torture and repression generated what I call terror economies.
>
> *(2010, p. 26)*

How Beautiful We Were also provides grounds for discussing the validity of some of the arguments found in social science writings regarding the pertinence and legitimacy of foreign NGOs and civil society organizations in general in political and economic development. Thula's and the Children's thoughts and opinions—especially in their exchange of letters while she resides in the United States—are a rebuke of de Tocqueville's (2004) postulate that societies strive politically and economically when they are able to build strong and nurturing social capital through a vibrant civil society. Research on Africa and in country contexts under autocratic governments such as the one described in the novel shows that civil society remains an elusive concept, with foreign NGOs often contributing negatively to social capital, democratic consolidation, or economic well-being (Monga 2009).

As in certain Richard Attenborough movies where one knows from the start that the end will be tragic but where one is still totally captivated by the suspense of the action and the ambiguity of the unpredictable characters (his 1982 film *Gandhi*, for instance), the reader knows in advance that Mbue's novel will not end well. Still, one is surprised by the turn of events. Thula returns to Kosawa convinced that the real problem is not Pexton, but rather the country's autocratic and ruthless leader. Six months after her return home, she gives up on nonviolence, provides money to people to buy guns, and inspires a new generation into warfare. The resistance strategy followed by the villagers and the Children includes actions that devolve into violence and mayhem. They engage in random killings of their perceived adversaries:

> We knew none of these people. We executed them only to pass a bit of our pain along to our tormentors. After every kill, those of us who had taken part in the act accepted palm wine from the others. While the killers got drunk, the sober ones pondered whom to kill next. We were now the spears of the people.
>
> *(p. 307)*

When The Five, the angriest and most desperate group of villagers, kidnapped another oil company executive and his wife to try to force negotiations, they explicitly requested in their letters that the government soldiers be kept out. For once, Pexton appears willing to oblige, as "it wanted its man and his wife free to return to their children in America, it wanted no more blood on its hands" (p. 349). Unfortunately, the country's authoritarian leader does not agree. "His Excellency did not take orders, particularly from women." Even when Pexton's top executive at headquarters in New York calls the presidency to warn that if he sent soldiers and there was bloodshed, the company would have to stop doing business with his country, His Excellency is said to have laughed and responded that he had no time to waste. Another massacre ensued. Kosawa is destroyed by government forces.

20.3 Discussion

Some salient themes of Mbue's novel are worth exploring further in the light of economics and other social sciences. To begin with, there is the issue of property rights. As the owner of all the underground resources of the countries—a common feature of most countries, whether developed or developing—the central state is entitled by law to award their exploitation to any competent firm. In a well-functional democracy, the state is expected to set the terms of the contract with the selected firm in such a way that the welfare of the general population, and the local population in particular, is maximized. Benefits are obtained through taxation of the firm's profits at a level that affords it sufficient profitability to make the investment attractive. Assuming that there is no national firm possessing the technology and know-how required for the resource extraction, the contract is signed with a private foreign firm with which an agreement has to be found. To achieve the purpose of collective welfare maximization, the tax proceeds collected by the state ought to be redistributed across the population according to some fairness principle, and this should imply that the population residing in the area where the resource is located is not bypassed.

But there is a second duty of the state, which is to monitor all negative externalities, or noxious effects, resulting from the exploitation of the resource and compel the firm to compensate local inhabitants for any harm caused to them. In the case of oil drilling, because such externalities are huge and they take the form of severe damages to health, the role of the state also consists of requesting the firm to take all measures necessary to prevent their occurrence.

What Mbue depicts is the worst possible situation in which the state has not only abstained from redistributing income toward the local population but also eschewed the fulfilment of its most basic duty, namely, to block any transfer of resource exploitation costs to this population. In view of such glaring failures, the rebellion of local inhabitants is perfectly understandable. The key problem, however, is that, the state being autocratic, these people have no institutional channel available to air their grievances and put pressure on the ruler. Most revealing in this regard is the tragic destiny of Malabo, the father of Thula. Full of frustration, anger, and despair, he discusses with his brother Bongo his decision to travel to Bezam, the capital city, to try to meet with government officials and raise the issue of water poisoning by Pexton in his village. In a country where citizens have no voice and the ruler is accountable to no one, Malabo knew that it was a risky trip. But he feels the urge to go and to try anything which may help save his people. He was right to be suspicious because this was, indeed, his very last trip. He never came back, and his family never recovered from his disappearance. The fact of the matter is that the autocrat does not want to hear about any complaint because he is eager to maintain his rent from the Pexton operations.

The question in the minds of the villagers is therefore fully legitimate: "Is the government a rock, a thing with neither brain nor heart? Is the government not humans like us—people who have children, mothers and fathers who know what it's like to have a sick child?" (p. 41). Given the absence of democratic institutions and the aloofness of the despot at the helm of the country, there are only two options left for them: submit and passively accept the ordeal imposed on them by human actions, or engage in some violent action, initially unarmed, in the hope of ending it or at least negotiate improvements in their condition. This dilemma confronting them is at the heart of Mbue's novel, the epilogue of which suggests that a violent revolt is doomed to fail owing to the highly asymmetrical balance of forces.

Following the author's account, the villagers have well understood their hopeless position and this is why they were initially reluctant to get involved in any kind of struggle against the multinational firm and the colluding state power. It is no coincidence that the rebellion was actually sparked, and in a sense forced on them, by the village's madman, that is, by an outcast excluded from participation in local decision-making processes. And that it was later supported by the group of Five and morphed into deadly terrorism when no other option was left and their lives were filled with despair and anger. Perhaps less expectedly, Thula, whose character plays an important role in the novel as she steers the Children, undergoes a gradual transformation of her ideas as a result of her studies in the United States. Essentially non-violent, she nevertheless indulged momentarily into violence by facilitating the purchase of guns by the group of Five. However, upon her return to her country, and before the tragedy that destroyed her village, her followers, and herself, she becomes an active non-violent militant campaigning across the whole country for Kosawa but also for the rights of poor and ill-treated people, without drawing particular attention from the autocrat. In this way, Mbue suggests that such campaigning is essentially harmless to his rule.

A correct deciphering of the mechanism of violence depicted by Mbue reveals that there were, in fact, two distinct steps in its escalation process. First, at the instigation of the madman, violence was directed against the multinational firm through the kidnapping of the driver of a firm's delegation sent to the village. And second, in reaction against the brutal repression at the hands of the regime's military, violence spread in the village through the actions of the Group of Five and others. A major observation is that this ominous escalation of violence could have been stopped when, in the last sequence of tragic events, the firm's representatives at last manifested some willingness to negotiate with the villagers and to give in to some of their central demands. Yet the implacable Excellency would not hear about any concession to the rebels and vindicated further use of state violence. This was a major turning point and, certainly, one that motivated Thula to get irremediably radicalized. Autocracy thus comes out as the ultimate culprit for the chain of violent events that led to horrifying massacres of innocent people.

Clearly, the autocratic ruler is not a "stationary bandit" concerned with the country's long-term economic growth from which he could extract a regular and reasonable income share for himself (Olson 1993). He instead behaves as a "roving bandit" whose short-time horizon prompts him to indulge in theft and plunder without any attention paid to their long-term effects. This is the extractive or predatory regime analyzed by scholars like Nobel Laureates Acemoglu and Robinson (2012), and Dixit (2004). How can we reconcile such a character (or preference) profile with the empirical observation that not infrequently autocrats rule over rather long periods of time? One plausible answer is that, owing to political instability, the autocrat feels continuously threatened by rival contenders (perhaps belonging to their own clique) or by opposition forces, thereby living in the constant fear of being dislodged from power and thus deprived of access to sources of extractable rents. In the novel's story, political instability stems from the perceived possibility of popular rebellion, hence the autocrat's inflexible attitude toward, and brutal repression of, any manifestation of dissent.

The question then arises as to whether, in the absence of disciplining by the national state of the country of operation, the multinational firm could have been brought to heel by the justice system or by NGOs from its country of origin. Mbue's novel touched on the two aspects of this question. Regarding the former, it bears emphasis that the US Department of Justice declined the motion by Kosawa's lawyer to indict Pexton under the Foreign Corrupt Practices Act. The consequence was immediate: the company walked off talks of a settlement with the villagers. Moreover, the American judge who rendered the final verdict did not deny that Pexton had ruined the land in Kosawa and that it was even likely that the collusion between the oil company and the government of His Excellency had caused serious crimes. However, it was judged that the case should be left to the jurisdiction of the country where the company operated on the ground that "America had to respect other countries' boundaries" (p. 343). In short, the US judiciary washed its hands in circumstances where the despotic power of His Excellency meant that the victims stood no chance of getting reparations and receiving a fair treatment.[2]

As for the NGOs, Mbue's narrative seems to indicate that, despite all their goodwill and their mobilizing power, foreign NGOs are unable to effectively come to the rescue of the villagers harmed by the firm's actions in a foreign country. They discover painfully that the outsourcing of their resistance strategy to some foreign actors (American newspapers and NGO) was a costly illusion and moral innocence cannot win over evil. The problem, here, is in part that foreign organizations have their own agenda which do not necessarily coincide with the objectives of local protest movements. At the same time, mention is made of the remarkable achievement by the American NGO, which consisted of indicting a powerful multinational into a major US court for damages caused to victims living in a distant country.

Finally, the question of decentralization of political power as an alternative to concentrated power at the centre emerges in some places of the novel. Some of the Children thus dream of living in a country where all important decisions would be made at the level of villages like Kosawa. Leaders would be selected by them and held accountable for the quality and effectiveness of their leadership, and removed from office through elections when their performance would be viewed as unsatisfactory. Such a view is consistent with the analysis by Myerson (2018, 2024) who studies power relations within countries and argues that successful states tend to maintain a functional relationship between local politics and national politics. According to him, "when the question is how to find responsible leadership to improve the provision of essential public goods and services for a whole nation, we should not ignore the supply of leadership that is available locally." This is true despite the fact that "local governments in poor communities might not have the most modern administrative technology, and the potential constituency of some local politicians might be limited by their identification with one side of an ethnic rivalry."

In short, local politics might not be democratic. Yet the important point is that "economic development depends on political leadership, and trusted leaders can be found in local politics. The great successes of modern economic growth began in nations where local leadership was regularly integrated into national politics" (Myerson 2018). Myerson's approach seems to underpin Thula's and her friend's faith in the intrinsic goodness or superiority of political systems dominated not by corrupt autocrats in the capital city but by accountable stakeholders in rural areas.

Unfortunately, a number of empirical works on decentralized governance in the African context do not confirm the optimism of Myerson's view. The corrupt behaviour exhibited by Woja Beki, the local village chief of Kosawa, is actually not exceptional. Rent-seeking of the type described in *How Beautiful We Were* appears to be quite prevalent in African countries where governance is mainly grounded in "retail politics." A case in point is provided by the Democratic Republic of Congo (DRC), the development challenges of which are very similar to those chronicled in Mbue's novel. Although it is rich in natural resources, the DRC remains one of the world's lowest income countries. This paradox happens in a context where its precious minerals are exploited by large firms or produced in artisanal and small-scale operations which subject the workers to extortion, human trafficking, child labor, and violence perpetrated by many armed groups. Just like in Mbue's novel, water pollution and other destructive policies followed by firms in charge of resource extraction have caused serious environmental damages in several regions.

Would the political decentralization recommended explicitly or implicitly by the main characters in *How Beautiful We Were* deliver good results in the DRC where the problems are similar to those of the fictional Kosaxa village? Englebert and Kasongo Mungongo (2016) supply some clues. They study the effects of the decentralization reforms adopted in 2006 with bold objectives: to improve governance and accountability; undermine predation, corruption, and personal rule; bring government closer to the people; and promote local development. They conclude that despite some regional variations, Congolese decentralization

> had instead increased the degree to which the state extracts the resources and incomes of its citizens. It had also fostered provincial centralization at the expense of local governments, produced largely unaccountable provinces governing with little transparency, and unleashed self-serving provincial elites.

Englebert and Kasongo Mungongo provide original empirical evidence for these claims and suggest that decentralization was thwarted by the failure of formal reforms to affect informal ruling institutions and by an erroneous diagnosis of Congo's governance failures. Such a diagnosis singled out the abuse of elites without identifying the generalized nature of the instrumentalization of sovereignty by officeholders at all levels of the state.

When we bear in mind those serious lessons from the empirical literature, the hopes of Thula and her followers seem to be misplaced and their characters seem to be those of innocent children who have not grasped the complexity of the challenges confronting the common people in their country. The autocracy of roving bandits comes out of the novel as a vicious regime that is hard to displace and replace by a more people-centered system of governance.

20.4 Conclusion: The unbearable cost of innocence

How Beautiful We Were is a dazzling work of fiction with several unforgettable characters who stay with the reader long after the book has been shelved in one's library. Its elegant, powerful, and original construction and surgical precision of its writing style—most notably the daring decision to have the story told from several perspectives by different characters—provide the reader with many opportunities to go beyond the details and the suspense of the plot so as to pause and reflect about the key underlying issues. Through its endearing characters, the novel is also replete with strong philosophical undertones, which challenge the reader to confront the big questions raised in the novel.

The story of the courageous but losing fight of the Kosawa villagers who try to reclaim their land from unscrupulous business leaders and a ruthless political leader is a chronicle of a death foretold. But it is also a sober breviary of political immorality under autocracy and a frightening reminder that certain kinds of moral character have no place in politics. Afflicted by their moral innocence and fears, the Kosawa revolutionaries find themselves engaged in the struggle by accident—after the village madman confronts them unexpectedly, kidnaps the Pexton team's driver, confiscates their car keys, and triggers an unplanned movement of resistance. But, in the end, a spiral of violence is unleashed because of the brutal reaction of the autocrat, derisively called "His Excellency." Villagers who, if one excepts the truly atypical madman, are initially peaceful and willing to negotiate are then gradually and inexorably transformed into fighters increasingly ready to take up arms against their oppressors.

Mbue's tragedy is the result of the uncompromising stance of the autocrat, which has the effect of shutting down all possibilities of negotiation and compromise. This is especially tragic because such possibilities actually exist and could have improved the lot of the population. Instead of this path of compromise, the autocrat has chosen the path of confrontation which is doomed to inflict on the people the huge costs of asymmetrical violence. His short-termist approach, combined with his self-serving preference profile, wreak havoc in his country. Villagers are just innocent people who are then trapped in a deadlock of misery and hopelessness with no effective exit which they can devise by themselves. In other words, they are the victims of an oppressive system of political governance, and whatever their actions, their predicament is set to last.

The economy of moral innocence and betrayal has been studied in the literature, from Shakespeare's *Henry VI* to Sony Labou Tansi's *The Antipeople* and *Life and a Half*. Mbue has brought to it a new, contemporary twist, which invalidates our collective faith in political progress.

Acknowledgments

The author is grateful to François Bourguignon and Jean-Philippe Platteau for their careful reading and substantive suggestions on the previous draft of this chapter.

Notes

1 Praising "the novel's incisive appeal to the reader's empathy" and Mbue herself as "masterly at shading in the spaces where greed and guilt intermingle," *The New York Times* named her new work as "One of the 10 Best Books" of 2021. Her previous novel *Behold the Dreamers*, which won the PEN/Faulkner Award for Fiction, was a *New York Times* bestseller.

2 Mbue's novel seems to be mimicking similar real-life situations. Thus, in the Kabwe case, the South African high court threw out a lawsuit brought against the multinational mining company Anglo American on behalf of 140,000 Zambian women and children who suffered lead poisoning from one of its mines. The judge said:

> The applicants seek permission to advance an untenable claim that would set a grave precedent. The precedent is that a business could be held liable half a century after its activities have ceased, to generations not yet born, as a result of being tested against future knowledge and standards unknown at the time.
>
> *(quoted by Johnson 2023)*

References

Acemoglu, D., and J.A. Robinson, 2012. *Why Nations Fail: The Origins of Power, Prosperity, and Poverty*, New York, Crown Publishing Group.

De Tocqueville, A., 2004. *Democracy in America*. (Edited by O. Zunz and translated by A. Goldhammer), New York: Library of America.

Dixit, A.K., 2004. *Lawlessness and Economics: Alternative Modes of Governance*, Princeton, NJ, Princeton University Press.

Englebert, P. and E. Kasongo Mungongo, 2016. "Misguided and Misdiagnosed: The Failure of Decentralization Reforms in the DR Congo." *African Studies Review*, vol. 59, no. 1, pp. 5–32

HRW, 2023. "Zambia: Clean Up Lead Contamination in Kabwe," https://www.hrw.org/video-photos/video/2023/07/18/zambia-clean-lead-contamination-kabwe

James, E.C., 2010. *Democratic Insecurities: Violence, Trauma, and Intervention in Haiti*, Los Angeles, CA, University Press of California.

Johnson, S., 2023. "Judge Throws Out Kabwe Lead-poisoning Case against Anglo American Mining." *The Guardian*, December 18.

Mbue, I., 2021. *How Beautiful We Were*. New York: Penguin Random House.

Monga, C., 2009. *Uncivil Societies A Theory of Sociopolitical Change*, Policy Research Working Paper no. 4942, Washington, DC, World Bank.

Myerson, R.B., 2018. *Village Communities and Global Development*, Working Paper No 300, Abidjan, African Development Bank.

Myerson, R.B., 2024. *Local Politics in Nations and Empires*, University of Chicago, https://home.uchicago.edu/~rmyerson/research/niehandbk.pdf

Olson, M., Jr., 1993. "Dictatorship, Democracy, and Development." *The American Political Science Review*, vol. 87, no. 3, pp. 567–576.

21

FRANK HERBERT'S *DUNE*

Mark Koyama

21.1 Introduction

Dune, Frank Herbert's 1965 science fiction classic, narrates the rise of a hero—a freedom fighter and a prophet—Paul Atreides. The setting is the planet Arrakis, or Dune, one of countless planets within a vast Galactic Empire knitted together by spice—the drug that allows for interstellar travel, but which also entraps its users in addiction and has the potential to unlock untapped psychic abilities.

Dune is among the most influential works of science fiction ever written. Its setting, visual style, and its combination of advanced technology with an archaic or feudal political relationship created a whole new genre of science fiction. The massive commerce franchise, that is, Star Wars, and the more niche offerings, such as the Warhammer 40,000 universe, are directly inspired by it.

The outlines of the plot are as follows. As the book opens, the Duke Leto Atreides has been granted Arrakis, previously the possession of his rivals the Harkonnens, by the Galactic Emperor.

Arrakis is an inhospitable desert, but the planet plays a unique role in the Galactic Empire because it is the only place where spice can be harvested.

This "gift", the Duke suspects, is a trap. Nonetheless, he is obliged to accept it, transporting his family, including his son Paul and companion the Lady Jessica, with him. Once in possession of the planet, he encounters corruption and passive resistance. He is betrayed by a member of his household to an attack by the Harkonnens, secretly aided by the Emperor. The Duke is killed while Paul and Jessica escape into the hostile desert where they are taken into by the rebellious and ungoverned natives of Arrakis, the Fremen, a fierce tribal people resembling to a degree the Arab tribesmen of antiquity or the Berbers of the North African desert, who are likewise destined to play an outsized historical and geopolitical role.[1]

DOI: 10.4324/9781003534358-26

Among the Fremen, Paul is hailed as a messiah: Paul Muad'Dib. After drinking the Water of Life, he obtains prophetic powers, specifically the ability to see possible futures. From the Fremen, he trains a fearsome army of guerrilla fighters who enable him to defeat Harkonnens and liberate Arrakis. In so doing, he deposes the Galactic Emperor and establishes a regime based on the newly unleashed power of the Fremen.

Like all science fiction, *Dune* is a hodgepodge, a melange. Nonetheless, though imaginary, Herbert's fictional universe is firmly rooted in history and in social science.

Many of the analogies to our own world or to our history may appear obvious. But, as I shall hopefully draw out, others are subtle and illuminating. Spice plays the same crucial role in the universe created by Herbert as oil does in our own time. As one reads on, other analogies become apparent. These operate at different levels. There is an ominous religious order—the Bene Gesserit—named to rhyme with the Jesuits—who seek to control mankind's genetic heritage. Atreides, the family name of Paul, conjures images of Greek mythology: Agamemnon and Menelaus, the sons of Atreus, doomed to tragedy. But Paul is also the name of the apostle to the gentiles, and his real significance, as becomes apparent in the novel, is that he is destined to become a prophet and to launch a jihad. Paul will conquer the galaxy. But the focus of the sequels to *Dune* written by Herbert is less to trace his story than to narrate that of the planet Arrakis.

And, as I shall demonstrate, *Dune* can be used to explore some key ideas in classical works of political economy and economic history. In this chapter, I will draw on Herbert's space opera to discuss insights from Ibn Khaldun, perhaps the first historical social scientist, Adam Smith, Thomas Malthus, and other classical and modern economic thinkers.

21.2 Poverty and autocracy

Economists reading *Dune* will no doubt be struck by the fact that poverty is endemic on Arrakis. Despite being set many thousands of years in the future, the economic problem of scarcity has not been solved. Dying of thirst is common. The majority of ordinary people are poor, despite technological advances that would awe people in the 21st century. Herbert has been celebrated as an ecological thinker, concerned about man's impact on the natural environment, and at first glance, the reasons for this poverty appear to be ecological.

Poverty is the normal baseline condition for human societies. In the late 18th century, the political economist Thomas Malthus proposed a simple explanation for this. For humans, as for other species, population growth eats up the economic surplus. New machinery or technological progress might temporarily raise living standards. But in the long run, ordinary people would live close to subsistence. The key assumption that drives this result is the law of diminishing returns applied to labor: adding more hands increases total output but at a diminishing rate.

So it is in *Dune*. Long-distance space travel has been invented. Humanity has colonized thousands of planets. Yet ordinary people remain poor, just as Malthus might have predicted. In Herbert's universe, as in the thinking of the classical economists: "All growth was therefore limited growth, almost one might say conditional growth" (Wrigley, 1988, 19).

Why is this? Malthus believed that population growth was the reason for enduring poverty; specifically, the rate of population growth relative to resources. And ecological themes are important to Herbert and to the story of *Dune*. Arrakis, a desert planet, seemingly lacks the resources, the carrying capacity, and especially the water, to sustain the population it has at any higher standard of living. But a deeper investigation reveals that the reasons for Dune being a desert are institutional rather than ecological or even technological. The technologies exist to transform Arrakis into a garden world. The planet is kept an inhospitable desert because of how it is governed.

In other words, *Dune*'s ecological crisis cannot be separated from Herbert's analysis of the political system that governs the planet. Arrakis, at the start of the novel *Dune*, is a water despotism—a concept Herbert borrowed from Karl August Wittfogel (1957) who wrote of "hydraulic despotism". Wittfogel, in turn, borrowed from Karl Marx's *Asiatic Mode of Production* and from John Stuart Mill's, and Adam Smith's contrast between the process of growth in Europe and in Asia. The idea is that in societies where there is a scarce resource like water that is needed for the society to function, centralized control of that resource will result in despotic power. In ancient Egypt, for example, all agriculture relied on the flooding of the Nile Delta. Ownership of the irrigation systems thus made the Egyptian Pharaohs unconstrained, despotic rulers.

Wittfogel's (1957) link between hydraulic agriculture and autocracy (that so evidently influenced Herbert) has drawn tremendous scholarly criticism. Nonetheless, there is empirical support for it. Looking across countries, Bentzen, Kaarsen, and Wingender (2017) establish a strong empirical relationship between irrigation potential and autocracy. They argue simply that a monopoly of water in conjunction with easy monitoring reduced the economic and political power of the general population in hydraulic societies compared to their rulers. These effects are persistent: today, countries with greater irrigation potential are more likely to be autocratic.

Here, it is interesting to contrast the different personal economics of the Harkonnens and the Atreides. The former use coercion to extract as much spice as possible. The latter rely on rewards and high wages, with Duke Leto cultivating a reputation for caring about the safety of his men. In an important scene at the beginning of *Dune*, Leto is willing to sacrifice spice and equipment in order to save his crew (a fact he also wants to be publicized). Leto's actions suggest that good governance is possible and thus emphasize the tragedy of

Atreides' rule in the long run which despite his (and Paul's) personal efforts will result in the long run in a system of government that is at least as autocratic and tyrannical as that of the Harkonnens.

Herbert does not consider autocracy in isolation in the *Dune* novels. While the governance of Arrakis is autocratic, the overall political economy of the *Dune* universe is feudal. The Galactic Empire, vast though it is, is reminiscent of medieval Europe. Indeed, aspects of it recall the medieval Holy Roman Empire as much as it does the Roman or Persian empires; it has a Landsraad that comprises noble houses, such as the Atreides and their arch enemies, the Harkonnens, who govern planets "in fief".

A key characteristic of the feudal world was the absence of a monopoly on violence (see Desierto and Koyama, 2024). There is an emperor—Shaddam IV of House Corrino—who possesses the elite Sardaukar warriors. But each of the great houses also has its own staff, military forces, and traditions. Like Japanese daimyo or the most powerful feudal lords in 10th century Europe, their rule in their fiefs is described as "unchallenged". In the absence of any monopoly of legitimate force, the problem of political violence is unresolved, and the institutions of the Empire, both under the "Old Imperium" and in the subsequent empire created by Paul and his Fremen, are best understood as responses to this problem.

21.3 Institutions

The institutional framework of *Dune* can be illuminated using concepts from institutional analysis. For example, North, Wallis, and Weingast (2009) introduce the concept of limited access orders. All societies, they argue, face a problem of political violence, but they resolve this problem through different means. Limited access orders control violence and achieve a measure of social order by generating rents for elites through the control of markets and the creation of monopolies.

> …through the formation of a dominant coalition whose members possess special privileges. The logic of the natural state follows from how it solves the problem of violence. Elites—members of the dominant coalition—agree to respect each other's privileges, including property rights and access to resources and activities. By limiting access to these privileges to members of the dominant coalition, elites create credible incentives to cooperate rather than fight among themselves. Because elites know that violence will reduce their own rents, they have incentives not to fight. Furthermore, each elite understands that other elites face similar incentives. In this way, the political system of a natural state manipulates the economic system to produce rents that then secure political order.
>
> *(North et al., 2009, 18)*

Limited access orders constrain violence and produce political order through the creation and maintenance of economic rents. But the process through which these rents are generated is costly. It typically involves the creation of monopolies and hence produces both deadweight losses in the wider economy and a competition for the control of the rents themselves. In a related vein, Johnson and Koyama (2019) distinguish between general rules and identity rules. Reliance on identity rules complements limited access orders. In contrast, moving to general rules requires dismantling barriers to competition and eroding rents for insiders.

In the *Dune* universe, monopolies are ubiquitous. The extreme expense of space travel, which is controlled by the monopoly of the space guild, exemplifies this. Identity rules are pervasive. Humanity has not escaped the limited access order despite conquering the stars.

We see this in Herbert's depiction of economic life on Arrakis. While the vast deserts are populated by the Fremen—who live ungoverned, outside of the shield wall and outside of the purview of the state (and whose numbers are massively underestimated by the Harkonnens), there are cities and denser settlements: notably Arrakeen and Cartag. These settlements depend for their existence on water, specifically on water shipped from the poles of the planet. Soon after Duke Leto Atreides arrives on Arrakis, he hosts a banquet for local elites in the capital. Among these elites is a banker—a "water magnate" and financial advisor to the Water Peddlers Union. His power rests on the exclusive control of water; in other words, on monopoly power. Those in power in Arrakis benefit from the scarcity of water; that is, they obtain economic rents from their politically granted monopoly power.[2] Duke Leto's plan to establish an orderly cycle of water threatens these rents. Unsurprisingly, therefore, the water magnate and those like him conspire with Harkonnens against the Duke, keeping Arrakis poor. Poverty is a political problem. It is also an institutional one.

21.4 Political cycles

To more fully understand the role of institutions in *Dune*, we need to consider Herbert's sequel novels, especially *Children of Dune* (1976) and *God Emperor of Dune* (1981).

Throughout these novels, the role of water contrasts with that of spice. Water is a necessity for life; spice is a luxury for individuals but essential for space travel. Arrakis is initially almost devoid of water, but abundant in spice. Extracting the spice is both capital intensive (requiring expensive haulers and equipment) and dangerous. Sandworms are responsible for countless lost crews. Due to the high fixed costs involved, it is a natural monopoly. This, again, lends to itself to the reproduction of despotism (though there is some smuggling, and this smuggling preserves the possibility of liberation).

Spice and water have an inverse and mirroring relationship in Herbert's novels. Paul and his family come to Arrakis from the water-abundant world of Caladan. The sandworms that create the spice are poisoned by water. The reclamation of the desert undertaken in Paul's reign and completed during the three thousand years long reign of Leto II means the near extinction of the sandworms, the source of the spice.

The presence of spice on Arrakis resembles a resource curse, the subject of extensive literature in political economy (Isham et al., 2005; Mehlum et al., 2006; Alexeev and Conrad, 2009; Haber and Menaldo, 2011). This literature distinguishes between an economic resources curse (such as in models of "Dutch Disease") and a political resource curse. The latter occurs when the presence of the valuable resource induces rent-seeking behavior by political agents (Desierto, 2018). A prominent example of this is conflict, for example, as over mineral resources in sub-Saharan Africa (see Berman et al., 2017). Under Harkonnen rule, extracting spice on Arrakis involved the ruthless suppression of the native population and ensured that the planet would be the seat of ongoing conflict.

History often appears cyclical in the *Dune* universe. The climate of Arrakis changes from desert to oasis and back to desert again. But despite these cycles, and despite the promise of liberation brought by Paul to the Fremen, autocracy of some form appears to be a constant.

Cyclical theories also have a long provenance in the social sciences. Cyclical theories come in at least two variants: institutional and non-institutional. Kondratiev waves are an example of a technological-based, non-institutionalized theory of cycles, and modern economists have (in my view) correctly rejected these ideas. The writings of Thomas Malthus (1802) also offer the basis for demographic-based economic cycles.

Institutional-based cycles are more pertinent for understanding *Dune*. Ibn Khaldun, another inspiration for Herbert, articulated one of the most influential such cyclical theories.[3] Khaldun was concerned with how nomadic groups went from raiding sedentary societies to being able to take them over before declining through decadence and slipping back into obscurity. Khaldun's concept of *asabiyya*—a potent form of social solidarity—has special resonance when applied to describe the Fremen. Harnessing this power catapults Paul into power as a Galactic Emperor. But once the new regime is in place and the initial fury of the jihad has exhausted itself, the energy of the Fremen begins to dissipate.

Important themes that Herbert took from Khaldun include the tension between desert nomads and city dwellers. Luxury and the comforts of city-living corrupt the city dwellers. In contrast, the desert is the breeding ground of the toughest of warriors. To survive there, the nomads need to band together (in the "sietch"), economize on resources ("water discipline"), and trust one another with their lives. Thus, for Khaldun and for Herbert, the desert produces the greatest fighters, the fighters with the most asabiyya. Once they leave this harsh environment, their asabiyya begins to dissipate; we already see the corrupting effects of urban life on the Fremen in *Dune Messiah* set just decades after the events of *Dune*.

Polybius, Machiavelli, Vico, and Oswald Splenger were also cyclical theorists. The most obviously influential thinker on Herbert was Arnold Toynbee, whose multi-volume *The Story of History* was published in numerous volumes from the 1930s to the 1960s and attracted a huge readership, though it is neglected nowadays. Certainly, Toynbee emphasizes several themes evident in the *Dune* novels, such as the role of the desert (e.g., Toynbee, 1934).

The concept of cycles in history has also been taken up by Peter Turchin (2003), Turchin and Nefedov (2009), and Turchin (2023)). There are different stages to the secular cycles that one observes historically. Turchin combines a demographic component—during demographic expansions wages fall—with an analysis of the social structure—as wages fall, rents rise, and this means that elite incomes initially increase with population growth. The initial increase, however, in elite incomes generates elite overproduction and inter-elite competition, and this results in political crisis and even civil war.

The spice-water cycle and the rise and fall of Paul Atreides similarly speak to the ubiquity of such structural cyclical forces in the *Dune* universe. The conflict between the Atreides and the Harkonnens is an intra-elite struggle for the rents generated by spice. Paul frees Arrakis from the tyranny of the Harkonnens, but recreates an autocracy in their place. A new elite—based on his Fremen warriors—replaces the old elite, and the cycle will begin again. To break this cycle, his son Leto II will establish a still more all-encompassing tyranny that will keep the galaxy in quasi-medieval stagnation. He temporarily frees Arrakis both from the resource curse and from related political cycles via the Golden Path. But this comes at the expense of technological, economic, and cultural progress. These contrasting fictional histories—one of violent cycles; the other of stagnation and stasis—bring to mind Toynbee's and others' depictions of the histories of Europe, on the one hand, and China on the other.

While Herbert articulated the notion of a "Golden path", recent work in institutional economics emphasizes the idea of a "narrow corridor" (Acemoglu and Robinson, 2019). That is, there is the possibility of liberty and prosperity when the state is strong enough to provide order from anarchy and free individuals from what they call the "cage of norms", i.e., oppressive customs and familial practices, but not so strong to entirely dominate society. In other words, there needs to be a Leviathan (a powerful state), but for humanity to flourish, this has to be a "shackled Leviathan".

This argument resonates with the institutional reading of the *Dune* novels that I have proposed here. The Fremen, though they live free of the state, represent the potentially oppressive forces of custom. Their harsh environment has imposed on them an unforgiving social code (e.g., "the bond of water").

In contrast, the rule of the Harkonnens is nakedly despotic. They treat the population of Arrakis as slaves and use repression, torture, and murder as routine instruments of control, thereby behaving as an unshackled Leviathan. In contrast, at the beginning on the Dune novels, the Atreides offer the possibility of "life in the corridor". That is, we have the impression that the rule of Duke Leto Atreides on his native Caladan combined good governance with a large measure of liberty for the population. But as Acemoglu and Robinson (2019, 184) note, "life in the corridor is never tranquil" and it can be easily destabilized. The death of Duke Leto and the rise to power of Paul set off a train of events that sees life on Arrakis (and in the galaxy) spiral out of the corridor and into a kind of theocratic despotism.

21.5 Religion

Religion is central to *Dune*. This observation deserves attention. Religion is absent in much 20th century science fiction. Religion doesn't feature in HG Wells' *War of the Worlds*. Religion is not a major theme of Isaac Asimov's *Foundation* series. This is in keeping with mid-to-late 20th century scholarly thinking and its adherence to some form of the secularization thesis (see Bruce, 2002).

Subsequent social scientific opinion has come to think, in contrast, that aspects of religious belief may be perennial (or at least receptivity to such belief may be).[4] In the *Dune*-inspired, Warhammer 40k universe, religion and the nature of religious belief are similarly foregrounded, in contrast to much mid-20th century science fiction.

For the people of *Dune*, Paul Atreides is the "Lisan al-Gaib" or Mahdi. Their religious belief is a powerful force, a bond that unifies the disparate Fremen tribes. At times, we are given to believe that this religion is fake, seeded thousands of years earlier by the Bene Gesserit. But in a sense, this is a red herring. Paul *does* possess the powers of a god, and he *does* deliver the Fremen from Harkonnen rule, thereby fulfilling the ancient prophesies. The question of his humanity or divinity, we are told (by Paul himself), is meaningless for "[t]here exists no separation between gods and men; one blends softly casual into the other".

While Adam Smith was very interested in the relationship between church and state (see

Anderson, 1988), religion dropped out of the purview of economic scholarship for much of the 20th century.[5] Within economic history, religion occasionally featured, for instance, in the form of interest in the Weber hypothesis, but otherwise was seen as of secondary importance. This gradually changed with the institutional turn in economic history, associated largely with the work of Douglass North. North directed the attention of scholars to institutions, which he defined as the man-made incentive structures that guide human behavior or, more concisely, "the rules of the game".[6] This, in turn, eventually led many economic historians to examining both religion and the relationship between religious institutions and the state (see Johnson and Koyama, 2013; Platteau, 2017; Rubin, 2017; Johnson and Koyama, 2019; Becker and Pfaff, 2022; Bentzen and Gokmen, 2023).

Religion matters both because it was an especially important form of consumption in preindustrial economies and because of its central role in the political economy of these societies. Religious institutions played the preeminent role in legitimating political authority (e.g., Rubin, 2017). Religious authorities shaped legal systems (Berman, 1983; Kuran, 2010) and priests and members of religious orders provided education and, in many past societies, staffed bureaucracies and state organizations. Autocratic political leaders can co-opt religious leaders as an "opposition suppression strategy" (Auriol and Platteau, 2017; Platteau, 2017) resulting in state control of the religion and in a religion that supports the autocratic regime.

The perilous relationship between Church and State in Herbert's universe comes to the fore in his second book *Dune Messiah*. The religious establishment in place by *Dune Messiah* is a repressive bureaucracy. There is a chief priest, an inquisition that suppresses dissenting thought. Paul, despite his foreknowledge and fears, has become the head of an authoritarian theocracy. He only "escapes" this fate when an assassination attempt results in his blinding. Paul then retreats in the desert alone, traditionally a death sentence for the Fremen. When Paul reappears as a wandering preacher in *Children of Dune*, he is viewed as a dangerous heretic.

This religious establishment is in keeping with the kind of hydraulic despotism described above. In the societies Wittfogel studied, the ruler was a high priest, and the correct rites had to be practiced in order to guarantee the correct flow of water; so it is in the Arrakis of Paul Muad'Dib.

21.6 The curse of the leader

Heroic fantasy and indeed much science fiction speak to our need for heroes—figures capable of changing the course of history. In contrast, one recurrent and most important idea found in the writings of classical political economists, notably Adam Smith, is the central role of structural factors in history and the relative weak influence of political leaders, particularly the so-called great men. This is evident in Smith's famous critique of the man of systems:

> The man of system, on the contrary, is apt to be very wise in his own conceit; and is often so enamoured with the supposed beauty of his own ideal plan of government, that he cannot suffer the smallest deviation from any part of it. He goes on to establish it completely and in all its parts, without any regard either to the great interests, or to the strong prejudices which

> may oppose it. He seems to imagine that he can arrange the different members of a great society with as much ease as the hand arranges the different pieces upon a chess-board.
>
> *(Smith, 1759)*

By such men of systems, Smith is thinking of Colbert, Controller-General of Finances under the French king Louis XIV, or Frederick the Great, Holy Roman Emperor and monarch of Prussia. He also anticipated the grandiose ambitions of leaders such as Napoleon, Lenin, or Mao. On this topic, the classical political economists were directly opposed by romantics such as Thomas Carlyle, who lauded the prospective man of systems in the following terms:

> They were the leaders of men, these great ones; the modellers, patterners, and in a wide sense creators, of whatsoever the general mass of men contrived to do or to attain; all things that we see standing accomplished in the world are properly the outer material result, the practical realisation and embodiment, of Thoughts that dwelt in the Great Men sent into the world: the soul of the whole world's history, it may justly be considered, were the history of these.
>
> *(1–2 Carlyle, 1941)*

Is there a better description of Paul Atreides?

Even before Paul gains prescient powers when he drinks the Water of Life among the Fremen, he is trained as a human computer capable of calculating extremely complex probabilities and thus forecasting future events.[7] It is widely understood that Herbert sought to subvert the classic notion of the hero—Joseph Campbell's hero of a thousand faces. Paul combines the abilities and virtues of a warrior, a general, a political leader, and a religious messiah. He has Bene Gesserit training. He sees visions of the future. Nonetheless, he is unable to truly shape history. He cannot prevent the murderous jihad that he foresees. Nor is he able to prevent the death of his lover Chani.

Campbell called the archetypical hero story that he saw as present, to a degree, in almost all human societies the monomyth. The hero is forced by a crisis to leave his familiar or ordinary world and to pass into a supernatural world:

> Prometheus ascended to the heavens, stole fire from the gods, and descended. Jason sailed through the Clashing Rocks into a sea of marvels, circumvented the dragon that guarded the Golden fleece, and returned with the fleece and the power to wrest his rightful throne from a usurper. Aeneas went down into the under-world, crossed the dreadful river of the dead, threw a sop to the three-headed watchdog Cerberus, and conversed, at last, with the shade of his dead father.
>
> *(Campbell, 1949, 28)*

In this supernatural world, they face a great struggle in which the hero must overcome challenges and ordeals. For this, he is granted some kind of boon or supernatural reward that he can return with to the ordinary human world.

The monomyth provides the apparent or external structure to Herbert's novel. At the beginning of *Dune*, Paul is obliged to leave his home world of Caladan and travel to Arrakis. There, with the Harkonnen attack on his family and the death of his father, Paul is forced to flee with his mother, Jessica, into the unforgiving desert. To survive in this hard environment, Paul and Jessica have to establish themselves among the Fremen. Paul faces down and kills the Fremen Jamis. Surmounting this challenge, he is accepted by them as Lisan al-Gaib or "the Voice from the Outer World" and a Mahdi, or prophet, Paul Muad'Dib. Finally, Paul defeats the Harkonnens and avenges the death of his father.

Paul's "boon"—his ability to foresee future events is, of course, a curse. And, as we have already noted, Paul's family name alludes to the tragedy that will inevitably befall him and the universe.

But just as JRR Tolkien's *Lord of the Rings* is only fully appreciated as the product of an author who had lived through both World Wars (and fought in one of them), so *Dune* is a modernist iteration of the monomyth.[8] The particular form of his myth and the particular tragedy that engulfs its hero could only have been conceived after Hiroshima and the Holocaust.

Thus, Paul's heroic quest culminates not just in personal tragedy but in the world-ending death of billions. By his own account, Paul has "killed sixty-one billion, sterilized ninety planets, completely demoralized five hundred others", a death toll that he explicitly compares to Hitler's (*Dune Messiah*, p. 138). The motto of Dune is that:

> No more terrible disaster could befall your people than for them to fall into the hands of a Hero.
>
> *(221/271/276)*

21.7 Conclusions

Reading *Dune* through the lens of institutional economics is an intriguing exercise. Behind the exotic setting, it allows for the examination of several classic themes in history, economics, and political science.

Dune is an important reminder (if we need it) of the importance of ideology and religion and other non-material factors in human societies, topics that economists have only begun to grapple with. *Dune* also undercuts narratives that focus on heroic individuals. The dictum that power corrupts has become a cliché, but it is a message that accords with much of classical political economy and public choice. Herbert was similarly skeptical of heroes and of politicians.[9]

Economists and political scientists have devoted a lot of attention to the problem of democratization. This literature has focused on the threat of revolution from below (as in Acemoglu and Robinson, 2006) but also on the role played by political elites in democratization. But many revolutions do not produce stable democracies, and the academic literature has less to say on this phenomenon. On this point, *Dune* contains both important warnings about reliance on a single, messianic figure and caution about belief in the allegedly deterministic nature of history and of our ability to predict it.[10]

At its heart, *Dune* is a novel that recognizes the constraints imposed by geography, technology, and human psychology. Reading it is, therefore, not pure escapism; its lessons inform and are informed by our own understanding of history and of the study of society.

Acknowledgments

I am grateful for the excellent comments from Avinash Dixit, Francois Bourguignon, Jean-Philippe Platteau, and Marcus Shera.

Notes

1 Though as pointed out by Herbert (2003), and more recently by Immerwahr (2022), the Fremen also resemble Native Americans in important respects.
2 It is implied that water could be brought in from off planet but that this would not be politically expedient.
3 See Irwin (2018, 200–201) who notes that Herbert mentioned reading Khaldun in a radio interview.
4 See for various discussion Altran (2002), Bloom (2007), and Banerjee and Bloom (2013).
5 See Koyama (2020) for a discussion of this. See Platteau and Aldashev (2014) for a survey of the recent scholarship.
6 See, in particular, North and Thomas (1973), and North (1981, 1990).
7 Computers and artificial intelligence are prohibited in the *Dune* universe as a consequence of the Butlerian Jihad, which takes place hundreds of years before the beginning of the novel.
8 See Shippey (2000) for a discussion of the role World War 1 played in shaping Tolkien's world view.
9 See Herbert (2003, 191–192) for details of his skepticism, including toward John F. Kennedy.
10 Indeed, as other scholars have noted (e.g., Scigaj, 1983), Paul's prescience traps him in inaction. He is obsessed with preventing a jihad but every action he takes makes it more likely. Indeed "If Paul had the dexterity to control a giant sandworm, perhaps he could have averted at least some of the ravages of the holy war?" (Scigaj, 1983, 342).

References

Acemoglu, D. and J. A. Robinson (2006). *The Economic Origins of Dictatorship and Democracy*. Cambridge: Cambridge University Press.

Acemoglu, D. and J. A. Robinson (2019). *The Narrow Corridor to Liberty: States, Societies, and the Fate of Liberty*. New York: Penguin.

Alexeev, M. and R. Conrad (2009). The Elusive Curse of Oil. *The Review of Economics and Statistics 91*(3), 586–598.

Altran, S. (2002). *In Gods We Trust: The Evolutionary Landscape of Religion*. Oxford: Oxford University Press.

Anderson, G. M. (1988). Mr. Smith and the Preachers: The Economics of Religion in the Wealth of Nations. *Journal of Political Economy 96*(5), 1066–1088.

Auriol, E. and J.-P. Platteau (2017). Religious Co-option in Autocracy: A Theory Inspired by History. *Journal of Development Economics 127*, 395–412.

Banerjee, K. and P. Bloom (2013). Would Tarzan Believe in God? Conditions for the Emergence of Religious Belief. *Trends in Cognitive Sciences 17*(1), 7–8.

Becker, S. O. and S. Pfaff (2022, May). *Church and State in Historical Political Economy*. CEH Discussion Papers 03, Centre for Economic History, Research School of Economics, Australian National University.

Bentzen, J. S. and G. Gokmen (2023). The Power of Religion. *Journal of Economic Growth 28*(1), 45–78.

Bentzen, J. S., N. Kaarsen, and A. M. Wingender (2017). Irrigation and Autocracy. *Journal of the European Economic Association 15*(1), 1–53.

Berman, H. J. (1983). *Law and Revolution, the Formation of the Western Legal Tradition*. Cambridge, MA: Harvard University Press.

Berman, N., M. Couttenier, D. Rohner, and M. Thoenig (2017, June). This Mine Is Mine! How Minerals Fuel Conflicts in Africa. *American Economic Review 107*(6), 1564–1610.

Bloom, P. (2007). Religion Is Natural. *Developmental Science 10*(1), 147–151.

Bruce, S. (2002). *God is Dead: Secularization in the West*. Oxford: Basil Blackwell.

Campbell, J. (1949). *The Hero with a Thousand Faces*. New York City: Pantheon Books.

Carlyle, T. (1941). *On Heroes, Hero-Worship, & the Heroic in History: Six Lectures*. London: James Fraser.

Desierto, D. and M. Koyama (2024). Feudal political economy. *Economic Theory*, 1–40.

Desierto, D. A. (2018, August). Formal Models of the Political Resource Curse. *Economics of Governance 19*(3), 225–259.

Haber, S. and V. Menaldo (2011). Do Natural Resources Fuel Authoritarianism? A Reappraisal of the Resource Curse. *American Political Science Review 105*(1), 1–26.

Herbert, B. (2003). *Dreamer of Dune*. New York: Tor.

Herbert, F. (1976). *Children of Dune*. New York: Putnam.

Herbert, F. (1981). *God Emperor of Dune*. New York: Putnam.

Immerwahr, D. (2022). The Quileute Dune: Frank Herbert, Indigeneity, and Empire. *Journal of American Studies 56*(2), 191–216.

Irwin, R. (2018). *Ibn Khaldun*. Princeton, NJ: Princeton University Press.

Isham, J., M. Woolcock, L. Pritchett, and G. Busby (2005). The Varieties of Resource Experience: Natural Resource Export Structures and the Political Economy of Economic Growth. *The World Bank Economic Review 19*(2), 141–174.

Johnson, N. D. and M. Koyama (2013). Legal Centralization and the Birth of the Secular State. *Journal of Comparative Economics 41*(4), 959–978.

Johnson, N. D. and M. Koyama (2019). *Persecution & Toleration: The Long Road to Religious Freedom*. Cambridge: Cambridge University Press.

Koyama, M. (2020). The Institutional Foundations of Religious Freedom. *Journal of Economics, Management and Religion 01*(02), 1–35.

Kuran, T. (2010). *The Long Divergence*. Princeton, NJ: Princeton University Press.

Malthus, T. R. (1992, 1802). *An Essay on the Principle of Population* (2nd ed.). Cambridge: Cambridge University Press.

Mehlum, H., K. Moene, and R. Torvik (2006). Institutions and the Resource Curse. *The Economic Journal 116*(508), 1–20.
North, D. C. (1981). *Structure and Change in Economic History*. New York: Norton.
North, D. C. (1990). *Institutions, Institutional Change, and Economic Performance*. Cambridge, UK: Cambridge UP.
North, D. C. and R. P. Thomas (1973). *The Rise of the Western World*. Cambridge, UK: Cambridge University Press.
North, D. C., J. J. Wallis, and B. R. Weingast (2009). *Violence and Social Orders: A Conceptual Framework for Interpreting Recorded Human History*. Cambridge: Cambridge University Press.
Platteau, J.-P. (2017). *Islam Instrumentalized*. Cambridge: Cambridge University Press Press.
Platteau, J.-P. and G. Aldashev (2014). Religion, Culture, and Development. In V. A. Ginsburgh and D. Throsby (Eds.), *Handbook of the Economics of Art and Culture*, Vol. 2, pp. 587–631. Amsterdam: Elsevier.
Rubin, J. (2017). *Rulers, Religion, and Riches: Why the West got rich and the Middle East did not*. Cambridge: Cambridge University Press.
Scigaj, L. M. (1983). "Prana" and the Presbyterian Fixation: Ecology and Technology in Frank Herbert's "Dune" Tetralogy. *Extrapolation 24*(4), 340.
Shippey, T. (2000). *J.R.R Tolkein: Author of the Century*. New York: Harper Collins.
Smith, A. (1759). *The Theory of Moral Sentiments*. Cambridge: UP.
Toynbee, A. J. (1934). *A Study of History: The Growth of Civilizations*, Vol. 3. Oxford: Oxford University Press.
Turchin, P. (2003). *Historical Dynamics*. Princeton, NJ: Princeton University Press.
Turchin, P. (2023). *End Times: Elites, Counter-Elites and the Path of Political Disintegration*. London: Penguin Books.
Turchin, P. and S. A. Nefedov (2009). *Secular Cycles*. Princeton, NJ: Princeton University Press.
Wittfogel, K. (1957). *Oriental Despotism: A Comparative Study of Total Power*. New Haven: Yale University Press.
Wrigley, E. A. (1988). *Continuality, Chance and Change. The Character of the Industrial Revolution in England*. Cambridge, UK.: Cambridge UP.

Made in the USA
Coppell, TX
03 August 2026

86152046R00188